The Fortress of Salvador
in Colonial Brazil

Luiz Walter Coelho Filho

The Fortress of Salvador
in Colonial Brazil

Translated by Catherine V. Howard

1ª Edição
POD

KBR
Petrópolis
2014

Publisher **Noga Sklar**
Translation **Catherine V. Howard**
Text edition **KBR**
Cover design **KBR**

Copyright © 2014 *Luiz Walter Coelho Filho*
All rights reserved.

ISBN: 978-85-8180-324-1

KBR Editora Digital Ltda.
www.kbrdigital.com.br
www.facebook.com/kbrdigital
atendimento@kbrdigital.com.br
55|21|3942.4440

HIS033000 - History, South America

Luiz Walter Coelho Filho was born in Salvador, Bahia, in 1961. He is a lawyer and a senior partner at Menezes, Magalhães, Coelho & Zarif Associates. Coelho Filho has published other books in his areas of expertise, such as *Jurisprudência Fiscal* (1995) and *A Capitania de São Jorge e a Década do Açúcar* (2000). In 2012, he received the Thomé de Souza Medal from the Municipal Council of the City of Salvador in recognition of his excellent research work in *A Fortaleza do Salvador na Bahia de Todos os Santos*, which *The Fortress of Salvador in Colonial Brazil* now makes available in translation for an international audience.

E-mail: luizwalter@mmcz.adv.br

Catherine V. Howard is a Portuguese-to-English translator who specializes in the social sciences. Her previous translations include *From the Enemy's Point of View: Humanity and Divinity in an Amazonian Society* (1992) and numerous articles in edited volumes.

E-mail: catherine@translationcraft.com

I dedicate this book to my twin daughters, Catarina and Sofia. A spiritual union with the land and a fascination for knowledge inspired the choice of their names. Love for the land and for knowledge produced every line of this essay.

"The architect should be equipped with knowledge of many branches of study and varied kinds of learning, for it is by his judgment that all work done by the other arts is put to test. This knowledge is the child of practice and theory. Practice is the continuous and regular exercise of employment where manual work is done with any necessary material according to the design of a drawing. Theory, on the other hand, is the ability to demonstrate and explain the productions of dexterity on the principles of proportion [...].

"An architect ought to be an educated man so as to leave a more lasting remembrance in his treatises. Secondly, he must have a knowledge of drawing so that he can readily make sketches to show the appearance of the work which he proposes. Geometry, also, is of much assistance in architecture, and in particular it teaches us the use of the rule and compasses, by which especially we acquire readiness in making plans for buildings in their grounds, and rightly apply the square, the level, and the plummet. By means of optics, again, the light in buildings can be drawn from fixed quarters of the sky. It is true that it is by arithmetic that the total cost of buildings is calculated and measurements are computed, but difficult questions involving symmetry are solved by means of geometrical theories and methods.

"A wide knowledge of history is requisite because, among the ornamental parts of an architect's design for a work, there are many the underlying idea of whose employment he should be able to explain to inquirers."

Marcus Vitruvius Pollio (1 BCE)

I would like to express my gratitude to my friends, Edgard da Silva Telles Sobrinho, who conducted a meticulous critical review of the manuscript of this book, and Sonia Cardoso Dórea, who was the enthusiastic editor; to Professor Francisco Senna and the professional staff of the Department of Culture and Tourism of the State of Bahia, who demonstrated great interest in publicizing this essay; and, finally, to my colleagues at MMC & Zarif Attorneys, who, for so many years, put up with a lawyer who insisted on talking about the history of urbanism, and to my family, especially Luíza, Luciana, Luiz Artur, Catarina and Sofia, patient interlocutors.

Table of Contents

Index of Figures and Tables • 15

Foreword • 21

Introduction • 23

1. Air, water, and place • 29
2. Selection of the site • 37
3. Polybius versus Vegetius • 49
4. Regular and Irregular Cities • 57
5. The Portuguese Renaissance Era • 65
6. The Military Inspiration of the Project • 73
7. The Missionary Paradise • 83
8. The Beach and the Harbor • 89
9. Fountains and Pools • 99
10. The Twin Access Roads • 107
11. The Perimeter of the Fortress • 117
12. The Southern Boundary of the Fortress • 125
13. The Northern Boundary of the Fortress • 135
14. The Eastern Boundary of the Fortress • 149
15. The Sacred Origin of Walls • 161
16. Areas Outside the Fortress • 167
17. The Fence and the Wall • 175
18. The Gates of the Fortress • 181
19. From Tower to Bulwark • 189
20. The Evolution of the Bulwark • 209

21. Bulwarks and Stations in the Fortress • 215
22. From Bombards to Culverins • 225
23. Artillery in the Fortress • 235
24. The Four Corners of the Fortress • 243
25. Symmetry and the Human Body • 249
26. The Urban Design • 259
27. Blocks and Lots • 269
28. Streets • 279
29. The Plaza • 287
30. The Pelourinho District • 297
31. The Citadel and the Governor's House • 305
32. Municipal Council Building, Jail, and Butcher's Market • 311
33. Infrastructure at the Harbor • 321
34. The Sé Cathedral • 331
35. Construction of the Cathedral • 339
36. The Churches of Our Lady • 345
37. The Peripheral Churches • 349
38. The Hospital and the Infirmary • 355
39. The Jesuits' Buildings • 361
40. Cemeteries • 367
41. The Anguish of the Master Architect • 377

Documentary Appendix

Table Appendix

Bibliography • 405

Index of Figures and Tables

Figure 1 - Page in Codex 112 referring to the Fortress of Salvador, 1549 • 25

Figure 2 - The Fortress of Salvador was constructed on two plateaus, Sé (to the north) and Ajuda (to the south) • 46

Figure 3 - Plan of the Aztec city of Mexico and its monumental plaza, 1524 • 54

Figure 4 - Plan of the city of Carlentini, Sicily, founded in 1551 • 55

Figure 5 - Diagram in Rojas (1591) to illustrate that "the plaza that seems to be the strongest and most perfect of all is the pentagon" • 61

Figure 6 - The hexagonal city, according to Cataneo, 1554 • 62

Figure 7 - Fortress of Mazagan, Morocco, 1542 • 69

Figure 8 - Members of a company, also called a bandeira (1588) • 77

Figure 9 - Cove where the present-day Yacht Club of Bahia is located • 90

Figure 10 - Port of the city of Salvador. Oldest known drawing, dated 1605 • 95

Figure 11 - Fountain on Praia da Preguiça, the former fishermen's beach • 104

Figure 12 - Fountain at Ladeira da Misericórdia • 106

Figure 13 - Ladeira do Pau da Bandeira, the southern access road to the upper city, linking the Conceição Church to the main plaza, 1860 • 108

Figure 14 - Ladeira da Misericórdia. Below, the Fonte do Pereira, before being demolished • 109

Figure 15 - Model of the city of São Sebastião in 1567 • 111

Figure 16 - Francesco di Giorgio Martin's models for cities on hills, with ascent roads shown as circular, spiral, diagonal, and criss-crossing • 114

Figure 17 - Plan of the Fortress of Salvador in 1549, as conceptualized by Teodoro Sampaio • 120

Figure 18 - Original borders of the Fortress of Salvador, as reconstructed by the author • 121

Figure 19 - Present-day plan of the city of Salvador • 121

Figure 20 - Southern boundary of the Fortress of Salvador, at the top of the Ajuda plateau • 126

Figure 21 - Present-day plan of the city of Salvador, superimposed with the southern boundary of the fortress and the demarcation of the lots belonging to Judge Baltazar Ferraz • 130

Figure 22 - Detail of the southern boundary of the plan of the city of Salvador, 1605 • 134

Figure 23 - Present-day plan of the city of Salvador showing the northern boundary of the fortress superimposed in black • 136

Figure 24 - Aerial view of Terreiro de Jesus. In the background is the Church of San Francisco • 146

Figure 25 - Current plan of the city of Salvador • 153

Figure 26 - Stamp "City of Salvador, 1624," which illustrates the book by Henry Hondius • 154

Figure 27 - Present-day view of Terreiro de Jesus and Largo de São Francisco • 156

Figure 28 - Terreiro de Jesus, on the northern border, originally outside the city walls • 170

Figure 29 - Praça Castro Alves, on the southern boundary of the fortress, a space originally outside the walls where building was prohibited • 171

Figure 30 - Probable location of the first Santa Catarina gate • 184

Figure 31 - Plan of the city of Caesarea, Israel • 192

Figure 32 - Illustration of the Tower of London, England • 192

Figure 33 - Plan of the city of Aigues-Mortes, France • 193

Figure 34 - Square tower in the Castle of Guimarães, Portugal • 194

Figure 35 - Transitional style from tower to bulwark at the beginning of sixteenth century. Model of a sturdy circular tower by Francesco di Giorgio Martini • 196

Figure 36 - Transitional style. Fortress of Salses, according to Francisco de Holanda, 1538 • 198

Figure 37 - Transitional style: the Portuguese fortress at Aguz in Morocco, built in 1519 • 199

Figure 38 - Bulwarks of the Portuguese Fortress in Diu, India, 1546 • 203

Figure 39 - Portuguese Fortress of Ormuz, 1558-1560 • 206

Figure 40 - Illustrations by Martini representing various types of "bombards" used in the late fifteenth century • 226

Figure 41 - Portuguese *verso*. Artillery piece widely used on the coast of Brazil in the mid-sixteenth century • 241

Figure 42 - Fortress of Poggio Imperiale in Italy, showing anthropomorphic conception of the fortress (1488-1511) • 244

Figure 43 - Design of the Fortress of Poggio Imperiale and the ramparts • 245

Figure 44 - The relationship of body and city, in the view of Francesco di Giorgio Martini • 253

Figure 45 - Vitruvian Man as reconceptualized by Leonardo da Vinci • 258

Figure 46 - Simplified city plan of Priene, Greece • 261

Figure 47 - Plan of the Roman city of Timgad, Algeria • 263

Figure 48 - Plan of Eximenes's theoretical city • 270

Figure 49 - Plan of the Portuguese city-fortress of Daman, India • 273

Figure 50 - Model of city with straight streets that cross in the main plaza, according to Martini • 283

Figure 51 - Fortress of Mazagan, showing plaza in a trapezoid shape, 1757 • 291

Figure 52 - Piazza Pio II, in Pienza, Italy, in the shape of a trapezoid, 1459-1462 • 292

Figure 53 - Current view of the Municipal Plaza of the city of Salvador • 293

Figure 54 - Location of the original Sé Cathedral in the city of Salvador • 338

Figure 55 - Corner where the first hospital in the city of Salvador was built • 360

Figure 56 - Probable location of the Jesuits' buildings in the present-day Praça da Sé • 363

Table 1 - Variation in Sea Level in the Bay of All Saints • 30

Table 2 - Sites of Cities and Towns on the Coast of Brazil • 42

Table 3 - Strategic Requirements for Choosing a Site for a City • 43

Table 4 - Structures of the Spanish Tercio and the Portuguese Ordenança • 76

Table 5 - Distribution and Allotment of Staff in the General Administration, 1549 • 80

Table 6 - Bulwarks in Fortress of Mazagan and Fortress of Salvador, 1542-1549 • 85

Table 7 - Properties Belonging to Jesuits in Praça da Sé • 140

Table 8 - Width of Streets in Historic Center of City of Salvador • 158

Table 9 - Measurements in the Cities of Salvador and Rio de Janeiro, 1596-1652 • 158

Table 10 - Division of Entities According to Justinian's Institutes and the Seven-Part Code • 164

Table 11 - Fortification of the City of Salvador: Events 1587-1613 • 172

Table 12 - Costs of Walls and Bulwarks in Fortress of Salvador, 1549 • 179

Table 13 - History of Gates in the City of Salvador, 1549-1796 • 187

Table 14 - Measurements of the Wall of Beseta, Jerusalem • 191

Table 15 - Comparison of Measurements of Portuguese Fortresses • 205

Table 16 - Evolution in Distance Between Bulwarks, 1542-1598 • 211

Table 17 - Data on Fortresses of Mazagan, Diu, Salvador, and Ormuz • 219

Table 18 - Classification of Artillery According to Spanish Standards, 1607 • 228

Table 19 - Classification of Martini's "Types of Bombards" • 233

Table 20 - Items for Defense Required in Captaincies and Plantations • 237

Table 21 - Prices for Weapons and Supplies • 239

Table 22 - Blocks in the Fortress of Salvador: Proportions and the Human Body • 256

Table 23 - Linear Measurements with Anthropomorphic Roots • 268

Table 24 - Measurements of Lots in Fortress of Salvador • 276

Table 25 - Measurements of Streets in Greek, Spanish, and Portuguese Cities • 281

Table 26 - Theoretical Measurements of Streets • 284

Table 27 - Dimensions of Plazas in Selected Cities in the Americas • 294

Table 28 - Standard Proportions in Length of Plazas and Cities • 296

Table 29 - Measurements of the Fortress of Daman • 307

Table 30 - Progress of Work on Jail and Municipal Council Building, 1626-1639 • 317

Table 31 - Buildings Constructed on Góes stream, 1549-1552 • 323

Table 32 - Measurements of Storehouses in the Fortresses of Safi and Salvador • 325

Table 34 - Location of the Main Temple: Theoretical Patterns • 335

Table 35 - Location of Main Cathedral in Selected Spanish Cities • 336

Table 36 - Cathedral Location in Selected Portuguese Cities • 337

Table 37 - Hospital: Orders of Payment, 1549-1552 • 358
Table 38 - Correlation of Units of Measurement • 403

Foreword

The construction of Portuguese America in the New World represents an era of civilization that synthesized knowledge acquired by Christian Europe as it embarked on a revolutionary path during the Renaissance after a prolonged period of territorial expansion and consolidation. The city of Salvador emerged from a political project, through a regulation dated December 17, 1548, which instituted powers and obligations, activities and limitations, form and content. This gave birth to a "fortress and large settlement" with a "governor and captain-general" to civilize the heathen, to promote justice, governance, security, settlement, trade, and conversion to the Holy Catholic Faith, to exploit its riches, and to serve the King.

In this book, Luiz Walter Coelho Filho contextualizes the planned city of Salvador by situating it in time and space, and analyzes its design, urban plan, and purpose, presenting it as an integral part of the social, political, and economic state of affairs at the time. His research utilizes documents and analyzes facts, interprets texts and urban layout, and draws on history, science, rationalism, and fiction. *The Fortress of Salvador in Colonial Brazil* is the fruit of research and passion, knowledge and adventure, dedication and perseverance. The book goes beyond borders for its sources, turning to Miguel Arruda and Luis Dias, King Dom João III and Tomé de Souza, Hippocrates and Aristotle, the Middle Ages and the Renaissance, Leon Battista Alberti and Vitruvius, Plato and Thomas Aquinas, as well as Caramuru and the Tupinamba Indians, Portugal and Brazil, Salvador and the Bay of All Saints.[1]

Anyone who wishes to understand the city of Salvador should read this book; it will unravel various enigmas and propose new paradigms.

Francisco Senna

---

[1] Ed. note: Bahia de Todos os Santos.

Introduction

All people by nature desire to know.

Aristotle

This essay investigates the military and urban conceptualization of the Fortress of Salvador, built on the Bay of All Saints, in the land of Brazil, in 1549. The construction of the city was planned, with each detail concealing two thousand years of knowledge and reflection. The design had unity and style, reflecting the most refined vision of the Portuguese builder-engineer-military figure-architect-urban planner of the first half of the sixteenth century. Is it a Renaissance design? Yes, but such a label says little. It is better to consider the city through the lens offered by the archeology of knowledge, in which the Greek and the Roman, the medieval and the modern, represent sediments that are deposited in layers, offering the reader a broad historical retrospective of urban forms and its relationship to Mediterranean society.

The use of the term "fortress" (*fortaleza*), without prior explanation, may lead to a mistaken understanding of the city. In sixteenth-century Portuguese, the word also referred to a fortified city or town. The fortress was a center of trade, which had a commander, residents, streets, a church, a plaza, soldiers, and Crown officials. Salvador was born as a fortress and city, but, over time, the former faded from view. The title of this book did not arise from the author's imagination, but was inspired by and copied from Codex 112, the registry book of the acts of the Governor General, opened on January 1, 1549. The heading on page 171 reads, "Of the fortress of Salvador on the bay of all Saints in the lands of brazil"—this being the vision of the scribe assigned the task of recording the official acts that preceded the voyage of Tomé de Souza's fleet. "Brazil" was not yet a proper name (Fig. 1).

The whole is best understood by distinguishing and studying the parts; this is the principle method used in this study. Each aspect of the city has a distinctive history: the choice of the site, the determination of the perimeter, the construction of the entry points, the articulation between the upper and lower sections, the urban layout, the location of the main cathedral, the position of the main plaza, the symmetry of shapes, the conceptualization of the bulwarks, and many others. The study of these various aspects begins with Hippocrates, passes through Plato and Aristotle, takes on architectonic form with Vitruvius, and blossoms in the Renaissance rationality of Alberti, Martini, and Cataneo. It involves a mosaic of influences in which the classical is usually dominant, the medieval appears here and there, and, in other places, the modern, that is, the Renaissance, can be seen. The superimposition of various eras in the same design demonstrates the rich evolution of knowledge.

The design of the Fortress of Salvador revealed unity and style. For this reason, it is an excellent historical model. The works of the Roman author Vitruvius exercised extensive influence on the design. It is not coincidental that, in the 1540s, his work, *The Ten Books of Architecture*, was distributed and translated in Portugal. The writings of Vitruvius, who lived just before the Christian era, were embraced by King Dom João III and his court. The term "architect" arose in Portugal at this time. Vitruvius detailed, step by step, the theoretical framework that should guide the planning of a city; we can see a certain resemblance between the Vitruvian guidelines and the work undertaken on the Bay of All Saints.

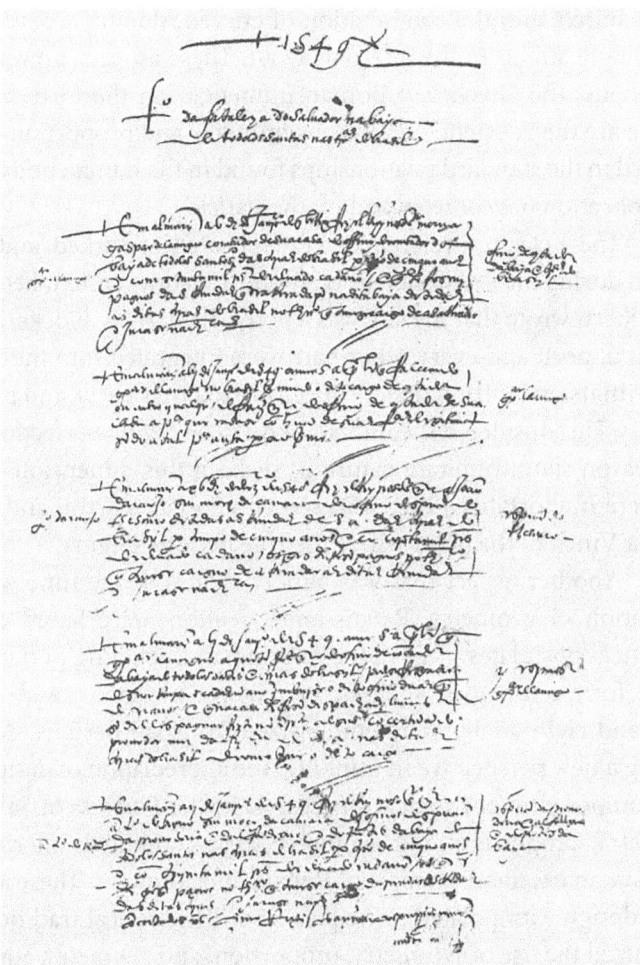

Figure 1 - Page in Codex 112 referring to the Fortress of Salvador, 1549, showing the entry that inspired the title of the present work. Source: Arquivo Histórico Ultramarino Português, Códice 112 [Portuguese Overseas Historical Archive, Codex 112].

The classical influence is present in certain elements of the urban design. For example, Hippocrates commented extensively on the choice of a site, to which Vitruvius lent objectivity, stating that the ideal locale should be moderately high, without much frost or cloudiness, and specified the location of the main plaza, the position of the church, and the combination of curved, sloping access streets and straight streets in the internal layout. These aspects, however, do not exhaust the Greek and Roman influences on the fortress. Also notable are the aesthetic notions of symmetry and proportion—both adjusted to the standard relationships found in the human body—and the application of geometry and mathematics.

These classical references were repeated, reworked, and exaggerated during the Renaissance era. In the fifteenth century, Leon Battista Alberti wrote that the city was a body. The streets, blocks, plazas, cathedral, port, and every other part were integrated into the whole, each with its proper function, relationship to other parts, and proportionality. He considered the human body to be divine perfection, and said reason should imitate nature in seeking this dimension—ideas that were immortalized by Francesco Di Giorgio Martini and Leonardo da Vinci, to the point where the rule became dogma.

Another aspect that was almost radical at the time was the application of geometry. Renaissance treatises were based on the theoretical postulates of Euclid, exploring and detailing perfect geometric forms: triangles, squares, pentagons, hexagons, and circles. Lines and right angles were emphasized in urban designs, demonstrating a new perspective in thinking: the appreciation of design and well-composed mathematical structures. In the Fortress of Salvador, symmetry, proportion, and geometry were combined, offering the historian an excellent example of Renaissance thought. These aspects of the design extrapolated principles from the classical tradition and radicalized the use of symmetry, proportion, and geometry, adjusting them to the topography in a manner that demonstrated a new style, one that involved a search to create something that did not yet exist, an experimentation by someone anxious to imitate the classical and, at the same time, supersede it—an attitude typical of a scientist, an artist, or an entrepreneur.

The design was based on the classical and the Renaissance. The former provided objective principles for choosing the site for the city and the distribution of its parts. The ancients also contributed aesthetic notions concerning proportion, symmetry, and mathematics. And what was the contribution of the modern? The answer appears straightforward: the reprocessing of such knowledge. The bulwark, for example, was a geometric creation typical of the sixteenth century, originating from the tower. The notion of the city as having perfect forms was another Renaissance creation. Symmetry, proportion, and the human body were combined with the method of division into a series from one to ten, a vision of metaphysical mathematics that was favored by the Pythagoreans—aspects that can be identified in the Fortress of Salvador, representing the greatest intellectual treasure of the design.

Contrary to popular opinion, the model of constructing the city in two levels, an upper and a lower, was not derived from a Medieval pattern. It was, rather, Greek, much favored by Aristotle, and survived through the end of the sixteenth century as the preferred option in the choice of an urban site. The Medieval influence was present in only one feature: the identity of cemetery and church, a Christian pattern that stemmed from the Middle Ages, representing a radical break with Roman practices.

The Fortress of Salvador represented an evolutionary synthesis of the concept of the city up through the sixteenth century, bearing its own unique stamp on the combination of influences. It established direct links among features from the Greek world, here and there the Roman, a subtle detail from the Medieval, and the great flowering of aesthetic, military, and mathematical rationality of the Renaissance. The latter determined the style and unity of the urban design, leaving a permanent mark on the construction of the city. The architect who designed the Fortress of Salvador had never heard the word "Renaissance," but he was conscious of creating something new based on knowledge systematized by Vitruvius and on ideas derived from Italian, Spanish, and Portuguese sources. It embodies the adventure of human knowledge.

Fortunately, the design of the Fortress of Salvador is still evident in the historic city center. The layout has been preserved: a few streets were widened, the access ramps were divided by a new access street, and the main cathedral was demolished, but the basic design is still there for us to contemplate. This fact is significant. The main plaza is now a public parking lot, which devalues the historical dignity of the space.

This essay is a quintessential outsider work. It lies off the beaten path and outside the work of research centers, institutes, academies, and universities. It was pieced together during spare time, in hours spent pleasantly pursuing a hobby. It did not have external funding. It has an underground spirit—not one of rebellion or destruction, but one reflecting the choice to preserve a certain intellectual independence. This helps maintain fidelity to the project as well as focus and motivation: without distractions or concessions to others, it arose from an idea, research, books, and an attempt to write an engaging book. This project went on day after day, week after week, year after year.

Spirituality can exist without God, and this essay is a product of such a search. Perhaps the notion of humanism best conveys this world view. The values that inspired this essay have nothing to do with materialism, money, or titles; neither vanity, nor position, nor business, only the desire to create something that gives lasting intellectual form to something hidden. My only hope, perhaps without foundation, is that the work may be read over the next hundred years. It strives for longevity, like a child's notion of immortality, spurred by so much motivation, so much passion, so many pleasant hours.

1. Air, Water, and Place

For fortified towns the following general principles are to be observed. First comes the choice of a very healthy site. Such a site will be high, neither misty nor frosty, and in a climate neither hot nor cold, but temperate.

Vitruvius

How did people learn how to select the best place to build a city? Plateaus, hills, and mountains have long inspired a sense of safety and healthfulness. Philosophers and scholars such as Hippocrates, Aristotle, Vitruvius, Vegetius, Aquinas, Ibn Jaldún, Alberti, Martini, and Cataneo analyzed this preference; likewise, the documents that guided the choice of the site for the Fortress of Salvador in Brazil discussed it as a strategic choice. The founding of every city in the world has required taking particular geographic conditions into account. The historical city of Salvador on the Bay of All Saints is a good example of the tactical knowledge accumulated by Mediterranean culture and applied to a vision of reality to be created.

Human beings are afraid of the sea and now, more than ever, fear its rising level and the sudden fury of its waves. Stories of a great flood, immortalized in *Genesis* and recounted by Plato,[2] provoke a certain degree of anxiety. Plato invited the listener to imagine what happened to the inhabitants who survived the disaster, concluding that "those who then escaped would only be hill shepherds—small sparks of the human race preserved on the tops of mountains." In his account, he assumed that all cities located on the plains and near the sea were destroyed. A vast, terrifying loneliness overcame the earth's surface, and most animals were destroyed, with only a few herds of cattle and flocks of goats surviving to provide sustenance to people.

Although the veracity of the flood may be questioned, the geology of South America does raise troubling concerns. At the height of the Ice Age only 17,000 years ago, the Bay of All Saints was a valley, and the sea lay one hundred meters below the current tide level. During subsequent millennia, the water rose five meters above the current level, leaving its marks on the rocks. Analysis shows that the sea fell, rose, and fell again, then stabilizing for an unknown period of time (Table 1).

Table 1 - Variation in Sea Level in the Bay of All Saints

Time (years)	Sea Level	Observation
17,000	100 meters below current level	climax of Ice Age
7,000	same as present level	—
5,000	5 meters above current level	—
4,000	same as present level	—
3,500	2 meters above current level	—

Source: Leite, Osmário Rezende. *Evolução Fisiográfica e da Ocupação do Território da Baía de Todos os Santos [Evolution of Physiography and Occupation of the Region of the Bay of All Saints]*, pp. 17-22.

Although people are afraid of the sea, a succession of tranquil days allows their fears to take a long rest in their unconscious. Thus, Plato concluded that people forgot the flood and returned to life on

---

2 He also mentions, "The traditions about the many destructions of mankind which have been occasioned by deluges and pestilences, and in many other ways, and of the survival of a remnant." PLATO. *As Leis* [Laws], pp. 136-137.

the plains, giving the example of the city of Ilion (Troy), founded on a low-lying hill by the primitive peoples who descended from higher regions. The settlement was close to the many rivers that had their sources in the heights of Ida[3]—invoking a few of Homer's verses, their words suggestive of the human epic:

> *Dardania's walls he raised;*
> *for Ilion, then [...] was not.*
> *The natives were content to till*
> *The shady foot*
> *of Ida's fountful hill.*
> (Iliad, XX, 216-218)

Their fear of the sea was forgotten and survival required a reconciliation of life on the mountains, plains, and rivers. The world grew increasingly interrelated, while the choice of sites became a matter of health and safety. Upon this scene entered Hippocrates, known as the "Father of Medicine." He wrote a brief essay[4] dealing with the influence of the seasons of the year as they changed, as well as the effects of winds, both hot and cold, and of water sources on human health. Upon arriving in any unfamiliar city, he said, a doctor should study its position in relation to the winds, the rising of the sun, and its exposure to the elements. With regard to the elements, he should ascertain whether the city site is protected and sweltering, or elevated and cold. He should also investigate the quality of the water, the type of soil, and the activities pursued by the inhabitants, observing whether the drinking water is murky and bland or if it comes from high, rocky places, and whether the type of soil is arid and dry, or moist and fertile. In short, he advocated studying the conditions of life for the inhabitants, using these criteria for evaluating the healthfulness of a particular locale.

---

3 This refers to the mountain range in western Mysia, Phrygia, and Crete. (BRANDÃO, *Dicionário Mítico-Etimológico* [Dictionary of Myths and Etymology], I, p. 591)

4 HIPPOCRATES. *Sobre los Aires, Aguas y Lugares* [On Airs, Waters, and Places]. *Tratados Hipocraticos* [Hippocratic Treatises], II, Editorial Gredos, Madrid, 1997. This essay is considered by some to be the "golden book" of the Hippocratic Corpus. It bears an obvious similarity with other works by the same author in the way it deals with the influence of the environment on human beings.

The Hippocratic notion of the influence of the environment on people is a theory that many researchers are still pursuing today, perpetuating ideas about the effects of the sun and cold temperatures on human behavior. Hippocrates believed that "Astronomy contributed to Medicine, not merely to a slight degree, but a very large degree." In general, he concluded that cities facing the direction where the sun rises are healthier than those facing the north, south, or west, since heat and cold coming from the east are more moderate. The same principle holds for waters facing the east, which he argued are clearer and have a more agreeable odor. He stated poetically that "fog is not produced in these cities, since the sun prevents it when it rises and shines."

Hippocrates did not limit himself to identifying the ideal locale for living: he also created typologies that combined the factors of location, diseases, and human behavior. In the ideal site, facing the sunrise, the inhabitants enjoy "good color and vigor, better than in any other site." They have "clear voices and their attitudes and intelligence are better." Cities oriented in this way bear many similarities "with springtime," they have fewer infirmities, and their women are more fertile and "give birth with great ease." This ideal site, however, creates people who are more accommodating in temperament. Hippocrates describes them as "cowardly and lethargic spirits." By contrast, people living in locations subject to greater variations and adversities are vigorous. In his opinion, temperament is rooted in the degree of exertion required of the body, an idea that is still provocative today.

Hippocrates demonstrated his knowledge on the subject of health, but, among the known historical texts, Aristotle was the first to analyze appropriate sites by taking into consideration all significant factors.[5] He recommended four criteria, in order of importance: healthfulness; protection against strong winds; suitability of the locale for both administrative and military activities; and natural abundance of water sources and springs. In discussing these criteria, he identified air and water as the sources of health. He also examined the relationship between topography and defense, leading him to speculate

---

5 ARISTOTLE *Política* [Politics]. 1330, b, and 1331, a.

The Fortress of Salvador

about each type of government and its ideal site: hilltops for monarchical and oligarchical governments; flat places for democratic governments; and fortified positions in scattered places for aristocracies.

Aristotle's thinking was speculative and dynamic, reflecting various factors in the social organization of his time and its tenuous equilibrium between internal and external peace based on the type of power structure in the city. His vision was, above all, that of a political scientist who investigated and attempted to arrive at the truth, respecting the factual circumstances. This was the source of his genius as well as his current relevance.

Aristotle investigated these issues at a general level, but it fell to the Roman Marcos Vitruvius Pollio, called the "Father of Architecture," to thoroughly detail the ideal relationship among sites, healthfulness, and buildings. Vitruvius lived in the first century B.C. and wrote *The Ten Books on Architecture*, a work that had far-reaching influence on Renaissance architects. It was also the main theoretical source for the construction of the Fortress of Salvador.

In the beginning of his work, Vitruvius dedicated a chapter to the selection of healthy places to settle.[6] The most important criterion was the healthfulness of the site, the first requirement being that it should be located at a height: "[…] we cannot but believe that we must take great care to select a very temperate climate for the site of our city, since healthfulness is, as we have said, the first requisite." A high site would protect residents from excessive heat or cold. A temperate climate was the best expression of the physical well-being of the citizens.

Vitruvius emphasized two other aspects: avoiding places near lagoons and those next to the ocean facing the direction where the sun sets. Proximity to lowlands and marshes would subject the city to "heavy, unhealthy vapors," and the direction toward the sunset would favor exposure to the midday heat, especially in summer, which he described as "hot at noon, and at evening all aglow." Vitruvius coined a poetic image when he described the rigor of the sun's rays sucking out the "natural strength" of things. To support his contention, he in-

---

[6] POLLIO, Marcus Vitruvius. *Los Diez Libros de Architectura* [The Ten Books on Architecture], p. 14.

voked some common sense of the era: people moving from a cold region to a hot one will waste away, while those going in the opposite direction will not fall ill from the change, but become stronger instead.

According to the perception of these classical writers, the effect of heat on people was harmful and weakened them. The best expression of this truth, they believed, was the metaphor of iron: it is hard by nature, but the heat of fire softens it in such a way that it can be molded into any form; however, if it is then placed in cold water, it hardens and returns to its original rigidity. According to Vitruvius, echoing Hippocrates, the human body reacts in the same way to heat.

The site of a city should thus be on an elevation, with a temperate climate, without nearby marshes, and, if close to the ocean, facing the direction where the sun rises—rules for living well that are still valid today when choosing a place to live.

Vitruvius discussed a final parameter: the quality of pastures and water. The positive or negative properties of places depended equally on the nature of the surrounding fields, rivers, and water sources. The ancients, according to Vitruvius, practiced a ritual for verifying the healthfulness of a site. Before building a settlement, they observed the livers of some cattle they sacrificed, having kept them only in the pastures of the site they were considering; if they found the liver of the first animal to be abnormal, they sacrificed others through a series of trials until they found ones indicating pastures and waters that were healthful. If this could not be verified, they concluded that the waters and pastures of those places were prejudicial to people as well and sought another locale.

Unlike Aristotle, Vitruvius did not discuss the quality of a site from a military perspective. This aspect is richer and more complex, since, in addition to health factors, it concerns administrative, military, and commercial questions, in addition to issues of supply and communications.

Aristotle's and Vitruvius's ideas were ratified and transcribed literally by Saint Thomas Aquinas,[7] who also relied on another important Roman author: Flavius Vegetius Renatus.[8] The theories of the

---

7 AQUINAS, Saint Thomas. *Escritos Políticos* [Political Writings], pp. 169-172.
8 RENATUS, Flavius Vegetius. *Instituciones Militares* [Military Institutions].

three classical authors lent support to Medieval theological conclusions, which also recommended a temperate region and healthy climate for building cities. These authors were simply transcribed in the Middle Ages, when Greek and Roman knowledge was neither amplified nor altered. Europeans continued to propound theoretical models drawn from the experience of the Greeks and Romans. However, this knowledge was not limited to Europe; it was a reality throughout the Mediterranean world.

Ibn Jaldún, born in Tunis in 1332, was the author of a formidable compendium entitled *Introduction to Universal History*, which portrayed the Arab vision of history and knowledge. In a certain passage, he wrote about the construction of cities designed "for the enjoyment of well-being and the satisfaction of the requirements of luxury."[9] Defense and healthfulness are crucial interrelated points, he argued. To counter the deleterious influences of the atmosphere, a place should have pure air and not be prone to illnesses, an idea that merged with the notion of the wind, as he condemned locales where the air was still and of bad quality. He likewise criticized cities situated near contaminated or swampy waters, arguing that water sources should be pure and abundant. Finally, he called attention to the necessity of having fields, pastures, and forests nearby for the inhabitants' use.

For this Arab author, a city should be erected high up on a steep mountain, on an ocean peninsula or a river, so that its access points could be well defended. For cities on the coast, this feature was indispensable as a means of protection against maritime attacks.

During the Renaissance, such concepts were not altered. Alberti[10] devoted at least three chapters to the subject, exhaustively examining past history to conclude that the most advisable environment should have a humid, warm climate. Martini[11] commented specifically on the terrain, water, air, and wind, establishing principles

---

9 JALDÚN, Ibn. *Introducción a la Historia Universal* [Introduction to Universal History], p. 617.
10 ALBERTI, Leon Battista. *L'Architettura* [Architecture], pp. 14-26.
11 MARTINI, Francesco Di Giorgio. *Trattati Di Architettura Ingegneria e Arte Militare* [Treatise on Architecture, Engineering, and Military Arts]. II, pp. 302-309.

concerning their quality. Cataneo[12] explained that the success of a city depends on the selection of a good site, listing salubrity, land fertility, security, and convenience as factors. He defined salubrity as the good quality of the air, waters, and fields.

The Mediterranean universe conceptualized the ideal site for any city on the basis of widely shared criteria: health, defense, and a good logistical position, as well as avoiding the direction where the sun sets and lowlands filled with swampy or stagnant waters. For the first criterion, the factors that writers recommended examining were the healthfulness of the climate, the quality of the waters, and the availability of fields, pastures, and forests. The second criterion, strong defense, entailed a location on a height, without any surrounding elevations that could give the enemy an advantage, and in a place that allowed an escape route. The third required a suitable location in terms of trade routes and administrative services. All three were rational criteria considered by Hippocrates, Aristotle, Vegetius, Vitruvius, Ibn Jaldún, and Aquinas, and which served as raw material for Renaissance thinkers. Based on these authors, the Portuguese and Spanish built their cities in the New World. The idea of what constituted a good dwelling place had apparently not changed much over the past 2,500 years.

---

12 CATANEO, Pietro *Dell'Architettura* [On Architecture], pp. 188-197.

2. Selection of the Site

Life is short, science long, opportunity fleeting, experiment dangerous, judgment difficult.

Hippocrates

In Amsterdam in 1648, Guilherme Piso published his book *Natural History of Brazil*, the first work dedicated to the study of tropical diseases on the coast of Brazil.[13] The first chapter, echoing Hippocrates, was entitled, "On Airs, Waters, and Places."[14] According to Piso, Hippocrates was the best author "of all that is good in this art," and, like him, recommended that the first thing a doctor should do upon arriving in a city was to observe the setting and its relationship to the direction of the winds and sunrise, the location of springs and their type of water, and the inhabitants' way of life. This was what he did himself, concluding:

---

13 Guilherme Piso lived in Pernambuco for six years, serving as a doctor on the team of Mauricio de Nassau. He collected a vast amount of material as part of the project's scientific objectives.

14 He opened his book by saying, "No better guide could be devised for organizing or instituting medicine among remote peoples than that handed down by Hippocrates, the best author on all that is good in such arts."

"The continent of Brazil is considered, with good reason, to be the largest and most excellent area in the entire New World; upon accurate examination, it will also be seen as the most pleasant and healthy."[15]

Over the course of forty pages, Piso analyzed the sea, winds, geography, and the inhabitants' temperament, trying to determine what could be learned, revealing the knowledge and vision of an educated man concerning each phenomenon of nature. His conclusions were an eloquent homage to his love of Brazil's natural surroundings: the temperature was excellent, the soil fertile, and the renowned healthfulness of the place "attracted not a few aged men and those of less robust health from Spain, the Indies, and other remote places, to the air and waters bestowed by these skies." The children of "Brazilians" were healthy and had been raised with exposure to the climate, bathed in cold water and exposed uniformly to the air and the winds, implying the "logical" conclusion that heat weakens health and cold strengthens it.

In a certain passage, Piso described the ideal location in which to live. Everyone should choose to settle in "a place that is somewhat elevated, closed to the west and open to the east," which could keep "the thick wind from the continent" away from the settlement and allow inhabitants "to receive the advantages of the light sea breeze that always accompanies the sun." Even today there can be no wiser recommendation.

The choice of a good site, according to Piso, followed a basic logic. It should be an elevated location, but not so extreme that it might expose the population to excessive cold and wind. Headwaters should flow toward the east so they can receive the first rays of the morning sun. A site overlooking the sea was the healthiest, especially if it faced the east. If a city was on a hill, it was best to have it on the side facing the east. In short, the ideal was always the sunrise, always the early exposure to the morning warmth.

---

15 PISO, Guilherme. *História Natural e Médica da Índia Ocidental* [Natural and Medical History of the West Indies], p. 30.

Piso's ideas showed notable parallels to the regulations contained in Spanish legislation. The *Seven-Part Code*, a set of normative rules codified in the Renaissance, dedicated an entire chapter to warfare, detailing the locale where an army should camp during a campaign. The text recalls that the Romans called a military encampment a *castra*, meaning "a strong camp organized for defense against the enemy." In military thinking, the site should be healthful, strong, and well-supplied with water, a place that would make a suitable choice for "building a good town,"[16] close to water, pastures, and firewood. The criteria listed in the *Seven-Part Code* were almost literal repetitions of Vegetius's text.

The instructions given to Hernando Cortez on June 26, 1523,[17] for settling New Spain (now Mexico) contained clear rules about choosing a site:

> "One of the main things you must examine closely is the setting where sites might be built."[18]

The sites should be healthful, not inundated, with good air, close to hills and good soil for cultivation, and near the sea to facilitate loading and unloading. Regarding the port, the instructions stated that the settlement should be built on the coast, in places suitable for security and resupplying ships. When it was necessary to settle the interior, the locale to be chosen should be served "by some river" that would allow "things to be brought from the sea to the settlement."

Signed by Carlos I, these instructions were expanded and improved, eventually incorporated into the *Ordinances* issued by King

---

16 LEI DAS SETE PARTIDAS *[Seven-Part Code]*, Segunda Partida, Título XXIII, Lei XIX.

17 COLLECCION DE DOCUMENTOS INÉDITOS [Collection of Unpublished Documents], II, 167. The summary described the text as "Instructions given to Hernando Cortes, Governor and Captain General of New Spain, concerning the settlement and pacification of that land and the treatment and conversion of its natives."

18 COLLECCION DE DOCUMENTOS INÉDITOS [Collection of Unpublished Documents], II, p. 176.

Felipe II in 1573.[19] One of the laws presented detailed rules about the choice of sites for cities, towns, and settlements, clearly indicating the influence of Vitruvius. On the seacoast, the site should be elevated, healthful, and strong, taking into consideration shelter, the depth and defense of the port, and, if possible, it should avoid facing "the sea at midday[20] or at sunset." Water should be located nearby. The places chosen should not be too high because of the "discomfort of the winds and the difficulty they impose on work, nor in places that are too low," since they are diseased. He concluded that "they should be founded on somewhat elevated places that are open to winds from the north and south."

Towns or settlements in mountains, he directed, should be constructed in places that were not prone to fog; if built on the banks of a river, the settlement should be situated in such a way that "the sun should shine first on the settlement rather than on the water." We can see this rule debated in a historical example: the city of Santo Domingo on Hispaniola was founded in 1496 on the left side of the Rio Ozama so that the town would first receive the sun's rays. In 1504, it was transferred to the right side of the river, since this facilitated communication by land with other settlements and towns located on the western side of the island. Oviedo[21] and Bartolomé de las Casas,[22] famous historians with contrasting ideological profiles, were unanimous in criticizing the change in the settlement's location, for two

---

19 RECOPILACION DE LEIS DOS REYNOS DE LAS ÍNDIAS [Compilation of the Laws of the Kingdoms of the Indies]. In the second volume, the seventh heading deals with the settling of cities and towns. Law I deals specifically with the ideal site, corresponding to ordinances 39 and 40 issued by King Felipe II in 1573.
20 In the northern hemisphere, this meant facing south.
21 OVIEDO, Gonzalo Fernandez. *Historia General y Natural de las Indias* [General and Natural History of the Indies]. I, p. 76. The text contains the following passage: "In truth, it would necessarily be better to settle and live on the other side rather than on this one, where the Ozama River passes between the sun and the city, making the morning mists, as soon as the sun appears, pour down or spill over the city."
22 CASAS, Bartolomé de las. *Historia de las Indias* [History of the Indies], II, p. 234. The text also stated, "In truth, however, for health reasons, the Admiral chose a better site in the other part or side, which was in the east where the rising sun chased away the vapors, mists, and humidity."

reasons: the sun shone first on the river, and the water sources lay on the abandoned side.

In Portugal, the same basic recommendations contained in the *Seven-Part Code* were reiterated in the "Rules of War," an integral part of the Alfonsine Ordinances, which were in effect until 1512. In military jargon, what the Romans meant by *castro* was called by the Spaniards *hoste* and, by the Portuguese, *arraial*, i.e., "village." The Portuguese text said that an *arraial* should be settled in a strong place that could be defended, was close to water, and lay near food sources for animals.[23]

It is intriguing to observe how the logic of healthfulness and abundant resources was manipulated on the military level when selecting a site. The construction of the Fortress of Mozambique by the Portuguese is a good example. In 1545, Dom João de Castro sailed toward India, stopping over on the island of Mozambique. The Portuguese had a small fortress on the southern end of the island. As a defense against the Turks, the Viceroy made the strategic decision of transferring the Portuguese fortification to the northern side. The island is low and small, but the northern end has a higher bluff, a location that he considered to be ideal for the construction of the fortress. The reasons behind his recommendation for the move are worth examining.

At the entrance of the port, the high, steep cliff ensured good protection when landing and defending the site. It was also a healthier place because it was "exposed to the winds and washed by the sea and was founded on a cliff and rocks." If the Turks were to invade, they would not be able to stay for long, since the surrounding land was sterile and lacking food sources. The Viceroy said the Turks were men who "were gluttons and were prone to vices and indulgences." Moreover, the local airs were unhealthy and intemperate, and "the waters scarce and foul."[24]

The reasoning followed for the island of Mozambique was an

---

23 ORDENAÇÕES AFONSINAS [Alfonsine Ordinances], livro primeiro, título LI, p. 291.
24 SANCEAU, Elaine. *Cartas de D. João de Castro* [Letters of Dom João de Castro], pp. 97-98.

exception. For a settlement, the ideal site was high, suitable for defense, and well-served by water and fertile lands. When the first towns and cities were built by the Portuguese along the Brazilian coast, sites located at high elevations predominated, with the ports facing the southern or eastern quadrants. The choice of a site on an island was common, demonstrating the search for protection against indigenous peoples in the area. Of a total of nine towns, six were founded with their main ocean front facing the south or east. The predominance of this orientation, besides being determined by geography, demonstrates the apparent rationality in the choice of the locale, keeping in mind that the east, southeast, and south in the southern hemisphere are the favored directions in terms of winds and exposure to the sun (Table 2).

Table 2 - Sites of Cities and Towns on the Coast of Brazil

Name	Founded	Direction of Port	Location	Position
Salvador	1549	Northwest	tableland	mainland
Olinda	1534	Southeast	tableland	mainland
Itamaracá	1534	South	tableland	island
Ilhéus	1540	West	tableland	mainland
Porto Seguro	1534	East	tableland	mainland
Vitória	1534	South	plains	island
Rio de Janeiro	1565	East	hill	mainland
Santos	1540	North	plains	island
São Vicente	1532	South	plains	island

Source: The author.

Vitruvius criticized the choice of sites facing the south (midday) or west (sunset). His reason was to prevent greater exposure to hot winds and the sun's heat. His rule makes sense in the northern hemisphere, which explains the pattern found in India. On the coast of Brazil, northeastern winds predominate, as do the "mild, benign eastern wind coming with the morning breezes" and, in the colder season, from April to October, the southern and southwestern winds. Apparently, the Philippine rule contained in Ordinances 39 and 40, which recommended avoiding a southern orientation, clearly inspired by Vitruvius, were not appropriate for cities situated in the southern hemisphere. In Brazil, emphasis was placed on careful observations of potential sites.

Table 3 - Strategic Requirements for Choosing a Site for a City

Requirement	Rule in Charter for Tomé De Souza	Aristotle's Model
Defense	"[...] with knowledgeable people, look for a place that will be best endowed for building a strong fortress that can be well defended [...]"	With regard to military actions, the locale "[...] should afford easy egress to the citizens, and at the same time be inaccessible and difficult of capture to enemies."
Quality of Region	"[...] and which has the best conditions and qualities so that, henceforth, a large settlement can be built [...]"	"Special care should be taken of the health of the inhabitants, which will depend chiefly on the healthiness of the locality and of the quarter to which they are exposed."
Administrative Center	"[...] and it is fitting that it be so, in order that it can supply the other captaincies [...]"	"The site of the city should likewise be convenient both for political administration and for war."

Healthfulness	"[...] and should be in a healthy site with good airs [...]"	"In respect of the place itself [...] its situation should be fortunate in four things. The first, health—this is a necessity."
Water Supplies	"[...] and have an abundance of water [...]"	"There should be a natural abundance of springs and fountains in the town."
Good Port	"[...] and a port in which ships may easily be tied up and beached when needed [...]"	"As for its position, if we wish to build a city, as we may desire, we should locate it favorably with regard to the ocean as well as to the land [...] we often see in countries and cities dockyards and harbors very conveniently placed outside the city, but not too far off; and they are kept in dependence by walls and similar fortifications."

Source: MENDONÇA, Marcos Carneiro de. *Raízes da Formação Administrativa do Brasil* [Roots of the Administrative Formation of Brazil], p. 38; Aristotle, *Política* [Politics]. 1330 b.

The Fortress of Salvador

The city of Salvador faces the ocean in the northwestern quadrant, which was an exception to the usual siting of early Portuguese settlements. The sunset reaches the port at a 45-degree angle, which makes the beach area stifling, being poorly served by winds during the summer months. However, the upper city is favored by northeastern and eastern winds coming from the ocean, which ensure healthfulness to the site. We must not forget the good advice offered by Oviedo and Las Casas: when the sun rises, it should first shine on the city. In choosing the site, other vital aspects prevailed, such as conditions for defending the locale, an abundance of water, access to fertile land, and a good port.

The charter granted to Tomé de Souza, which defined standards that must be observed in choosing a site, were quite detailed and precise. The fortress should be "large and strong, in an advantageous place."[25] The charter praised the Bay of All Saints as the most appropriate place to settle on the coast of Brazil, due to the layout of the port and rivers as well as the good quality, abundance, and healthfulness of the land. One chapter analyzed the locale thoroughly, reflecting the complete mastery of all the aspects recommended by Aristotle, Vegetius, and Vitruvius (Table 3).

The *Seven-Part Code* required that the choice fall on the "best place that can be found in the place as it is."[26] This sentence is redundant and sounds strange, but that was exactly how the choice was made on the Bay of All Saints. The site chosen for the Fortress of Salvador was perfect in the strategic terms that were dominant in the sixteenth century, adopting the criteria from Greek and Roman knowledge. The fortress was built on a plateau, with a small, central depression above the slope where the access road called the Ladeira da Misericórdia was built. On the western side, a sixty-meter escarpment overlooks the ocean; on the eastern side, a valley ends in a marsh, across from two nearby hills known as Palma and Desterro; to the north is a flat, dry spit of land, then a gentle descent to Pelourinho,

---

25 MENDONÇA, Marcos Carneiro de. *Raízes da Formação Administrativa do Brasil* [Roots of the Administrative Structure of Brazil], p. 35.
26 LEI DAS SETE PARTIDAS [*Seven-Part Code*], Segunda partida, título XXIII, Lei XIX, p. 88.

with Mount Calvário on the other side; and, to the south lies the sloping street from the Praça Castro Alves and the heights of São Bento (Fig. 2).

Figure 2 - The Fortress of Salvador was constructed on two plateaus, Sé (to the north) and Ajuda (to the south).

When the governor Tomé de Souza and the master architect Luis Dias showed the plateau to the men who had to be consulted about this important decision, inviting them to examine it and offer advice, it was easy for them to demonstrate that it would be the ideal locale. It had a high, open, exposed area with an agreeable climate, and water sources and springs on the eastern slope and the side facing the ocean; the port lay at the foot of the city and could be connected through sloping streets; overland paths would allow movement of merchandise, people, and emergency escape; and the access points could be easily defended.

Over the millennia, choosing a place to live has involved a sort of intuitive apprenticeship for humankind. The Tupinamba Indians liked to build their huts near places supplied by water and firewood. Gabriel Soares de Souza reported that, when the Tupinamba founded a village, they looked for a "site that was high and free of winds," with nearby water and land suitable for making their gardens around the village.[27] In this regard, there was not much difference between the Tupinamba and the Portuguese. For our purposes here, however, the relevant links are those spanning more than two thousand years of Western history, especially those involving the complex examination of the various desirable criteria applied to the process of site selection.

With regard to location, Aristotle wrote that, to build the ideal or desired city, the site should be well positioned in relation to both the ocean and the land. One of the decisive factors was that the city should be able to easily communicate with the rest of its territory for the sake of protection; another was that it should be easily accessible for receiving the fruits of the land from its territory.[28] Sixteenth-century Portuguese applied the same type of rationality advised by the Greeks, representing an inheritance from the ancients, even though this knowledge had crystallized into something that, to them, seemed quite natural. The Greeks theorized, the Romans refined, the Middle Ages conserved, and the Portuguese applied such knowledge. The result was the first large fortress on the coast of Brazil.

---

27 SOUZA, Gabriel Soares. *Notícia do Brasil* [Report from Brazil], II, capítulo CLI, p. 246.
28 ARISTOTLE, *Política* [Politics], p. 234.

3. Polybius versus Vegetius

> *The Greeks used to seek strong sites, and would never have put themselves where there was not a ditch or a riverbank or a multitude of trees, or another natural shelter that might defend them. But the Romans encamped securely not so much from the site as from art. Nor would they ever have encamped in places where they would not have been able to extend all of their men according to their discipline.*
>
> Machiavelli

In 1521, Niccolo Machiavelli published *The Art of War*, in which he defended Roman military practices and proposed ways of adapting them to the contemporary reality of sixteenth-century Italy. One of his most intriguing discussions concerned the organization of military encampments, which can be summarized as follows: the Romans would choose sites where they could apply the same arrangement of streets, blocks, and troop movements, while the Greeks always chose protected places, adapting the organization of the encampment to the topography of the locale. The Portuguese and the Spanish shared common roots for planning sites, but, starting in the sixteenth century, their practices diverged. The Spanish adopted the Roman pattern, referred to here as the Polybian pattern, while the Portuguese followed the Greek pattern, here called the Vegetian pattern.

Salvador is an excellent example of a fortified city that is adapted to the topography of the chosen site. According to Machiavelli, the Greeks sought secure places where the site was protected by a gorge, river, forest, or other natural defense. The Romans, he said, relied more on engineering, favoring tactical formations and a single pattern for military encampments: straight paths that crossed each other to form a grid; a plaza close to the center; a hierarchical arrangement of the tents; and regular dimensions at all points.[29] Machiavelli's book achieved renown and influenced military thinking.

In Spain, Diego de Salazar's *Treatise on Warfare*, published in Alcalá in 1536, was an adapted translation that simply changed the names of the characters in the dialogues and a few historical examples.[30] However, the creation of the typology of Greek and Roman patterns cannot be attributed to Machiavelli. He simply repeated the Greek historian Polybius, following a typical Renaissance phenomenon: after the renewed interest in the Greek language, sixteenth-century humanists became more interested in the period of the Roman Republic rather than the Empire as a source of knowledge about warfare and strategy in ancient Rome. Polybius belonged to the Republic, while Vegetius was from the Empire.

Flavius Vegetius Renatus and Polybius wrote about the choice of sites from a military perspective, exercising enormous influence on Medieval and Renaissance military thought. Vegetius, a Hispano-Roman, lived in the fourth century A.D. and wrote a work entitled *Military Institutions*. Polybius, a Greek historian, lived in the second century B.C. and wrote an extensive history of Rome, in which he discussed at length the military organization of Greek and Roman armies. Six centuries separate the two in time and differentiate them in terms of the influence they exerted over the Middle and Modern Ages. Vegetius was consulted the most during the Middle Ages, while the work of Polybius, written in Greek, was rediscovered during the Renaissance, guiding, for example, Justus Lipsius,[31] author of *On Ro-*

---

29 MACHIAVELLI, Niccolo. *Del Arte de la Guerra* [The Art of War], p. 146.
30 Idem, estudo preliminar, XXXV.
31 RENATUS, Flavius Vegetius. *Instituciones Militares* [Military Institutions], p. 23.

man Warfare, subtitled *Commentary on Polybius*. Lipsius, in turn, guided the military thinking of Machiavelli.

Vegetius lived through the decline of the Roman Empire and attempted to revive the teachings of earlier authors.[32] Polybius, a member of the military, first fought against the Roman army and then ended up joining it, experiencing the apogee of the institution. Polybius presented a radical model based on offensive strategy. Although both wrote about Roman military organization, the standard of excellence in the ancient world, they differed in their views about site selection.

Vegetius wrote his essay around 400 A.D. In 378, the Goths had defeated the Roman army in Adrianopolis, a few years before the destruction of Rome by Alarico (410 A.D.), king of the Goths. The intention of Vegetius's essay was apparently to revive the ancient glory of the Roman army. He explained that recruits should be taught the principles of fortification, since the art of fortifying encampments had been lost. No one took such precautions any more, so the barbarians' cavalry "took our armies by surprise several times, both by day and by night."[33]

The basic principle was simple. The choice of site should fall upon an advantageous location where "water, wood, and fodder" were near at hand. If the army intended to stay longer at a camp, the site should also be "a healthy stopping place." He further recommended the avoidance of "places dominated by prominences,"[34] since these would be exposed to the enemy; locations subject to flooding; or sites dominated by steep slopes that would hinder escape. In another chapter, Vegetius warned of the danger of lagoons and swamps, which "cause many illnesses," and suggested avoiding arid terrains and wide open spaces where soldiers could not "enjoy the shade of trees." Furthermore, the location had to be the best choice so that the enemy would not invade.

While Vegetius based his work on readings, Polybius had direct experience of the Greek and Roman practices. The Roman en-

---

32 Idem, p. 21. Cato the Censor, Cornelius Celso.
33 Ibidem, p. 50.
34 Ibidem, pp. 50-51.

campment was constructed on a site that allowed for observation and the transmittal of orders:[35] a good place was at the intersection of routes and highways. The Romans sought certainty that each soldier would know exactly where he should be in the camp during successive changes of its site. The location would change, but the organization of physical space within the camp was always the same, which, according to Polybius, constituted the main difference between the Greeks and the Romans. The Greeks believed that the crucial aspect of a siting an encampment was to adapt it to the particular features of the terrain, taking advantage of natural defenses; however, adaptation to the site made the organization of the encampment uncertain. The Romans, by contrast, preferred the "toil of building an entrenchment and what it contained, since doing so resulted in an encampment that was always identical and familiar."

Polybius did not favor one or the other criterion, but simply compared them. The Roman standard, suitable for the time of the Republic, could only be employed by a victorious, offensive army. To a certain extent, the Spanish Empire repeated this offensive concept in building its cities in the Americas.

The description of the Roman military encampment contained in the work of Polybius was confirmed and enriched by another historian, Flavius Josephus, author of *Antiquities of the Jews*, who also witnessed the military standards of Rome. According to Josephus, the Romans fortified a site in a "quadrangular form" and, if the land was uneven, leveled it out. The space within the encampment was divided into blocks where the lodgings of officials and soldiers were built. The exterior of the encampment resembled the "walls of a city," with "equidistant towers," in between which were machines to launch rocks and spears. It had four sections divided by wide roads, while in the middle were the leader's lodging, the market, workshops, and the court.[36] Josephus, who was Jewish, lived during the time of the emperor Vespasian (70-79 A.D.), when Roman military discipline still reigned.

---

35 POLYBIUS. *Histórias* [Histories]. Livro V, pp. 27-42.
36 JOSEPHUS, Flavius. *História dos Hebreus* [Antiquities of the Jews]. Livro Terceiro, capítulo 6.

The Fortress of Salvador

If Polybius and Vegetius wrote about military encampments, to what extent can their principles be applied to the building of cities? Vitruvius, the Roman architect who gave instructions on building cities, temples, and houses, did not ignore features of the terrain. He stated that the site chosen should obey the main criteria ensuring health, but that defense was also a vital aspect; in this regard, his advice was similar to that of Vegetius. Both Vegetius and Vitruvius favored cities built on heights, replete with contours and natural defenses, thus diverging from the vision of straight lines and wide spaces described by Polybius and approved by Flavius Josephus.

Machiavelli argued that fortresses embedded in places that were easily scaled were vulnerable to artillery and explosives; he therefore tended to prefer erecting them "on a plateau, to be artificially fortified,"[37] a type of thinking that reflected the influence of the Polybian pattern. The classical period was idealized to a certain extent: if the Romans used a particular practice and were strong and powerful, the Renaissance world thought it should follow their example.

The typology distinguishing Vegetius and Polybius is echoed in the cities erected in the Iberian Americas. We can see clearly that the Spanish freed themselves from limitations imposed by the terrain, while the Portuguese continued to favor hills and cities on heights. Subservience to the topography of the terrain meant that the urban design took second place, necessitating adaptations and concessions to uneven levels. This reduced the size of city blocks, so the settlement ended up being smaller, an imposition of the model of a defensive city.

The Spanish, based on their conquest of Mexico, pursued an important change in the relationship between the urban design and the terrain. Previously, they had chosen elevated sites suitable for protection; subsequently, flat terrains were deemed more suitable to the design. They followed the Polybian pattern and freed themselves from the defensive stance, encouraged by a number of factors: by their confidence, since Spain had become the greatest empire in Europe; by the offensive nature of the military campaigns they pur-

---

37 MACHIAVELLI, Niccolo. *Del Arte de la Guerra* [The Art of War], p. 175.

sued; by the fact that they occupied areas in the interior rather than on the coast; and, especially, by the grandiosity of the central plaza in the Aztec city of Mexico, which influenced the new pattern. The large, new cities of Spanish America were built with spacious plazas and square blocks, with various areas allowing for subsequent enlargement (Fig. 3).

Figure 3 - Plan of the Aztec city of Mexico and its monumental plaza, 1524. Source: Benevolo, Leonardo. História da Cidade [History of the City], p. 477.

A new way of planning cities arose, similar to Roman military encampments, a Hispanic-American pattern that did not, however, extend to the entire Spanish Empire. The city of Carlentini, founded in Sicily in 1551, for example, was constructed on top of a plateau and adhered to the defensive logic suggested by Vitruvius, also applied to the Fortress of Salvador (Fig. 4).

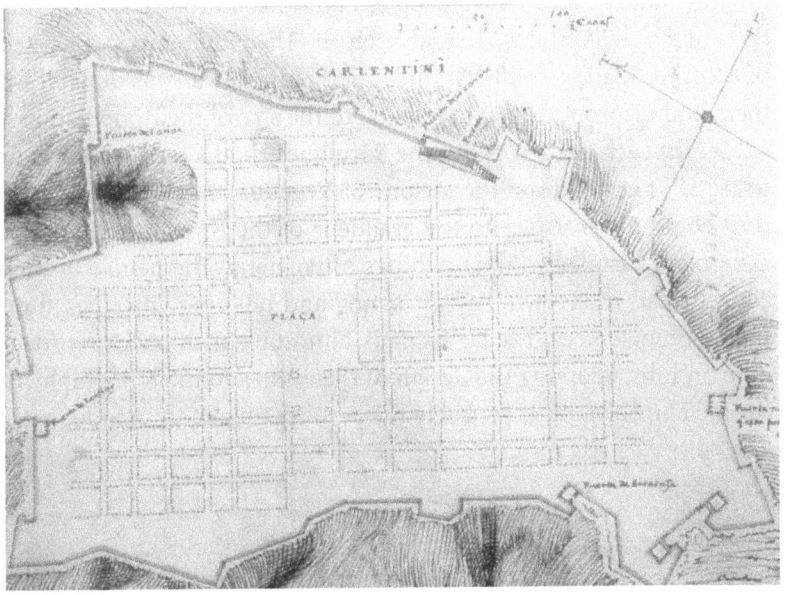

Figure 4 - Plan of the city of Carlentini, Sicily, founded in 1551. Source: BLOND, José Ramón Soraluce. Las Fortificaciones Españolas de Sicilia en el Renacimiento [The Spanish Fortifications of Sicily in the Renaissance], p. 69.

The Polybian pattern was suited to the profile of the Spanish conquistador. In the first half of the sixteenth century, Spain was the strongest military power in Europe. Its territorial domains included part of Italy, Germany, the Netherlands, and some forts in northern Africa, Spanish America, and the Philippines. The wars in Italy brought respect and confidence to the noblemen and soldiers who fought in them. Wealth, power, and glory allowed the Spanish to follow the example of the Roman armies. The Spanish reasoned that, if the Romans used certain practices, why shouldn't they?

Such a notion could never be shared by the Portuguese. Their country was small, their population was limited, and their domains were scattered widely across the globe: the Portuguese therefore opted to defend them. The symbol of a Lusitanian occupation overseas was the fortress, which demonstrated the need for protection, defending the inhabitants from native peoples and other Europeans, including the French, Dutch, British, and Spanish. Their diplomacy consisted of accommodating conflicts, since conducting a war was difficult for them and disproportional in relation to the size of their population.

In each of their ports, the Portuguese had a castle, hillock, or fortress. They followed the lessons of Vegetius and Vitruvius, since they could never aspire to the grandeur of the Roman military encampment detailed in the teachings of Polybius. The people of each country had their own ways of acting and building cities based on their circumstances. The Lusitanians, almost by instinct, felt more secure on hills, adapting the design of their cities to the topography of the terrain. Salvador is probably the best example of this tendency.

4. Regular and Irregular Cities

Sites are flat, mountainous, or maritime, or have all three features. A site refers to the circumference of the city or castle with some space around it.

Cristóbal de Rojas

What is the best site for constructing a city: mountain, plateau, or beach? This was a question addressed in Renaissance treatises. The concept of regular or irregular cities arose from ideas about their location, and the topic became controversial: on the one hand were the adherents of the Roman pattern and perfect geometric forms, defending the choice of flat places and perimeters that were square, pentagonal, hexagonal, and the like; on the other hand were advocates of the pragmatic, who defended the notion of elevated cities and the resultant adaptation of the perimeter and design to restrictions imposed by topography.

Once again, the dilemma of models arose: the Roman or the Greek pattern? The Fortress of Salvador followed the Greek model: it was constructed on a height and its design was adapted to the topography of the plateau.

In 1554, Cataneo wrote an essay that reflected well the clash of ideas in the fifteenth and sixteenth centuries:

"Many arguments have arisen among military engineers and architects about what is more secure, a city built on a mountain or one erected on a plain, and which of these sites would be stronger, more useful, more pleasing, and less expensive."[38]

The controversy of that era can be described through the ideas defended by Alberti, Martini, Machiavelli, and Cataneo: the choice of site determined the possibility of a city being regular or irregular. In the latter half of the sixteenth century, a theory took shape arguing that cities could be geometrically regular or irregular depending on the nature of the site; this more complex doctrine was a typically Renaissance theoretical construction, even though many of the examples were taken from the ancient world.

Leon Battista Alberti apparently initiated the controversy:

"The most important thing is to decide if it is better to construct the site on a plain, a mountain, or on a beach."[39]

He believed that each alternative had positive and negative aspects. To his way of thinking, many cities were built on mountains because their founders probably thought that such a position was the most secure; however, it did not furnish sufficient water. By contrast, cities on plateaus had rivers or other means for obtaining enough water, but the climate was hotter and the sites were more exposed to enemy attack. The seacoast allowed the movement of goods, but facilitated enemy attacks.

In expressing his opinion, Alberti showed some preference for flat zones situated on mountains or on higher parts of plains, but he considered various other locations, such as river banks, valleys, or beaches, without limiting himself to ideal positions. His only recommendation throughout was to avoid constructing cities near hills, slopes, rivers, marshes, or any other feature that could serve as a hiding place for the enemy or that present-

---

38 CATANEO, Pietro. *L'Architettura* [Architecture], p. 211.
39 ALBERTI, Leon Battista. *L'Architettura* [Architecture], p. 147.

ed some disadvantage to the residents. Although Alberti initiated theoretical reflections during the Renaissance on the best site, he did not propose any new ideas. In his view, the perimeter of a city and the layout of its parts varied according to the location.[40] If the city was constructed on a mountain, there would be no possibility of "giving the circumference of the wall"[41] a circular or quadrangular shape.

Martini, who wrote after Alberti, maintained the tradition of evaluating a city according to the locale. It could be built on a flat area without a river, entirely on a flat area with a river in the middle, entirely on a mountain, entirely in a valley, and so on, combining the possibilities. Like Alberti, he argued that a city erected on a plain should have a perfect geometric form: triangular, rhomboid, pentagonal, hexagonal, or orthogonal.[42]

These Renaissance architects did not defend extreme theoretical positions. They determined the format of a city by examining the available terrain. Their approach was very different from that of Machiavelli, who was, above all, ideological, almost megalomaniac: he valued strength and the principles of the Roman army, a perspective that molded his thinking. He argued that, while fortresses were always useless,

> "[...] nowadays they are even more so, due to the artillery, which impedes the defense of closed spaces, where new bastions cannot be erected to replace those that were destroyed."[43]

To ratify his point of view, he invoked the Roman practice:

> "The authority of the Romans is enough for me: they razed the

---

40 Idem, p. 152.
41 Ibidem.
42 MARTINI, Francesco Di Giorgio. *Trattati Di Architettura Ingegneria e Arte Militare* [Treatise on Architecture, Engineering, and Military Arts]. II, p. 366.
43 MACHIAVELLI. *Comentários sobre a primeira década de Tito Lívio* [Discourses on Livy], p. 268.

strong places in the countries they wished to hold, and never built any new ones."[44]

Machiavelli's arguments stemmed from his point of departure: princes and republics with strong, regular armies could dispense with the need for large fortifications. Those who could not depend on "a good army" might get prepared against an attack, but only for as long as it would take to negotiate or receive outside assistance. Machiavelli's preference for sites located on plains suggests the controversy raised by Cataneo, who, however, preferred elevated positions if there were no towering mountains in the vicinity. The cost of defending the site was lower. Cataneo's work was practical. It dealt with creating the shape of regular cities—square, pentagonal, hexagonal—as well as that of irregular ones.

If we study the development of shapes in Western history, we can see that urban designs revealed a marked evolution in the elaboration of forms. Two aspects are noteworthy: the design itself, which, as an expression of an idea and technique, was gradually perfected, and the shape of cities, which became more geometric. Geometry constituted the theoretical foundation, while design was the physical expression of the underlying ideas. These two variables were historically combined in ways that led to the theory of regular or irregular cities. Military architects, who determined the ideal geometric forms for fortresses or cities, formulated patterns that eventually were included in manuals, a typical Renaissance phenomenon. The two great innovations in military architecture in the sixteenth century were the bulwark and the theory of the ideal shape of cities and fortresses.

The regular polygon was attractive to architects and facilitated design. The shape was derived by applying the geometric demonstrations contained in Euclid's work, leading to the appropriate pattern for planning a fortress or city. For example, the triangle and the square were recommended for fortresses: the proper distance between corners did not allow for large areas. The pentagon was suited to small

---

44 Idem, p. 270.

cities or large fortresses. The hexagon and even the dodecagon were perfect figures for cities.

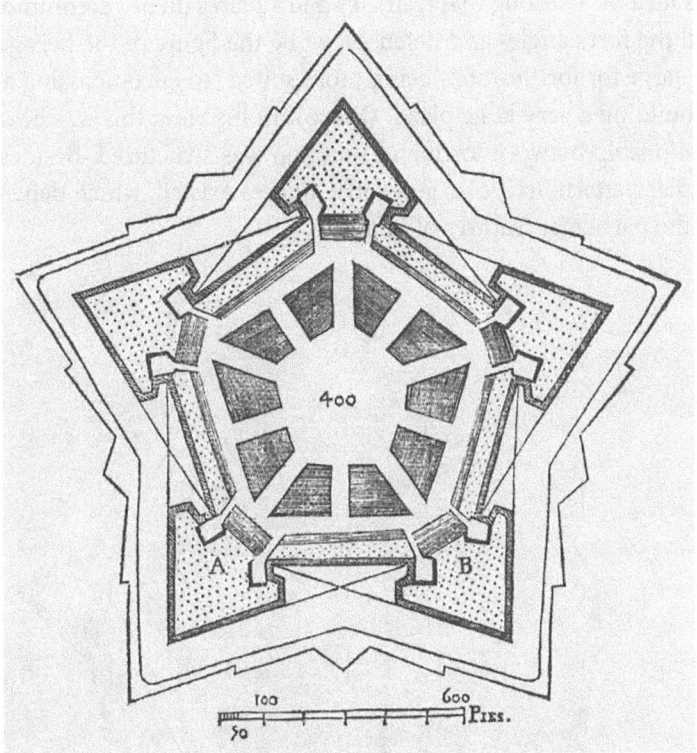

Figure 5 - Diagram in Rojas (1591) to illustrate that "the plaza that seems to be the strongest and most perfect of all is the pentagon."
Source: ROJAS, Cristóbal de. Teorica y Pratica de Fortificacion [Theory and Practice of Fortification], p. 102 (quotation) and p. 111 (illustration).

Such a theory was well developed in the work of Cristóbal de Rojas, published in 1598.[45] He defined regular figures as those with equal sides and angles, and irregular ones as those with "unequal sides and angles in which circles cannot be inscribed."[46] The pentagon, Ro-

---

45 Source: ROJAS, Cristóbal de. "Teorica y Pratica de Fortificacion" [Theory and Practice of Fortification]. In: *Tres Tratados sobre Fortificación* [Three Treatises on Fortification].
46 Idem, p. 76.

jas wrote, "is more appropriate for fortification than all other figures because it is in between large and small plazas" (Fig. 5).⁴⁷ He amplified this idea by asserting that triangles and squares do not accommodate well the fort's angles and defenses, while the figure of the hexagon is too large for fortification, being more suited "to encompassing a city or building a very large plaza" (Fig. 6). In his view, this was how the relationship between form and function was structured. Besides the regular pattern, irregular geometric figures existed, which depended on the particular features of each site.

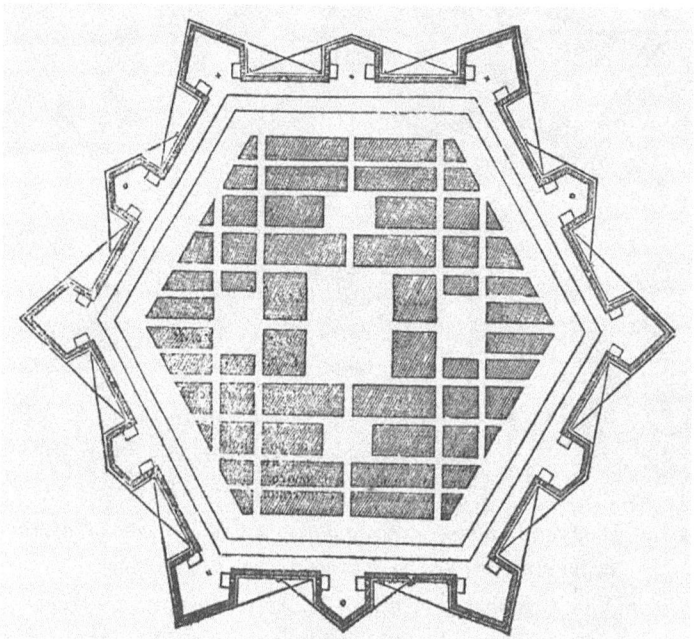

Figure 6 - The hexagonal city, according to Cataneo, 1554.
Source: CATANEO, Pietro. L'Architettura [Architecture], p. 222.

The notion of an ideal site from a military perspective was clear in Rojas. Flat terrain, he said, is suitable for sites when bordered by a lake or rivers that can surround them with water, or when they are located on open plains and far from any feature overlooking them.

---

47 Ibidem, p. 68.

The Fortress of Salvador

A mountain site is ideal when it is located at the highest point, so it cannot be controlled from any nearby elevation, and when it has cliffs on several sides and is built of stones that cannot be destroyed. A coastal site is strong when it is surrounded by the sea and moats.[48] In practice, these conditions were combined. The controversy lost steam as agreement emerged about the basic requirements: the absence of towering mountains and the presence of natural protections surrounding the chosen site.

The Fortress of Salvador was constructed on a plateau: in the front was the sea, in the rear, a marsh, and its entry points were restricted to the northern and southern edges—in short, a pattern chosen according to the ideas defended and accepted in the sixteenth century. It was an irregular city, despite its geometric design. It followed the principle of adapting to the location, a condition recommended by Vitruvius and defended by Cataneo. Geometry was applied to produce the polygon and the design. In this respect, it is an excellent example of Renaissance knowledge, exploiting geometry to the maximum on the basis of the topography.

---

48 Ibidem, p. 325.

5. The Portuguese Renaissance Era

Among all princes ancient and modern, King Dom João the Third of Portugal of glorious memory may be considered to be eminent in this art, and who, according to all the masters of stonework and masonry, had great skill in knowing how to design palaces, fortresses, or any other work.

Francisco de Monçon[49]

Pedro Nunes (1502-1578) was one of the greatest Portuguese mathematicians. He lived in the court of King Dom João III and authored many works. In October, 1541, he wrote *Sobre o Crepúsculo* ("On the Dawn"), in which he mathematically demonstrated the duration of the sun's movement across Lisbon. The preface is an excellent example of the intellectual milieu in Portugal and of the King's commitment to knowledge. Pedro Nunes called Dom João III a "patron and promoter of the sciences" and a sponsor of letters and "the lettered."[50] The ded-

---

49 MONÇON, Francisco de."Livro Primeiro del espejo del Príncipe christiano" [Book One of the Mirror for the Christian Prince]. In: *Da Pintura Antiga* [On Ancient Painting], by Francisco de Holanda, Lisbon, 1571 (according to the note by Angel González Garcia), p. 10.
50 NUNES, Pedro.*Sobre o Crepúsculo* [On the Dawn].This reference is in the preface to the work and is dated October 17, 1541.

ication, he said, was a way of apologizing for the delay in his "translation of Vitruvius," which had been commissioned by the monarch, and was only halfway done. He asked for clemency and pardon, promising to complete the work shortly. Pedro Nunes's awkward sentiments suggest an intellectual climate in which the desire to read Vitruvius's work was strong, revealing the spread of concepts of classical architecture in Portugal.

Two classical works in the field of architecture in the sixteenth century stand out: *The Ten Books on Architecture*, by Vitruvius, and *Elements*, by Euclid (in the field of geometry). To these should be added the book by Vegetius on military arts, and two or three other books by Aristotle on philosophy and politics, works that were fundamental to the technical training that originated from the knowledge developed in Greece and Rome. This menu of classics can be complemented by at least one Italian work written during the Early Renaissance: *Da re aedificatoria* ("On the Art of Building"), by Leon Battista Alberti. The spread and debate of the ideas advanced in these books in Portugal made possible the theoretical basis for the construction of the Fortress of Salvador.

Various other works, not yet cited, are worth mentioning, at least to illustrate certain details. The work *Historia General y natural de las Indias* ("General and Natural History of the Indies"), written by Gonzalo Fernandez de Oviedo and completed in 1546, cited Vitruvius four times, Aristotle nine times, and Vegetius twenty-six times.[51] Pedro Nunes, in the preface to *On the Dawn*, stated that, for ten years, he taught mathematical sciences to the king's brother, Prince Dom Henrique, who, in a short period of time, learned *Elements of Arithmetic and Geometry*, by Euclid, *Treatise on the Sphere*, *Theories of the Planets*, part of Ptolemy's *Almagest*, and Aristotle's *Mechanics*.[52]

This intellectual framework was complemented by literature and historical chronicles, but its distinguishing characteristics lay in its practical uses—in the construction of churches, monasteries, fortresses, and palaces—and in the continual application of geometric

---

51 OVIEDO, Gonzalo Fernandes de.*Historia General y natural de las Indias* [General and Natural History of the Indies].Tomo V, pp. 425, 478, 476.
52 NUNES, Pedro. *Sobre o Crepúsculo* [On the Dawn].

principles to the technical tradition advanced by Vitruvius. This was the best way to transmit the intellectual forces at work in the sixteenth century in the field of architecture.

Geometry and the mathematical ideas underlying the notions of symmetry and proportion were revived from the work of Vitruvius. The vision of the city as a body, with its internal division into parts and organs harmonized with the measurements of the whole, had its origins in Vitruvius and was perfected by Renaissance thinkers. The practical application of geometry in construction can be attributed to the systematic study of Euclid's books. The mystique of numbers and the poetry of architecture, which Vitruvius mentioned, originated in Egypt. It was developed by the Pythagoreans, perfected by Plato, and amply discussed by Aristotle, representing the great imagination of classical and Renaissance writers, conveyed through Vitruvius and especially influenced by Martini. It is worth noting the extent to which the intellectual climate in the court of King Dom João III was receptive to these ideas.

The word "architecture," a neologism taken from Vitruvius, began to have new applications in this era. Master builders, through their accumulation of specialized knowledge, began to acquire the status of architects. From 1541 onwards, King Dom João III took a special interest in construction projects. He wrote to Cardinal Gaddi in 1550, thanking him for the plans he sent from Rome, noting the "singular pleasure" it gave him to study the models "due to the affection I have for the science of architecture." According to Rafael Moreira, stressing this point, "the king became an architect"[53] and, from then on, supported the publication of architectonic treatises.

In 1541, the mathematician Pedro Nunes translated Vitruvius's work *De Architectura* ("On Architecture") into Portuguese. In the same year, the royal bookseller Luís Rodrigues published *Medidas del Romano* ("Roman Measurements"), by Diego Sagredo, which essentially copied the precepts recommended by Vitruvius. In 1551, the humanist André de Resende translated the work of Alberti. Other im-

---

53 MOREIRA, Rafael. "Arquitectura: Renascimento e classicismo" [Architecture: Renaissance and Classicism]. In: *História da Arte Portuguesa* [History of Portuguese Art], p. 350.

portant works, such as Albrecht Dürer's *Befestigungslehre* ("Treatise on Fortification"), which was translated in 1552, can be highlighted. Intense intellectual exchanges were underway, promoting the development of what Rafael Moreira called "mathematized architecture"[54] and preceding the diffusion of written works, whether translated or not. For example, Francisco de Holanda traveled to Italy and wrote some influential theoretical works; the towers and bulwarks in Holanda's design are similar to those proposed by Martini. The meeting between Benedito de Ravena and Miguel de Arruda in Mazagan in 1542 is well-known (Fig. 7); Miguel de Arruda became the master architect of the Kingdom in 1548 and was responsible for drawing up the city plan of the Fortress of Salvador.

At some point in 1549, Miguel de Arruda met with Antônio Ferramolino, a famous Italian military engineer who was responsible for the fortification of Sicily. Miguel de Arruda also worked on designs for various fortresses: Mazagan, Mozambique, Ceuta, Seinal, and Salvador. During his initial training, he collaborated with the French sculptor Nicolau Chanterene in work on the Convent of Grace, a pantheon inspired by Vitruvius, Bramante, and some Italian authors such as Luca Pacioli, who wrote *Divine Proportion*.

In 1549, King Dom João III asked Miguel de Arruda to create a model of the Seinal hill and its fortress, following proportional measurements[55]—proof that mock-ups and scaled replicas were elements used at the time in an architect's work. Technical expressions such as *montea*, which means the design of a profile, and *traça*, designating a ground plan, were abundant in their correspondence, attesting to the spread of strictly technical knowledge.

---

54 Idem, p. 351.

55 ANDRADE, Francisco de. *Crônica de D. João III* [Chronicle of Dom João III], p. 994. The text contains the following passage: "And because they also expressed other doubts about Seinal, which Miguel d'Arruda raised, which they could not verify fully without more complete information, he told him to make of model of the mountain and the work built on it, and of what he planned to build, with all its measurements, and explaining all his doubts."

The Fortress of Salvador

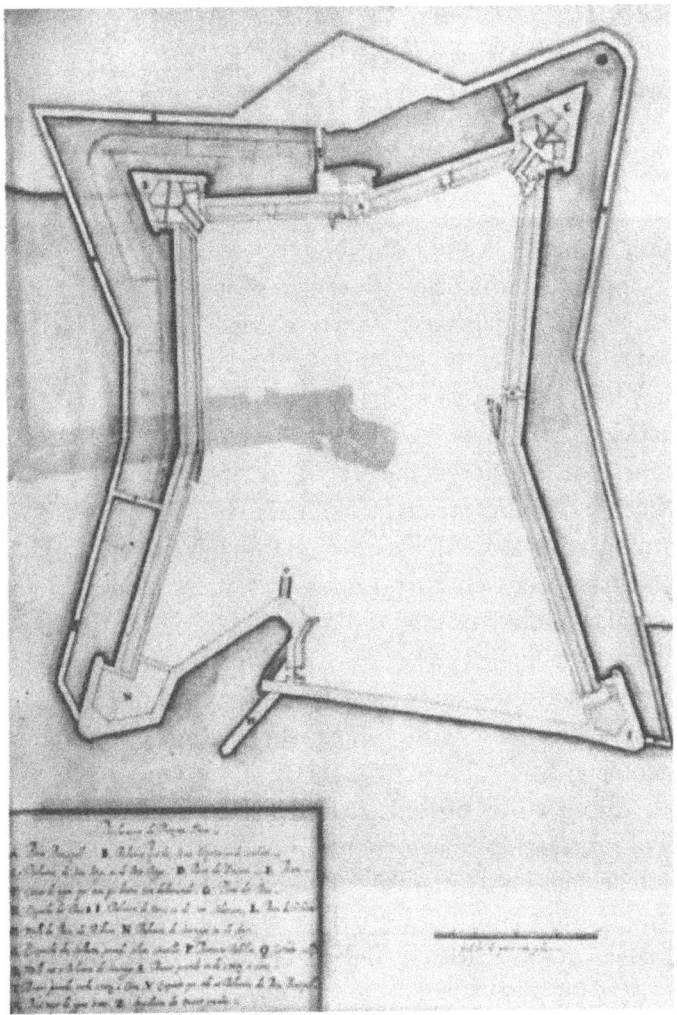

Figure 7 - Fortress of Mazagan, Morocco, 1542. The first Portuguese fortress to include bulwarks, designed by Benedito de Ravena with assistance from Miguel de Arruda.[56]

---

56 NOTES: The city plan of Mazagan carries the following legend in the lower left-hand corner: "Declaration of the Present Design: A, Main Port; B, Bulwark called Holy Spirit or Combat Bulwark; C, Saint George or Dom Diogo Bulwark; D, Gate of Treachery; E, Bridge; F, Water pipe entering inside, now demolished; G, Gate for Cattle; I, North or Saint Sebastian Bulwark; L, Riverside Gate; M, Pier for Riverside Gate; N, Saint James or Angel Bulwark; O, Calheta Stairs, where horses climb up; P,

Source: "Códice da Casa de Cadaval (M-7, nº 26). ANTT. Farinha, Antonio Dias. "Plantas de Mazagão e Larache no início do Século XVII" [Plans of Mazagan and Larache at the beginning of the 17th century]," pp. 159-161. In: A Abertura do Mundo [...] [Opening the World], fig. 12.

Among a myriad of noteworthy aspects, one of the most intriguing is the application of geometry associated with proportion, which applies in particular to the Fortress of Salvador. The city exemplifies the "mathematized architecture" suggested by Rafael Moreira, who cites evidence of this tendency in the surge in publications in the fields of mathematics, geometry, and astronomy: *Prática d'Aritmética* ("Practice of Arithmetic")], 1540, by Rui Mendes; *Tratado da Prática d'Arismetyca* ("Treatise on the Practice of Arithmetic"), 1541, by Gaspar Nicolas; e *De Crepusculis* ("On the Dawn"), 1542, by Pedro Nunes. According to Moreira, "this sudden interest in a theory of architecture and its strong geometric tendency—with its astronomical and cosmological connotations that would be interesting to explore—had its counterpart in applied architecture produced in the following years." Moreira's observations indicate great sensitivity and comprehension, addressing the intense relationship that prevailed between proportion and geometry.[57]

Another way of understanding the milieu is to retrace the circle of relationships that were based on professional acquaintances and intellectual similarities. Miguel de Arruda, the master architect,

---

First Ravelin; Q, Covered street; R, Pier to the Saint James Bulwark; S, Conduits used for filling and emptying the pit; V, Stairs ascending to the Bulwark of the Main Port; X, High tide area; Z, Anchorage for large ships." In the lower right-hand corner is a scale divided into 10, 50, 100, 200, 300, and 400, with the legend, "measurement of four hundred spans."

57 MOREIRA, Rafael. "Arquitectura: Renascimento e classicismo" [Architecture: Renaissance and Classicism]. In: *História da Arte Portuguesa* [History of Portuguese Art], p. 351: "The rules for multiplying the figures, the equal size of the areas in different forms, proportionality and its musical and cosmological implications, the symbolic importance of certain numbers and derivations from them, created a Renaissance architectonic culture that was specific to Portugal, with a typically Portuguese taste for spaces in unusual forms and for an intricate interplay among replicated figures."

traveled with Dom João de Castro to Ceuta in 1543. They rebuilt the fortress and, while there, the former introduced the latter to André de Resende, a renowned humanist who was familiar with Latin and Greek, and who studied classical topics. In 1545, Dom João de Castro went to India as governor, preparing his will before traveling; Lucas Giraldo, merchant and future donee of the Captaincy of Ilheus, was his friend and executor of his will, and Tomé de Souza, who would later become the first governor of Brazil, was a witness to its signing. Dom João de Castro, enthusiastic about Vitruvius's treatise, invited André de Resende to work with him in India. These relationships formed a complete circle revolving around the king and his taste for architecture and science.

All illustrious men seek knowledge, wrote Gaspar Nicolas, paraphrasing Aristotle, adding that, among the liberal arts, arithmetic was the foundation of all the others, because it opened the doors of understanding, imprinting a natural desire for speculation in order to perceive in reality all that depends on arithmetic. The development of mathematical knowledge arose in large part from its potential applications: for commerce to expand, it requires arithmetic; naval engineering and architecture are improved through studying geometry; and navigation makes use of astronomy—all being branches of mathematics.

Classical authors called rational knowledge "the philosophical sciences," dividing them into four fields: logic, physics, metaphysics, and "the mathematics." The latter were divided into four branches: geometry, arithmetic, music, and astronomy—a structure of mathematics that held sway among the classical and Arab authors, and which could still be observed in the sixteenth century. Pedro Nunes proposed teaching another brother of Dom João III, the child prince Dom Luís, the subjects of arithmetic, geometry, music, and astrology, which, according to Vitruvius, were four branches of mathematics with which the architect must be familiar.

Mathematics and architecture came together in those whose minds were open to knowledge, enabling the creation of the Fortress of Salvador. The design of the new city was an exercise in geometry and symmetry. Its symmetry took inspiration from the proportion existing between the human body and its parts, while its geometry was expressed in the straight lines of its streets and blocks. The design was adapted to the topography, but it sought regularity. The spatial arrangement of each part followed historical patterns, in which each component had its own logic. The play of elements was complex but systematic. The fortress was a logical whole, while its parts were determined by the unfolding of intellectual principles. This expansive rationality had its beauty, presupposing intentionality and a climate favorable to its creation—requirements that certainly existed in the court of King Dom João III.

6. The Military Inspiration of the Project

Novelty and surprise throw an enemy into consternation; but common incidents have no effect.

Vegetius

At the front of our squadron went the priests of the Society of Jesus, one of whom carried a large cross on his back, accompanied by many tears, which inspired devotion in the Christians and no small admiration in the natives, who did not understand.

Francisco de Andrade

Codex 112[58] is a book recording normative acts and appointments, which was created specifically for the government on the coast of Brazil. Started on January 1, 1549, it was part of the bureaucratic effort to create an administrative structure for the Governorate General. The heading on page 171 reads, "Of the fortress of Salvador on the bay

---

58 Name given by the Portuguese Overseas Historical Archives to the Book containing records of the rules, provisions, official letters, and pardons issued by the King to people who went to Brazil, opened in Almeirim on January 1, 1549.

of all Saints in the lands of brazil" (Fig. 1). The title reveals the perspective of the scribe who made entries in the book: the new city was a fortress. Indeed, Salvador was born more as a fortress than a city. When they disembarked, Tomé de Souza's men practiced the rituals typical of warfare.

Governor Tomé de Souza and his men, "positioned in a well-armed ordenança," disembarked on the third day after landing;[59] at the front of the squadron walked the Fathers of the Society of Jesus, one of whom carried a large cross. *Ordenança* ("ordinance") and *esquadrão* ("squadron") are terms belonging to the Iberian military vocabulary, and their meanings are strictly correlated with the field organization of the infantry and cavalry. An ordenança refers more to the order followed in a march, battle alert, or combat, while a squadron designates a certain unity in the troop formation in battle. These are key terms for understanding military organization in the sixteenth century, revealing that the revival of the Greek and Roman traditions, so typical of the Renaissance spirit, occurred in the domain of military arts as well. The wars that took place in Italy in the early sixteenth century, involving the French, Italians, and Spanish, enabled a resurgence of an approach to organizing infantry in terms of efficiency. This was illustrated in what were known as the "Swiss brigades" and their famous "pike columns," which can be traced back to the Macedonian phalanxes: close ranks of large numbers of uniformed soldiers bearing long lances, forming compact rectangular units. This tactic was incorporated and perfected by the Roman army, although it was diluted during the Middle Ages. Nevertheless, the Swiss cantons conserved the formation, called "Swiss brigades," "the Swiss model," or "Swiss infantry," which, in the late fifteenth century, emerged as a great tactical innovation.

The hegemony of the Swiss infantry in Medieval cavalries was reinforced in the war of Burgundy, from 1476 to 1477, and thereafter was widely adopted as a guarantee of victory. Their success motivated Pope Alexander VI to use "Swiss pikemen and halberdiers" for his personal guards, a tradition that has survived up to the present day.

---

59 ANDRADE, Francisco de. *Crônica de D. João III* [Chronicle of King Dom João III], p. 976.

Macedonians, Romans, and the Swiss adopted similar formations, which demonstrates the revival of Greek and Roman knowledge. On the subject, Machiavelli formulated some interesting correlations: "The Greeks did not arm so heavily for defense as did the Romans, but in the offense relied more on this staff than on the sword, and especially the Phalanxes of Macedonia, who carried staffs which they called Sarisse, a good ten fathoms in length, with which they opened the ranks of the enemy and maintained order in the Phalanxes." He then speculated that "a Macedonian Phalanx was nothing else than a battalion of Swiss is today, who have all their strength and power in their pikes."[60]

In 1496, Gonzalo Fernandez de Córdoba, called "The Great Captain," initiated reforms in the infantry of the Spanish army, after his first battle at Seminara when he had seen the effectiveness of the Swiss brigade. Following the "Swiss model,"[61] he mixed pikemen with swordsmen, riflemen, and harquebusiers. The process of reform was consolidated in 1534 with the creation of a type of troop that the Spanish called a *tercio*. Thereafter, squadrons, companies, and tercios became the hierarchical and operational units of their armies.

The Portuguese copied the Spanish model to a certain extent, but adapted it to their own needs, instituting the troop regiment known as an ordenança, but there were significant differences between a tercio and an ordenança. The Spanish pattern was employed by professional armies, while the Portuguese system was used to standardize civilian militias in each town or city in the empire (Table 4).

A little-known fact is that a company, a tactical organization composed of 10 squadrons and 265 men, came to be known in Brazil as a *bandeira*, meaning "flag" (Fig. 8). The reason is simple: each unit had its own flag, which was carried by the ensign. The strength and use of militias reinforced the name; units that went into the backlands and manifested clear paramilitary organization also came to be known as *bandeiras*, and their members as *bandeirantes*. Their origins go back to the *Regimento das Ordenanças* mandated by King Dom Sebastião.

---

60 MACHIAVELLI, Niccolo. *Del Arte de la Guerra* [The Art of War], p. 42.
61 BLANCO, Ricardo Román. *Las Bandeiras* [The Flag Companies], p. 71.

Table 4 - Structures of the Spanish Tercio and the Portuguese Ordenança

	Spanish	Portuguese
Year Created	1534	1570
1st Level (Squadron)	25 men commanded by a leader	25 men commanded by a leader
2nd Level (Company)	Company commanded by a captain and composed of 10 squadrons (250 men). Support unit: page (1); ensign, whose duty was to carry the flag (1); sergeant (1); quartermaster (1); drummer (1); fifer (1); chaplain (1); and squadron leaders (10). Total number of men: 267	Company commanded by a captain and composed of 10 squadrons (250 men). Support unit: ensign flag-bearer (1); drummer (1); sergeant (1); magistrate (1); scribe (1) and squadron leaders (10). Total number of men: 265
3rd Level (Tercio or Ordenança)	Tercio commanded by a field commander, composed of 10, 12, or 15 companies. Support unit: sergeant major (1); quartermaster major (1); munitioneer (1); drum general (1); first captain (1); first lieutenant (1); physician (1) surgeon (1); apothecary (1); chaplain (1); honor guard with German halberdiers (8). Total: 18	Ordenança commanded by a captain major (1), composed of companies of the city or town. Support unit: sergeant major (1). Total: 2

Source: BLANCO, Ricardo Roman. *Las Bandeiras [The Flag Companies]*, pp. 155-156, 444-461.

It should be noted that the deployment of military organization was not merely a question of organization charts; it involved an entire context of conduct and discipline, summarized well by a noted field commander of the era. In his definition, repeating classical writers, a militia was composed of three aspects: the first, the instrumental aspect, which consisted of recruiting, arming, paying, and accommodating troops; the second part, the troop aspect, which involved the march to the camp and the encampment; the third, the combat aspect, which was summed up in issuing good, firm, and appropriate orders, forming squadrons.[62]

Figure 8 - Members of a company, also called a bandeira (1588). Representation of all elements that tactically integrated a company: captain, fifer, drummer, ensigns or flag-bearer, followed by pikemen and harquebusiers. Source: BLANCO, Ricardo Roman. Las Bandeiras [The Flag Companies], fig. 12 (engraved by B. Dolendo).

The mission of the field commander, which, in the Portuguese structure corresponded to the captain major, consisted of obtaining "secure order on the march, a good mode of shelter, and order in bat-

---

62 VALDÉS, Francisco de. *Espejo y Disciplina Militar* [Mirror of Military Discipline], pp. 38-39.

tle."⁶³ Ordenança, therefore, referred to order in marching, order in combat, order in training, and discipline in the corps of soldiers, with each one positioned according to a certain standard. The squadron leader, for example, had the responsibility of assembling his troops and going with them "in an ordenança of five by five or of three by three, all with their weapons,"⁶⁴ to find the captain and join him. Here, ordenança carries the same meaning as order on the march.

Such order on the march, however, does not encompass the full meaning of the word "ordenança." In 1508, Dom Manuel created a special corps of guards with "a hundred lances" and called them "ordenança members."⁶⁵ Each soldier was required to have a halberd, armband, helmet, and armor on the head and shoulders, and he could be recruited to the "pike ordenanças" or required to shoot with rifles. In this sense, "ordenança" meant the corps of soldiers formed in the Swiss pattern, something that was differentiated from the usual pattern in terms of their clothing, type of weapons, manner of organizing themselves in a group on the march, and by their form of combat.

A few documents after 1550 criticized the abandonment of the ordenança model, especially in India, and denounced the decadence of the Portuguese Empire due to its lack of military order. A certain report, written at the end of the sixteenth century, denounced a strand of thought prevailing in India, according to which an ordered battle would favor the enemies, since it would be "much easier" to kill the Portuguese.⁶⁶ It claimed that they were few in number, while their opponents were many, a fact that would justify an attack "in a scattered way because going together and united" was dangerous due to the large number of arrows.⁶⁷ The author blamed the lack of protective gear for the body, as well as the long, powerful lances, the harquebuses and muskets, and asserted that "a small squadron, well

---

63 Ibidem, p. 38.
64 "Regimento dos capitães-móres [...]" [Rule of captain majors]. BLANCO, Ricardo Román. *Las 'Bandeiras'* [The Flag Companies], p. 451.
65 Rule of ordenança members, 1508. BLANCO, Ricardo Román. *Las 'Bandeiras'* [The Flag Companies], p. 441.
66 MEMÓRIAS de Um Soldado da Índia [Memories of a Soldier in India], p. 35.
67 Idem, p. 36.

ordered and equipped" had a much greater impact than another that was "very large but lacked the necessary order."[68]

A squadron had a meaning that differed from that of an ordenança. Francisco de Valdés, the Spanish field commander, defined a squadron as a "congregation of soldiers usually positioned in such a way that each one has his own place where, without interference from others, he is able to do battle and to unite his strength with everybody together, in order to achieve the main purpose and goal, which is to make them invincible."[69] Squadrons were formed with a large number of soldiers, varying according to the size of the army. Depending on the site, the formation could be square, have a broad frontline, or form a long line—one of which was best suited to the particular circumstances of each combat or march, determining a rapid mathematical calculation that enabled troop numbers to be distributed in perfect formation.

In 1549, when Tomé de Souza landed in Brazil with well-armed soldiers positioned in an ordenança, with a Jesuit holding a cross at the head of the squadron, he had at least one company in his service. The payment records show that, during 1549, the General Administration maintained a small, structured military corps, comprised of men at arms (pikemen), riflemen, crossbowmen, trumpeters, and drummer. Perhaps it could be considered a company, despite the absence of corporals, sergeants, and second lieutenants. The average numbers of personnel indicate a certain proportion in the mixture of lances and firearms (Table 5).

The staff of the General Administration in 1549 was composed of at least 234 offices: salaries, wages, and provisions were paid out of the royal purse to the professional staff members who were responsible for founding and maintaining the fortress during the first year. This number probably represented a quarter of the total number of people who landed at the site. Of the total number of offices allocated to the staff of the General Administration, 95 fulfilled functions that were exclusively military. Such numbers provide evidence of the

---

68 Ibidem, p. 37.
69 VALDÉS, Francisco de. *Espejo y Disciplina Militar* [Mirror of Military Discipline], p. 38.

military nature of the enterprise, reflected as well in the adoption of modern techniques of organizing militias in service to the Crown.

Table 5 - Distribution and Allotment of Staff in the General Administration, 1549

	Group	Average Number of Personnel	Total
Officials	High-Ranking Officials	Governor general (1), purveyor major (1), captain major (1), and ombudsman general and chancellor (1)	5
	Intermediate Officials	Treasurer (1), accountant (1), magistrate (1), and manager of supplies and provisions storehouse of Salvador (1)	4
	Technical Officials	Master architect (1), stonemason (1), physician and surgeon (1), and barber (1)	4
	Scribes	Those assigned to the governor (1), purveyor major (1), inspectorate and chancellery (1), treasury (1), accounting (1), navy (1), general registrar (1), and manager of supplies and provisions storehouse of Salvador (1)	8
Salaried personnel	Military Men	Drummer (1), crossbowmen (3), trumpeters (5), bombardiers (10), riflemen (26), men at arms (pikemen) (50)	95
	Seamen	Captains (3), masters (4), pilots (3), navy overseer (1), navy scribe (1), sailors (15), grumetes (apprentice sailors) (15), pageboys (2), river superintendent (1), caulkers (5), and cooper (1)	51

Salaried personnel	Construction Workers	Masons (13), carpenters (10), navvies (2), sawyers (2), and laborers (15)	42
	Noblemen[1]	Diogo Moniz Barreto and Duarte de Lemos	2
	Servants[2]	Servants remained at the service of the nobleman, who was often appointed to a post in the colony.	18
	Clergy	Only the Jesuits followed, without salaries, only provisions.	6
	Total		234

Source: DOCUMENTOS HISTÓRICOS [Historical Documents]. Bibliotheca Nacional, V. 12, 13.[70]

---

70 Table notes: (1) It was common for noblemen to exercise duties without a defined role, receiving a specified salary. (2) Each nobleman had the right to bring a certain number of servants and a paid man-at-arms.

7. The Missionary Paradise

> *The blessed Thomas, apostle of the Lord, steadfast in the peace of Christ, traveled throughout India; and since he taught the Gospel of Christ to all in a temple, he was crowned with martyrdom and reached the kingdom everlasting.*
>
> Breviary of Braga

The fortress was christened "Salvador." The name is an adjective, but it also serves antonomastically to designate Jesus Christ. The word has become a noun, but it has not lost the sense of a qualifier, conveying the notion of catechizing and converting souls to the Catholic faith, which suggested that the fortress would serve as a house of God. Each church would enjoy the protection and care of the Our Lady, the Mother. The bulwarks were dedicated to warrior saints and missionaries: Saint James, Saint George, and Saint Thomas. While the bastions were masculine, the only gate we know of was named after a female saint: Saint Catherine. The names chosen all had something in common: they were associated with missionary and warrior spirits, synthesizing the notion that they were united in the Portuguese Crown's project of expanding Catholicism.

The fortress could have been named "City of Jesus" in honor of the Son of God, promoting memories of how he died on the cross, but

King Dom João III preferred the descriptive name Salvador, "He who saves." The religious symbolism reveals the ideology that motivated the enterprise of building the new capital, evoking divine entities engaged in the ideal of conversion and catechism, which are clearly associated with the function of the fortress-city. The objective was to impose and expand the Catholic order, which, at the time, was rendered fragile by the expansion of Lutheran and Calvinist sects.

If the house belonged to the Savior, the Son of God, the religious temples were consecrated to the Mother of Christ. Every point of access on the southern side of the Fortress of Salvador had a church: Nossa Senhora de Ajuda, "Our Lady of Help," whose name reveals the desire for assistance; and Nossa Senhora da Conceição, "Our Lady of the Immaculate Conception," an importation of the Patroness of Portugal to the New World. The Ajuda and Conceição churches were the first built in Salvador, revealing the special relationship the Portuguese had with maternal protection. At a great distance from the homeland, the places of prayer were dedicated to the worship of Mary.

The bulwarks and stations received names of the saints traditionally associated with combat and conquest, a fact that is not fortuitous: it is related to a moment in Portugal's history and the commitment of the kingdom to preserving the Catholic faith, threatened on various sides by the expansion of new Protestant currents. The incorporation of new peoples and territories into the Catholic faith served as a strong motivating element, a sort of spiritual compensation for Catholic losses in Europe.

Another suggestive fact is the identity of the names of the bulwarks in the Fortress of Salvador, on the Bay of All Saints, and the Fortress of Mazagan (Mazagão), on the coast of Morocco, both constructed in the 1740s. São Jorge and São Tiago, for example, are widely used names, revealing a preference for saints with a strong military appeal.

In the Fortress of Salvador, the bulwark located on the southeastern corner is named São Tiago (Saint James), patron and apostle of Spain, who is represented as a pilgrim grasping his staff. The war cry "Santiago" served as a spiritual motivator when the Iberian Christians launched into battle against the Moors. It is said that the saint, also represented as a crusading knight,[71] showed up at the Battle of Clavijo in 834 and routed the Moors. To this day, the pilgrimage he made to Spain and the location of his tomb in Compostela still fuel the folklore surrounding the "road to Santiago."

Table 6 - Bulwarks in Fortress of Mazagan and Fortress of Salvador, 1542-1549

Position in Relation to Harbor	Name of Bulwark	
	Fortress of Salvador	Fortress of Mazagan
Entrance to harbor	São Tomé	São Sebastião
End of harbor	São Jorge	Santiago or Anjo
Interior entrance to harbor	São Tiago	São Jorge
Interior end of harbor	—	Santo Espírito

Source: The author.

The second saint and apostle who lent his name to the São Tomé bulwark in the Fortress of Salvador was Saint Thomas. As an apostle of Jesus, he was given the mission of preaching in India:

> "The Lord appeared to Thomas in a night vision, saying, "Do not be afraid, go to India, I will not abandon thee."[72]

Based on this interpretation, a certain tradition has grown up claiming that the tomb of the saint is in India. The Portuguese located it in Meliapor in 1517, based on information from Armenian merchants, or at least, that is what they reported. In the context of the great voyages, Saint Thomas became the spiritual link to the new lands and "our patron in those parts of India, just as Santiago is for Christianity in Spain."[73] His name was adopted as a war cry in the Orient.

---

71 LEITE, José. *Santos de Cada Dia* [Saints for Every Day]. VII, p. 463.
72 THOMAZ, Luís Filipe F. R. *A Lenda de São Tomé* [The Legend of Saint Thomas], p. 355.
73 Idem, p. 401.

In one of the first letters he wrote upon arriving in Brazil, the Jesuit Manuel da Nóbrega reported seeing footprints of Saint Thomas in rocks on the Bay of All Saints and in São Vicente. The Indians told Nóbrega that the saint, whom they called Zomé, fled from their arrows; the sea opened up and he passed through it to India. Thomas promised the natives that he would return, and Nóbrega asked the saint to watch over their interests before God, "so that they may come to know Him and receive the Holy Spirit, as they hope."[74]

Saint George—called the "great martyr"[75] in the East and, during the Middle Ages, the protector of crusading knights—lent his name to the third bulwark, São Jorge. The story of the dragon he killed with his lance and the idolatrous people he converted with a beautiful sermon has become legendary. For the deed, the king offered him a great sum of money, but he gave it all away to the poor and continued on his way, wishing nothing for himself. Among the Portuguese people, the assistance given by the Duke of Lancaster (son of Edward III in England) to King Fernando in the battle against Castela enhanced the cult of Saint George. The Portuguese substituted the war cry "São Jorge" for that of "Santiago" used by the Spanish.[76]

As for Saint Catherine, for whom the only gate (Santa Catarina) in the fortress is named, tradition relates that she overcame the arguments of fifty wise men who were defending the philosophy of Alexandria and thereby converted them to Christianity. For this deed, she was put to death by the emperor. She was born of nobility, and it was said that her body, when struck by the deadly blows, spurted blood and milk. The saint was revered by the Portuguese aristocracy in the Renaissance. Moisés do Espírito Santo suggests that this worship arose from the fact that "the philosopher saint who defeated the arguments of the Neo-Platonists of Alexandria represented a reaction

---

[74] Information from Lands of Brazil from Father Manuel da Nóbrega, dated August 1549. LEITE S. I., Serafim. *Cartas dos Primeiros Jesuítas do Brasil* [Letters of the First Jesuits of Brazil]. I, p. 154.
[75] LEITE, José. *Santos de Cada Dia* [Saints for Every Day]. I, 508.
[76] Idem, I, 509.

against the humanist and liberating ideas of the time."[77] She was the patroness of King Dom João III.

The names chosen reveal the Portuguese need to affirm and expand the Catholic faith throughout the world. The undertaking was not only economic and political, but also religious, an aspect that should not be underestimated. The ideological strength of faith spurred the process of territorial expansion and motivated those behind it. Catholicism was more than a religion; it was also an ideal that united a large portion of the Portuguese, creating a unity of thought capable of propelling the formidable effort of crossing the ocean.

---

77 ESPÍRITO SANTO, Moisés do. *Origens Orientais da Religião Popular Portuguesa* [The Eastern Origins of Portuguese Popular Religion], p. 189.

8. The Beach and the Harbor

[On] the subject of the usefulness of harbors [...] If their situation has natural advantages, with projecting capes or promontories which curve or return inwards by their natural conformation, such harbors are obviously of the greatest service.

Vitruvius

Anyone who navigates between the harbors of Barra and Comércio can attest to the beauty of the hillside, one of the loveliest places in the world. For those who live there, every day is a delight being in the midst of such sights, among the most pleasing that can be found anywhere. The sea licks the foot of the hillside; the beaches are so narrow that they hardly exist. At various points, small upwellings of healthy fresh water emerge from cracks in the hillside. It is difficult to disembark from boats due to the enormous stones and flat rocks, which make it almost impossible to walk. The narrow strip of beach along the coast is noteworthy, since Tomé de Souza chose a section of it for the port of the Fortress of Salvador. Certain details of the location, such as the presence of springs and reefs, and the curves of the cove, explain why the site was chosen and integrated with the fortress.

To get an idea of how the beach originally looked when it was chosen for the port of the Fortress of Salvador, we can contemplate the old photo of the cove (where nowadays the Yacht Club of Bahia is located) through the eyes of an adventurer (Fig. 9). We can see a large number of stones, some short sections of smooth beach, imposing flat rocks, and some upwellings of water from rocky floor below. We can also see the curvature of the cove, which was probably the location of the original port of the hamlet of Pereira. This settlement was linked to the Largo da Vitória, the center of the village headed by Francisco Pereira Coutinho, who had received the property through a land grant. However, Tomé de Souza and his colleagues did not like the site; according to Gabriel Soares, the port was unsuitable due to the lack of protection against the southern winds. This was certainly a problem, causing terrible undertows in the entrance to the Bay of All Saints. They continued sailing ahead and stopped at the site of Conceição da Praia, where they found three good springs.

Figure 9 - Cove where the present-day Yacht Club of Bahia is located. High above is the Vitória Church; on the right, the Ladeira da Barra and the English Cemetery.
Source: FERREZ, Gilberto. BAHIA—Velhas Fotografias 1858/1900 [BAHIA—Old Photographs 1858-1900], p. 122.

The Fortress of Salvador

The site was dominated by three coves and numerous reefs. It is difficult to reconstitute a picture of the beach, since the documents are vague, but we may speculate on the local topography. When someone enters the Bay of All Saints and approaches the port, Preguiça beach will be visible on the nearest end. There, the hill projects into the ocean, then curves in a gentle half-moon toward the present-day Lacerda Elevator. The first cove leads to five houses before reaching the elevator. The current view is deceptive, since the Conceição Church projects into the ocean, covering up the original curvature. The second cove starts shortly before Lacerda Elevator and follows a new curve to a point near the Corpo Santo Church. From there, the third curves around to the foot of the Ladeira da Montanha.

Landfills that were repeatedly built up on the beach make it difficult to identify the original topography. Each half-moon curve contained a beach, but large flat rocks in suitable places determined the choice of sites selected for constructing bulwarks. A few paths can still be seen along the curvature of the hillside, which causes the line of houses to meander from the Largo da Preguiça to the entry of the Ladeira da Montanha. A slight elevation can be observed in front of the churches of Conceição and Corpo Santo, but it is difficult to ascertain whether it is natural or the result of some human intervention. At any rate, the present shape of the hillside and the three coves seem to be compatible with that described in the available documents.

In the middle of the first cove is the Conceição Church, the oldest in the city, built by Tomé de Souza soon after landing. Its original site was further up the hillside. The available descriptions indicate that reefs lay to the south and the land was narrow: "[...] in front of the fort where Nossa Senhora da Conceição is located are some rocky reefs [...] lying in the southern part, where weirs can be placed to catch fish."[78] This information suggests that the beach beyond the Conceição Church met up with a certain number of reefs, although how far they extended is unclear. The smooth beach, without rocks, ended at the edge of Conceição da Praia.

The documents further indicate that, in front and toward the

---

78 LIVRO *Velho do Tombo* [Old Register of Charters and Deeds], p. 26.

north, there was a beach that also served as a place for beaching boats and as a port.

> "A piece of land in this city on the beach of Nossa Senhora da Conceição was given as a place for beaching boats where goods could be unloaded, which measured twenty fathoms in length along said beach and place for beaching boats, and six fathoms in width on dry land [...]."[79]

The place where boats were beached for repairs had to be dry and free of any rocks that might damage the hull. Gabriel Soares noted that the Ladeira da Conceição was a passageway for "the general wharf for merchandise."[80]

Documents from the period between 1586 and 1604 are unanimous in indicating the existence of a fort on the edge of the sea, near the Conceição Church, on the southern side. According to a certain land title dated 1604, the parties descended the Ladeira da Conceição to the point where "[...] it comes out on the place for beaching boats, next to the fort located there, and we continued on to the reef along the foot of said fort on the side of the sea and from there we went to the beach to the side of Nossa Senhora da Conceição."[81] The fort, which took advantage of the reefs at the site, was also mentioned in another land title dated November, 1586, a document that

> "[...] gave him title to the reefs and beach, as contained in said letter, in front of the bulwark where Nossa Senhora da Conceição is located on the southern part [...]"[82]

In front were reefs that were located "where I have the old bulwark," explained Governor Manuel Telles Barreto.[83] It is likely that

---

79 LIVRO *Velho do Tombo* [Old Register of Charters and Deeds], p. 318.
80 SOUZA, Gabriel Soares de. *Notícia do Brasil* [Report from Brazil], p. 256.
81 LIVRO *Velho do Tombo* [Old Register of Charters and Deeds], p. 362.
82 Idem, p. 27.
83 Ibidem.

this fort, platform, or bulwark corresponded to the original station of Santa Cruz, built by Governor Tomé de Souza. Oddly, the site was not the best; the far end of the cove, nowadays known as Praia da Preguiça (Lazy Beach), would have been better, since it overlooked the entire expanse of sea. However, the boundaries of the city probably mandated its construction on the southern side of Conceição, jutting out into the ocean.

If an observer of the era stood in front of the Conceição da Praia Church and looked out at the ocean, he would have seen a fort to the left and, beyond it, the beach and reefs. In front would have been a beach, apparently quite smooth, with a good place for anchoring boats. Looking toward the north, a little more than a hundred meters beyond, were flagstones in the sea that could be touched by wading waist-deep, where a small fortress was built around 1620, called the Royal Fort of the São Felipe Sea. The location of these flagstones corresponds nowadays to the gardens of the Port Authority, near the guardhouse and next to the harbor.

At the end of the second cove, the hillside and the reefs form a cape, which was the place that jutted out the most into the ocean. This site probably had the best views, affording good defense of both the northern and the southern sides of the fortress, being the only position where gunfire could protect the beachfront as a whole. This is most likely the reason it was chosen as the spot for the Góes bulwark. Luís Dias, the master architect, wrote,

> "And thus we built two bulwarks, one on the Góes stream, a very strong one, above the cliffs, which, as Your Highness will see in the illustration, looks out over the entire bay [...]"[84]

The oldest map of the city, dated 1604, indicates that there used to be a fortification at this locale (Fig. 10). The Santo Alberto Fort was built at some time between 1583 and 1593 in honor of Cardinal Archduke Alber-

---

84 LETTER from Luís Dias to the King Dom João III, dated August 15, 1551. In: DIAS, Carlos Malheiros. *História da Colonização Portuguesa no Brasil* [History of Portuguese Colonization in Brazil]. III, p. 363.

to D'Austria, Governor of Portugal, by the King of Spain, which explains the origin of the fort's name. In 1660, a list of fortifications referred to it as "useless" for defending the city, which led to its being sold at auction to Domingos Pires de Carvalho[85] in 1673. We can surmise that the Santo Alberto Fort was built by taking advantage of the space and perhaps the ruins of the Góes bulwark, a hypothesis worth considering.

In the old engravings, we can see that the Santo Alberto Fort occupied a position that jutted out in relation to the beaches on either side. Likewise, the place where it was situated is still, to this day, higher than the land in front of it. In this regard, it is similar to the Church of Conceição da Praia.

The picture above shows a northern end at the height of the Corpo Santo Church, with a full view of the ocean, and, in the south, the reefs encroaching on the beach, to the left of the Conceição Church. On both ends of this cove, small fortifications stood at crossfire, protecting the port: the Góes bulwark on the north side, and the Santa Cruz station on the south. The first stood by the Góes stream, which was named by Tomé de Souza in honor of Pero de Góes, his captain general, who directed the construction of the fortification. The master architect Luís Dias said, "And thus we built two bulwarks,

---

85 The auction letter contains some illuminating references. The order from the Governor and Captain General of the state of Brazil includes the following passage: "Inasmuch as I have been informed that on the beach of this city is a site where formerly there was a fort called Santo Alberto, which today is in ruins and without artillery [...]" The Commission charged with examining the military expediency of the site made the following remarks in its report: "[...]on March 18 of said year [1673], we went to the beach of this city and the site referred to earlier, which is next to the Corpo Santo called Santo Alberto, and, examining it well and traversing it, we found that it would not be useful for any defense of the plaza or of the harbor and its beach, because it is small and almost ruined, and because on both flanks (sides) there are houses, where people are residing, that extend out to the sea, and so it lies far back behind them, and for many years it has had no cavalcade artillery, nor anything in it, and, on the side of the sea, there were only two very low embrasures that were incapable of being of any service for defense, nor is there a wharf, since in front of it is the São Marcelo fort and Nossa Senhora do Populo, and on the beach is the Royal Fort of São Felipe, and that of São Francisco, and other platforms [...]" The São Marcelo fort did not exist in 1660, but is mentioned in this reference of 1673, so it was built at some point during the interval. The legal title to the building was issued on July 18, 1673.

one on the Góes stream, very powerful, above the cliff"[86] and on "the other end of the stream we built another station, which is called Santa Cruz."[87] An order of payment stated that the Santa Cruz station was next to the Pescadores stream, that is, near Preguiça.[88]

Figure 10 - Port of the city of Salvador. Oldest known drawing, dated 1605. From right to left: the Conceição Church; a set of houses where the Royal Storehouse and other services operated; the flagstones; the wharf; the water "reservoir" or fountain; and a bulwark.
Source: RAZÃO do Estado do Brasil [Reason for the State of Brazil] (c. 1616). Códice 126 da Biblioteca Pública Municipal do Porto [Codex 126 of the Porto Municipal Public Library], p. 57.

Repeated landfills made over the centuries hid all this evidence. The section of the beach between the Conceição and Corpo Santo churches was probably relatively free of rocks, although the two ends, mentioned above, were not. Also built on the Góes stream were the Treasury, Customs House, Storehouse, Powder Vault, and

---

86 LETTER from Luís Dias to the King Dom João III, dated August 15, 1551. In: DIAS, Carlos Malheiros. *História da Colonização Portuguesa no Brasil* [History of Portuguese Colonization in Brazil]. III, p. 363.

87 MOREIRA, Rafael. "O arquiteto Miguel de Arruda e o primeiro projeto para Salvador" [The architect Miguel de Arruda and his first project for Salvador]. In: *Anais do 4° Congresso de História da Bahia*, v. I, p. 141. Letter from Luís Dias to Miguel de Arruda, dated July 13, 1551.

88 DOCUMENTOS HISTÓRICOS [Historical Documents], v. XIII, Biblioteca Nacional, mandado de pagamento nº 655.

Blacksmith Shop. Located two or three houses beyond the Church of Corpo Santo was the other side of the river, forming the start of the third cove, which sheltered the wharf where people disembarked. A little more than halfway along the third cove could be found the Pereira Fountain, where the second access road was built leading to the upper city.

According to Vitruvius, the best harbor was a cove protected by capes or reefs on the sides, where a ship could be naturally sheltered from ocean forces. A harbor is a shelter, which requires some sort of cove. This association was undoubtedly understood by Tomé de Souza and his colleagues, although it is not always perceived as such by modern society. The project of building the Fortress of Salvador took advantage of the topographic characteristics of the beach and integrated the system of defense and access to the upper city with great ingenuity, using the buildings constructed between the two bulwarks of the Góes stream, one large, the other small, and the access roads on the northern and southern sides of the Bay of All Saints. The boundaries are clearly defined in the upper city, where the bulwarks protected the access points and the fortifications on the beach, which could defend against a maritime invasion.

This system of integrating the upper and lower parts of a city was described by Aristotle. His text suggests that it was common for the Greeks to situate a city on high, with the harbor below by the beach, which is sensible:

> "[...] we often see in countries and cities dockyards and harbors very conveniently placed outside the city, but not too far off; and they are kept in dependence by walls and similar fortifications."[89]

One of the most fascinating aspects of the Fortress of Salvador is the near-perfect marriage between the topography of the upper city and the arrangement of coves along the coast—a gift of nature noticed by men who wished to build something that could protect them from pirates and native peoples. The sheltered harbor, located between two

---

[89] ARISTOTLE, *Política* [Politics], 1327b.

promontories, was aligned with the two plateaus where the city was constructed, allowing the fortress to have an integrated layout (Fig. 2). This unity was intentional and well thought out; the best way to perceive the rationality that guided its construction is to study the positioning of its main points of access, the Ladeira da Conceição and the Ladeira da Misericórdia.

9. Fountains and Pools

> *There should be a natural abundance of springs and fountains in the town.*
>
> Aristotle

To the right of the modern-day Lacerda Elevator, there used to be a natural fountain. The water emerged from fissures in the mountain range and cascaded down the hillsides, flowing toward the beach. The oldest engraving of the city shows that the water was channeled for a certain distance, ending in a sort of pool.[90] This fact, not yet described in any books, is useful for reconstructing the scenario surrounding the choice of this particular site and the logic behind its settlement. Nowadays, anyone who ascends the Ladeira da Montanha can see infiltrations of water here and there in the high, thick walls on the left. These are springs that are resisting the asphalt and concrete against all odds. In the past, this natural fountain supplied the ships of Tomé de

---

90 Source: RAZÃO do Estado do Brasil [Reason for the State of Brazil] (c. 1616). *Códice 126 da Biblioteca Pública Municipal do Porto* [Codex 126 of the Porto Municipal Public Library]. The design is dated 1605. The plan of the city of Salvador, shown on page 57, contains a collage superimposed on the harbor region. The first image portrays the phase before reforms were made; the second, the completed project afterwards. The first drawing, appearing below, is not well known.

Souza's fleet, and was a decisive factor in the choice of the harbor and site where the Fortress of Salvador was erected.

The year 1549 heralded two striking episodes in the history of military engineering: the construction of the city of Salvador on the Bay of All Saints, on the Brazilian coast, and the abandonment of the city of Alcácer-Ceguer and the mountain fort overlooking it, called Seinal, on the Moroccan coast. These two settlements were subjected to the same technique of site evaluation, which involved assessing the harbor, the elevations, and especially the supply of water. At the Salvador fortress, water was abundant and readily available within its borders; at the Seinal fortress, it was scarce and distant. The former prospered; the latter was abandoned. A comparison of the two can enhance our understanding of Portuguese military thinking.

On February 12, 1549, only two days after the departure of the fleet commanded by Tomé de Souza, news reached Lisbon that the city of Fez in Morocco had been seized by the Sharif named Muley Hamete. With this conquest, he became the head of the kingdoms of Sus, Fez, and Morocco. This state of affairs made King Dom João III most apprehensive about the risk it posed to the Lusitanian fortresses situated along the coast of Morocco. Information indicated that the Sharif had great military strength, including large-scale artillery, and that he would attempt to conquer Portuguese cities.[91]

Alcácer-Ceguer seems to have been his immediate objective. The site was inherently weak and required immediate fortification. When the King's Council examined the problem, the members concluded that the main risk was an enemy occupying the neighboring hill of Seinal. Since the hill was higher and overlooked the city, whoever gained control of the hill could conquer the city. The Council approved a measure for a military occupation of the hill by constructing a fort, where a subsequent evaluation of the site could be conducted. Dom Afonso de Noronha was appointed to lead the military action, involving 5,300 men, of whom 4000 were soldiers, 1000 were laborers, and 300 were stonemasons, carpenters, and navvies, plus 6 master architects who were personally directed by Miguel de Arruda, the

---

91 ANDRADE, Francisco de. *Crônica de D. João III* [Chronicle of Dom João III], p. 980.

royal master architect. These figures indicate that the operation was at least five times larger than that planned for the coast of Brazil, the destination of the armada sailing at the time, heading for the Bay of All Saints.[92]

On April 4, 1549, Dom Afonso landed in Alcácer-Ceguer with some noblemen and found the city already filled with a thousand soldiers from Lisbon, along with many ships containing provisions. With them was Miguel de Arruda, who was the superior of Luís Dias, the master architect who was on Tomé de Souza's fleet sailing to Brazil. To meet the needs of the construction project, the King ordered that decisions would be based on the report of four people: Dom Afonso, Miguel de Arruda, Álvaro de Carvalho, captain de Alcácer-Ceguer, and Luís de Loureiro, an experienced military man. The Portuguese occupied the hill, celebrated Mass, and began to build a fort of "wood, branches, and rubble on top of the hill, where they found the site to be larger and better suited to fortification."[93]

The fort was constructed without difficulties, but the knowledge gained about the site triggered a strategic reevaluation. The purpose of maintaining a fort was to prevent the Sharif from getting access to the river and harbor of Alcácer-Ceguer, since, from there, he could attack the Portuguese ships. Doubts arose, however, about its costs and benefits, leading the builders to conclude that building a rock castle on Seinal would be sufficient. The King summoned all those involved to a meeting in Lisbon, asking Miguel de Arruda to make a "model of the hill and the works that were completed [...] with all their measurements"[94] and to return to the Court.

The issue of Seinal subsequently became subsumed in a wider consideration of the policy of maintaining Portuguese settlements on the Moroccan coast, due to the high costs and difficulty of maintaining so many settlements in enemy territories. After numerous debates, the Court leaned in favor of abandoning the places where the harbors were insufficient to serve as shelter from the "galley ships of

---

92 Idem, pp. 981-982.
93 Ibidem, p. 991.
94 Ibidem, p. 994.

the Moors,"[95] or inherently so weak that they could not be fortified without great expense. This line of reasoning led to the abandonment of Arzila. Its harbor offered poor conditions for disembarking, which was always difficult, so reinforcements might not be able to land if bad weather hampered access. If the harbor at Arzila was not useful for the Portuguese, it would also not serve as shelter for their enemies. In June, 1549, a notice was issued from Lisbon ordering the evacuation of the city of Arzila.

King Dom João III needed more technical information to decide what to do about the city of Alcácer-Ceguer and the fort of Seinal. The next step, taken the same month, was to send an armada to Morocco, composed of three ships and six peoples (two military men, two engineers, and two sailors), with the mission of studying and evaluating precisely the characteristics of the site. The group included Captain Dom Pedro de Mascarenhas; his nephew, Dom João de Mascarenhas, captain of the Fortress of Diu during its second siege and therefore an experienced military man; Miguel de Arruda, master architect; Diogo Telez Português, an engineer who had served in Germany for the king of Spain; and two experienced sailing masters.

This appointed group examined the site and concluded that the harbor of Alcácer-Ceguer was inadequate to serve as a shelter for galley ships, so it would be better to clog the harbor with rocks to prevent navigation by enemy ships. The harbor was exposed to the wind in almost all directions, while the former harbor that used to serve the city was too far away to be protected by the fort's buildings and was thus subject to enemy attack. The site at Seinal was poor because it lacked readily accessible fresh water, which could be supplied only by cisterns. The available wells were paltry and distant from the fort, so they risked exposure to enemies. With this technical report, the fate of Alcácer-Ceguer and the Seinal fort was sealed. The city and the fort that was supposed to defend it were abandoned because of the characteristics of the harbor and the lack of accessible water.

The opposite conditions prevailed at the Bay of All Saints: the advantages of the harbor and the ready availability of fresh water de-

---

95 Ibidem, p. 995.

termined the choice of the site. Gabriel Soares stated that Tomé de Souza landed at the original site and ordered the fleet to search for a better and more sheltered harbor. They found a "clear and sheltered" harbor and, on land, "a large spring close to water's edge that would provide fresh water for ships and service the city."[96]

Everybody praised the location chosen. The Jesuit Manuel da Nóbrega stated that the site was very good, surrounded by "water around the fence"[97] and with many other "springs rising from the ocean and from land."[98] The best description of the availability of water for the site comes from a later description by Gabriel Soares, who said the city had large wharfs "with three fountains on the beach at its foot,"[99] from which sailors got their water supplies. On the eastern side there was a "stream of water"[100] coming from a spring, and other fountains in various other places. Everyone took drinks of water from different sources that varied by taste and location.

Two of the fountains described by Soares are well-known: one is on the slope of the Ladeira da Preguiça (Fig. 12) and the other, known as the Pereira Fountain, at the foot of the Ladeira da Montanha. Where might the third fountain have been? It was probably in front of the harbor, between the Corpo Santo Church and the present-day Lacerda Elevator. This hypothesis draws on the documentary references described above as well as a third source, the old plan of the harbor area, which indicates a spot with a structure that appears to be a fountain.[101]

According to Vilhena, the entire hillside "is gushing with wa-

---

96 SOUZA, Gabriel Soares de. *Notícia do Brasil* [Report from Brazil]. Tomo I, p. 247.
97 LETTER from Father Manuel da Nóbrega, dated August 10, 1549. LEITE S. I., Serafim. *Cartas dos Primeiros Jesuítas do Brasil* [Letters of the First Jesuits of Brazil]. I, p. 135.
98 Idem.
99 SOUZA, Gabriel Soares de. *Notícia do Brasil* [Report from Brazil]. Tomo I, p. 264.
100 Idem.
101 Source: RAZÃO do Estado do Brasil [Reason for the State of Brazil] (c. 1616). *Códice 126 da Biblioteca Pública Municipal do Porto* [Codex 126 of the Porto Municipal Public Library], p. 57.

ter, and few are the houses that do not have their own well to take advantage of it."[102] Even today, it is possible to see small springs in different places, varying in intensity according to the seasonal rainfall. The picture shown in the 1605 plan[103] indicates that it was constructed from a catchment, which apparently ended in a reservoir. When the wharf was renovated, shown in the next picture, the fountain or reservoir ceased to exist, for unknown reasons.

Figure 11 - Fountain on Praia da Preguiça, the former fishermen's beach.

On the eastern side of the fortress were two ditches: the smaller one was at the intersection of Rua da Oração and Rua Três de Maio, while the larger was on the Ladeira da Praça Luís Dias, where a sizable

---

102 VILHENA, Luiz dos Santos. *Recopilação de Notícias Soteropolitanas e Brasílicas* [Compilation of Reports from Salvador and Brazil]. I, p. 104.
103 Razão do Estado do Brasil [Reason for the State of Brazil] (c. 1616). *Códice 126 da Biblioteca Pública Municipal do Porto* [Codex 126 of the Porto Municipal Public Library], p. 57.

well was built. Luís Dias described it as follows: "Two small ditches have created embankments inside the city, and at the larger one we built a very large well, being twenty palms [4.4 meters] long, which has excellent water that in summer is six palms deep [1.32 meters] and nine [1.98 meters] in the rainy season."[104] Its exact location is difficult to determine, but we can state with some certainty that it lay in the first half of the lowlands that run parallel to the Ladeira da Praça—keeping in mind that the floodplain invaded a large part of that area—which is compatible with the military pattern that guided the construction of the well or cistern within or near the citadel. Martini's first recommendation was this: there must be a well or cistern sufficient to supply the entire fortress.[105]

This well was apparently short-lived and figured in a curious episode that resulted from a rumor that circulated among the Indians: "Concerning a well that they opened in the city for their needs, that is, for drinking water and washing clothes, they said that we would throw them in and drown them."[106]

The Ladeira da Misericórdia is frozen in time. It is a quiet, melancholy space, although it is pleasant to spend time there. The water is clear, with a well here and there, surrounded by the silence of the mountain range. A certain apprehension hangs in the air. The local vegetation is abundant, and the ruins confuse the visitor's sight. Anyone who dares to climb it will find a fountain at the second bend in the road (Fig. 12). Water emerges from various spots and flows over the thick walls—the same waters that used to course down and help form the fountain known as the Fonte do Pereira. There may have been another fountain, which Vilhena called the Fonte dos Padres, although one by the same name was also found in Tabuão. At any rate,

---

104 MOREIRA, Rafael. "O arquiteto Miguel de Arruda e o primeiro projeto para Salvador" [The architect Miguel de Arruda and his first project for Salvador]. In: *Anais do 4º Congresso de História da Bahia*. V. I, p. 141. The letter from Luís Dias, the master architect, is dated July 13, 1551.
105 MARTINI, Francesco di Giorgio. *Trattati Di Architettura Ingegneria e Arte Militare* [Treatise on Architecture, Engineering, and Military Arts]. II, p. 429.
106 LETTER from Father João de Azpilcueta,, dated March 28, 1550. LEITE S. I., Serafim. *Cartas dos Primeiros Jesuítas do Brasil* [Letters of the First Jesuits of Brazil]. I, p. 181.

at that bend in the road, the visitor can imagine the beauty of the cascade that once flowed in the rocky river bed, covered by vegetation, and which moistened the beach area with fresh water.

Figure 12 - Fountain at Ladeira da Misericórdia.

10. The Twin Access Roads

The roads should be encompassed at steep points, and planned so as to approach the gates, not in a straight line, but from the right to the left; for as a result of this, the right hand side of the assailants, unprotected by their shields, will be next to the wall.

Vitruvius

The historic center of Salvador preserves segments of the two original sloping access roads from the beach to the upper city. They start from opposite points of the fortress on the strip of beach and terminate at the main plaza: on the south side, the Ladeira do Pau da Bandeira, formerly known as Palácio, and, on the north side, the Ladeira da Misericórdia (Figs. 13 and 14). Both are currently divided in two places, so it is not possible to see the connection between their winding paths and the original boundaries of the Fortress of Salvador. As military strategy suggests and historic documents confirm, they were roads that obeyed military patterns by being built within city limits and linking up to the central plaza. These ascents are steep, taking advantage of certain features of the hillside and articulating symmetrically with the urban plan of the upper part of the city. They represent twin offspring of the military rationality used by the people who planned and constructed the Fortress and should be viewed as crucial parts of the original design of the city.

Figure 13 - Ladeira do Pau da Bandeira, the southern access road to the upper city, linking the Conceição Church to the main plaza, 1860. Source: FERREZ, Gilberto. BAHIA - Velhas Fotografias 1858/1900 [BAHIA - Old Photographs 1858-1900], p. 43.

These ascending roads wound back and forth up the slope, with curves in places still close to the beach. These are the facts: but is there some logic behind them? Or did the master builder simply adapt them to the terrain, without any guidelines or principles? Military strategy suggests that these questions deserve closer examination.

The upper city, being situated on elevated ground, occupied a privileged military position: the means of access had to be defended and, in turn, contributed to the defense of the beach. The ascents facilitated the coordination of defending the lower part and assured an escape route for the defenders. At the same time, the layout had to make access difficult, so that any enemy who tried to ascend would be exposed to fire power from the upper part of the city. This meant that the ascent had to be steep and parallel to the hillside, which is exactly what the builders did. Enemies who might ascend along the Ladeira da Conceição would be exposing their right side, since their shields would be held in their left hands. If they opted to take the Ladeira da Misericórdia, they would not expose their right side, but the distance would be longer. These military aspects demonstrate the logic of the urban infrastructure of the Fortress of Salvador, which at first glance might appear fortuitous or poorly planned.

Figure 14 - Ladeira da Misericórdia. Below, the Fonte do Pereira, before being demolished. Above, the second curve on the way to the upper city, 1880. Source: FERREZ, Gilberto. BAHIA - Velhas Fotografias 1858/1900 [BAHIA - Old Photographs 1858-1900], p. 25.

The fact that the ascents end at the central plaza of the fortress is also a military feature. The present-day Praça Tomé de Souza was once the center of the fortress, while the citadel was its heart. The military authorities assigned under ordinary circumstances to command the defense forces would be stationed in that observation post. Looking over the plan of the fortress, we can see that all the roads go through the city plaza, a design that enabled rapid, efficient troop movements. All communication with the beach would have to take place by means of the protected, winding ascents. Those in the command post above would coordinate the movements of the troops in all directions.

The idea of having two ascending roads that wind back and forth, coming to an end at the main plaza on the upper level, was not unique to the Fortress of Salvador. The city of São Sebastião of Rio de Janeiro, founded in 1565, had an identical design: two symmetrical ascents on opposite sides, which began at the beach and terminated at the central plaza above. To one side was the citadel; in a separate space was the church plaza. These features reveal illuminating similarities (Fig. 15).

In the case of Salvador, the central plaza was conceptualized as being the military center, the best defensive position. The significance of the main plaza as the center of the city's defense can be found in the teachings of Aeneas Tacticus:

> "The commander-in-chief and his bodyguard should be stationed round the town hall and market place, if this position is a defensible one, otherwise, he should have previously occupied the strongest place in the city, and the most conspicuous from all quarters."[107]

Another intriguing aspect is the way in which the design is adapted to the logic of the Roman military encampment. The command point lay in the center, where all the paths crossed. When the lowest section of the beach was integrated into the design, the plaza was also central. In Salvador, the central plaza was not situated on the beach next to the harbor, as Vitruvius recommended; rather, it was kept in the upper part of the city and articulated with the roads that led to vital

---

107 TACTICUS, Aeneas. *Poliorcética* [Poliorketika], p. 82.

points of the fortress. This made the design superior to any theoretical model, since it took advantage of the terrain's characteristics.

Figure 15 - Model of the city of São Sebastião in 1567, showing the two ascending access roads, the plaza, the school, two bulwarks, and the church plaza in a distinct, isolated space.
Source: NONATO, José Antonio; SANTOS, Nubia Melhem. Era uma Vez o Morro do Castelo [Once Upon a Time there was a Castle on a Hill]. Rio de Janeiro: IPHAN, p. 16.

In the case of a siege, two basic rules guided the defense of the city: first, always maintain positions that are higher than those of the attacker; second, ensure that an escape route exists for both defenders and attackers. The logic is to avoid a situation in which the invader becomes trapped and thus redoubles his will to fight.

Vegetius recommended that those besieged should not abandon the ramparts, towers, or other high parts, because residents of any age and sex could throw "rocks and other things from the windows and roofs" down onto the enemy.[108] In the famous episode of Epirus's attack on Argos, King Pyrrhus died after he was struck in the head by a roof tile thrown by the Argos women, who fought from the roofs of the houses by hurling various objects at the enemy.[109]

The ascent roads were used for communication and troop movements. From any direction that an attack might occur, situating access roads on the sides ensured better conditions for defense because they offered a protected escape route to the upper city for the rearguard. The defenders could withdraw to the farthest boundary of the fortress and ascend to the citadel while being protected by those at the highest position of the access road. Military strategists reiterated that this position should be occupied, and, according to many reports, it was used as a crucial point of defense in Salvador.

Ensuring an escape route was a tradition in ancient warfare, with its famous maxims: Scipio said, "If the enemy wants to withdraw, disperse and open an escape route for their retreat";[110] Rabelais immortalized the proverb in *Gargantua and Pantagruel*, "Open, therefore, unto your enemies all the gates and ways, and make to them a bridge of silver";[111] and Lycurgus recommended to the Laconians that, when enemies flee, they should not be slain, so they will be "apt to think flight more advantageous than resistance."[112]

---

108 RENATUS, Flavius Vegetius. *Instituciones Militares* [Military Institutions], p. 129.
109 POLYAENUS. *Estratagemas* [Strategems], p. 564.
110 RENATUS, Flavius Vegetius. *Instituciones Militares* [Military Institutions], p. 106.
111 Idem.
112 POLYAENUS, *Estratagemas* [Strategems], p. 188.

The ascent roads were winding not simply because of the steep, uneven terrain; their curves were also part and parcel of a military strategy that made it possible to assault enemies multiple times from a higher position. In this respect, the fortress was impregnable. One of the first Greek treatises on the tactics of military sieges recommended that an army on the march should take into account the nature of the terrain and whether or not there were "elevated positions to their right." Greek soldiers carried their shields in their left hand, leaving their right flank exposed to their enemies. According to Philo of Byzantium, this logic lay behind the construction of fortifications with gates and towers placed in such a way as to force invaders to expose their right side.[113] This rule was repeated by Vitruvius in his guidelines for building access roads to the city:

> "Special pains should be taken that there be no easy avenue by which to storm the wall. The roads should be encompassed at steep points, and planned so as to approach the gates, not in a straight line, but from the right to the left; for as a result of this, the right hand side of the assailants, unprotected by their shields, will be next the wall."[114]

History records some episodes that allow us to evaluate the military significance of the sword and the shield, and of the rituals associated with the right hand and the left. When Scipio, the Roman general, saw a soldier proudly displaying his ornamented shield, he said, "It is a shame [...] for a Roman to pride himself more on the ornament of his left hand than of his right."[115] Similarly, during the civil war that the Roman Republic waged against Pompeii, Caesar's soldiers marched along a road by the sea and were wounded by arrows shot from ships that pursued them. In response, the general ordered the soldiers to switch their shields from their left hand to their right.[116]

---

113 TACTICUS, Aeneas. *Poliorcética* [Poliorketika], p. 68.
114 POLLIO, Marcus Vitruvius. *Los Diez Libros de Architectura* [The Ten Books on Architecture], p. 18.
115 POLYAENUS. *Estratagemas* [Strategems], p. 514.
116 Ibidem, p 527.

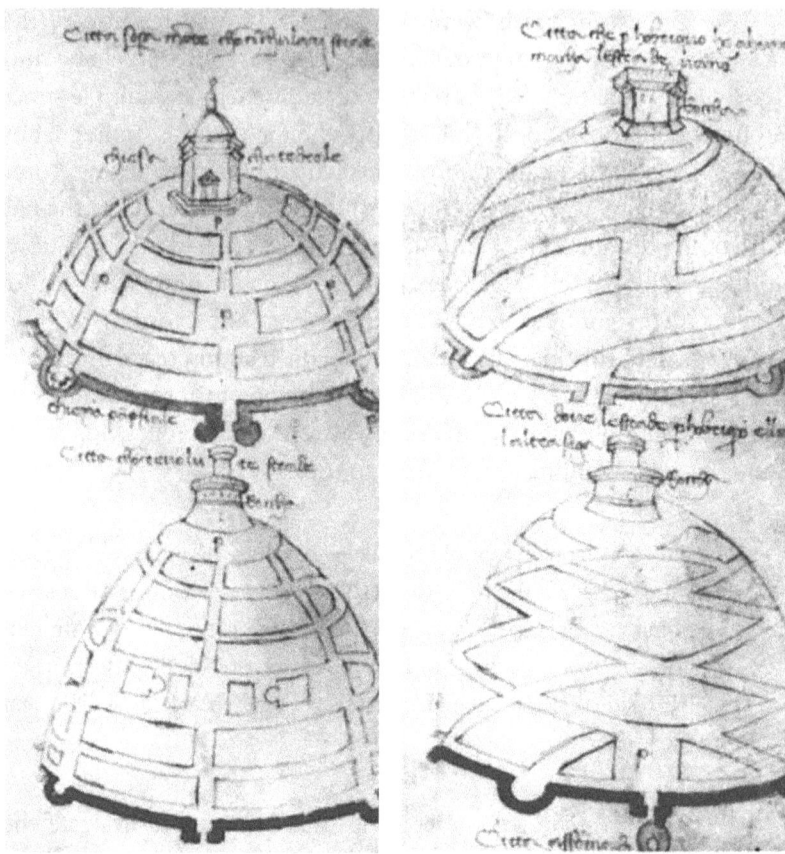

Figure 16 - Francesco di Giorgio Martin's models for cities on hills, with ascent roads shown as circular, spiral, diagonal, and criss-crossing. They all converge on the main plaza, almost always in straight lines.
Source: MARTINI, Francesco Di Giorgio. Trattati Di Architettura Ingegneria e Arte Militare [Treatise on Architecture, Engineering, and Military Arts], I, folha 7 tábua 9.

According to the model of urban planning envisioned by Martini, ascent roads in cities built on hillsides should be winding, until they reached the vicinity of the central plaza, where they converged in straight lines, thus lending a certain harmony to the design. This pattern is identical to that used in the Fortress of Salvador (Fig. 16).

The Fortress of Salvador

There is another curious explanation possible for the steep curve in the Ladeira da Conceição, which was the most strategic road in military terms, since it was situated on the side facing the sandbar of the Bay of All Saints; furtive attacks could occur on a farther beach. The access road could have been built on three levels, with a less severe slope, but the master builder Luís Dias preferred that it have only one curve and a long inclining section: this would expose the right side of any enemies who came up this road, rendering them more vulnerable to the defenders' attacks. The Ladeira da Misericórdia, on the other side, has two curves and a gentler slope, exposing invaders on only one level but, in compensation, extending their exposure on a long section of the road. The curves in the ascent roads are situated at the farthest boundaries of the Fortress, where the upper level began to exercise total domination of the surroundings. This is obviously a case of pure military logic.

11. The Perimeter of the Fortress

> *Cities and forts are either fortified by nature or by human hand, or by both, which is considered stronger. By "nature" is meant places which are elevated, precipitous, surrounded by sea, morasses or rivers; by "hand," fosses and a wall.*
>
> Vegetius

The location of the original perimeter of the Fortress of Salvador is a contentious issue. At least three different theories have been proposed for identifying landmarks along the early boundaries. All three are unanimous in recognizing the military purpose behind the design of the fortress and the rationale for the city's outline, but its precise shape remains uncertain. Although the issue may not incite passionate debate, having fallen into obscurity long ago, it is worthwhile to take it up again and propose some new hypotheses. In these, the Terreiro de Jesus, the Praça Castro Alves, the Ladeira da Misericórdia, and the Ladeira do Pau da Bandeira acquire new significance.

The first approach, championed by Teodoro Sampaio,[117] argued that, when the walls were built, they started at some point along

---

117 SAMPAIO, Teodoro. *História da Fundação da Cidade do Salvador* [History of the Founding of the City of Salvador], p. 184.

the slope down to where the Praça Castro Alves is now located, continuing along the line running through the dip now called the Baixa dos Sapateiros, then climbing up along the Ladeira da Praça, and ending at the dip that separates Misericórdia from the Praça Tomé de Souza. The second approach, advocated by Edison Carneiro,[118] asserted that the "boundaries of the city were natural—the ocean, the mountain, the marsh";[119] with certain variations, the wall continued past the Baixa dos Sapateiros and down the valley to Pelourinho at the current Rua do Tabuão. The third theory was succinctly articulated by José Teixeira de Barros; in his view, the "early wall must have gone from Ajuda along Rua do Tesouro, then behind the Ladeira da Praça to the low area, there forming a wide angle and then continuing on the other side toward the São Domingos Church, in the rear; from there, past the front of the School of Medicine to the bluff behind the cathedral; and then turning back along the top of the hill to Rua Chile."[120] Teixeira de Barros commented briefly on the location of the fountain on the eastern side of the city, but did not offer relevant technical support for his theory.

Among scholars, the position defended by Teodoro Sampaio predominates. In his work, *História da Fundação da Cidade do Salvador* (History of the Founding of the City of Salvador), he presented an urban plan that reconstituted the boundaries of the original city (Fig. 17). His drawing, enriched with details on scale and contour lines, altered the angle of presentation to make it easier to visualize the streets, blocks, and hills. It was based on another urban plan, the oldest one available, which was drawn up around 1605 and delivered to the king "in order to proceed with the fortification"[121] of the city. In recognition of this native son and his abilities, the city reproduced his plan in a bronze plaque, which was mounted on the side of a monument at the Praça da Sé.

---

118 CARNEIRO, Edison. *A cidade do Salvador 1549* [The City of Salvador, 1549], pp. 62-63.
119 Idem, p. 90.
120 BARROS, José Teixeira. *Muros da cidade do Salvador* [Walls of the City of Salvador]. Revista do IGHB, v. 36, pp. 76-77.
121 RAZÃO do Estado do Brasil [Reason for the State of Brazil] (c. 1616). *Códice 126* da Biblioteca Pública Municipal do Porto, p. 51, verso.

Sampaio's intellectual authority carried great weight, leading later Brazilian and Portuguese authors to propose similar theories. Pedro Calmon[122] incorporated his approach; Américo Simas Filho[123] cited Sampaio by name; Paulo F. Santos,[124] who propounded his own position, also affirmed Sampaio's point of view; and Manuel C. Teixeira,[125] in a fascinating work on the evolution of Portuguese urbanism, did not diverge from the dominant opinion.

The opposing position, based on Edison Carneiro's theory, is currently advanced by some followers, most prominently by Rafael Moreira in a conference paper presented at the Fourth Congress of the History of Bahia.[126] The third theory, defended by Teixeira de Barros in 1909, is supported by Braz do Amaral, who holds that the path of the wall in the upper city was very similar up to "the Terreiro or surroundings," adding a significant detail:

> "[...] the section from the hillside down to the ocean divided, forming two paths or sloping access roads, one following more or less the outline of the present-day Ladeira da Misericórdia, and the other going along the spit called Pau da Bandeira [...]."[127]

In a theory independently proposed by Father Serafim Leite, the northern boundary was the same. According to him, the boundary of the Fortress of Salvador went "from the Barroquinha to the Terreiro de Jesus, the precise spot where, later, the priests of the Society of

---

122 CALMON, Pedro. *História da Fundação da Bahia* [History of the Founding of Bahia], pp. 163-164.
123 EVOLUÇÃO FÍSICA DE SALVADOR [Physical Evolution of Salvador], pp. 34-35.
124 SANTOS, Paulo F. *Formação de Cidades no Brasil Colonial* [Formation of Cities in Colonial Brazil], p. 83.
125 TEIXEIRA, Manuel C. *O Urbanismo Português* [Portuguese Urbanism], p. 225.
126 MOREIRA, Rafael. *O arquiteto Miguel de Arruda e o primeiro projeto para Salvador* [The Architect Miguel de Arruda and the First Project for Salvador]. Anais, I, p. 133.
127 SILVA, Ignácio Accioli de Cerqueira e. *Memórias Históricas e Políticas da Província da Bahia* [Historical and Political Memoirs of the Province of Bahia], notes by Braz do Amaral. I, 334.

Jesus founded their school [...]."¹²⁸ In Serafim Leite's view, the Terreiro thus formed "a gentle hill outside the first wall of the city."¹²⁹ With a few remarks and additional considerations, this theory appears to be correct.

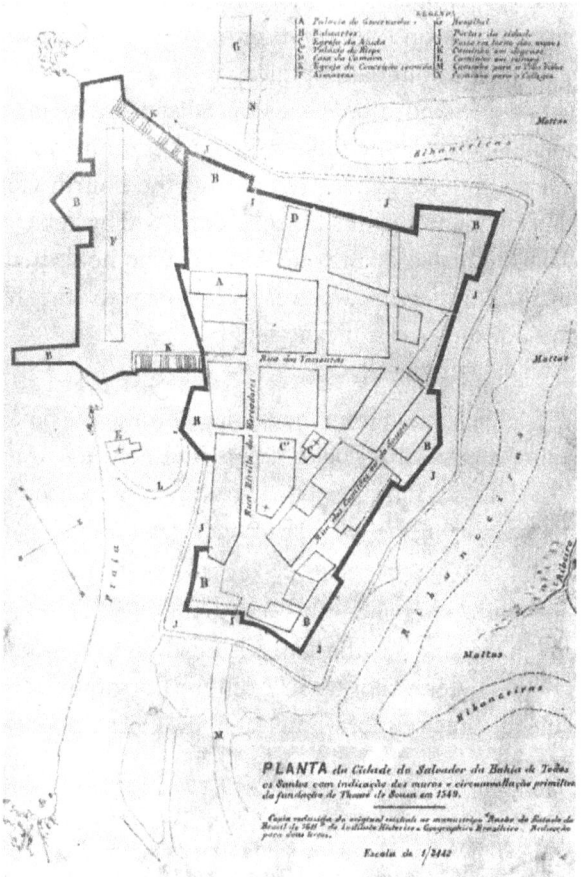

Figure 17 - Plan of the Fortress of Salvador in 1549, as conceptualized by Teodoro Sampaio.
Source: SAMPAIO, Theodoro. História da Fundação da Cidade do Salvador [History of the Founding of the City of Salvador], p. 185.

---

128 LEITE, Serafim. *História da Companhia de Jesus no Brasil* [History of the Society of Jesus in Brazil]. I, p. 21.
129 Idem, p. 22.

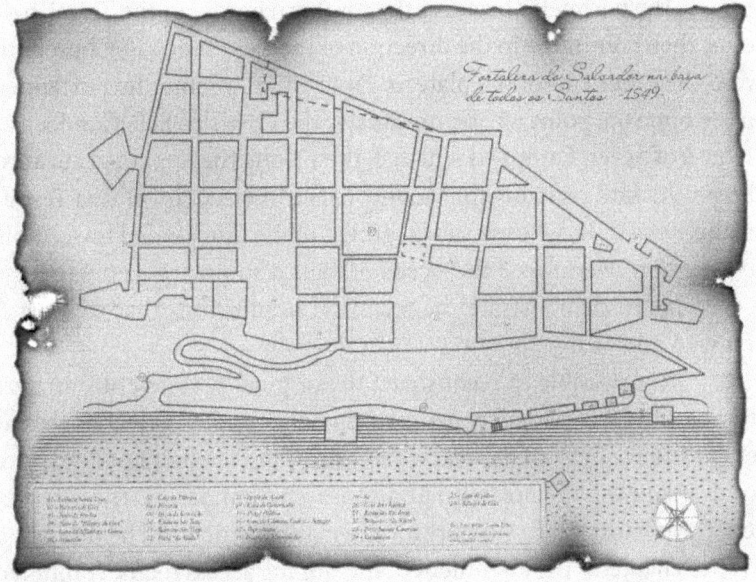

Figure 18 - Original borders of the Fortress of Salvador, as reconstructed by the author.

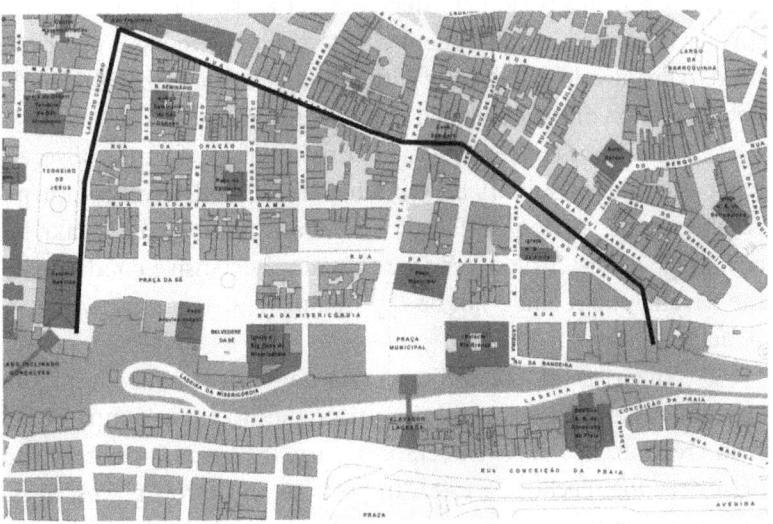

Figure 19 - Present-day plan of the city of Salvador. The dark line indicates the original perimeter of the Fortress of Salvador.

The perimeter began at the southern border of the Terreiro de Jesus, then continued in the direction of the São Francisco Church toward the other end of the plateau. From there, another line extended to the opposite point where, nowadays, the Casa dos Sete Candeeiros (House of Seven Lamps) is situated, then along the upper part toward the south, until reaching the vicinity of the intersection of Rua Tesouro and Rua Chile, where a new segment of the line headed toward the hillside that overlooked the ocean. This is a summary of the theory; it remains to demonstrate the technical foundations that support it (Figs. 18 and 19).

It is possible to reconstruct the original perimeter by analyzing the physical evidence, geometry, and strategic issues, as well as letters and writings of the era, which constitute the point of departure for determining the northern and southern boundaries. These represent the documentary support for the matter, which will be discussed in later chapters. The alignment of the sloping access roads, combined with the arrangement and symmetry of the urban design, assured unity to the project. The geometry of the design leaves no doubt as to the rationality behind the plan, allowing us to determine the perimeter of the fortress with a reasonable degree of certainty. These issues will be further examined in subsequent chapters. First, two basic principles need to be introduced, dealing with military concepts that guided the determination of the polygonal outlay of the Fortress of Salvador.

Decisions concerning the perimeter of any fortress observed two basic rules of military tactics, which together determined the perimeter of the Fortress of Salvador: the construction had to take full advantage of the curves, bends, and natural defensive conditions of the terrain, and it could not be exposed to view from nearby hills or structures.

Theorists of the military arts developed the concept that strongholds and castles owed their resistance to either nature or human creation. In the seventeenth century, the Spanish military theorist Cristobál Lechuga wrote, "In posts set in narrow places, in the mountains or in valleys, it is necessary to guard what is desirable, even if the fortress built there has to be high in some places and low in others [...]" and its parts should be "[...] interlocking in such a way that

The Fortress of Salvador

all of them protect each other and each one ensures the rest, with a high point overlooking the fortress."[130] This theoretical consideration is perfectly applicable to the Fortress of Salvador. The entire system of defense was developed in a coordinated fashion to "guard what is desirable," a rule recommended for protecting cities and strongholds in accordance with military strategy.[131]

One of the fundamental tactics consisted in building walls in inaccessible places. Vitruvius recommended that "Special pains should be taken that there be no easy avenue by which to storm the wall [...]. The roads should be encompassed at steep points [...]."[132] Such a tactic required taking advantage of the perimeter of the plateau at its highest point. This orientation also involved a second tactic: protecting the fortress against any neighboring position that, in the language of the era, could serve as a *padrasto* (literally, "step-father"), that is, a higher place overlooking another, which could expose the bulwarks and walls to view from nearby hills.

In the site chosen for the fortress, certain problems were posed by the plateaus of São Bento and Carmo, at the time called Monte Calvário. The tactic discussed above prescribed guidelines for determining the boundaries, but allowed an exception on the eastern side. At the top of the Ladeira da Praça, the hillside descended precipitously to the marshland below. The adjacent plateaus of Palma and Desterro were separated by the marsh and were difficult to reach, making this side the least dangerous one of the site. In this setting, the base of the city had to incorporate part of the lowlands within the walls. Residents of the Fortress of Salvador needed a well for water, a place to plant gardens, and an area for discarding waste materials.

Upon examining the site and determining its boundaries, the master architect Luís Dias noticed that the northern and southern sides required special attention, being the most vulnerable points of

---

130 LECHUGA, Cristóbal. *Tratado de la Artillería e Fortificacion* [Treatise on Artillery and Fortification], p. 418.
131 LECHUGA, Cristóbal. *Tratado de la Artillería e Fortificacion* [Treatise on Artillery and Fortification], p. 418.
132 POLLIO, Marcus Vitruvius. *Los Diez Libros de Architectura* [The Ten Books on Architecture], p. 18.

entry by land. He therefore placed bulwarks above, leading to inevitable restrictions on construction in areas outside the wall. This was the origin of the Praça Castro Alves and Terreiro de Jesus.

For similar reasons, he deliberately made the northern and southern access roads, which ascend from the beach, coincide with the upper boundaries of the fortress. When we examine the historic iconography of the city, we can see that the two farthest curves in the Ladeira do Pau da Bandeira and Ladeira da Misericórdia are aligned in relation to the southern boundary—the upper part of the Praça Castro Alves—and the northern one—the Plano Inclinado Gonçalves.

The issue of occupying the highest point is critical in military theory, a rule included in the *Seven-Part Code* and systematically revisited in Renaissance treatises. Alberti recommended extreme caution in deciding on the perimeter so that there would be no peak, hill, or other point in neighboring areas that could afford refuge or protection to enemies.[133] Cataneo asserted that adequate defense required the absence of higher points and the existence of clear ground in front of the walls.[134]

It was essential that the Fortress of Salvador overlook and dominate adjacent land, a crucial strategic factor in determining the perimeter and the reason why the northern and southern boundaries were the most essential to secure. They had to be situated in elevated places with a good view overlooking the outside fields; similarly, they had to be out of sight from external areas so that residents would be protected in case of attack. These constituted the tactical concepts of fortification that were used to determine the original boundaries. It now remains to provide details on each of these boundaries.

---

133 ALBERTI, Leon Battista. *L'Architettura* [Architecture], p. 152.
134 CATANEO, Pietro *L'Architettura* [Architecture], pp. 209-210.

12. The Southern Boundary of the Fortress

The camp should not be [...] commanded by any eminences from which it may be annoyed by the enemy's weapons.[135]

Vegetius

In military theory, the advantage of an elevated position consists of three elements: first, the highest point is a natural obstacle to the enemy's approach; second, the height boosts the range of firepower; and third, the observer has a better view of the surroundings. These tactical aspects explicate the value of the southern side of the fortress and the attention given to determining its boundaries. The location of Praça Castro Alves on a height exemplifies these three elements (Fig. 20).

The southern boundary of the fortress began above at the Praça Castro Alves, shortly beyond the intersection of Rua do Tesouro and Rua Chile, and descended the hill toward the ocean below until reaching the Largo da Conceição da Praia, facing the Largo da Preguiça. In the upper city, the intersection of Rua do Tesouro and Rua Chile mark the highest point of the southern side, constituting the

---

135 RENATUS, Flavius Vegetius. *Instituciones Militares* [Military Institutions], pp. 51-52.

dominant position in the Fortress of Salvador, with the greatest strategic importance—being the side that overlooked the ocean, the harbor, and the neighboring hill of São Bento. Any enemy attack would most likely occur in this sector due to the ease of access to the sandbar in the Bay of All Saints.

Figure 20 - Southern boundary of the Fortress of Salvador, at the top of the Ajuda plateau.

Examining the topography of this tract, the southern face of the plateau was narrow, measuring no more than fifty meters. On the western side, the tract abruptly descended to the ocean and, on the opposite side, sloped down more gently to the marsh. The site lay on one end of the plateau, which the perimeter had to encompass. Military logic suggests that the wall occupied the edge of the crown, since any descent in the direction of the neighboring high point of São Bento would have made the fortress vulnerable to enemy fire coming from São Bento, which overlooked the fortress.

Another militarily significant aspect was the declivity of the Praça Castro Alves. To reach the outer rampart, an attacker would have had to climb the hillside; in tactical terms, the ramp was a natural obstacle to approach. The quality of the harbor, the abundance of springs, and the defensive perimeter on the upper part were defining characteristics of the site for the fortress.

We can hypothesize that the southern side was the starting point, since the end of the plateau and the harbor coincided on this side, a feature lacking on the northern side. On one extreme, the fortress ended at the Terreiro de Jesus—where it could have continued, since the plateau extended further out—while the other extreme marked the end of the high ground, requiring the Praça Castro Alves to form a corner on one side in order to align the defensive structures with the harbor. These features provide theoretical support to the thesis concerning the southern perimeter on top of the plateau.

By virtue of the vulnerability of the southern boundary, it is reasonable to posit that two bulwarks were constructed in this location, defending a narrow piece of land and a gate. A deed preserved by the Benedictines indicates that this was where the São Tomé station was situated; it was also mentioned by Luís Dias in one of his letters, in which he said that sections of the wall had fallen from the "São Tiago bulwark down to the São Tomé station."[136] In another passage, he noted that the size of the loss was not large. These bulwarks were therefore near each other, so such documentary references make sense, considering the tactical precepts applicable to cities built on irregular sites, which dictated that bulwarks be constructed at the most vulnerable points. Cataneo presented a theoretical model in which bulwarks on the narrowest, most dangerous side should be close to each other precisely to protect the most fragile access point.[137]

Gabriel Soares remarked that Rua Chile was a lovely street, with many residents, at the end of which lay the chapel of Santa Luzia and a station with artillery.[138] He further wrote that Rua Ajuda ran

---

136 MOREIRA, Rafael. *O arquiteto Miguel de Arruda e o primeiro projeto para Salvador* [The Architect Miguel de Arruda and the First Project for Salvador]. Anais, I, p. 133.
137 CATANEO, Pietro *L'Architettura* [Architecture], p. 230.
138 SOUZA, Gabriel Soares de. *Notícia do Brasil* [Report from Brazil]. I, p. 3.

alongside the chapel: hence, this was where the two streets met and where the first bulwark was situated.

The deeds preserved by the Benedictines in the *Livro Velho do Tombo* (Old Register of Charters and Deeds), covering the late sixteenth century and early seventeenth, clearly indicate the location of the São Tomé station as well as the system of defensive structures located on the beach. These deeds were land titles belonging to Judge Baltazar Ferraz, a rich and powerful man in the city of Salvador, who acquired three plots in the area of Conceição da Praia, where he built a house. His aim was to improve the natural harbor and construct some buildings that could serve as warehouses; this was the origin of the Baltazar Ferraz port.

At the end of the sixteenth century, the city grew. After three decades of peace, pirate incursions spurred the construction of new walls. The southern boundary of the rampart descended a bit toward the Praça Castro Alves in order to protect the new blocks that were laid out below Rua do Tesouro. This situation explains the donation of lands that were part of the original defense system of the city.

The three lots may have totaled up to ninety-four fathoms (206.8 meters), covering a continuous area of land, beach, and reef, starting before the northern boundary of the Conceição da Praia Church and ending on the other side of Preguiça. It is not possible to determine how much overlap there was among the plots, which could reduce this estimated measurement. Identifying each property is crucial for an adequate understanding of the facts. Analyzing the three land titles allows us to speculate with a reasonable degree of certainty on the military structures found on the site. Below is a description of them, from north to south, from the Elevador Lacerda toward Avenida do Contorno (Fig. 21):

> — In 1596, Luis Rodrigues gave Judge Ferraz a piece of land, in gratitude, "on the beach of Nossa Senhora da Conceição over to the boat beaching site where merchandise is unloaded from ships."[139] The plot had originally been given

---

139 LIVRO *Velho do Tombo* [Old Register of Charters and Deeds], p. 318.

to the donor as a land grant by Governor Francisco de Souza around 1592. The lot was a large one, measuring 44 meters along the beach and the site for beaching boats, and 13.2 meters going toward the hillside. The donor had built small thatched-roof houses on the lot The description reveals the state of the natural harbor at the beach in front of the Conceição Church. This constituted the first lot.

— The second lot was one that Judge Ferraz bought from Maria Fernandes Coelho on an unknown date. This piece of land was located at the "Santa Luzia gate of the aforementioned city where the São Tomé bulwark used to be [...]." The documentation concluded by stating that the lot descended the hillside from the "Santa Luzia gate over to the path running along the ocean beach [...]."[140] The lot was perpendicular to the beach, beginning in the upper city and ending at the narrow path on the beach. The original owners were Estevão Lopes Da Gram and Francisco Vaz. The former held the post of river steward. Payment records indicate that Estevão Lopes Da Gram was already in Bahia around 1552.[141]

This plot was a strip of land that began in the upper area and descended to the beach. We can identify its northern and southern boundaries: on the northern side, a line that ended in the area surrounding the Conceição da Praia Church; on the southern side, probably the original curve in the Ladeira da Conceição, where it took on the name Ladeira do Palácio.

— Finally, Judge Ferraz asked Governor Diogo Botelho in 1603 to give him a land grant consisting of the "tongue of land," 4-6 meters across, located between the path and the beach. This tract bordered the plot that Maria Fernandes Coelho had purchased. He also asked for another piece of land "farther ahead" toward the port known as the "Porto dos Pescadores," heading toward Avenida do Contorno, which consisted of 110 meters of beach and reefs. These two strips of

---

140 Idem, p. 360.
141 DOCUMENTOS HISTÓRICOS [Historical Documents], v. XIII, Bibliotheca Nacional, mandados de pagamentos n. 1189, 1321, 1349, 1360.

beach comprised the third lot Judge Ferraz acquired. On the plot was an area of landfill where two pieces of artillery were situated; in his request, Judge Ferraz agreed that, if necessary, he would extend the landfill out into the sea.[142]

Figure 21 - Present-day plan of the city of Salvador, superimposed with the southern boundary of the fortress and the demarcation of the lots belonging to Judge Baltazar Ferraz.
Source: CENTRO Histórico de Salvador, Bahia: patrimônio mundial [Historic Center of Salvador, Bahia: World Heritage Site].

In 1604, Judge Ferraz took ceremonial possession of his property on the beach. Although we do not know about the transfer of the plot that began in the upper city, it is reasonable to surmise that he had already obtained it. The present ceremony began on the sloping access road that went from "the House of His Majesty to the beach of Nossa Senhora da Conceição."[143] Note that the Ladeira do Pau da Bandeira curved around and emerged onto another sloping road, the Ladeira

---

142 LIVRO *Velho do Tombo* [Old Register of Charters and Deeds], p. 360.
143 Idem, p. 362.

da Conceição. The record of the ceremony identified exactly where the property lay: the "place where a wooden cross is erected and the path goes back to the house of Nossa Senhora da Conceição."[144] The curve was the initial point of the trajectory followed in the ceremony.

The description was meticulous. The land transfer ceremony began with the lands granted by Luis Rodrigues. The distance was 44 meters "going from the aforementioned cross along the old path that goes to the site for beaching boats [...] until reaching the sea, turning back to Nossa Senhora da Conceição." The notary public stated that they "walked from the aforementioned cross [...] toward the site for beaching boats" and that the Judge was given possession of the lands lying "on the aforementioned path toward the sea"; from there, they continued until they reached "the site for beaching boats next to the fort located there." From this point, they went to the reef that lay at the "foot of the aforementioned fort on the side facing the sea," and from there went across the beach to the "side by Nossa Senhora," completing the distance of 44 meters.[145] The description suggests that the fort lay in front of the Conceição da Praia Church in a north-south direction and, facing downhill, to the left of the Ladeira da Conceição.

The land transfer ceremony was not yet over. The scribe was requested to present the land title for the third lot, consisting of the "tongue of land" and the 110 meters of beach, awarded as a land grant by Governor Diogo Botelho. The scribe stated that the "tongue of land" was "contiguous" to the plots that were transferred and next to the lot that descended the hillside. To begin the ceremony, the scribe and Judge Ferraz returned to the "Varadouro beach" (where boats were beached) and positioned themselves next to the fort "on the side by Nossa Senhora," that is, on the side toward the hill, "in front of the house" where Antonio Mendes lived, indicating that they were at some spot near the upper part of the Largo da Conceição on the southern side.

In this passage of the record of the land transfer ceremony, Judge Ferraz stated that Antonio Mendes's house sat on the piece of land sold by Maria Coelho that descended from the upper city. He

---

144 Idem.
145 Ibidem, pp. 361-364.

further asserted that this spot—possibly at some intersection on the upper part of the Largo da Conceição—was part of the land grant given by Luis Rodrigues, which was why he had already taken possession of it, and also led to the lot granted by Governor Diogo Botelho. From this spot, they headed out in a southerly direction "along the reefs of the beach and the tongue of land that lies between the saltwater and the path inside as well as outside the trench over to the pit that comes out from the Santa Luzia gate." This description of 1604 indicates that, in addition to the Conceição fort, there was a sort of trench that ran down from the upper city by the Santa Luzia gate to the area surrounding the Largo da Preguiça. Similarly, another trench ran along the beach, parallel to the coast, ending at the Conceição fort. The ceremony did not conclude at the juncture of the two trenches; the participants continued toward the Praia dos Pescadores until completing the perimeter of the land parcel.

This document does not exhaust the available documentary sources. In 1612, Judge Ferraz faced a legal conflict with the Benedictines, who sought to gain ownership and title to part of the plots located on the beach. In support of their property claim, the Benedictines presented two deeds for land grants conceded to them on the strip along the ocean. Examining these documents complements the available information about the site on the Conceição da Praia and Largo da Preguiça.

The oldest title dates back to 1586 and was awarded to Manuel Dias de Seita by Governor Manoel Teles Barreto. The area, according to Manuel Dias, was "in front of the fort where Nossa Senhora da Conceição is" and consisted of "rocky reefs [...] running along the southern side where weirs can be laid to catch fish." In the document, Governor Teles Barreto asserted that "the reefs are where I have the old bulwark and, on the side where said bulwark lies, is land where said fort stands."[146]

The second title is a letter for a land grant awarded by Governor Dom Diogo de Menezes in 1612. The Benedictines claimed that they needed a house on the beach for supporting their work, located

---

146 Ibidem, pp. 26-28.

on a strip of land along the ocean from "the Baltazar Ferraz port" going southwards for 440 meters. The land title was conveyed in 1612, and conflict ensued.[147] Judge Ferraz challenged the document, claiming that he had ownership and title to the "grounds, beach, and reefs," that he had owned them for many years, and that there he had built a house and a sugar dryer made of rock and lime. He alleged usurpation and requested the annulment of the land title awarded the Benedictines. In his allegations, he made some noteworthy statements: the area in question had been in his possession for more than eight or ten years and was "next to the port called Baltazar Ferraz";[148] and he had removed large rocks from the site that used to damage boats.

The deeds demonstrate that the São Tomé bulwark lay above, coordinated in some way with another fort on the beach [Fig. 22]. According to Governor Teles Barreto, this was "the old bulwark." Could this be the same one built by Tomé de Souza? Apparently yes. The "old bulwark" was built on the reefs, which concurs with the information conveyed in a letter by Luís Dias.

Near the São Tomé station, on the western side, the São Tiago bulwark was erected. An examination of the urban network laid out in the old maps of the city reveals that Rua Rui Barbosa was based on the path that encircled the bulwark. Between the two bulwarks was a narrow strip of the wall and perhaps the southern gate of the fortress as well. Following the recommendations of military strategy, this defensive line had two projecting bulwarks overlooking the area from which an invasion would probably occur. Any attack originating from neighboring hills, or any attempt to scale the open area in front, where the Praça Castro Alves was located, would be struck by crossfire coming from the bulwarks.

The configuration of the southern boundary of the fortress indicates that there were three bulwarks, more or less aligned, to defend that side. Two were situated above. defending the harbor, wall, and plot that led down from the Praça Castro Alves, and overlooking the beach and the Ladeira do Pau da Bandeira. The third was on the beach, taking advantage of the favorable state of the plot near the end

---

147 Ibidem, pp. 41-42.
148 Ibidem, p. 44.

of the second cove, and served to defend the harbor and its surroundings. The defensive line was built on a narrow strip of land, which was advantageous for defense and, theoretically, would bear the probable impact of an invasion. This seems to have been the military logic that guided the determination of the southern perimeter of the Fortress of Salvador.

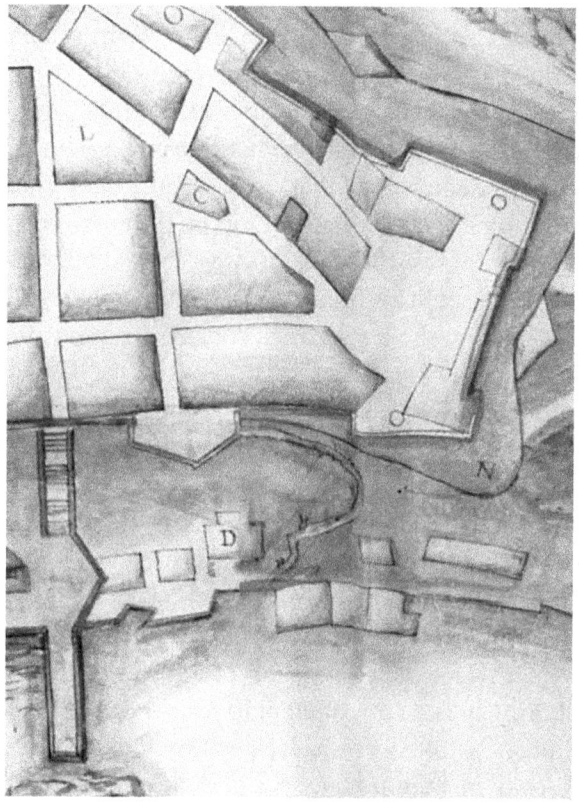

Figure 22 - Detail of the southern boundary of the plan of the city of Salvador, 1605. The last city block on the hillside reproduces the original format of the São Tomé bulwark.
Source: RAZÃO do Estado do Brasil [Reason for the State of Brazil] (c. 1616). Códice 126 da Biblioteca Pública Municipal do Porto, p. 57.

13. THE NORTHERN BOUNDARY OF THE FORTRESS

The fortress or fortified city should be designed in such a way that there is no place around or near it from which it can be discovered and flanked from many sides.[149]

Simão Madeira

Military strategy prohibited buildings in the area outside fortresses, so many plazas and public squares arose as a result. The Terreiro de Jesus in Salvador is a good example. The wall on the northern boundary of the fortress overlooked the plateau that gently descended to Pelourinho. On the outside, no building was allowed. The Jesuits wanted the piece of land outside the wall, which eventually they succeeded in acquiring. The name "Terreiro de Jesus" arose in honor of the Society of Jesus. At some unknown date, Mem de Sá demolished what remained of the original city wall and established new standards for streets and blocks. This is how the Pelourinho quarter was created. The Terreiro de Jesus and the street leading to the São Francisco Church were conceived as connecting points between two distinct levels of the historic center of the city of Salvador.

---

149 VITERBO, Souza, *Dicionário Histórico e Documental dos Arquitetos [...]* [Architects' Historical and Documentary Dictionary]. II, p. 118. This passage is included in a manuscript entitled, "Thesis on Military Architectonics," written around 1660.

By focusing on the alignment of houses on the southern side, an observer standing in the door of the São Francisco Church can see an angle in the middle of the Terreiro de Jesus, then a straight line going toward the Plano Inclinado Gonçalves. This alignment is what remains of the original design, embodied in the line of the wall. At the site, Luís Dias chose three widely separated points that would be good places to set up defenses, then laid out two straight streets that intersected each other (Fig. 23). At the midpoint where they converged, he constructed a bulwark. Between the wall and the line of houses, there was a street that was approximately 5.5 to 6.6 meters wide.

This thesis can be demonstrated initially through the correspondence of Father Manuel da Nóbrega and through certain titles to land that belonged to the Society of Jesus. Such evidence can be complemented and confirmed through the analysis of Renaissance standards of symmetry and proportion that guided the construction of the Fortress of Salvador. Finally, we must examine the geometry of the design of the city and the differences in the size of blocks and streets on opposite sides of the Terreiro de Jesus.

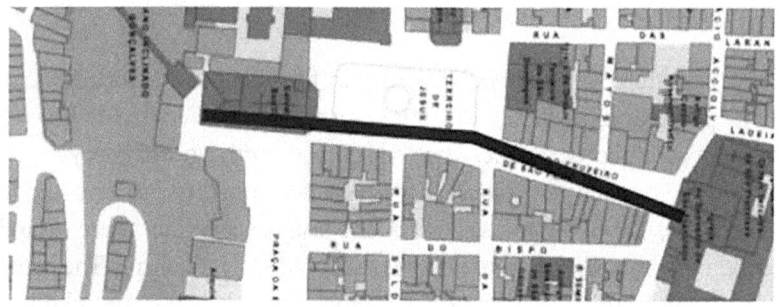

Figure 23 - Present-day plan of the city of Salvador, showing the northern boundary of the fortress superimposed in black. Two straight lines intersected in the middle of the Terreiro de Jesus.
Source: CENTRO Histórico de Salvador, Bahia: patrimônio mundial [Historic Center of Salvador, Bahia: World Heritage Site].

These various sources of proof are in agreement. The thesis they demonstrate begins with the documentary evidence: letters by Manuel da Nóbrega and certain deeds, which establish the grounds for determining the northern boundary with some degree of certainty. Studying the strategy of constructing fortified cities enables us to understand the connection between the sloping access roads and the defensive measures on higher ground. The heights defended each access road, which, in turn, served as their boundary. Finally, using a ruler and compass demonstrates patterns of symmetry between the human body and proportions in city blocks. Vitruvius's ideas, taken to an extreme by Martini, provide theoretical support for these conclusions in reconstructing the northern boundary of the Fortress of Salvador.

Manuel da Nóbrega referred to the matter in two letters written in 1549 and 1557. In August, 1549,[150] he discussed the existence of the wall and the Jesuits' intention of occupying the higher ground, on the upper part of the hill, outside the wall. By that time, the plots of land within the fortress had already been distributed. Nóbrega made an effort to "find a good place" for the school, but he could only find one spot. He then proceeded to enumerate three inconvenient aspects of the spot: a) it was "very close to the Sé Cathedral and having two churches together" was not good; b) the plot was small and depended greatly on the city; and c) the hill was very steep.[151]

The high ground that Nóbrega wanted also overlooked the ocean, but it had fresh water all around and a place for gardens and orchards. But Governor Tomé de Souza did not agree to grant the site because it lay outside the city and he feared a possible attack by the "pagans."

---

150 LETTER from Father Manuel da Nóbrega, dated August 9, 1549. LEITE S. I., Serafim. *Cartas dos Primeiros Jesuítas do Brasil* [Letters of the First Jesuits of Brazil]. I, p. 125.

151 Idem, I, p. 125. The text reads as follows: "I endeavored to choose a good place for our school within the wall and only found one, which serves to show Your Highness how many inconveniences it poses, because it lies right next to the Sé Cathedral and having two churches next to each other is not good, and it is small because the only place to build a house is no bigger than 10 fathoms, although 40 would be needed in length; and there is no place to open a garden, or anything else, because every side is very steep and the city presses in on it greatly. Furthermore, all of us believe the area of high ground that lies shortly beyond the wall to be much better, in the part where the city should be expanded [. . .]."

Years passed. In 1557,[152] Father Nóbrega complained that the Jesuits' houses in the city were cramped and did not allow adequate separation between priests and boys. The solution he proposed revolved around "our dismantling the city wall and building some houses in the area outside the site assigned to the School." He concluded with a note of doubt about whether or not they had authorization to "dismantle the wall." In Nóbrega's opinion, it would be better to return the site they were assigned, in which case the Crown would build "a simple shelter in the area outside the wall at the place chosen for this."[153]

In another passage in the letter, Nóbrega indicated more precisely the location of the Jesuits' house: "it abuts the Sé so closely that, no matter how softly people speak, one can hear in one church what happens in the other."[154] This information leaves no doubt that the Jesuits initially had their houses in the Praça da Sé, near the present-day Excelsior Cinema. When Manuel da Nóbrega stated that the new house should be built "on the other side of this site where we are now, so it can be farther from the Sé," he revealed his intention to move to the opposite side, that is, where the Basílica Cathedral was built. The letter of 1557 shows that the Jesuits were seeking a ruling about the location where they could construct their permanent buildings. There was no more correspondence about the walls, but on May 23, 1572, the Jesuits' new church, constructed by Mem de Sá, was inaugurated.

Documentary proof concerning the northern boundary of the fortress is not confined to Manuel da Nóbrega's letters. The *Register of Deeds of the Society of Jesus*[155] contains eight deeds involving plots situated between the Praça da Sé and Pelourinho, all on the side toward the ocean. The documents are dated or refer to events that

---

152 LETTER from Father Manuel da Nóbrega to Father Miguel Torres, dated September 2, 1557. LEITE S. I., Serafim. *Cartas dos Primeiros Jesuítas do Brasil* [Letters of the First Jesuits of Brazil]. II, pp. 407-410.
153 Idem, p. 409.
154 Ibidem, p. 410.
155 DOCUMENTOS HISTÓRICOS [Historical Documents], v. LXIII LXIV, Bibliotheca Nacional, Códice I - 19, 18, 2.

occurred between 1566 and 1619. Three of the deeds, drawn up between 1573 and 1581, deal with properties located at the Praça da Sé, and prove the following: a) the Jesuits' house stood near the original Sé and above the Ladeira da Misericórdia; and b) the Jesuits acquired the plots that bordered the Pereira Fountain. Considered jointly, the deeds give evidence of chronologically successive acquisitions by the Jesuits of properties moving away from the Praça da Sé and toward Pelourinho.

The most interesting one is dated 1581. The Jesuits sold Helena Borges a set of houses on the "street of Paulo Serrão coming from the Sé." They were located "next to the Sé" and, in 1575, were described in a list of the Jesuits' property as a "set of houses" that lay between "our school and the Sé Cathedral."[156] The houses were made of wattle and daub, covered with tiles, with walls facing the following sites: on one side, the house belonging to Antonio Rodrigues Vaqueiro; on another, that of Gaspar Luis and his wife, Maria Rabela; on another, the public street; and, on the side toward the ocean, "the road that goes to the Pereira fountain," in other words, the Ladeira da Misericórdia. The set of houses sold to Helena Borges in 1581 represented the Jesuits' first site, a location chosen by Manuel da Nóbrega and Tomé de Souza (Table 7).

The Jesuits moved from the house "next to the Sé Cathedral" to the Terreiro de Jesus in search of more space. They wanted direct access to the ocean, a place for gardens, and their own fountain. To realize this goal, they bought some properties situated on the northern edge of the Praça da Sé.

In 1573, Felipa Álvares—daughter of Diogo Álvares Caramuru and wife of Paulo Dias Adorno—sold the Jesuits a small house and garden "abutting the fence of the Jesuit Monastery." In the same year, Paulo Adorno, grandson of Paulo Dias Adorno, also sold the Jesuits a few "houses" he had received as an inheritance from his grandfather, located "on the street that runs alongside this school," with sides facing the houses of Gaspar Álvares and Baltazar Barbuda; the gardens extended "below as far as André Pereira [...]."

---

156 LEITE, Serafim. *História da Companhia de Jesus no Brasil* [History of the Society of Jesus in Brazil]. I, p. 152.

Table 7 - Properties Belonging to Jesuits in Praça da Sé

Date	Parties	Boundaries/ Comments
September 3, 1573	Felipa Álvares sold the Jesuits "[...] a set of houses with gardens [...]."	The lot "abuts the fence of the Jesuit monastery." Felipa Álvares was the widow of Paulo Dias and daughter of Diogo Álvares Caramuru.
September 17, 1573	Paulo Adorno sold the Jesuits "[...] houses he inherited from his grandfather Paulo Dias, which are on the street that runs along the school."	The house bordered Baltazar Barbuda on one side, and the garden extended below it as far as "André Pereira."
August 12, 1581	The Jesuits sold Helena Borges a set of houses on the street "of Paulo Serrão coming from the Sé Cathedral." The houses were made of "[...] wattle and daub on pylons, covered with tile, and a large house in front."	They were bordered on one side by "[...] the houses of Antonio Rodrigues Vaqueiro and, on the other, by the houses belonging to Gaspar Luis and his wife Maria Rabela and, on the other, by a public street and, on the side toward the sea, part of the road that goes to the Pereira Fountain." The Jesuits had received the houses in payment of the royal dowry.

Source: DOCUMENTOS HISTÓRICOS [Historical Documents]. V. LXIII, pp. 357-363; LXIV, pp. 23-27.

Paulo Dias Adorno had a house in the city, described in some orders of payment. Between 1551 and 1553, he was always referred to as a resident of the city of Salvador.[157] Some of Diogo Álvares Caramuru's family remained in the village of Pereira, but Dias Adorno

---

157 DOCUMENTOS HISTÓRICOS [Historical Documents], v. XIII, Bibliotheca Nacional, mandados de pagamento n º 829, 1073, 1337.

moved to the new city, although he kept his house and fields back in Pereira. He and his wife lived in an elite area, with a beautiful view of the harbor, on a piece of property slightly to the left of the Plano Inclinado Gonçalves, extending down to the edge of the property belonging to one André Pereira.

The houses purchased from the Adorno family in 1573 allowed the Jesuits to take up residence around the Plano Inclinado Gonçalves and the adjoining hillside almost as far as the curve in the Ladeira da Misericórdia. This made sense since, in September, 1572, the Jesuits' new church had been inaugurated at the old "high ground"; the wall no longer existed, and the Jesuits bought plots near the wall to expand the southern side of the monastery. The old group of houses next to the Sé Cathedral were rented out and subsequently, in 1581, sold to Helena Borges.

A few observations can be made regarding the Pereira Fountain, which lay at the bottom of the Ladeira da Misericórdia, where nowadays the Ladeira da Montanha begins. To this day, a plaque marks the site, indicating that it was destroyed in 1912 to make way for the construction of the Ladeira da Montanha. What is the origin of the fountain's name? Was it a reference to André Pereira, the first owner of the lands next to the fountain?

On board Tomé de Souza's armada was a man named André Pereira, who served as a blacksmith in Salvador, receiving a regular salary from the Crown. The Blacksmith Shop was established in the lower part of the city. It is plausible that André Pereira received some land near the fountain, leading to the correlation with the place name. Paulo Dias Adorno had a plot bordering that of André Pereira and situated close to the northern boundary of the fortress.

Serafim Leite's research in *História da Companhia de Jesus no Brasil* (History of the Society of Jesus in Brazil) is rigorous. In his view, the northern boundary of the fortress was the Terreiro de Jesus; in referring to the subject, he situates the boundaries of the city from "the Barroquinha to the Terreiro de Jesus."[158]

The evidence for the northern boundary is not exhausted by

---

158 LEITE, Serafim. *História da Companhia de Jesus no Brasil* [History of the Society of Jesus in Brazil]. I, p. 21.

the above documents and Serafim Leite's research. The classical Renaissance pattern of military urban design provides further evidence that merit consideration.

The Ladeira da Misericórdia and Ladeira do Pau da Bandeira demarcate the boundaries on the side toward the beach. As discussed earlier, the upper level protected the access roads, a fact that was compatible with the standards of military architecture. Vitruvius recommended that access roads should be twisting and close to the walls so that invaders could be attacked as they climbed them. Martini recommended that cities built on hills have their roads form loops or spirals, never straight lines, to ensure more comfortable travel for residents. In simple terms, the logic was as follows: on flat land, build straight and direct roads; on hills, build spiral or interwoven roads that allowed the gentlest slopes possible.

The Plano Inclinado Gonçalves lies at one end of the hillside. The terrain permitted good defense, forming a sort of natural bulwark, that is, a projection jutting forward from the general line of the hillside, an excellent configuration from a military perspective. Slightly more than forty meters below, to the left, was the curve in the Ladeira da Misericórdia, with its passage totally controlled by the bulwark located above. As in the case on the southern side, the sloping road was situated within the boundaries of the fortress.

Another critical fact was the supply of water. On the Ladeira da Misericórdia, there is still a spring that emerges above and flows over the flagstones down to the foot of the hill, where the Pereira Fountain used to be. Since every fortress had to be well supplied with water, it was inevitable that this water source would be incorporated within its boundaries. This may have been the reason for placing the northern boundary a bit beyond the fountain—suggesting that maintaining complete control over it took precedence—at a site where the hillside projects toward the ocean, favoring strong surveillance. The southern boundary was chosen because the site was excellent for defense, taking into account the characteristics of the harbor.

On the end opposite the projecting angle of the Plano Inclinado Gonçalves is a site currently occupied by the São Francisco Church. At this point, the plateau forms another corner and descends toward the Ladeira da Praça and the Baixa dos Sapateiros. These were two excellent vertices, which, in military jargon, served to guard "whatever was needed." A noteworthy question arises: why did the master architect Luís Dias not follow the natural curves of the terrain and fix the boundary of the fortress 150 meters farther, at the point where the land starts to slope downward toward Pelourinho? He could have done this and would have had a fortress that dominated the top of both plateaus.

One answer to this intriguing question may lie in the desired size of the fortress. Martini recommended that the *rocca* or city should be compact and narrow in order to allow better defense and security. In the mid-seventeenth century, Simão Madeira spoke to the War Council, arguing in favor of certain concepts about military architecture. The goal of fortification was to remain safe in a site and to resist a large number of invaders, even with fewer people, causing great losses among the enemy. To attain this goal, "cities with oversized circumferences" could not be well defended without problems, even if they had many people.[159] Furthermore, it should be remembered that another factor limiting the size of a fortress was the costs associated with walls and bulwarks.

In comparative terms, the Fortress of Salvador was larger than Mazagan, constructed in 1542, and somewhat smaller than Daman, built in 1572. The Fortress of Salvador was built with dimensions appropriate for its needs: it was a large fortress by Portuguese standards.[160]

If we consider the Terreiro de Jesus, we will notice that, after Rua da Oração, the alignment of houses that run toward the Church of São Francisco stops forming a straight line and turns toward the south. An angle is formed that compromises the rectangular space of

---

159 VITERBO, Souza. *Dicionário Histórico e Documental dos Arquitetos [...]* [Architects' Historical and Documentary Dictionary]. II, p. 118.
160 The Fortress of Mazagan was initially planned as a quadrant, with sides measuring fifty or one hundred fathoms. The measurements were determined by the site. The result was a rectangle of 175 and 155 fathoms, on the larger sides, and 135 and 109 fathoms on the smaller ones. In: MOREIRA, Rafael. *A Construção de Mazagão* [The Construction of Mazagan], p. 51.

the Terreiro de Jesus, raising certain speculations. Upon first thought, it seems that it may have been an artifice devised to ensure that the Church of São Francisco had greater visibility. However, the oldest engravings and city plans showed that the angle already existed. Around 1605, the Church of São Francisco did not have the same characteristics it currently has, and the blocks on either side already had this peculiar morphology. What may have motivated this decision to break the harmony of a square in favor of an irregular quadrilateral?

The answer to this question requires the solution of another enigma: where was the fourth bulwark of the fortress built? The natural solution would have been on one of the far corners. Would it be the place where nowadays the Church of São Francisco stands? Apparently not. The distance between one bulwark and another—250 meters—would have been too great, making mutual defense difficult. Comparative studies show that the average distance between the bulwarks was less than 120 meters. If the bulwarks existed in pairs that mutually defended each other, nearby and linked together as required by military strategy, it is improbable that another building would have been farther away than that, a strategically inadequate location. The reason is simple: a distance greater than 120 meters would have made it difficult to take aim and shoot an enemy.

The two bulwarks would have to project out toward the area where the enemy would probably emerge. If there were a gate between the two, the necessity for defense would have increased, and both would have the task of guarding the access point. We know that the Santa Catarina gate used to be there. The only place possible was the passage between the Praça da Sé and the Terreiro de Jesus: on the Plano Inclinado Gonçalves was the bulwark overlooking the sea; fifty meters farther, the Santa Catarina gate; in another fifty meters, the fourth bulwark. These measurements coincide with the angle found in the turn in the street going toward the Church of São Francisco, and the symmetry between the two bulwarks is a mathematical fact that can be confirmed with a ruler and a compass.

The seeming disorder in the symmetry of the Terreiro de Jesus is a consequence of the original order that guided the construction of the fortress. As long as the wall existed, buildings could be found in blocks lying inside and outside the wall, establishing the layout of the streets, which could not be redone later.

Another curious aspect is that bulwarks were supposed to be built where danger was likely to emerge.[161] On the esplanade that existed before the Terreiro de Jesus was created, the main road bordered the hillside as far as the junction with the Ladeira do Tabuão. Danger would have arisen in front of the Santa Catarina gate, and any threat would have to be contained on that front. The fourth bulwark, built in the middle of the northern boundary, also permitted defense of the curtain of wall that extended to the Church of São Francisco. Another tactical detail was that the inner angle pushed the line of the wall toward the south, allowing greater exposure to shots fired from the fourth bulwark.

In 1551, the fortified city of Carlentini in Sicily was designed and built, which bore many similarities to the city of Salvador. In the former, we can see how bulwarks were built to protect the means of access, projecting over the area where an attack would likely come, but without any relationship to the far end of the perimeter of the fortress. In the Fortress of Salvador, the bulwarks were built symmetrically in relation to the Santa Catarina gate, as demonstrated earlier.

The plaza replicates the angle in the northern boundary, a fact that suggests symmetry between the polygon of the fortress and the plaza. Another curious aspect is that the measurements of the plaza, especially the two northern lines, correspond to one-third of the two sides facing the Terreiro de Jesus. This fact may be simply a coincidence, but the main public space forms a miniature version of the format and perimeter of the northern side of the fortress.

The final technical considerations concern the difference in the standard lengths of the streets and in the dimensions of the blocks, with the Terreiro de Jesus being the divider between two distinct standards (Fig. 24). On one side, the blocks are more or less 46 meters on each side and the streets are 5.5 meters wide; on the other side, in Pelourinho, the blocks are larger and the streets are 6.6 meters wide, that is, three fathoms, the subsequent standard in the city. It is obvi-

---

161 The ideal format of the city, in Martini's vision, included a projection on the most vulnerable side.

ous that these were two distinct stages, both planned. A curious detail in this regard is that the Sé Cathedral, formerly the Jesuits' church, was built 6.6 meters beyond the edge of the first block to the south of the Terreiro, which means that the demarcation of the plot followed the standard width of the streets applied in Pelourinho. Apparently, the way this new area was handled was a technical decision, which dictated new patterns for laying out streets and measuring blocks.

Figure 24 - Aerial view of Terreiro de Jesus. In the background is the Church of San Francisco. Note the angle and alignment of houses on the right.
Source: CENTRO Histórico de Salvador, Bahia: patrimônio mundial [Historic Center of Salvador, Bahia: World Heritage Site], p. 34.

The Terreiro de Jesus and Rua São Francisco were designed together as a transition between two distinct sections. Anyone who contemplates the map of the historic center will perceive a certain harmony. The perimeter of the Fortress of Salvador, which formed the boundaries of the first pattern of the urban network, was lost to memory, but it has still left its traces. The northern boundary is probably the richest aspect.

The fortress became a city and, by 1586, Gabriel Soares de

Souza, a well-informed citizen, could not say exactly where the old walls and bulwarks had been located. The absence of historical memory also buried wisdom; hence, recuperating this knowledge is almost a revelation, enabling us to comprehend the order beneath apparent chaos and, at its foundation, the ideas and values that were typical of the Renaissance.

14. The Eastern Boundary of the Fortress

> *Among the sites on hills, the strongest one will be on the highest part of the hill, with cliffs on all sides, or on some of the sides, and without having another hill near it that is taller.*
>
> Cristóbal de Rojas

In 1634, Jacques Raynard, a French captain and merchant, wrote a little-known report on the city of Salvador. In a certain passage, he commented on seeing a snake that measured twenty-seven spans (5.94 meters) in length, with a proportional width, in a chapel dedicated to Our Lady of Exile.[162] This fact demonstrated the stranger's surprise and reveals something about the settlement history of the hills near the eastern boundary of the Fortress of Salvador. The swamp, hills, and forests were natural defenses. Snakes and alligators continued to live for a few more decades in the untouched areas where nowadays the neighborhoods of Nazaré and Palma are located.

On the plateau next to the Fortress of Salvador, someone built a small, rustic chapel around 1560 and placed an image of Our Lady

---

162 SERRÃO, Joaquim Veríssimo. *O Tempo dos Filipes em Portugal e no Brasil* [The Philippine Dynasty in Portugal and Brazil], pp. 303-310.

of Exile in it, an invocation that recalls or pays homage to the flight of Joseph, Mary, and the infant Jesus into Egypt. The classical iconography shows Mary with her son in hand, in a walking pose, representing their exile. The place chosen for the chapel was a site where, decades later, the Santa Clara convent was built, better known as the Convent of the Exile.[163]

The small chapel was constructed of planks and covered with thatch; the land around it was kept clear and free of weeds. Years passed. Due to fear of dangerous, poisonous animals, attendance at the chapel fell off and it was eventually abandoned. Because people were afraid of the snakes and alligators that inhabited the nearby lakes, they would only visit the locale with firearms.

Local tradition has it that a man, riding horseback toward the area, asked some native people walking there what the building was; they responded that it was the "house of Our Lady of Exile" and added that he should not go there, because it was dangerous. The man decided to dismount his horse and entered the chapel to pray and ask for protection. When he was finished, he exited the chapel, sat down in the gateway, and fell asleep. He soon awoke, startled, and found himself wrapped by a huge boa constrictor or anaconda, which was getting ready to devour him. In the short time he had left facing this danger, he invoked the help of Our Lady of Exile and, perhaps inspired or comforted by his faith, remembered the knife he was carrying. He struck the snake with such precision that it fell, decapitated and dead. Before he could catch his breath, he looked over the frightening animal and contemplated what had just happened. He entered the chapel and gave thanks. Then he arranged the snake as best he could on top of his horse and returned to the city plaza, proclaiming his good luck.

The tough skin of the snake was opened, its insides were stuffed with cotton, and the small knife was placed in its mouth, in memory of the man's good fortune. The miracle inspired renewed devotion, and the chapel was rebuilt with stones and lime. In 1635,

---

163 MARIA, Frei Agostinho de Santa. *Santuario Mariano e História das Imagens Milagrosas de Nossa Senhora* [The Marian Sanctuary and History of Miraculous Images of Our Lady], pp. 28-30.

Jacques Raynard saw a snake that was 5.94 meters long in the chapel dedicated to Our Lady of Exile, a place he thought had been abandoned.[164] The snake was probably stuffed, since it does not seem logical for someone to simply stumble over an animal of this size, alive in a church.

This report helps confirm the truth of the episode related by local tradition and illustrates the exuberant wildlife in the hills near the eastern boundary of the fortress. The area known as the Baixa dos Sapateiros was a vast swamp, filled with forests and lakes, snakes and alligators, with high and low grounds that were difficult to reach or occupy. This inhospitable area simplified the plans for defense in the east; in a certain respect, it rendered dispensable the construction of any bulwark on that side, since the wall was sufficient. On a strategic plane, the function of a bulwark was threefold: a) it ensured adequate space for moving artillery pieces; b) it protected the curtains of wall and the bulwark on the opposite side, as a projecting citadel; and c) it served as a point of defense, projecting out toward the area from which an attack would probably come.

Behind the bluff and the marsh was another plateau, which was also difficult to access, resulting in a simple military equation: it was not necessary to build any bulwark there. In principle, it would have been wasteful to build complex defensive structures on the eastern side. The risk of attacks lay in the harbor and on the southern and northern boundaries.

Even though bulwarks were not necessary on this side, we still need to determine the probable line of the wall. We can reconstruct the eastern perimeter through a combination of five elements: a) brief documentary references and the history of settlement represented in historical maps and engravings; b) tactical concepts employed in the military arts in the sixteenth century; c) an examination of the measurements of surviving streets; d) the topography of the terrain; e) and the proportions and symmetry between the perimeter and the main plaza.

The eastern side began above the Praça Castro Alves, bor-

---

164 The information provided by Jacques Raynard can be found in Document 5 in the Documentary Appendix.

dered by the São Tiago bulwark. The line of the wall started from the bulwark and headed northeast, following the hill along the Rua do Tesouro (Fig. 25). The wall probably followed the sides of the plateau all the way to the end, where nowadays the Casa dos Sete Candeeiros is located. There, at the corner of the plateau, the terrain drops off about twenty meters; below is the valley of the Ladeira da Praça. From the corner and the top of the plateau, an observer can easily see the Church of São Francisco on the other side of the valley, located on the highest point, which was formerly the northeast corner of the fortress. To complete the perimeter, the wall would have to cross the swamp, nowadays the valley at the foot of Ladeira da Praça, and continue on from there. What direction might the wall have taken, straight ahead or bypassing the lowland?

The only documentary reference to the eastern boundary of the Fortress of Salvador can be found in a letter from Luís Dias to Miguel de Arruda, his superior, in which the architect reported on the main events associated with the project. In a certain passage, he commented on the drawing he was submitting, stating that it showed "two small valleys that are inside the city, and, in the larger one, we made a very large well."[165] The larger of the two valleys corresponded to the present-day foot of the Ladeira da Praça, and the smaller, to the final section of Rua Três de Maio. Both, according to Luís Dias's description, lay within the perimeter of the fortress. The well was dug somewhere near the Ladeira da Praça.

The engravings and old maps portraying the city of Salvador reveal that there was no urbanization around the foot of the Ladeira da Praça. The two blocks presently located there were settled in the second half of the seventeenth century. A decision passed by the Municipal Council, dated April 1, 1626, prohibited anyone from throwing trash or "small game in the Praça da Sé, or in any other street or alley whatsoever." The only place where this was permitted was "the

---

165 MOREIRA, Rafael. "O arquiteto Miguel de Arruda e o primeiro projeto para Salvador" [The Architect Miguel de Arruda and the First Project for Salvador]. In: *Anais do 4º Congresso de História da Bahia*. V. I, p. 141. The letter from Luís Dias, the master architect, is dated July 13, 1551.

marsh, which is behind Rua Direita."[166] For a long time, the foot of Ladeira da Praça was a "marsh," also described as a "dike." The settlement of this area was not orderly, which explains its disproportional format and the lack of regularity in the two blocks.

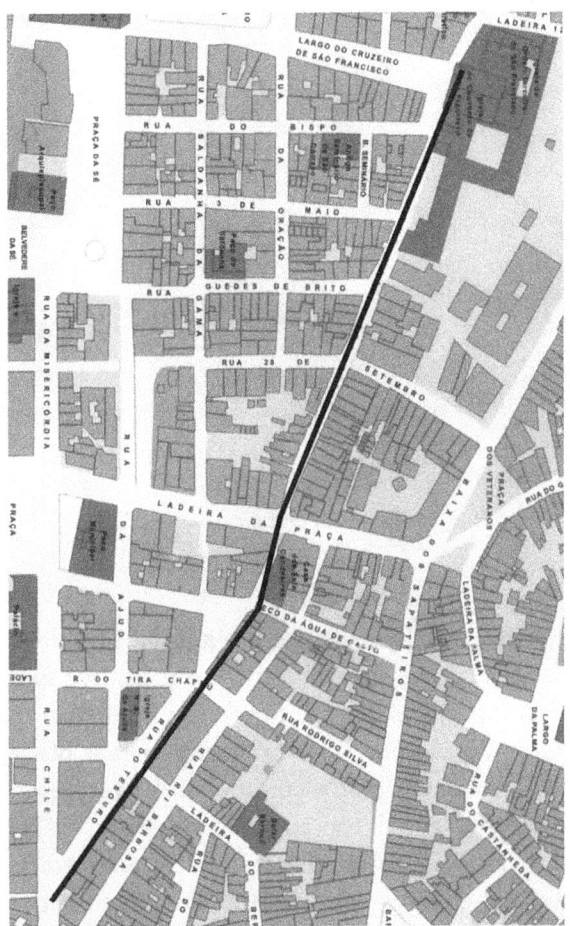

Figure 25 - Current plan of the city of Salvador. Dark line indicates eastern boundary of the fortress.
Source: CENTRO Histórico de Salvador, Bahia: patrimônio mundial [Historic Center of Salvador, Bahia: World Heritage Site].

---

[166] DOCUMENTOS HISTÓRICOS do Arquivo Municipal [Historical Documents of the Municipal Archives], V. 1°, p. 33.

The lack of urbanization in the valley at the foot of Ladeira da Praça does not exclude the line of narrower blocks that lay on the left-hand side of this street. These smaller blocks are visible in the oldest engravings, especially in the city plan by Henry Hondius,[167] dated 1625 (Fig. 26).

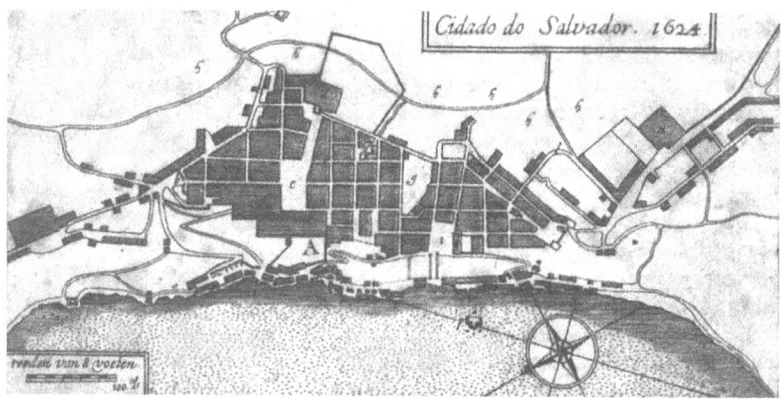

Figure 26 - Stamp "City of Salvador, 1624," which illustrates the book by Henry Hondius. This was the best map of the city of Salvador in the seventeenth century.

In the foreground, the details indicate that the height and edge of the two plateaus (Sé and Ajuda) were utilized to the greatest advantage. However, it is difficult to determine whether the line that linked the Alto do São Francisco to the present site of the Casa dos Sete Candeeiros was straight or curving. Both hypotheses should be considered. A sinuous wall was advisable from a tactical perspective; curves and angles were part of military strategy. In fortresses, military architecture kept straight lines short and confined between angles. This gave angles the function of defending the curtain of wall; the preferred form consisted of tooth-shaped angles. High terrain with steep slopes was considered excellent. The perimeter ideally exploited

---

167 HONDIUS, Henry. Stamp of the city of Salvador, dated 1624, which illustrates the author's book. In: *Imagens de vilas e cidades do Brasil Colonial* [Images of the Towns and Cities of Colonial Brazil], by Nestor Goulart Reis, p. 24.

curves in the path, since they exposed an invader to attack from the side. The combination of these two factors was present in all theoretical considerations about fortifications. Vitruvius stated that "Special pains should be taken that there be no easy avenue by which to storm the wall" and that "The roads should be encompassed at steep points [...]."[168]

The Italian Renaissance produced many treatises on architecture and military arts. The subject was also taken up by theoreticians. Alberti reiterated many techniques used by the ancients. For him, the perimeter of the city and the distribution of its components should vary according to the location. The walls should have sinuous contours, since they would make it dangerous for the enemy to penetrate the recesses. Martini, another Renaissance architect, believed that a large city should have angles determined by the site and the dimensions of its circumference. Martini's designs, portraying projects constructed on irregular terrain, showed a preference for perimeters in the form of triangles and stars, taking advantage of the characteristics of each part of the terrain.

Machiavelli also wrote about the subject: "The first industry is, to make the walls twisted and full of turned recesses; which pattern results in the enemy not being able to approach them, as they will be able to be attacked easily not only from the front, but on the flanks." Cristóbal Lechuga, a Spanish engineer active at the end of the sixteenth century, was the one who wrote with the greatest clarity: in mountains and valleys, the general rule was to follow the terrain in a manner that kept what was desirable, even if that meant the fortress would be high in some parts and low in others. In parts that could not be attacked or that were not prominent, a simple rampart, with a few turns but without bulwarks, would be sufficient. We can see the theoretical consensus between these two authors concerning the concept of twisting perimeters.[169]

Another curious aspect is the width of some of the streets in

---

168 POLLIO, Marcus Vitruvius. *Los Diez Libros de Architectura* [The Ten Books on Architecture], p. 18.
169 MACHIAVELLI, Niccoló. *Del Arte de la Guerra* [The Art of War]; LECHUGA, Cristóbal. *Tratado de la Artillería [...]* [Treatise on Artillery], p. 418.

the blocks at the base of the Sé plateau. This suggests there was a curve in the line of the wall uniting the Alto do São Francisco to the opposite end, where the Casa dos Sete Candeeiros is now located. On the eastern side of the Praça da Sé were thirteen blocks, of which nine were rectangular, almost square, and the remaining four were quadrilateral. At first glance, they seem to belong to the original outlay of the Fortress of Salvador, but the measurements of the streets suggest a different set of facts.

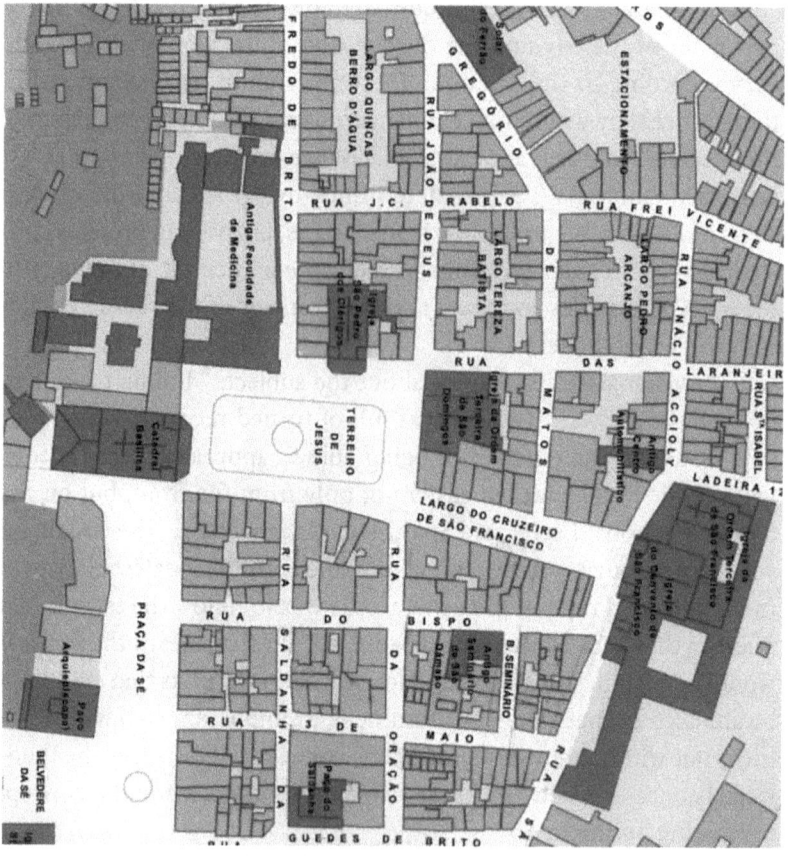

Figure 27 - Present-day view of Terreiro de Jesus and Largo de São Francisco. Below are smaller blocks and narrow streets. Above is the Pelourinho quarter, larger blocks, and wider streets.

The Fortress of Salvador

The measurements reveal that some streets are two-and-a-half fathoms in width, while others are three fathoms. This sort of measurement could conceivably be adopted in any fortress, with the size varying according to the importance or function of the street. However, the variation in the size of the streets in Salvador depended on the area. There are two groups: the first includes the blocks next to the Praça da Sé and the Terreiro de Jesus over to the intersection of Rua da Oração and Rua Três de Maio, in which the streets have an average measurement of two-and-a-half fathoms; the second, made up of the southern half of Rua da Oração and almost all of Rua Guedes de Brito, represents streets with a uniform measurement of three fathoms (Table 8). The latter measurement is the same width found in the streets in Pelourinho and is referred to in documents of the seventeenth century as the official standard in the city (Fig. 27). This fact suggests that the blocks situated below the intersection of Rua Três de Maio and Rua da Oração, which are part of the smaller valley, did not originally form part of the perimeter or else they were laid out at a later date, allowing the width of the streets to observe a new standard.

According to an old certificate contained in the *Old Register of Charters and Deeds of the Benedictines*, dated June 6, 1612, the usual width of ordinary streets in Salvador was three fathoms.[170] This information was provided by the Council Attorney, which leaves no doubt as to its veracity (Table 9). Later, in 1652, the Chamber arranged for Captain João Lobo to build a "road through the Forest of São João," where, in the past, "people drove cattle herds that were brought to this city."[171] The combined width of the road was sixty spans, exactly double the standard width of streets inside the city.

---

170 LIVRO *Velho do Tombo* [Old Register of Charters and Deeds], p. 415. The document contains the following statement: "[...] sixty-six spans across, which comprised the road, being equal to two ordinary city roads plus six spans to ease passage [. . .]." One fathom (2.2 meters) equaled ten spans; therefore, thirty spans were equivalent to three fathoms (6.6 meters).
171 DOCUMENTOS HISTÓRICOS do Arquivo Municipal [Historical Documents of the Municipal Archives]. V. 3º, p. 202.

Table 8 - Width of Streets in Historic Center of City of Salvador

Historically Preserved Blocks	Measurement in Meters	Measurement in Fathoms	Position
Rua do Bispo	5.40	2.45	1st perpendicular
Rua 3 de Maio	5.50	2.50	2nd perpendicular
Rua Guedes de Brito	6.50	2.95	3rd perpendicular
Rua Saldanha da Gama (public square)	5.09	2.31	2nd parallel
Rua Saldanha da Gama (Liceu)	5.60	2.55	2nd parallel
Rua da Oração (public square)	5.70	2.59	3rd parallel
Rua da Oração (2nd block)	6.60	3.00	3rd parallel
Rua São Francisco	5.90	2.68	—

Source: The author.

Table 9 - Measurements in the Cities of Salvador and Rio de Janeiro, 1596-1652

City	Type of Thoroughfare	Measurement in Fathoms (Meters)
Rio de Janeiro (1596)	Main avenue	3.5 (7.7m)
Salvador (1612)	Ordinary street	3.0 (6.6m)
Salvador (1652)	Path (for cattle herds)	6.0 (13.2m)

Source: LIVRO de Tombo do Colégio de Jesus do Rio de Janeiro [Register of Charters and Deeds of the Jesuit School of Rio de Janeiro], p. 250; LIVRO Velho do Tombo [Old Register of Charters and Deeds], p. 415; DOCUMENTOS históricos do Arquivo Municipal [Historical Documents of the Municipal Archive], v. 3°, p. 202.

The Fortress of Salvador

The combination of all these factors—the standards established by military arts, the symmetry between the fortress and the main plaza, the references contained in the letter of Luís Dias, the topography of the terrain, the history of settlement around the base of the Ladeira da Praça, and the differences in the size of the roads on the Sé plateau—suggest that the eastern line had four corners and at least one large curve. This curve may have had the shape of a tooth, which was common in Martini's designs, or it may have had more internal angles, taking advantage of the curvature of the terrain. On the northeastern corner, the perimeter would have had the shape of a shirt sleeve, a typical anthropomorphic design that was widespread in fortresses a few decades later.

The second hypothesis would posit a straight line descending Rua São Francisco until it reached the Ladeira da Praça. Hondius's plan (1624), the most exact one of its era, shows Rua São Francisco to be straight, crossing another street that descended from the Ajuda plateau. Curiously, where Rua São Francisco meets the Ladeira da Praça, it measures approximately 2.5 fathoms in width. Apparently, some changes and adaptations were made in that section, altering the original specifications. In light of our geometric reconstitution of the urban design, demonstrated in the plan of the Fortress of Salvador as formulated in this present essay, we have selected the second hypothesis as the strongest one. The first one, nevertheless, should also be considered, and has been indicated by the dotted lines.

Finally, there is another notable aspect related to the symmetry of the Fortress of Salvador. To the extent possible, the plaza of a city ideally followed the geometric shape of the fortress. The oldest engravings of the city of Salvador portray the main plaza as an irregular quadrilateral. The block where the Municipal Council Building was located yielded part of its space to the plaza, without any obvious rationale. A plausible justification was to maintain symmetry and proportion in relation to the fortress. The eastern part of the northern perimeter (i.e., the northern half of the fortress) is symmetrical with the plaza—an intriguing aspect that will be explored later.

15. THE SACRED ORIGIN OF WALLS

> *Sanctified things, such as city walls and gates, are also, in a certain sense, under divine law; they cannot become private property.*
>
> Justinian's Institutes

Certain ancient Roman traditions recount that Remus, to ridicule Romulus, scaled the walls of the recently-founded city of Rome; infuriated, Romulus killed him, saying, "So perish every one that shall hereafter leap over my wall."[172] This apparent cruelty can be explained by considering the sacred origin of the city wall, a concept that migrated into legislative texts and survived as a legal norm during part of the Middle Ages. Christian theology could not allow the pagan belief in a mystical respect for the walls to survive; thereafter, ramparts became basically an element of security. The conservation and restrictions against settling areas adjacent to the walls were observed with varying strictness, depending on the state of war or peace in each city. The intra- and extramural spaces in many cities became public spaces, squares, plazas, or greens.

Founding a city in ancient Greece and Rome was long considered a religious act. The ritual was replete with significance. Once

---

172 LIVY, Titus, *História de Roma* [History of Rome]. I, p. 28.

the location was chosen, a trench was dug, where some earth brought from the founder's place of origin was deposited: "This land will continue to belong to my parents; here lies my country."[173] This small trench was called *mundus*, and from it the souls of the ancestors were said to emerge three times a year, wishing to come back to see light for a few moments. After other rituals, the boundaries of the settlement were marked with furrows in the earth, where ramparts would be erected.[174]

The boundaries of the city were sacred because they derived from a basic principle of religion—the cult of ancestors. The place belonged to the family, and the dead inhabited that space forever: "What other place exists that is more sacred than the home of each person? It is there that the altar is placed; there glows the sacred fire; there lie sanctified things and religion,"[175] Cicero said. Anyone who penetrated the domicile committed a sacrilege. It was believed that the house god kept thieves away and protected the inhabitants against enemies. Each property was a territory lying under the protection of the house divinity; its boundaries were designated by the word *terminus* and, once consecrated, could not be removed.

The mixture of private property and religion led to the emergence of a certain legend, according to which Jupiter, wishing to secure a location on the Capitoline Hill where he could build his temple, was unable to do so because he could not dislodge the god Terminus from there.[176] Private property was sacred; sacred, too, was the city. Anyone who trespassed the walls was subject to capital punishment, as asserted in the precept in Justinian's *Institutes*: "Sanctified entities, such as ramparts and gates, are also, in a certain sense, under divine law; they cannot become private property."[177]

Care of the ramparts and gates fell to the person who was responsible for sacred buildings. Damaging them was forbidden, and

---

173 COULANGES, Fustel de. *A Cidade Antiga* [The Ancient City], p. 145.
174 Idem, p. 146.
175 Ibidem, p. 61.
176 Ibidem, p. 65.
177 *CUERPO DEL DERECHO CIVIL ROMANO, Instituta* [Corpus of Roman Civil Law, Institutes], livro II, título I, parágrafo 10.

habitations could only be built next to them with permission from the prince, since accidental fires were a risk.[178] The *Corpus Iuris Civilis*,[179] influenced by Christianity, dedicated much of Book I of the Code to the discipline of worship as taught to the Romans by the "divine apostle Peter." Nonetheless, it did not deny the sacred nature of the city walls: both the old and the new survived in the *Corpus Iuris Civilis*, which was then absorbed into the *Seven-Part Code*.

The *Seven-Part Code* contained the principle that "[t]he walls and gates of cities and towns are considered sanctified entities."[180] The place of ramparts and gates in the general classification of entities evinces some awkwardness, since they bear no relation to Christian doctrine. However, their survival as sanctified entities can only be attributed to the tradition and strength of earlier Roman law (Table 10).

In 1769, King Joseph of Portugal issued what was known as the *Law of Good Sense*, which sought to define and restrain the authority of Roman law applied in the kingdom. A jurist of the period, commenting on certain legal provisions, called attention to the pagan bias in the classification of ramparts and gates as sanctified things: "This and similar things that smell of Gentile superstition were unworthy of being inserted into Justinian legislation, as he was a Christian emperor."[181]

To explain the sacred nature of walls and gates, the *Seven-Part Code* invoked the historical notion that no person could cross them except through permitted points of access: "Emperors and philosophers established that no person may destroy them by breaking through them or forcing them open, or gaining entrance by scaling them or by other means, or entering by any means other than through

---

178 *CORPUS JURIS CIVILIS, Digesto* [Corpus of Roman Civil Law, Digest], Livro XLIII, Título VIII, Tomo 3º, p. 413.
179 Composed of the *Institutes, Digest, Code, Novels*, and *Constitutions*.
180 *LAS SIETE PARTIDAS* [Seven-Part Code], Terceira Partida, Título XXVIII, lei XV.
181 TELLES, José Homem Côrrea. "Comentário Crítico à Lei da Boa Razão" [Critical Commentary on the Law of Good Sense]. In: *Auxíliar Jurídico. Apêndice a Ordenações Filipinas* [Legal Guide: Appendix to the Philippine Ordinances]. Volume II, p. 437.

the gates."[182] Over time, walls lost their religious association and came to be viewed simply as elements of security. They required continual attention, carried high costs, and became especially important during times of war, which justified their maintenance and conservation.

Table 10 - Division of Entities According to Justinian's *Institutes* and the *Seven-Part Code*

Entities	Classification
Goods Belonging to All Creatures	Air, rainwater, ocean and beaches, rivers, harbors, and public thoroughfares.
Goods for Public Use, for Use by All Area Residents	Fountains, plazas where markets are held, stores, the place where the council meets, areas surrounding edges of the ocean and rivers, vacant lots, places where horses roam, hills, and areas of defense.
Goods in the City Used for Community Income	Fields, vineyards, gardens, groves of olives and other orchards, cattle, and servants.
Goods Belonging to the King	Income from harbors, saltworks, fisheries, iron and other metal foundries, tollgates for merchandise, and taxes.
Sacred Entities Belonging to No One, with Clergy as Guardians	Objects consecrated by the bishop, such as the church, cemetery, altars, crosses, chalices, books, vestments, and other things designated for use by the church.
Religious Entities	Hospitals, shelters designed to receive the poor, and other houses designed for acts of charity.
Sanctified Entities	"The walls and gates of cities and towns are considered sanctified things [...]"; oversight of these works, however, lies with the king, with the collaboration of everyone.

Source: CORPUS Iuris Civilis, Instituta [Corpus of Roman Civil Law, Institutes], Livro II, Título I; LAS SIETE PARTIDAS [Seven-Part Code], Terceira Partida, Título XXVIII.

---

182 LAS SIETE PARTIDAS [Seven-Part Code], Terceira Partida, Título XXVIII, lei XV

The Fortress of Salvador

In the sixteenth century, the divine nature of walls survived only in the texts on Roman law. The issue became secondary to the logic of security, associated with control by central or local authorities. In Portugal, building next to inner or outer walls of ramparts underwent a significant alteration in the law during the reign of King Manuel I: construction along the walls was allowed, but, if the city were faced with war or a siege, the property owner had to demolish the building and open up a corridor and passageway, while still being obliged to maintain the adjoining wall in good condition.

This change in the law signaled the coming of a new era, when walls would give way to urban expansion. A few exceptions to the rules were applied, however, such as restrictions on high points overlooking the city or in areas outside it, and the prohibition on buildings abutting ramparts or gates. The military factor determined the formation of urban spaces in the Fortress of Salvador, traces of which can still be seen today. In the city of Salvador, the walls lost their function and were demolished around the eighteenth century; in their place arose plazas, commons, and public squares, silent witnesses to the past.

16. Areas Outside the Fortress

The countryside around the city should be clear and without trees for a distance of a mile or more, depriving the enemy in wartime of any convenience which might facilitate an attack on the city.

Pietro Cataneo[183]

In various Brazilian cities, the plazas, squares, greens, and commons of today owe their origins to nearby ramparts, forts, or fortresses. The line and angle of defense for the fortification required the preservation of an extensive visual field in the surrounding countryside, where buildings were prohibited. Each urban space had its own dynamic of settlement. Usually some original area was preserved for the use and enjoyment of the population. In this context, the Terreiro de Jesus, Largo do Pelourinho, and Praça Castro Alves emerged—urban spaces that were inherited from the city's system of defense.

In areas outside the ramparts of a city, no buildings could be constructed that might serve as protection for enemies. The fields had to be clear, with special attention paid to high areas—a hill, convent, or tower from which an invader could shoot or injure those defending

---

183 CATANEO, Pietro. *L'Architettura* [Architecture], pp. 209-210.

the city. At the Portuguese fortress of Mazagan in Morocco, the monarch decided in 1621 that the wattle and daub walls and the ditches in gardens located far from the city wall had to be eliminated, since they served as hiding places for the Moors when they attacked the fortress.[184]

The manuals of military engineering in the sixteenth century established a certain basic circumference in which construction should be prohibited, as Pietro Cataneo described. Cristóbal de Rojas, a Spanish engineer, recommended that a fortification built on some high ground or mountain should occupy the entire site, or at least the upper parts of it, such that the enemy would not have any spot that overlooked the plaza, "unless at a distance of 1000 paces."[185] This strategic guideline became the norm. On February 22, 1545, Emperor Carlos established a law requiring castles and fortresses to keep the countryside always clear and uninhabited. Any obstacle within three hundred paces around the rampart had to be demolished.[186]

Was this strategic and normative scenario also transplanted to the coast of Brazil? Did Tomé de Souza adopt some restriction on building outside the walls? The answers are definitively yes. The first governor on the coast of Brazil was extremely cautious with the defensive system of the towns and fortresses. In a letter to King Dom João III in 1553, Tomé de Souza emphasized that all the settlements and plantations on the coast of Brazil had been surrounded by walls of "wattle and daub with their bulwarks."[187] The construction of walls required awareness about

---

184 REVISTA STUDIA, *Bibliotheca Virtual dos Descobrimentos Portugueses* [Virtual Library of Portuguese Discoveries]. Lisboa: Comissão Nacional para as Comemorações dos Descobrimentos Portugueses, volume 26, p. 51. CD-ROM.
185 Source: ROJAS, Cristóbal de. "Teorica y Pratica de Fortificacion" [Theory and Practice of Fortification]. In: *Tres Tratados sobre Fortificacion* [Three Treatises on Fortification], p. 98. In Spain, one pace equaled 0.65 meter; a thousand paces equaled 650 meters.
186 *RECOPILACION DE LEIS DOS REYNOS DE LAS ÍNDIAS* [Compilation of the Laws of the Kingdoms of the Indies]. Tomo I, Livro III, Título 7, Lei I.
187 Letter from Tomé de Souza to King Dom João III, dated June 1st, 1553. In: *História da Colonização Portuguesa no Brasil* [History of Portuguese Colonization in

The Fortress of Salvador

the effectiveness of defense measures, which ensured that exterior spaces would be kept clear.

If the countryside was supposed to be kept clear because of the system of defense, we need to consider how long it survived the pressures of urban expansion in the Fortress of Salvador. For example, in September, 1557, the Jesuits wanted to build some houses outside the wall "at the site where the school has been assigned," but they had doubts about whether they had permission to dismantle the wall.[188] Not long afterwards, the wall was dismantled; the date is unknown, but Governor Mem de Sá was definitely involved in the action.

Governor Mem de Sá consolidated the presence of the Jesuits in the Terreiro de Jesus, but the process was not simple. The city did in fact expand, causing new streets and blocks to be demarcated. The neighborhood of Pelourinho emerged; given the regularity of its design, the breadth of its streets, and the relative uniformity in the size of the blocks, we can see that the project was rational and intentional. After the Tupinamba Indians ceased being a threat around 1561, the fortress wall lost its function. At some point between 1562 and 1572, it tumbled down or was demolished.

The Terreiro de Jesus emerged as a deliberate project (Fig. 28). The intention was to ensure a recreation area for the school or a space large enough for cavalcades. It is not certain whether the well-marked plaza was intended solely for use by the Society of Jesus. The space was located where the old section of the fortress and the new blocks were integrated. A curious aspect, demonstrating the intersection between the old and the new sections, is the width of the means of access to the Church of São Francisco. The oldest engravings show that an avenue always existed there, a juncture accommodating two distinct sections—a situation produced when the blocks in Pelourinho were demarcated.

Brazil], Carlos Malheiros Dias, III, p. 364.
188 LETTER from Father Manuel da Nóbrega to Father Miguel Torres, dated September 2, 1557. LEITE S. I., Serafim. *Cartas dos Primeiros Jesuítas do Brasil* [Letters of the First Jesuits of Brazil]. II, p. 407.

Figure 28 - Terreiro de Jesus, on the northern border, originally outside the city walls. The plaza and the Largo do Cruzeiro de São Francisco served as a juncture between two distinct designs.

The Pelourinho area was conceived with geometric rationality when the high ground was demarcated and divided. On the side toward the Ajuda Church, a different process was used. Some settlement occurred on the side toward the ocean, and some streets and new blocks emerged below the Rua do Tesouro, but houses did not proliferate on the descending slope where the Praça Castro Alves now lies (Fig. 29). Expansion in this area was curtailed because of the new surge of fortifications that appeared starting in 1587.

The situation revealed the intense process of reconstructing the city's defenses. Conflicts among the Luso-Spaniards, British, and Dutch triggered a series of periodic attacks on the city, giving rise to the second ring of fortifications (Table 11), the Fortress of Salvador having been the first. The second ring expanded the original boundaries to some extent, due to the growth of the city. The southern boundary was partially preserved, but the walls and gates moved down the hillside. The city overflowed toward the valley.

On the northern side, the process of organized settlement was more intense, requiring defenses to be consolidated at the Largo do Pelourinho. The fortifications required empty spaces, so this second defensive boundary defense survived for almost a century. Improvements were made but, in essence, the fortifications began to be demolished in 1686, when they became obsolete because of risky exposure to shots fired from neighboring hills, and because of the excessive number of surrounding houses.

Figure 29 - Praça Castro Alves, on the southern boundary of the fortress, a space originally outside the walls where building was prohibited.

In 1686, the King gave the municipality a land grant for a plot of six fathoms (13.2 meters) situated in the Largo do Pelourinho, on the right side facing downhill, with the following boundaries: on the north, the Church of Rosário dos Pretos; on the south, the thick wall of the platform that defended the city, ending at the Carmo gate; and, on the east, the river known as Curtumes, nowadays the area called the Baixa dos Sapateiros. The grant was made with a condition, contained in the Ordinances, that, at any time, if it were necessary for the defense of the city, works on the plot could be demolished. That was where the second wall of the city of Salvador and the gate of Carmo were located.[189]

Table 11 - Fortification of the City of Salvador: Events 1587-1613

Period	Event
April 11, 1587 to June 1, 1587	Three English ships, commanded by Robert Witherington and Christopher Lister, attacked the city. Salvador did not have protective walls.
1591-1602 (?)	Governor Dom Francisco de Souza ordered walls of wattle and daub on pylons to be built around the city.
December 24, 1599 to February 20, 1600	Seven Dutch warships, commanded by Captains Hartmann and Broer, attacked the city. Álvaro de Carvalho placed his men in stations on the beach and in the city for defense.
July 20, 1604 to August 28, 1604	Eight Dutch ships, commanded by Paulus Van Caarden, attacked the port, seized a large ship, and burned another.
September 1604	Governor Diogo Botelho sent Sergeant-Major Diogo de Campos Moreno to Europe to request more artillery.
1605	A plan for fortifying the city of Salvador was presented to the King of Spain, with a proposal for a citadel, in a plan designed by Leonardo Torriani, the royal chief engineer.
1613	Baltazar de Aragão, the War Captain General, fortified the city, fearing threats from the French. He used stone and lime to rebuild the wall and the entry on the Carmo side, which, up to that point, had consisted of mud on pylons. He repaired and fortified the gates.

Source: SALVADOR, Frei Vicente do. História do Brasil [History of Brazil]; VARNHAGEN, Francisco Adolfo de. História Geral do Brasil [General History of Brazil]. Tomo II; MORENO, Diogo de Campos, Livro que dá Razão do Estado do Brasil [Book Giving the Reason for the State of Brazil]; HISTÓRIA Naval Brasileira [Brazilian Naval History].

---

189 LIVRO do Tombo da Prefeitura Municipal do Salvador [Register of Deeds and Charters of the Municipal Office of Salvador], pp. 66-76.

On the side by the Praça Castro Alves, exactly the same condition was imposed. In 1704, the King gave the municipality some property, in the form of a land grant, consisting of a site in front of the "São Bento gates," to create a plaza where fish could be sold. There, too, the structure could be demolished and the grant revoked if the building became necessary for defending the city.[190] In these examples, the King's ownership of the areas adjacent to the wall was indisputable, and his imprimatur was mandatory for concluding transactions.

The Terreiro de Jesus survived as a rectangular space for use by the general public. The Praça Castro Alves, which had once been a battlefield, lost its walls and the gates of São Bento, became a fish market, and ended up as an empty space without any clear purpose. Given the indeterminate nature of the space, it could have been named Market Square, Fish Square, Guarani Square, or Theater Square, but it so happened that, much later, someone erected a monument in one corner to honor the poet Castro Alves, whose name was bestowed on the plaza. On the northern side, the Carmo gate remained faithful to its origin and survived as a public square. The irregular triangle, another space for defending the city, became the Largo do Pelourinho.

---

190 Idem, pp. 104-105.

17. The Fence and the Wall

The wall is completed so that it can never be knocked down [...]. Two internal walls are built at intervals of twenty feet each. Then earth which has been dug out of the fosses is dumped between them and rammed solid with piles [...]. For no rams can breach a wall that is strengthened by earth [...].

Vegetius

Dom João de Castro, Viceroy in India from 1545 to 1548, led some of the great Portuguese military campaigns. A man of action and knowledge, he was familiar with Vitruvius's work and valued new techniques of fortification. He wrote recommendations on the art of war, acknowledging that he adopted modern techniques that were in vogue in Italy, Spain, and France—parts of the world, he said, where such matters were most advanced.[191] Under his orders, the Fortress of Diu was reconstructed in late 1546, and the fort in Salcete at the Mardol pagoda was constructed in 1547. These works illustrate well the techniques and measures utilized in building walls and bulwarks.

In reconstructing the Fortress of Diu, Dom João de Castro

---

[191] SANCEAU, Elaine. *Cartas de D. João de Castro* [Letters of Dom João de Castro], p. 131.

used the same design as Ceuta, a structure built in 1543 under the direction of the master architect Miguel de Arruda—who, it should be recalled, also drew up the plan of the Fortress of Salvador. Dom João de Castro and Miguel de Arruda belonged to an intellectual circle in Portugal in which the most advanced ideas about fortification circulated.

In Salcete, the master architect Francisco Pires built the fort in 1547 with a wall constructed in the following manner: "three spans across the top of the external layer and another three for the internal and four in the space between them to be filled with earth."[192] In total, the wall measured ten spans in width—which equaled one fathom (2.2 meters)—and twelve spans in height (2.64 meters). The width of the wall in the Fortress of Salvador is unknown, but we do know its height was originally sixteen to eighteen spans at the lowest point, and later lowered to eleven spans.

Vegetius wrote about the Roman style of constructing walls. The technique was simple. To make a rampart more solid, two parallel walls were erected, leaving a space of twenty feet between them. The dirt removed from the ditch was put in the empty space and compacted. The internal wall was lower than the external one.[193] The Roman writer Vitruvius recommended that the wall should be wide enough to allow two armed men to walk easily along the top. He also recommended that wooden braces should be placed between the two walls to ensure greater solidity.[194] This venerable technique of building two parallel walls filled with earth between them, which goes back to the tradition of the Roman armies, was evidently used in the Fortress of Salvador.

The fortress was built in three stages: in the first, a wooden fence was put up; in the second, houses of wood and thatch were constructed; and, in the third, ramparts and bulwarks were erected, along

---

192 VITERBO, Souza, *Dicionário Histórico e Documental dos Arquitetos [...]* [Architects' Historical and Documentary Dictionary]. II, p. 302.
193 RENATUS, Flavius Vegetius. Instituciones Militares [Military Institutions], p. 118.
194 POLLIO, Marcus Vitruvius. *Los Diez Libros de Architectura* [The Ten Books on Architecture], p. 18.

The Fortress of Salvador

with buildings having walls of wattle and daub, tiles, and, in a few cases, stone. To a certain extent, these phases were determined in the charter and integrated with the military context of the expedition, as evidenced in the orders of payment.[195]

Upon landing at the site, Governor Tomé de Souza and his men decided on the site for the fort, then built a wooden fence that was completed around May 12, 1549. Some of the wood was obtained from the Indians through barter. The amount of wood used and the time spent building it demonstrate that the project was a small one. The Portuguese bartered 9,831 objects—machetes, scythes, scissors, fishhooks, hoes—worth 17,458 réis, a little more than 10% of what would be bartered later for the construction of the permanent walls and bulwarks.[196]

After the palisade was built, the entire Portuguese workforce spent the next month and half, from May 1 to June 15, constructing public buildings and houses. The official stonemasons were paid monthly salaries, a form of remuneration that ended, by regulation, on June 15, 1549. On June 16, work on the permanent walls and bulwarks began using contract labor.

The best description of the sequence of construction projects came from Gabriel Soares de Souza: first, a strong palisade fence was built so that "laborers and soldiers could be safe from the pagans"; once this was done, "the city inside was fixed up, laying out orderly streets with houses covered with palm leaves 'in the pagan style' to serve as shelter for the soldiers and servants"; with that stage completed, the order was issued to surround the city with thick walls of wattle and daub, "which was done promptly, with two bulwarks along the ocean and four on the inland side [...]."[197] This information reveals that the time spent on the third phase took longer. The construction of the walls and bulwarks was not actually completed until December, 1551, in other words, two years and eight months after they were begun.

---

195 DOCUMENTOS HISTÓRICOS [Historical Documents], v. XII, Bibliotheca Nacional, pp. 271-272.
196 Idem, p. 272.
197 SOUZA, Gabriel Soares. *Notícia do Brasil* [Report from Brazil], I, capítulo III, p. 247.

The walls and bulwarks in the fortress were constructed of wattle and daub and of wood, for lack of other materials and in order to economize. The technique of building with wattle and daub by hand consists in creating a framework of wooden posts that is strong enough to retain dirt that has been moistened, packed, and dried. Vertical posts, called struts, thrust into the ground and crossed with horizontal wood bars, forming a mesh in which mud is packed in by hand. The fortress walls were constructed using this technique. The bulwarks, according to Luís Dias, were reinforced by "wood with wattle and daub inside [...]," a phrase suggesting that the space between the two faces of the wall was filled up with earth.

Nine official stonemasons were contracted to carry out the contract labor. We do not know whether the labor was paid by the fathom of wattle and daub or by a set price for each section; however, we do know that, for almost seven months—from June 15 until December of 1549—regular payments were made to various officials. By the end, the total cost added up to 172,100 réis, a considerable sum if we take into account that the same officials, had they been paid a monthly salary, would not have earned more than 71,200 réis, collectively, for this period (Table 12).

The wood necessary for the works was also acquired from the Indians through barter. The orders of payment indicate that, in the month of June, a large quantity was acquired in two lots, one of which was earmarked for the bulwarks. At the end of the year, in December, a new batch was acquired, probably to complete the project.

The work was completed in January, 1550, but in March of the same year, strong rains washed over the wattle and daub wall, causing a large part of it to tumble down. It became evident that the average height of sixteen or eighteen spans (3.52 or 3.96 meters) was excessive for the type of material used, requiring the stonemasons to lower the wall to around eleven spans (2.42 meters).

In the summer of 1550, before the rains, Pero de Carvalhaes was spurred by a special prize offered by Tomé de Souza to produce lime on Itaparica Island by burning mollusk shells. On March 1, 1550, the Procurator General authorized payment for eighteen *moios* (828 liters each) of lime that had been delivered to the Storehouse of Salvador. The lime was essential for making the wattle and daub waterproof and ensuring greater durability.

Table 12 - Costs of Walls and Bulwarks in the Fortress of Salvador, 1549

Month/Year	Contract Labor	Wood	Total
May 1549	—	17,458.00	17,458.00
June 1549	10,000.00	113,673.50	123,673.50
July 1549	4,000.00	—	4,000.00
August 1549	20,600.00	—	20,600.00
September 1549	25,000.00	—	25,000.00
October 1549	49,000.00	—	49,000.00
November 1549	13,500.00	—	13,500.00
December 1549	50,000.00	33,051.00	83,051.00
Total	172,100.00	164,182.50	336,282.50

Source: DOCUMENTOS HISTÓRICOS [Historical Documents], v. XII, Bibliotheca Nacional.

Rebuilding, lowering, and applying lime to the walls was a more arduous task than building them in the first place, lasting until at least December, 1551. When the work was completed, six bulwarks, gates, and approximately 1,500 meters of wattle and daub walls encircled the fortress.

Around 1586, Gabriel Soares de Souza wrote that the city had been "walled and towered" while Governor Tomé de Souza was in office, but that, afterwards, the walls fell to the ground, since they were made of wattle and daub and had never been repaired. The city had grown and no one remembered where the walls used to be.[198] In another chapter, Gabriel Soares beseeched the King to send help to repair the security of the city by encircling it with walls and fortifica-

---

198 Idem, capítulo VII, p. 256.

tions, since it had become exposed to raids by pirates and the various peoples scattered through the interior.

The first city wall lasted for ten or fifteen years—the period that the master architect had accurately estimated would be the duration of its usefulness. By the 1580s, no memories of its original location survived, having last been mentioned in 1557. Father Manuel da Nóbrega suggested that the wall be dismantled to make room for enlarging the Jesuits' school. That was the last that was heard of the first wall.

Around 1591 or soon thereafter, Governor Dom Francisco de Souza enclosed the city once again with walls of wattle and daub on pylons. The boundaries, however, were no longer the same: the urban nucleus, once squeezed onto the top of the plateau, had overflowed toward the hills, and authorities tried to adapt to this new reality. A new phase and another story then emerged: although the era when the Portuguese feared the Indians had come to an end, a greater danger appeared—English and Dutch pirates.

18. The Gates of the Fortress

When they come to the Town, if the City is noble and powerful, the Streets should be strait and broad, which carries an Air of Greatness and Majesty; but if it is only a small Town or a Fortification, it will be better, and as safe, not for the Streets to run strait to the Gates; but to have them wind about sometimes to the Right, sometimes to the Left, near the Wall, and especially under the Towers upon the Wall; and within the Heart of the Town, it will be handsomer not to have them strait, but winding about several Ways, backwards and sorwards, like the Coarse of a River.

Leon Battista Alberti

The walls were sacred. People, animals, and vehicles could only enter and leave the city through the gates. In an Etruscan ritual, two cattle hitched together traced a furrow in the earth, which was called a "fosse"; the mound on the inner side was the *murus* and the interior circle was the *orbis*. At certain points, the plowing was interrupted and the spaces between the furrows were referred to as *portae*. This place of passage from one world to the next, from the insecure to the secure, and from the universal to the familiar was always associated with war and the protection of the city. In the Fortress of Salvador, the gates were built and destroyed in three distinct stages—each one bearing a name and a memory.

The significance of gates can be understood only within in the context of the risks of war. The ancients taught that, if the city was put on alert, all gates should remain closed, except for one that should have a hatch through which men might leave one by one. This gate should be located in a place that was difficult to reach and where guards could see as far as possible to know when people were approaching the city. The moment when animals, carts, and merchandise entered the city was considered dangerous, so great precautions were taken. The gates could not be opened until dawn and, before doing so, the area around the walls had to be checked. Carts and people could not gather in the entrance of the gates, but, rather, had to keep farther away, a measure meant to prevent conspiracies and acts of betrayal.

During times of danger, the sentinels were not informed ahead of time about the day and place they would be assigned as guards, nor who their commander would be. They had to stand one in front of another; in the most accessible places, the guards had to be citizens who had the most to lose with an invasion. These rules for ensuring proper security were described in one of the first war manuals in Greece,[199] written in the fourth century A.D., and can profitably be transposed to the sixteenth century.

In 1546, during the second siege of Diu, João de Castro sent some written recommendations to the captain of the fortress, advising him not to open the gate for men to do battle outside the fortress.[200] In July, 1640, the Marquis Jorge de Mascarenhas ordered that certain rules for defending the walls and gates be recorded by the Municipal Council of Salvador: the keys to the gates should be entrusted to officials appointed by the Council; the act of opening and closing the gate should be conducted by these appointees and witnessed by the captain of the guards; the captain general should observe the changing of the civilian guards; and, finally, the Council Procurator should be responsible for the maintenance of the walls and repairs to the gates.[201]

---

199 TACTICUS, Aeneas. *Poliorcética* [Poliorketika], pp. 161-164.
200 SANCEAU, Elaine. *Cartas de D. João de Castro* [Letters of Dom João de Castro], p. 131.
201 DOCUMENTOS históricos do Arquivo Municipal [Historical Documents of the Municipal Archive], v. 1°, pp. 436-437.

Such provisions concerning guards and security were complemented by dozens of others related to architecture. The Greeks built their gates between two towers on the sides to provide lateral protection in case of an attack. In front of them lay drawbridges and moats, other common means of defense. Roman military encampments established the square format with four gates, each being located in the middle of each side, where the straight streets crossing in the main plaza came to an end. This simple geometric model survived during the Middle Ages, giving rise to various *bastides*, or palisades, and was disseminated through the writings of various Renaissance authors. Machiavelli recommended the model of the Roman encampment with the gates facing the four cardinal directions.

Renaissance architects proposed some small innovations. Alberti, underscoring the aesthetic function of the entrance, argued that, in a famous and powerful city, the street should be straight and wide, a pattern befitting its stature and dignity. In small towns or forts, however, the road to the city should lead indirectly to the gate after turning back and forth along the walls. Preferably, the entrance should be placed under ramparts.[202]

Francesco Di Giorgio Martini elaborated upon Alberti's ideas. He understood that the gate should be located on the most secure side where the least aggression would be directed. He suggested that it be built next to a protective tower or a bulkhead called a "ravelin," a structure built in front of the gate and designed to protect the entrance.[203] He also argued that each gate should be served by a main street, which should lead directly and without any curves to the opposite gate, with the main plaza being situated between the two. In Diu in 1546, the problem with security lay in the lack of a ravelin, which would have protected the men returning from the surrounding area.[204]

The Fortress of Salvador had at least two gates—to the south

---

202 ALBERTI, Leon Battista. *L'Architettura* [Architecture], p. 161.
203 MARTINI, Francesco Di Giorgio. *Trattati Di Architettura Ingegneria e Arte Militare* [Treatise on Architecture, Engineering, and Military Arts]. I, p. 9.
204 SANCEAU, Elaine. *Cartas de D. João de Castro* [Letters of Dom João de Castro], p. 131.

and the north—located on the walls that safeguarded the boundaries. The northern gate, called Santa Catarina, was located precisely on the path from Praça da Sé to the Terreiro de Jesus (Fig. 30), strategically positioned between two bulwarks exactly in the middle. The bulwark on the side toward the ocean was called the São Jorge station; the name of the other, situated on the land side, is unknown.

Figure 30 - Probable location of the first Santa Catarina gate.

There is little certainty about the gate on the southern border. Apparently this gate was not situated between two bulwarks. The master architect Luís Dias, in a reference to the spot, noted that pieces of dried mud from the wattle and daub structure of the São Tiago bulwark had fallen down on the São Tomé station.[205] In this passage, however, no gate is mentioned. Where might it have been located? Did it also tumble down? It is possible that it was located in the inner side of the São Tiago bulwark, facing the Ajuda Church—a hypothe-

---

205 Letter from Luís Dias to Miguel de Arruda, dated July 13, 1551. In: *Anais do 4º Congresso de História da Bahia.* I, pp. 140-144.

sis compatible with the technical criteria for positioning gates in fortresses, and which is supported by some of the evidence.

The gate in front of the Ajuda Church would have been located precisely opposite that of Santa Catarina; they would be visible even if the street were not perfectly straight. Positioning the church in front of the southern entrance would serve as an invocation for protection, corresponding to the Conceição da Praia church built at the bottom of the Ladeira da Praia. A third aspect suggests that the access roads were not straight, but winding and exposed to the walls and bulwarks. Rua Rui Barbosa started as a primitive path along the walls, its access being less steep than that of Rua Chile. It is reasonable to suppose that, in the early years, Rua Chile did not exist, and that access was possible only along Rua Rui Barbosa. The gate would have been behind the São Tiago bulwark, which would have served as a ravelin. The gentlest slope for entering would have been in front of the Ajuda Church.

The only drawback to this theory is the lack of a direct line to the plaza, but, even so, symmetry would have prevailed, since both gates would have been served by streets at right angles. Their placement in relation to the urban design revealed the efforts to ensure symmetry, but the topography made regularity impossible. The main street did not cross the fortress from one end to the other, but, rather, ended at the Sé Cathedral due to the curves of the hillside.

Another unknown aspect is the name of this gate. No reference to it exists, but nothing prevents us from calling it the Ajuda gate as a way of underscoring the theory presented here. Nevertheless, we should not discard the possibility that, in the original plan, there was a gate where Rua Chile now exists, called by some the Santa Luzia gate in honor of the nearby chapel that once stood there.

The original walls and gates ceased to exist around ten years after they were built. Only the São Tomé station remained, located on the side of the ocean along the southern boundary. In a place close to the old bulwark, a chapel was built and dedicated to Santa Luzia.

The decades of the 1560s, 1570s, and early 1580s went by in relative peace. The city grew and, while Mem de Sá was still in office, at least two sets of blocks were built that enlarged its boundaries. Without presuming to identify dates or precedence, we can refer to them as the "Pelourinho complex" and the "rectangles of Rua Rui Barbosa," both of which were built with a reasonable degree of planning and precision.

The city began to overflow toward the ramps to the north and south of the original plateaus, which was risky. In 1586, Gabriel Soares de Souza warned about the danger of pirate invasions. After this prediction, faced with Spain's wars against the British and Dutch, attacks began in 1587. The first was launched by three British ships commanded by Robert Witherington and Christopher Lister. A new cycle of fortifications began in the city of Salvador.

Governor Francisco de Souza arrived in Bahia in 1591 and took upon himself the task of rebuilding the city walls and gates, for which he used wattle and daub. The Santa Luzia gate appeared on the southern side, and that of Santa Catarina on the northern. The Santa Luzia gate descended the hillside and was built at some spot near the Teatro Gregório de Matos, and the Santa Catarina gate went up at the Largo do Pelourinho (Table 13). The placement of these gates is evident in the city plan drawn up in 1605, included in the book, *Razão do Estado do Brasil* (Reason for the State of Brazil).

In a deed dated April 9, 1603, the name of the Santa Luzia gate appeared for the first time. The document refers to the sale of a plot that extended down the hillside "from the gate known as Santa Luzia to the path that runs along the beach by the sea."[206] Around 1616, this gate was defended by two large stone cannons (known as *camelos*), while the Santa Catarina gate had only a small stone cannon (known as a *selvagem*), which indicated the need for greater defense on the southern side.[207]

In 1606, a deed referred to the street that ran from "the Santa Catarina gate along the wall [...]."[208] Another entry, made in 1619, mentioned the street that went from "the Terreiro de Jesus to the San-

---

206 LIVRO *Velho do Tombo* [Old Register of Charters and Deeds], p. 360.
207 Source: RAZÃO do Estado do Brasil [Reason for the State of Brazil] (c. 1616). Códice 126 da Biblioteca Pública Municipal do Porto, p. 53.
208 DOCUMENTOS HISTÓRICOS [Historical Documents], Bibliotheca Nacional, v. LXIII, pp. 383-384.

ta Catarina gate."[209] In 1640, a new deed referred to the Santa Luzia gate[210]—this being the last reference to it. After suffering the Dutch invasion, the city had to rebuild or renovate its gates. Starting in 1630, changes were set in motion. In the ensuing years, the Santa Luzia gate came to be known as that of São Bento, and the Santa Catarina was renamed the gate "of Carmo."

Table 13 - History of Gates in the City of Salvador, 1549-1796

Name of Gate	Probable Period	Approximate Location
Ajuda or Santa Luzia Gate	1549 -1560	Southern side. In front of Ajuda Church or in upper part of Rua Chile.
Santa Catarina Gate (first)	1549 -1560	Northern side. In front of Terreiro de Jesus.
Santa Luzia Gate	1591-1634	Southern side. In the middle of the present-day Praça Castro Alves.
Santa Catarina Gate (second)	1591-1635	Northern side. In the present Largo do Pelourinho.
São Bento Gate	1634-1796	Southern side. In the middle of the present Praça Castro Alves.
Carmo Gate	1635-1790	Northern side. In the present Largo do Pelourinho.

Source: The author.

On April 27, 1630, the Municipal Council received a directive from the governor ordering that work on the city gates begin.[211] To cover the costs of the project, a certain monopoly was set up for

---

209 DOCUMENTOS HISTÓRICOS [Historical Documents], Bibliotheca Nacional, v. LXIII, p. 378.
210 LIVRO Velho do Tombo [Old Register of Charters and Deeds], p. 192.
211 DOCUMENTOS históricos do Arquivo Municipal [Historical Documents of the Municipal Archive], v. 1°, pp. 153-154.

the sale of rum, called "honey wine," authorizing it to be sold upon payment of a certain levy earmarked for the gate project. This tax was placed on a commercial activity that had heretofore been prohibited. Four years later, in 1634, a request was submitted to suspend the additional charge, since "the city gates are finished."[212] One and a half years later, on August 27, 1635, the sale of "honey wine which is called rum" was blamed for causing "harm" to the city; the sale of rum, it was said, encouraged slaves to go night and day to places where it was sold, to steal from their masters, and to get into fights, sometimes deadly, among themselves. But the city gates, at least that of Carmo, were not yet finished.[213] The shortfall in resources for completing the work was overcome through charges imposed directly on residents, an act that brought an end to the rum levy.

The Carmo and São Bento gates survived until the end of the eighteenth century. The former was permanently demolished in 1790, while the latter survived a bit longer, until 1796. In a certain respect, the Terreiro de Jesus, Pelourinho square, and Praça Castro Alves owe their existence to these gates—structures that, in the past, had been passageways, points of transition between two worlds, and which then became open spaces given over to the public.

---

212 Idem, pp. 251-252.
213 Ibidem, p. 279.

19. From Tower to Bulwark

[...] each change and alteration always prepares the way and facilitates the next.

Niccolo Machiavelli

The square, circle, and pentagon are the geometric shapes that chronologically represent the evolution of towers, bastions, and bulwarks. At first, people observed that a tower projecting out from a rampart served as an anchor for the walls and a projecting point for defense of the sides. An attacker could be engaged in combat from the front and from the sides, or, in military jargon, the flanks. In a later stage, the square tower was superseded by a circular shape. A right angle was easily destroyed "by blows from a battering ram,"[214] as Vitruvius stated, while the circumference of a circle did a better job distributing the force of a blow; furthermore, it did not leave dead zones where enemies could hide. With the advent of bombards and canyons, the pentagon appeared, projecting out toward the probable field of attack. The pentagon inaugurated the era of the bulwark, the greatest innovation of military architecture in the Renaissance. The projecting

---

[214] POLLIO, Marcus Vitruvius. *Los Diez Libros de Archîtectura* [The Ten Books on Architecture], p. 19.

walls of the bulwark deflected shots, prevented dead zones, and, in geometric harmony with a paired bulwark, ensured mutual defense. Two nearby bulwarks defended each other, both pointing toward the field where the enemy would probably appear.

In the Greek world, towers, which had as their main purpose the provision of shelter to the guards, were not common in the first fortifications. With the advent of military machinery (for example, the catapult) and refinements in siege warfare, towers became the appropriate place for stationing this type of artillery. In relation to shapes, Lawrence asserts that at least 90% of known towers were rectangular. Towers with a semicircular plan may have been stronger, but they were more difficult to build.[215]

Vitruvius commented on the shift from the rectangle or square to the circle, recommending that towers should be "round or polygonal" because square ones suffered greater damage from military weapons. In a circular figure, he wrote, if the stones were wedge-shaped, the center of the tower would suffer no damage. In relation to the walls, the position of a tower should be projecting in such a way that the enemy could be attacked from openings on the sides of the tower, a strategy known as flank defense.

Before being destroyed by the Romans, Jerusalem was surrounded by three walls, the newest one being called "Bethesda, that is, new city,"[216] which was partially constructed by King Agrippa and subsequently completed by the Jews. It had ninety square towers with a height of 19.8 meters, each being 88 meters from each other; in other words, the ratio between the width of the tower and the wall curtain was 1:10 (Table 14).

According to Vitruvius, the distance between two towers could not be farther than "the shot of an arrow,"[217] since, if one tower were coping with enemy attacks, it could be defended by the other. In a study on the reach of different weapons, Gastão de Melo reports

---

215 LAWRENCE, A W. *Arquitetura Grega* [Greek Architecture], p. 177.
216 JOSEPHUS, Flavius. *História dos Hebreus* [Antiquities of the Jews]. Livro Quinto, capítulo 13, p. 645.
217 POLLIO, Marcus Vitruvius. *Los Diez Libros de Archîtectura* [The Ten Books on Architecture], p. 19.

that, in the case of an arbalest crossbow, the distance was 91 meters.[218] This measurement appears to be excessive, despite its compatibility with the distance observed between the towers in the Bethesda wall in Jerusalem. A few examples may illustrate the pattern found in some of the ancient and medieval fortresses.

Table 14 - Measurements of the Wall of Bethesda, Jerusalem[219]

City of Jerusalem	Wall of Bethesda	
	Cubits	Meters
Wall Measurements	—	—
Wall height	20	8.8
Parapet	3	1.32
Battlements	2	0.88
Total	25	11
Tower Measurements	—	—
Shape	Square	
Tower height	45	19.8
Tower width	20	8.8
Distance between towers	200	88
Number of towers	90	—

Source: JOSEPHUS, Flavius. *História dos Hebreus* [Antiquities of the Jews]. Livro 5°, cap. 13, p. 645.

Caesarea, a city of Judea built by Herod in honor of Julius Caesar, had towers that were square, although oblique (Fig. 31). There were at least fourteen towers, with a distance between them being no more than approximately 67 meters and no less than 28 meters.[220]

---

218 MATOS, Gastão de Melo de. *Memória sobre o alcance das armas usadas nos séculos XV e XVIII* [Memoir on the reach of arms used in the 15th-18th centuries], p. 108.
219 Author's Note: The cubit (*côvado*) corresponded to 1.5 feet; in the Italian system, 0.44 meters. See Appendix for information on correlations among different regional systems of measurements.
220 KAUFMANN, J. E. & KAUFMANN, H. W. *The Medieval Fortress Castles, Forts and Walled Cities of the Middle Ages*, p. 130.

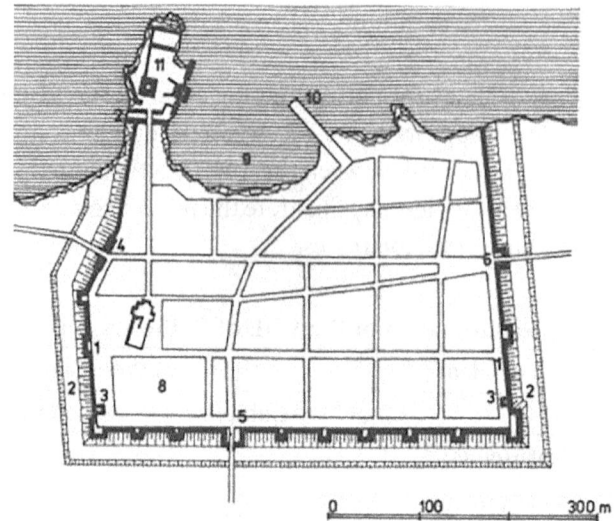

Figure 31 - Plan of the city of Caesarea, Israel.[221]
Source: KAUFMANN, J. E. & KAUFMANN, H. W. *The Medieval Fortress Castles, Forts and Walled Cities of the Middle Ages*, p. 130.

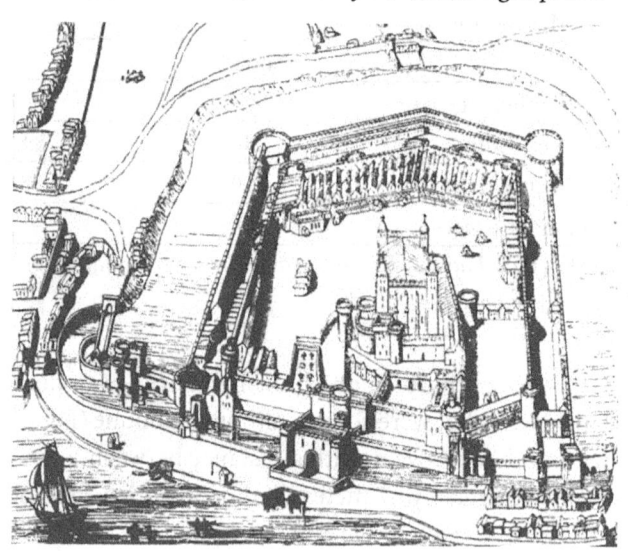

Figure 32 - Illustration of the Tower of London, England.
Source: KAUFMANN, J. E. & KAUFMANN, H. W. *The Medieval Fortress Castles, Forts and Walled Cities of the Middle Ages*, p. 190.

---

221 Numbers indicate the following parts: 1. Curtain of walls and towers; 2. Fosse; 3. Guard tower; 4. Gate facing the ocean; 5. Eastern gate; 6. Northern gate; 7. St. Peter's Cathedral; 8. Block of houses; 9. Port; 10. Wharfs; 11. Citadel.

The Fortress of Salvador

The Tower of London saw its first belt of walls built during the reign of Henry III in the thirteenth century (Fig. 32). It had twelve circular towers standing at variable distances, from a minimum of 19 meters to a maximum of 55.[222]

The French city of Aigues-Mortes, constructed in France by Louis IX between 1240 and 1250 (Fig. 33), had a rectangular perimeter and a city plan that was reasonably orthogonal, with access ensured by five gates flanked by semicircular towers. In each corner of the rectangle, there was a circular tower; along the ramparts were a few square or semicircular ones. The distribution of towers on each side of the rectangle displayed variations. On the three well-defended sides, the shortest distance between the towers was 40 meters and the longest was 100.[223]

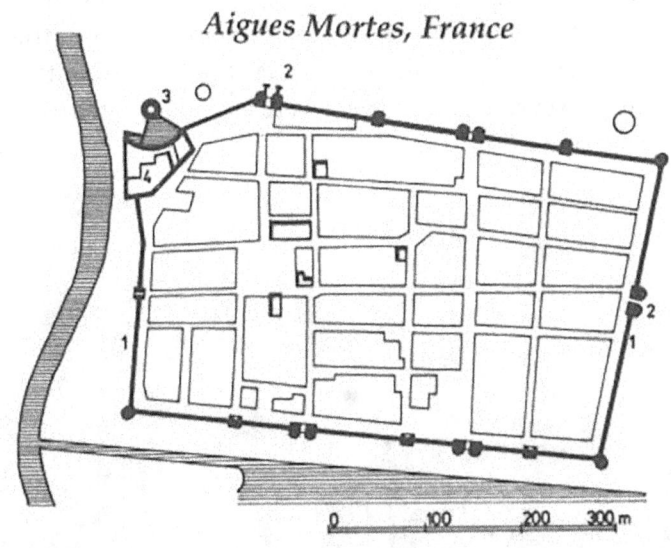

Figure 33 - Plan of the city of Aigues-Mortes, France.[224]
Source: KAUFMANN, J. E. & KAUFMANN, H. W. *The Medieval Fortress Castles, Forts and Walled Cities of the Middle Ages*, p. 227.

---

222 Idem, p. 190.
223 Idem, p. 227.
224 Author's Note: 1. Walls; 2. Gates; 3. Main tower; 4. Castle or citadel.

Another theoretical formulation of Vitruvius concerned the necessity of reinforcing walls with rammed earth.[225] According to the architect, using such reinforcement ensured greater security to walls and towers, since explosives, battering rams, and other machinery could not destroy them. However, they were only necessary in the most exposed parts of a fortress, that is, where areas outside the walls favored enemy attack. Similarly, Vegetius recommended that walls be built in two parallel lines, with the space between them being filled with earth, which would reduce the impact of battering rams.

This was the synthesis of knowledge in the classical period. During the Middle Ages, use of square towers persisted, although subsequently they gave way to round ones. In Europe, fortified cities such as Avila, in Spain, or Carcassone, in France, built around the twelfth century, featured circular or ultra-semicircular towers. In general, tall, circular towers predominated. In Portugal, however, square towers were abundant, such as the castle at Guimarães (Fig. 34).

Figure 34 - Square tower in the Castle of Guimarães, Portugal.

---

225 In military parlance, "terraplane" is earth that is filled, rammed down, and compressed inside a wall that holds it in.

The Fortress of Salvador

The term "tower" carries various meanings. It may refer to a prison tower, a central building, or one attached to a rampart, serving as living quarters and overlooking the rest of the castle, in which case a tower is similar to a citadel. The Italians called observation towers *torri de vedetta*, the best example of which is the famous Tower of Pisa. The third meaning refers to a structure attached to a rampart, built as a means of defending the circumference of a city or castle.

A smaller version of the tower was called a *cubelo*—a diminutive of "cube," which reveals its square origin—and was intended to offer intermediate protection for a rampart. Evolution, following the logic of the transformation of the square into the circle, gave rise to circular *cubelos*.

Apparently, towers in the Medieval setting did not undergo much modification until the advent of Alberti's work. He argued that walls should be defended by towers built fifty cubits (22 meters) from each other and should have a circular pattern, with the function of protecting the wall. Alberti called attention to the fact that the ancients used to build semicircular towers on a city gate in order to protect it, a pattern observed in the French city of Aigues-Mortes.

Alberti, who worked with Vitruvius's ideas, did not appear to be familiar with the devastating effects of bombards on walls and towers, so he did not make any contribution to the transformation of towers into bulwarks. However, the time for change was approaching. Someone who experienced these changes intensely was Martini, whose words reveal his fascination with the impact of bombards. He opened his treatise by stating that the fortress should be adapted so that could be defended against "the bombard machine."[226]

The bombard machine could only be combated, in Martini's view, by "divine ingenuity,"[227] and defense against it was quite difficult. For this reason, he argued for "a new formation for the city, fortress, or castle." He maintained that fortresses should be compact, narrow, and small in circumference. The preferential format was a rhomboid, but he also praised other regular polygons, such as the square or pen-

---

226 MARTINI, Francesco Di Giorgio. *Trattati Di Architettura Ingegneria e Arte Militare* [Treatise on Architecture, Engineering, and Military Arts]. I, p. 3.
227 Idem, I, p. 6.

tagon. He simply suggested that the shape be adapted to the terrain in such a way that the fort's angles would project outwards against the probable point of an attack and would require the least defensive resources.

Martini instructed that towers should be solid, with moats in front of them, and that the first escarpment should be tilted in a manner that would deflect shots. The format in his drawings suggests a preference for round shapes, with the hillside sloping up to a certain height, but he introduced innovations into ravelins and barbicans in the wall in front of the moat, serving as the first line of defense of the fortress. Martini's designs clearly indicate the "bulwarkization" of the barbicans, while towers remained round with a wide base and inclined (Fig. 35). Fortresses were supposed to have a ring of barbicons around them, and the shape could vary according to the place: round or angled, tall or short. In some places, they took the form of polygonal projections, suggestive of the five-sided format typical of bulwarks.

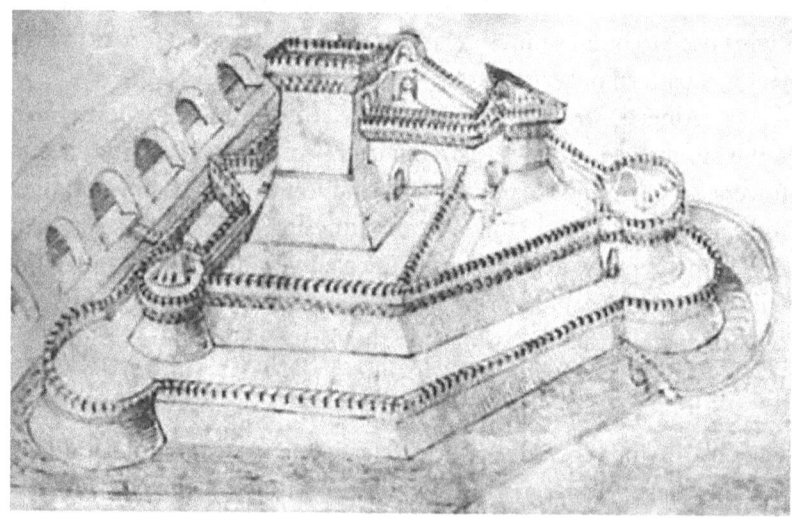

Figure 35 - Transitional style from tower to bulwark at the beginning of sixteenth century. Model of a sturdy circular tower by Francesco di Giorgio Martini. Source: MARTINI, Francesco Di Giorgio. Trattati Di Architettura Ingegneria e Arte Militare [Treatise on Architecture, Engineering, and Military Arts]. I, folha 5 tábua 5.

The Fortress of Salvador

In a certain passage, Martini clearly defended the round shape when he noted that the ancients preferred the circular shape for the city perimeter as well as for towers. However, but he only approved of the latter: "I assert that the tower is helpful and necessary, because it is more resistant and less apt to be penetrated by a bombard."[228] In short, he advised adding round towers on the ends of a fortress, facing the direction of a likely attack, and spaced in a manner allowing each tower to defend another. The turreted crown should measure 50 or 60 feet (15 or 18 meters) in diameter, he said, and the tower should be a solid structure, except on the flank, where there should be an opening for defense.

Martini innovated theoretical formulations about a fortification's defenses, but he did not propose the pentagonal format of the bulwark; round towers stubbornly persisted. Leonardo da Vinci offered theories about the superiority of the curved form over the angular bulwark. Subsequently, Albrecht Dürer, in his treatise *De urbibus, arcibus, castellisque, condendis, ac muniendis rationes aliquot, praesenti bellorum necessitati accommodatissimae* (Nuremberg, 1527; Latin translation, 1535), vigorously defended circular bastions and a circular plan for fortresses.[229] In various Italian and Portuguese fortresses constructed between 1500 and 1530, round bastions were still prevalent, having open embrasures on the first floor to defend the flank of the rampart, with a space above that protected the area surrounding the fortress.

In *Album of Designs in Antiquity*, written by Francisco de Holanda during his trip to Italy from 1538 to 1540, we can confirm the widespread use of large bastions that were round and reinforced, seen in the fortresses of Padova, Ferrara, Nice, and Salses (Fig. 36).[230] The format of the fortresses and bastions recalls the designs of Martini, indicating the style of the era. In the Portuguese world, the for-

---

228 Idem, II, p. 430.
229 MOREIRA, Rafael. "A Arte da Guerra no Renascimento" [The Art of War in the Renaissance] In: *História das Fortificações Portuguesas no Mundo* [History of Portuguese Fortifications Around the World], p. 149. Edited by Rafael Moreira, 1989.
230 HOLANDA, Francisco de. Álbum dos Desenhos da Antiguidade. [Album of Designs in Antiquity] 35r, 35v, 37r, 43v.

tresses of Aguz and Azamor in Morocco illustrate well the transitional style between the classical-Medieval and the modern (Fig. 37).

Figure 36 - *Transitional style. Fortress of Salses, according to Francisco de Holanda, 1538.*
Source: HOLANDA, Francisco de. *Álbum dos Desenhos da Antiguidade* [Album of Designs in Antiquity], p. 43v.

In the so-called "transitional style," military architects initially adapted existing designs for defense to the use of artillery: they lowered the height of ramparts; reinforced the walls using rammed earth in order to cushion the impact of projectiles; increased the width of towers to make them sturdier; and lowered bastions into trenches and casements to defend against shots close to the ground. Experience, however, led architects to realize that bullets ricocheted more easily on polygonal structures, an insight that gave rise to the bulwark.

The invention of the bastion is often attributed to the Italian architect Michele Sanmicheli, but we cannot ignore the contribution by Antonio da Sangallo (1484-1546), one of those responsible for building the St. Peter's Cathedral in Rome. In 1526, Sanmicheli and Sangallo traveled together to northern and central Italy, inspecting the fortresses belonging to the Papal State. Pope Clement VII's concern over military matters was closely correlated with the political environment arising from the League of Cognac, signed by France, Venice, Milan, and the Pontiff. The resulting conflict ended on May 6, 1527, when the troops of Emperor Carlos V of Spain sacked Rome.[231] The intensity of the war must have furthered the development of military architecture.

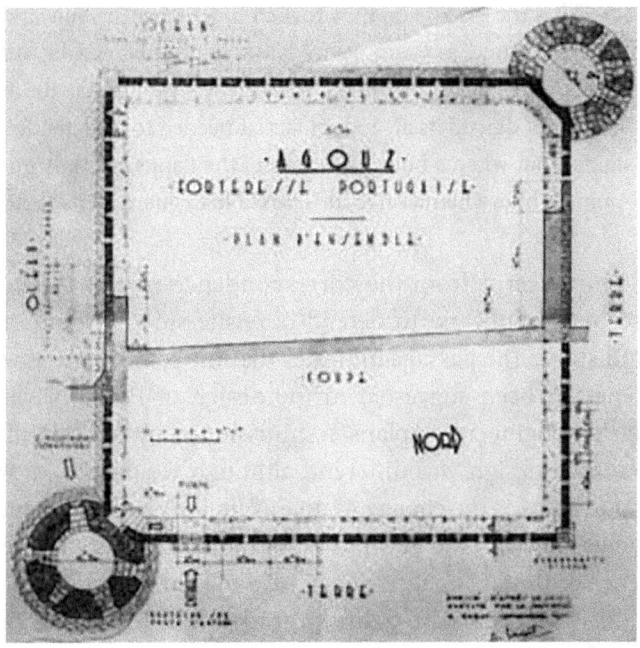

Figure 37 - Transitional style: the Portuguese fortress at Aguz in Morocco, built in 1519.
Source: História das Fortificações Portuguesas no Mundo [History of Portuguese Fortifications Around the World], p. 132.

A letter written by Machiavelli on June 8, 1526, dealing with the fortification of the city of Florence, reveals that pentagonal bulwarks had not been used previously, their superiority over circular structures being unknown. Machiavelli was the chancellor responsi-

---
231 LOTZ, Wolfgang. *Arquitetura na Itália 1500-1600* [Architecture in Italy 1500-1600], pp. 53, 67.

ble for rebuilding the city walls of Florence, when he received a visit from Vitello Vitelli, Captain General of the Florentine armies. They were awaiting the arrival of Antônio da Sangallo and Baccio Bigio to discuss the topic, and plans were drawn up by the Spanish military engineer Pedro Navarro. In one passage, the text states,

> "[...] the discussion then turned to whether the bulwark should be made round, as Count Pedro Navarro had planned, or with many facets. They agreed to make it faceted, arguing that the bulwark could not defend itself, and, in fact, it needed to be defended on the flanks, but when a bulwark is round, the flanks can only guard one point, while, when faceted, it is possible to guard all its façades." [232]

One excerpt from the correspondence reveals the essential purpose of the bulwark: to defend opposite sides without creating any blind spots. The passage indicates that the round format was still strong, having been suggested in the design of Pedro Navarro, an experienced engineer, for plans commissioned by the Pontiff; however, the final design was different, although we do not know who was responsible for the change. Captain Vitello Vitelli apparently was already familiar with the new notion of bulwarks, perhaps due to his experience or professional contact with Sangallo.

In 1526, the notion of the bulwark already existed, giving rise to the cycle of building modern fortresses. In 1534, Sangallo drew up plans for the Basso fortress in Florence, which featured the pentagonal model. Pietro Cataneo's treatise,[233] published in 1554, offers a good example of how quickly the use of the new tactic spread. In his book, the plans used designs that were perfectly geometrical. The fortresses had symmetrical bulwarks with embrasures on the flanks defending the curtains of wall and the opposite bulwark—a pentagonal model, proportionate and adjusted to the size of the fortress. The

---

[232] MACHIAVELLI, Niccolo. *Epistolário 1512-1527* [Correspondence 1512-1527], p. 335. Other passages in the letter contain significant references to details of the plan, notably the design of embrasures, trenches, and the measurements of bulwarks.
[233] *Dell'Architettura* [On Architecture].

bulwark, with its typical design of three projecting sides and five angles, was not the only feature to change.

In Cataneo, we can see the development of regular models of cities, with perimeters forming squares, pentagons, hexagons, and decagons. On each angle was a bulwark—a result of exploring geometric possibilities, which, up to then, had been limited to circular, square, or rectangular forms. Over a fifty-year period, the advantages of pentagonal bulwarks and regular perimeters around cities were consolidated, being the two great military innovations of the first half of the sixteenth century.

In Portugal, the tower was transformed into the bastion after 1500; in turn, the latter was substituted by the polygonal bulwark around 1540. This took place through a process of generalization after the bulwark first appeared at the Fortress of Mazagan on the Moroccan coast. This fortress was built in an almost rectangular shape, with four large bulwarks on the corners. The Italian engineer Benedito de Ravena, who assisted in the design of this fortified city, was famously praised for his contributions. His innovative design was heralded as something never before seen in Portugal, and his new knowledge gained him great admiration.[234] Miguel de Arruda represented the interests of the Portuguese Crown in the undertaking and, to a certain extent, participated in the project. After Mazagan, other fortresses were constructed, all taking advantage of the innovative type of design.

In 1543, the King ordered a new fortification to be built at Ceuta.[235] By 1545, Dom João de Castro called attention to the large expens-

---

234 In a letter to King Dom João III, dated June 7, 1541, Afonso de Noronha wrote: "[...] I reckon Benedito de Ravena to be a singular man and much knowledgeable about this manner of fortifying cities as well as every other manner of war ingenuities, and listening to him talk about this is like music, and he is so zealous in what he knows that he brought with him an expert in measurements in order to meet the expectations of Miguel de Arruda, who [...] praised him so for having accomplished well what Your Highness requested of him [. . .]. In: VITERBO, Souza. *Dicionário Histórico e Documental dos Arquitectos, Engenheiros e Construtores Portuguese* [Historical and Documentary Dictionary of Portuguese Architects, Engineers, and Builders]. I, p. 67.

235 On August 25, 1543, Dom João de Castro was appointed to go to Ceuta in the

es incurred by the work on the two fortresses. His interaction with Miguel de Arruda created strong synergy on the architectural plane: the famous politician and military man was also an intellectual who championed modern innovations in the realm of military architecture. When he went to India as governor in 1545, he brought ideas and experience concerning the new model, designing or constructing at least three fortresses that used the new features: Mozambique, Diu, and Salcete.

In 1545, Dom João de Castro suggested that the fortress at Mozambique be built.[236] King Dom João III ordered the project to be executed following Miguel de Arruda's design,[237] and to this end he sent the master architect Francisco Pires to India. Due to a chance turn in the weather, the ship carrying the master architect did not land in Mozambique but, instead, went on to Diu, where Governor Dom João de Castro was battling the siege imposed by the King of Khambhat. In the destroyed fortress, Dom João de Castro and Francisco Pires encountered each other. The Governor considered the master architect to be a man worthy of great honor due to the new knowledge he brought to the Indian world.

---

company of Miguel de Arruda to "fortify said city." It was a "new project," for which the King instructed him to make an assessment "about the design that Miguel de Arruda is bringing for the project." In: VITERBO, Souza. *Dicionário Histórico e Documental dos Arquitectos, Engenheiros e Construtores Portuguese* [Historical and Documentary Dictionary of Portuguese Architects, Engineers, and Builders]. I, p. 69.

236 Letter from Dom João de Castro to King Dom João III, written on the island of Mozambique, dated 1545. In it, he describes the location and appropriate form of the fortress: "[...] my opinion is that, if Your Highness wishes to build a fortress in Mozambique that is very strong and can be defended against the Turks if they besiege it, you should order that it be built on the tip of the island [. . .]." SANCEAU, Elaine. *Cartas de D. João de Castro* [Letters of Dom João de Castro], p. 97.

237 Letter from King Dom João III to Dom João de Castro, dated March 8, 1546: "I rejoiced greatly to see the draft of the fortress of Mozambique that you sent me [. . .]," ordering that it be built "[...] in the manner shown in the draft that you sent here, which I had ordered Miguel de Arruda to create, since, as you know, he is much practiced in such matters [. . .]." In: VITERBO, Souza. *Dicionário Histórico e Documental dos Arquitectos, Engenheiros e Construtores Portuguese* [Historical and Documentary Dictionary of Portuguese Architects, Engineers, and Builders]. I, p. 71.

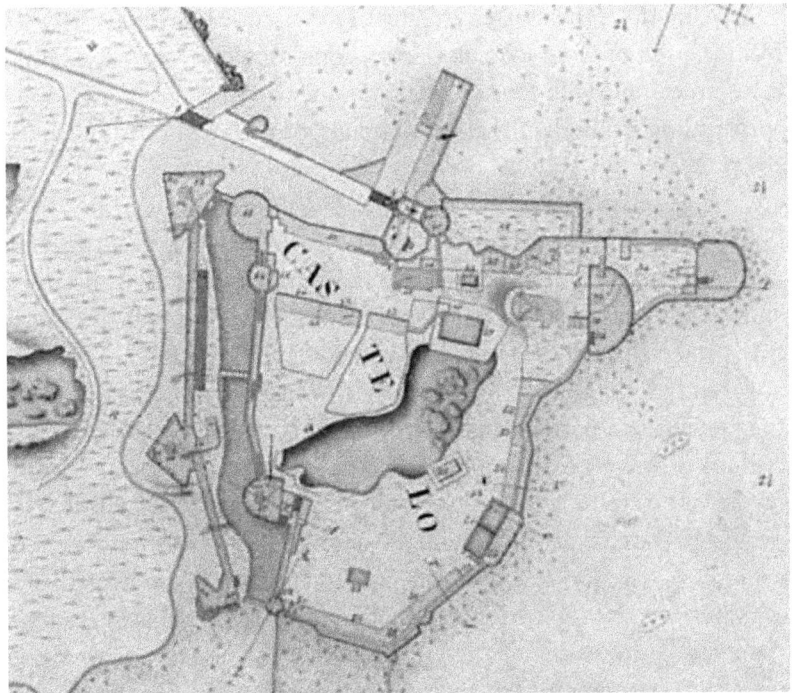

*Figure 38 - Bulwarks of the Portuguese Fortress in Diu, India, 1546.
Source: ROSSA, Walter. Cidades Indo-Portuguesas [Indo-Portuguese Cities], p. 73.*

In late 1546, the fortress of Diu was rebuilt with an external ring of ramparts and three bulwarks (Fig. 38). The project utilized in Ceuta served as a model[238]—a fact explicitly stated by Dom João de Castro, adding that it would cause great fear in people. Other references suggest that this fortress was the first in India to use the new design: "[...] and in the middle of the wall between these two bulwarks another one is built, just as large and strong, with a new appearance, for offense and defense. A thing of great skill, such as no other in these parts has been seen before, because the master was much knowledgeable in such work [...]."[239]

---

238 Letter from Dom João de Castro to King Dom João III, dated December 16, 1546: "The manner in which I design the fortress follows the sketch of Ceuta." SANCEAU, Elaine. *Cartas de D. João de Castro* [Letters of Dom João de Castro], p. 279.
239 In: VITERBO, Souza. *Dicionário Histórico e Documental dos Arquitectos, Enge-*

In 1547, the master architect Francisco Pires, with assistance from the son of Dom João de Castro, constructed the Fortress of Salcete, a rectangle with four bulwarks on the corners. The corners were "protruding points with their materials in a triangle,"[240] with each point defending "the wall on both sides" and "secure in defense and advantageous in offense."[241]

The walls and bulwarks at the fortresses of Mazagan, Diu, and, in certain respects, Salcete, had some characteristics in common, such as the triangular shape of the bulwarks. In Mazagan, the angles that projected farthest tended to be acute, while those in Diu were apparently right angles. The geometric model was not perfect, given the fact that no perfect alignment existed between the corner of the curtain of wall, the beginning of the opposite side, and the rampart of the opposite bulwark. Nevertheless, the opposite side, as a rule, protected the curtain of wall and the opposite bulwark, even if perfect symmetry were lacking, a characteristic common in later fortresses. Another aspect that the fortresses of Diu and Mazagan seem to have shared was the width of the bulwarks, which measured around 45 meters (20 fathoms) at the widest points (Table 15).

The Fortress of Ormuz was renovated in 1558-1560 (Fig. 39), when the original castle gave way to a quadrilateral with four triangular bulwarks on the corners. The shape and width of the bulwarks recall those of Mazagan and Diu; the distance between them was also close to that used at Diu. Miguel de Arruda held the office of master architect of the Kingdom until 1563, probably the year he died. Such facts demonstrate what could be called the "Arrudine style" typical of the second phase of the modern fortresses in Portugal. There was a lack of perfect geometric harmony in the integration and proportions between the walls and bulwarks; the latter, however, were triangular and offered mutual protection.

---

nheiros e Construtores Portuguese [Historical and Documentary Dictionary of Portuguese Architects, Engineers, and Builders]. II, p. 300.
240 Work certificate drawn up by Francisco Pires, dated August 18, 1547. In: VITERBO, Souza. *Dicionário Histórico e Documental dos Arquitectos, Engenheiros e Construtores Portuguese* [Historical and Documentary Dictionary of Portuguese Architects, Engineers, and Builders]. II, p.301.
241 Idem, p. 301.

The Fortress of Salvador

Table 15 - Comparison of Measurements of Portuguese Fortresses

Fortress	Year Founded	Distance Between Angles (Meters)	Distance Between Bulwarks (Meters)	Width of Bulwarks (Meters)
Fortress of Mazagan	1542	243 to 336	165 to 258	41 to 49
Fortress of Mozambique	1546?	—	72, 6, and 110.	—
Fortress of Diu	1546	110 to 148	67 to 126	24 to 48
Fortress of Salvador	1549	50 to 115	50 to 115	22 to 44
Fortress of Ormuz	1558-1560	116 to 209	70 to 155	30 to 46
Fortress of Daman	1570-1582	—	86 to 108	32 to 91
Fortress of Chaul	1570-1582	—	86 to 118	32 to 45

Source: *Códice da Casa de Cadaval (M-7, nº 26)*. ANTT. FARINHA, Antonio Dias. "Plantas de Mazagão e Larache no início do Século XVII" [City plans of Mazagan and Larache at the beginning of the seventeenth century]. In: *A Abertura do Mundo* [...] [Opening the World] pp. 159-161, fig. 12; BOCARRO, António. *O Livro das Plantas de Todas as Fortalezas, Cidades e Povoações do Estado da Índia Oriental* [The Book of City Plans of All Fortresses, Cities, and Settlements in the East Indies], p. 11; ROSSA, Walter. *Cidades Indo-Portuguesas* [Indo-Portuguese Cities], pp. 56, 73; MOREIRA, Rafael. "A época manuelina" [The Manueline era]. In: *História das Fortificações Portuguesas* [...] [History of Portuguese Fortifications], p. 114; BRITO, Raquel Soeiro de. *Goa e as praças do norte revisitadas* [Goa and the northern cities revisited], p. 127.

The Fortress of Salvador was constructed in 1549, chronologically following Mazagan (1542) and Diu (1546) and preceding Ormuz (1558). We may reasonably suggest that the walls and bulwarks of Salvador belonged to the Arrudine style, given that they had the shape and width of the bulwarks of Mazagan and Diu, even though they were made of wood and wattle and daub. It is possible to imagine them as being triangular or semi-triangular, measuring up to 45 meters in width, with a distance between them not greater than 160 meters.

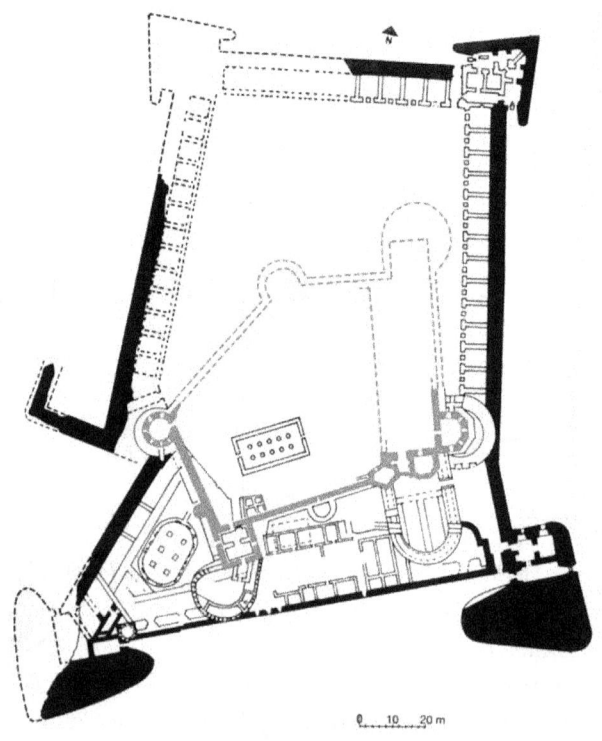

Figure 39 - Portuguese Fortress of Ormuz, 1558-1560.
Source: História das Fortificações Portuguesas no Mundo [History of Portuguese Fortifications Around the World], p. 114.

When the Fortress of Salvador was built, the model of fortresses with bulwarks was fully consolidated. The new technical concepts, so well absorbed and developed by Miguel de Arruda, had been incorporated into the Portuguese universe after ten years of practice and familiarity. The polygonal design of the bulwarks and the rectangular tendencies of the perimeter were amply applied. The bulwarks were not very large, and the typical distance between them was less than 160 meters. They were constructed on two levels: the lower story protected the flank while the upper one overlooked the surrounding area in front and to the sides. This was the tactical foundation that must have guided the direction taken in building the Fortress of Salvador.

20. The Evolution of the Bulwark

In the early days of artillery, Carlos Tetti, Geronimo Magi, and other authors arranged defenses according to the reach of a piece of artillery. When they saw that the distance from one wall to another was very large, they reduced it to the reach of a musket and arquebus, and thereby assured many things.

Cristóbal de Rojas

In 1598, the Spanish engineer Cristóbal de Rojas published the first treatise in Spanish on fortification, *Theory and Practice of Fortification, Following the Measurements and Defenses of Current Times*. The organization of the book was similar to many Italian treatises: it began with lessons in geometry and arithmetic, then turned to military topics. Rojas explained some intriguing historical aspects of the relationship between walls and bulwarks during the sixteenth century. At first, people believed that heavy artillery was capable of keeping any attacker away, but time and experience taught warriors how to outwit the power of the cannon. Little by little, fortresses were reduced in size. Their defenders had to combine the use of small arms with heavy artillery.

In the mid-sixteenth century, the bulwark-studded model of the fortress was firmly entrenched, but other technical questions arose and were debated through to the end of the century, such as the appropriate distance between bulwarks and the size of their front side in relation to the wall. These points were relevant because they represented cost and efficiency: what were the ideal distance and size? A greater distance required the use of cannons to defend the curtain and the front of the opposite bulwark, limiting the use of muskets, arquebuses, and rifles.[242] In the words of Pietro Cataneo, shots from the flanks required defense with "bronze pieces."[243]

Such cautions originated from experience. The art of war was considered a continuous process of evolution, with frequent changes and novelties. According to Rojas, the front sides of bulwarks and walls were large and defended by artillery before the changes proposed by Carlos Tetti (1569) and Geronimo Catanio (1571). Rojas presented data indicating that early curtains used to average 252 meters long, while the front side of bulwarks averaged 98 meters (Table 16). The measurements of the two largest curtains in the Fortress of Mazagan (258 meters and 227 meters) approximated those cited by Rojas, but in the later fortresses of Diu and Ormuz, the dimensions varied between 110 and 209 meters. Through experience, the Portuguese apparently learned the necessity of reducing the length of the wall curtains; however, they accepted the need to defend the flanks with cannons and supported it technically. A good example of this view comes from the letters of Dom João de Castro, who, in April, 1546, wrote some recommendations to follow in defending the Fortress of Diu.

---

242 On the evolution of this concept during the sixteenth century, Eduardo de Mariátegui formulated some fascinating considerations: "[...] bulwarks that were small and narrow-angled in the beginning gradually became larger and increased the size of the flanking angle. The lines of defense, which, in the beginning, cut across the curtain, had become flanking angles by the end of the century, and their distance diminished to the degree that the manufacture and handling of the musket were perfected, until they were reduced to the length this weapon could reach. The curtains become ever shorter, even though they were always flanked by the faces of the bulwarks [...]." In: MARIÁTEGUI, Eduardo de. *El Capitan Cristóbal de Rojas Engenheiro Militar do Século XVI* [Captain Cristóbal de Roja, Military Engineer of the Sixteenth Century], p. 58.
243 CATANEO, Pietro. *Dell'Architettura* [On Architecture], p. 216.

Table 16 - Evolution in Distance Between Bulwarks, 1542-1598[244]

Technical Standard	A Front Curtain	B Front of Bulwark	C Curtain and Bulwark	A+2B Front Total	A/B Ratio
Fortress of Mazagan (1542)	258.00	46.50	304.50	351.00	5.5
Fortress of Chaul	118.00	63.00	—	—	1.87
Opinion of early architects (before 1571)	252	98	350	448	2.57
Carlos Teti (1569) and Geronimo Catanio (1571)	210	86.8	296.8	383.6	2.41
Opinion of Cristóbal de Rojas (1598)	100.8	72.8	173.6	246.4	1.38

Source: ROJAS, Cristóbal de. "Teorica y Pratica de Fortificacion" [Theory and Practice of Fortification]. In: Tres Tratados sobre Fortificacion [Three Treatises on Fortification], pp. 33-36.

In summary, Dom João de Castro directed that artillery be placed in the bulwarks and not in the curtains of walls. The guiding principle was mutual defense between the bulwarks, using heavy artillery, since enemies would draw near hidden in trenches, and only powerful shots could impede their approach. He specifically rejected the use of small arms, such as the arquebus, recommending large artillery pieces even for small ammunition through the use of "lanterns (powder boxes) or hollow balls filled with rocks."[245]

The curtain of wall, situated in the space between the bulwarks, was gradually reduced during the sixteenth century. The no-

---

244 Author's note: The Spanish foot (0.28 cm) was used as a means of conversion.
245 Idem, pp. 133-135.

tion prevailed that the walls and bulwarks should also be defended with muskets, arquebuses, or rifles, which required shorter distances. According to Rojas, the reason was simple: the long reach of cannons allowed attackers to approach through trenches along the greatest angle projecting from the bulwark. If enemies crept in single file, the effectiveness of cannon fire was reduced. Moreover, cannon balls flew close to the ground, since the casements were low, which favored shallow trenches.

In the late sixteenth century, technical specifications for curtains limited them to 100 meters or less, while the front of the bulwarks was limited to 72 meters. The maximum reach of gunshot from muskets and arquebuses was about 176 meters and 105.6 meters, respectively.[246] The total measurements of the curtain of wall and the bulwark indicate that they were adjusted to the reach of these weapons. These technical aspects led to the gradual reduction of the front of each fortress: the curtains were reduced substantially and bulwarks were widened in the front. The results can be seen in many fortresses of the seventeenth century.

The architectural style used by Miguel de Arruda anticipated the use of shorter curtains, as seen in the fortresses at Diu, Mozambique, and Ormuz. However, they kept triangular bulwarks that were relatively small in relation to the size of the curtain of wall. The fortresses at Daman, Chaul, and Bassein, where the construction of walls and bulwarks began in 1570, revealed a distinctive style: the curtains were shortened, the front of the bulwarks was lengthened, and the ratio between the size of the curtains and bulwarks was reduced.

In Portuguese military architecture in the sixteenth century, walls and bulwarks went through three distinct phases: the first lasted

---

246 Fire from arquebuses and post muskets could reach a distance of 24 and 40 fathoms (52.8 and 88 meters), respectively. These distances represented the minimum reach of straight shots, when the weapons were fired from a horizontal position ("*livel de sua anima*"). When adjusting the aim, such measurements could be doubled, depending on "[T]he quality and type of artillery according to the foundry and the reach or direction of each one and its ammunition and gunpowder, length and weight." In: *Livro Primeiro do Governo do Brasil* [First Book of the Government of Brazil], pp. 30-31.

until the end of the 1530s; the second, a transitional style called Arrudino, was characteristic from the 1540s to the 1560s; and the last one, at the end of the century, used models that were geometrically more precise and better adapted to the capabilities of cannons. The implementation of so many changes within one century can be attributed to advances in the technology of firearms; nowadays, it is hard to appreciate the subtleties of each decade, but warfare was a dynamic process. In the words of Dom João de Castro, it was an art in which "one never stops learning" and "each day, from one hour to the next, new things and new secrets, for offense as well as defense, are discovered and invented."[247]

---

[247] Notes sent by Dom João de Castro to Dom João de Mascarenhas in April, 1546, concerning the defense of the Fortress of Diu in response to the siege imposed by the king of Khambhat. SANCEAU, Elaine. *Cartas de D. João de Castro* [Letters of Dom João de Castro], p. 136.

21. Bulwarks and Stations in the Fortress

> *Defense lines should be set according to the range of a musket, not that of artillery. No fortress can defend itself solely through artillery or through muskets. Both are definitely necessary and each one has its advantages over the other in relation to different effects.*
>
> Simão Madeira

The Fortress of Salvador was conceived with four bulwarks in the so-called "Upper City" and two more in the "Lower City." The names of some of them are well-known: on the beach were the Góes and Santa Cruz bulwarks, on the northern and southern sides, respectively; in the upper part, overlooking the ocean, was the São Bento or São Tomé bulwark, and, on the other corner, that of São Tiago; on the side toward the Terreiro de Jesus, guarding the open land beyond, was the São Jorge station, overlooking the ocean, and, in the center of the Terreiro de Jesus, a sixth one, the name of which has not been preserved. The shape and size of each one was adjusted to the topographical conditions of the terrain and its defensive purpose.

"Bulwarks" and "stations" are terms referring to different structures. A bulwark is a polygonal construction designed to protect the curtain and the opposite side of the fortress; a station is a smaller polygonal or rectangular construction, usually made of wood with posts and reinforced with packed earth, projecting forward from the line of the wall or facing the ocean. The difference between bulwarks and stations depends mainly on their size, shape, and position within the fortification. Bulwarks are larger, they defend the corners of the fortress, and their plazas are typically polygonal; however, the half-bulwark, having only one face and flank, has also been called a "station."

The *Regulations of the Fortifications of the City of Funchal, Madeira Island*, dated 1572, stated that the walls must follow the curves in the rivers and that stations, manned with arquebuses, must be built at the angles in order to protect the curtain of wall between them. The upper plaza had to be about 5.5 meters in width.[248] In this case, the stations were made of earth covered with stone. In technical terms, this type of construction was also called a *través*.

What did the words "bulwark" and "station" signify in the context of the construction of the Fortress of Salvador? Can the nomenclature help us differentiate fortifications in terms of their size and shape? In a letter to the King, the master architect Luís Dias used the term "bulwark" to designate structures that complemented the walls: "that is how we made two bulwarks, one on the Góes River, very strong, on top of the cliff."[249] Although the letter may have exaggerated the scale of the work, the orders of payment recorded expenses for "wooden bulwarks"—in this case, the term "bulwark" was apparently used for a class of structures, consistent with some dictionaries that define "station" as "a small structure in fortification, a type of bulwark, sometimes made of wood and posts."[250]

In another letter from Luís Dias, written to Miguel de Arruda,

---

248 CARITA, Rui. *O Regimento de Fortificação de D. Sebastião* [Regulations of the Fortification of D. Sebastião], p. 78.
249 Letter from Luís Dias, master architect, to King Dom João III, dated August 15, 1551. In: MALHEIROS DIAS, Carlos. *História da Colonização Portuguesa no Brasil* [History of Portuguese Colonization in Brazil]. III, pp. 362-363.
250 CARITA, Rui. *O Regimento de Fortificação de D. Sebastião*. [Regulations of the Fortification of D. Sebastião], p. 135.

The Fortress of Salvador

the use of terminology appears to be more technical. Dias had built a wooden station that, in accord with the Governor's request, was called the "Góes bulwark." On the other end of the stream, he built "another station," which was called Santa Cruz. The terminology used at the time also suggested a differentiation based on the intensive use of wood.

If etymology and terminology do not help us in reconstituting the size and shape of the bulwarks and stations in the Fortress of Salvador, we may make headway by using other criteria: first, by examining the land title for the São Tomé station and meticulously studying the oldest maps of the city; second, by crossing the resulting data with information about the geometric patterns utilized in the fortress; and finally, by comparing these results with surviving traces of the original plan. Some of the streets and buildings in the historic center of the city of Salvador preserve boundary lines that arose from secular activities—veritable images of the origin of the fortress.

The São Tomé station appears to be the key to solving the problem. Estevão Lopes da Gram, overseer of the river during the time of Tomé de Souza, and another man known as Francisco Vaz received a land grant of the grounds "where the São Tomé bulwark used to be."[251] The plot began in the upper city and ended at the beach, forming a strip that formed an approximate rectangle, with its width determined by the site where the bulwark stood. The bulwark ended up being sold around 1600 to Judge Baltazar Ferraz, who wanted to construct a private port with a place to store cargo bound for Europe. Through business dealings, he later acquired three different areas along the beach, totaling four plots, as described earlier in Chap. 12.

The Ladeira da Conceição used to have a sharp bend, and the upper edge of this curve coincided with the tip of the São Tomé bulwark. The alignment between this bend in the sloping access road and the corner of the bulwark was geometrically determined, a result of the strategy of preventing any access from being unprotected, congruent with the general pattern of integrating these access roads with the system of control from the upper level. However, there is another aspect that is even more significant. The distance between the edge of the wall of the for-

---

251 LIVRO *Velho do Tombo* [Old Register of Charters and Deeds], p. 360.

tress and the curve in the Ladeira da Conceição was 24 fathoms, which corresponded to the modular unit of 1/10 of the overall measurement of the fortress. The architect allotted the same length for the bulwarks that he had used for outlining the blocks; in other words, the length of the fortress was divided into ten sections. For the construction of the bulwarks on the outside, the architect laid out two more sections, each being 1/10. The result was 12 units of 24 fathoms each—a geometric hypothesis that can be confirmed by examining the oldest map of the city, included in the 1605 codex, *Reason for the State of Brazil*.

The version of the codex archived in the Porto Municipal Public Library[252] is the oldest and undoubtedly the best one, which includes a scale of measurements. If we examine the last city block on the side toward the ocean, just above the Praça Castro Alves, we will notice a corner, which is the far end of the São Tomé bulwark, with a format indicating a half-bulwark with a 90° angle. Below that, we will see the curve of the Ladeira da Conceição, reasonably well aligned with the São Tomé station, a format that has been preserved to this day in the shape of the plot currently occupied by the building that houses the Fundação Gregório de Matos. Part of its northern boundary was the curtain facing the ocean and extending to the corner.

The land grant that Baltazar Ferraz received reveals another significant aspect: the Santa Cruz station, constructed on the beach, was located outside of the wall alignment, but within the strip of bulwarks, as confirmed in the second parcel that the judge was granted. It was a tongue of land that was sinuous and irregular along its length. The judge made a request to extend it with landfill, if necessary, where two artillery pieces were situated on the platform at the foot of the Ladeira da Conceição, to the left. He wanted to build a pier and needed earth for landfill. In his proposal, he said he could extend the fort.

The platform on the beach (the Santa Cruz station) was most likely aligned with the city wall along a vertical line, demonstrating the rationality of the project. The platform protected the southern access to the city and, in turn, was protected by the São Tomé bulwark

---

252 RAZÃO DO ESTADO DO BRASIL [Reason for the State of Brazil], Códice 126 da Biblioteca Pública Municipal do Porto.

above, which had to project further out than the station in order to protect its southern side. The plots of land that lay between the Ladeira da Conceição and the ocean probably part of an easement for the bulwark, since any building in that area would have impeded the vista from the Santa Cruz station.

If we use a protractor, compass, and square, we can complete our exercise. The two front curtains of the bulwark lay at a right angle, as the map suggests. The third major face of the São Tomé bulwark, the lateral side, was aligned with the street, having a curtain that measured 20 fathoms (44 meters). Although the 90° angle and the measurement of the third side may be speculative, they represent standards that are compatible with the techniques utilized in some other fortresses of the era (Table 17). The measurements indicated for the Fortress of Salvador were, to a certain extent, also used in Mazagan (1542), Diu (1546), and Ormuz (1558).

Table 17 - Data on Fortresses of Mazagan, Diu, Salvador, and Ormuz

Fortress	Angle of Bulwarks	Bulwarks Curtains (in Fathoms)	Wall Curtains (in Fathoms)	Number of Bulwarks
Mazagan (1542)	60°, 62°, 62°, 60°	22 (16), 22, 22, 22	105, 118, 75, 103	4
Diu (1546)	91°, 89°, 90°	11, 14, 17	31, 54	3
Salvador (1549)	90°, 89°, 90°, 90°	20 (7.5), 20 (10), 20, 20	18, 50, 50	4
Ormuz (1558)	80°, 78°, 75°, 74°	12, 12, 21, 20	53, 34, 56, 70	4

Source: *Códice da Casa de Cadaval* (M-7, nº 26). ANTT. Farinha, Antonio Dias. "Plantas de Mazagão e Larache no início do Século XVII" [City plans of Mazagan and Larache at the beginning of the 17th century]. In: *A Abertura do Mundo* [...] [Opening the World], pp. 159-161, fig. 12; ROSSA, Walter. *Cidades Indo-Portuguesas* [Indo-Portuguese Cities], pp. 56-73; MOREIRA, Rafael. "A *época manuelina"* [*The Manueline era*]. In: *História das Fortificações Portuguesas [...]* [*History of Portuguese Fortifications*], p. 114.

It is worth noting the use of acute and right angles, the former being a characteristic of rectangular fortresses. The use of angles having less than sixty degrees was not recommended for such construction. Right angles were superior to obtuse ones, since they served to disperse projectiles more effectively. In the Fortress of Salvador, right angles were used for two reasons: the distance between bulwarks was not large, as we can see, for example, on the southern side; and shots fired from the fortress had to aim at the surrounding area in front, not to the sides. In case of attack, the targets would have been the Alto de São Bento and, on the opposite side, the Largo do Pelourinho; in neither of these would it have been possible to get a good aim from bulwarks having corners that formed acute angles in the front. Protection of the curtain would have suffered if the corners did not form right angles.

The Fortress of Diu is the most similar to that of Salvador, with a vast surrounding area located precisely in front of the bulwark corners. The wider the angles, the better the aim. Due to the characteristics of the site of the Fortress of Salvador, the São Tomé and São Tiago bulwarks had right angles. Having analyzed the first of these two bulwarks, let us turn to considering some features of the second.

The southern side of the fortress was the most vulnerable and hence was protected by two bulwarks. On the side opposite the São Tomé bulwark was that of São Tiago, both rising from the wall that ran between the inner part of the juncture of Rua do Tesouro and Rua Chile. The crest of the hill at that spot is narrow, a characteristic that the structures exploited. The outline of the São Tiago bulwark coincides with the block that lies between Rua do Tesouro and Rua Rui Barbosa. The design is obvious in the historical map in the book *Reason for the State of Brazil*: a block in the shape of a square, having a right angle and being set back in relation to the São Tomé station to avoid impeding its line of fire.

Since the site was narrow, the São Tiago bulwark was left with half a normal curtain, measuring only ten fathoms. Between the two bulwarks, a small open space was formed, which nowadays is located at the point where the Rua do Tesouro and Rua Chile come together, and which originated in the early bulwarks. Because the São Tiago bulwark formed a rectangular block, similar to the Anjo bulwark at the Fortress of Mazagan, a street ran along its lower side, which must have serviced the wall and offered a less steep means of access to the fortress's southern gate. This was the origin of the Rua Rui Barbosa. It is worth emphasizing that either streets are planned or they emerge from some practical activity. Along this wall, a service path arose that played a role in the formation of smaller blocks between Rua do Tesouro and Rua Rui Barbosa; the restricted dimensions in this area are obvious, clashing with the rest of the urban layout up to Pelourinho.

It was very common that curtains measured twenty fathoms between bulwarks. Although data from other fortresses are not exact, since they were taken from city plans of varied sources lacking complete rigor, they nonetheless indicate shared standards approximating this measurement—the figure that is the most consistent and most closely matching the measurements in the Fortress of Salvador. The modular unit was 24 fathoms, and the difference between the curtain and the standard measurement probably corresponded to the collar and casement of the bulwark, and the width of the wall. This figure, derived from the measurements of the São Tomé station, is geometrically consistent and correlates with the usual standard found in other Portuguese fortresses of the era.

The third and fourth bulwarks in the upper city, situated in the parcels occupied by the Basilica Cathedral and the Terreiro de Jesus, looked out over the surrounding area that extended to the Largo do Pelourinho, using its weapons to safeguard the wide expanse of the plateau. Between the two was the Santa Catarina gate.

The third one, the São Jorge station, protected the coast and access to the beach; its shots crossed those fired from the opposite bulwark at a 90° angle. Given the site it occupied, it must have been a half-bulwark, which justified its usual designation as a station. Its corner formed a 90° angle and the curtain on the eastern side measured 20 fathoms.

For the fourth bulwark, the name of which has not been preserved in any reference document, we can only reconstruct its dimensions by studying the urban site, techniques of fortification, and the geometric standards utilized in the Fortress of Salvador. Since the corners of bulwarks always had to project out toward the probable source of attack, we can eliminate the northeastern extremity of the fortress. If the bulwarks were located on the extremities, the distance between them would have been excessive (a little more than 100 fathoms, or 222 meters), compromising their mutual protection. It now remains to examine the site.

Along the sidewalk that goes from the corner of the Praça da Sé to the Church of São Francisco, there is a point where two straight lines cross and form a vertex—an obtuse angle that is incompatible with any military standard, since it would be impossible to view one side from the other. This strange vertex, situated in the middle of the Terreiro de Jesus, dates back to before 1600 and appears to have no plausible reason.

In the context of the geometry of the fortress, the only function of an angle was military: a long straight line was not advisable. The vertex lay in the middle of the north face, a fine example of the guiding symmetry. The bulwark arose precisely at this angle and protected the two curtains to the right and the left. In this position, both walls were of equal length, each having approximately 50 fathoms of curtain between the bulwarks—a measurement very similar to those seen in the fortresses of Diu and Ormuz. We may deduce that the fourth bulwark was designed with a 90° angle and a curtain length of 20 fathoms—such data being the result of geometric deduction based on the general patterns revealed.

Another technical detail is noteworthy: the curtain that projected out toward the Church of São Francisco emerged from the vertex of the fourth bulwark, having an outer angle greater than 180°. This prolonged the time that invaders were exposed to fire from the bulwark—a military detail used to expand the sweep over the probable area of attack. In 1545, Dom João de Castro recommended the use of this technique in the Fortress of Mozambique.[253]

---

253 Letter from Dom João de Castro to King Dom João III, written on the island of Mozambique, dated 1545. In: SANCEAU, Elaine. *Cartas de D. João de Castro* [Letters of Dom João de Castro], p. 99. The letter contained the following passage: "For the

The Fortress of Salvador

Having completed our examination of the bulwarks constructed on the upper level of the city, let us turn to the defense structures located on the beach: the Santa Cruz station and the Góes bulwark. These two fortifications sheltered a relatively complete set of artillery pieces for the primary purpose of protecting the harbor from an invasion by sea—a type of coastal defense that was usually served by long-range artillery intended for naval combat.

At the Góes bulwark were located two "larger types of esperas," two camels, two falcons, and a dozen versos. Esperas were long pieces (3.4 to 3.8 meters) weighing between 1,200 and 1,900 kilos. They shot iron balls, each weighing 4.59 kg, that could attain a maximum range (at 45°) of about 4,000 meters. "Espera" was the term typically used in Portugal, but its measurements apparently corresponded to a demi-culverin, which was a long, heavy piece using lightweight balls and having a long range, suitable for combat against ships. Camels were cannons that weighed about 822 kg and used stone balls weighing 6.43 kg. Their range was shorter than esperas, but the impact of their balls was greater, since they were larger and heavier. Falcons and versos served as support weapons, especially at close range to invaders, and were used during intervals when other pieces were being loaded. The smaller station called Santa Cruz was armed with one espera, two falcons, and half a dozen versos.

The spatial distribution of these pieces was probably as follows: the larger pieces (six in the Góes bulwark, three in the Santa Cruz station) were placed in the lower part of the structures, 2.2 meters above sea level, while the other pieces were on a higher platform, 2.5 to 4 meters above, which also served as protection from the sun and rain for the artillery below.[254] The physical space necessary for

---

curtain of this wall, I would make it somewhat curved in order to make it more difficult for the enemy to reach it as they could be wounded head-on or from the flanks; also so that the artillery does not fire straight ahead [...]."

254 These technical specifications are compatible with the standards recommended by Cristóbal de Rojas for platforms built for combat against ships. Source: ROJAS, Cristóbal de. "Sumario de la Milicia Antigua y Moderna" [Overview of Ancient and Modern Militias]. In: *Tres Tratados sobre Fortificacion y Milicia* [Three Treatises on Fortification and Militias], p. 351.

shelter was about 2-2.5 fathoms per piece; although the space could be square, circular, or polygonal, square platforms were better at accommodating the pieces. We might hypothesize that the São Tomé station measured 10 fathoms in front, and the Góes bulwark, 15-20 fathoms.

An intriguing fact emerges in relation to the casements. In 1550, a rumor arose among the Tupinamba Indians living near the Fortress of Salvador, to the effect that the Portuguese had built bulwarks to lock them up and a well in which to drown them. Although this was unfounded, the Indians' fears are suggestive of how the bulwarks must have appeared to be prisons or dungeons. The cannons and firearms must have added to the Tupinamba's suspicions, indicating that some bulwarks probably had two stories, the first one being a closed space. The observation in the Jesuit's text is perfectly congruent with the technical conceptions of the era.

In 1586, Gabriel Soares de Souza described the São Tomé bulwark at the end of Rua Chile. The plot of land was donated and houses were built on it, until incursions by English and Dutch pirates made it necessary for Governor Francisco de Souza to rebuild the city gates, walls, and bulwarks. On the southern border of the plot, formerly the corner of the São Tomé bulwark, new polygonal structures were constructed. This line of defense went down the hillside, making it less effective, since it was exposed to shots that might come from the Alto de São Bento. When this new cycle began, little was remembered about the walls and bulwarks of the Fortress of Salvador, but the vestiges of their influence on the evolution of the urban design survive to this day.

22. From Bombards to Culverins

Because of the extremely powerful cannon called the bombard, all the older machines can now be considered useless and superfluous.

Francesco Di Giorgio Martini

In 1490, Francesco di Giorgio Martini wrote about cannons, newly invented, which he designated generically as "bombards," "a diabolical invention and work beyond the human."[255] Martini was one of the first to outline a classification of artillery pieces (Fig. 40). In the late sixteenth century, the Spanish systematized their use, classifying them into two groups, culverins and cannons:

(1) culverins (a name derived from *colubrino*, an adjective meaning "serpentine," in an allusion to the long shape of the pieces) did not have high caliber, in order to avoid making them too heavy; they were a type of field artillery intended for attacking enemies on the move;

(2) cannons were shorter pieces with higher caliber, intended for destroying or defending fortifications.

---

255 MARTINI, Francesco di Giorgio, *Trattati Di Architettura Ingegneria e Arte Militare* [Treatise on Architecture, Engineering, and Military Arts]. II, p. 418.

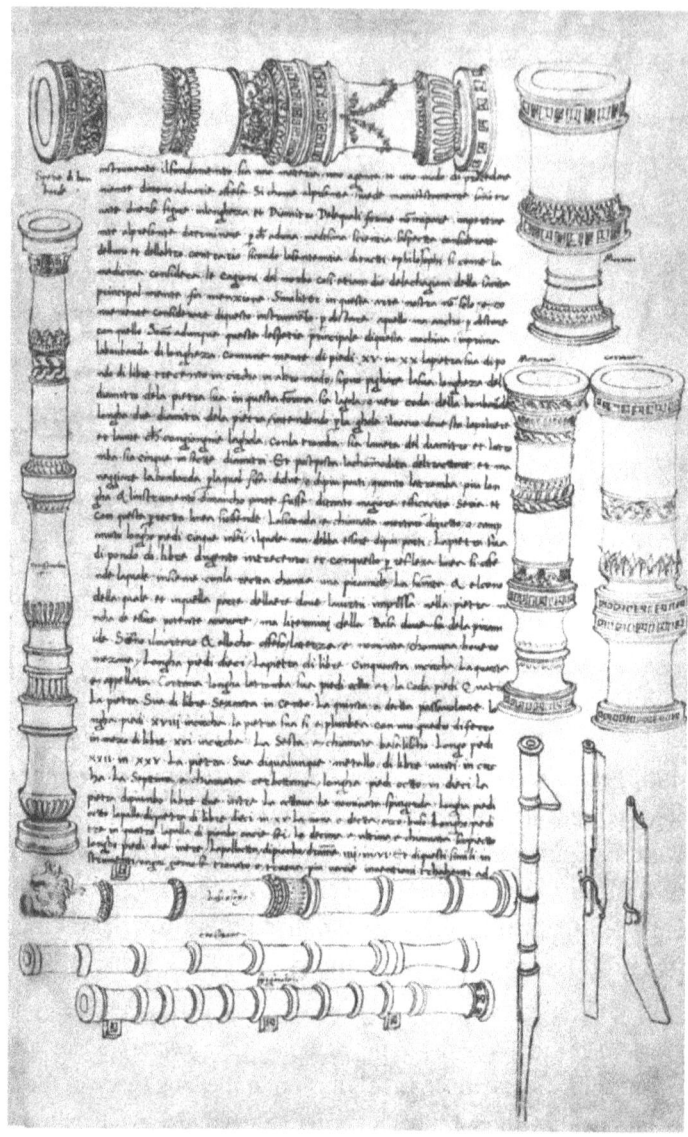

Figure 40 - Illustrations by Martini representing various types of "bombards" used in the late fifteenth century.
Source: MARTINI, Francesco di Giorgio, Trattati Di Architettura Ingegneria e Arte Militare [Treatise on Architecture, Engineering, and Military Arts], II, folha 48, tábua 241.[256]

---

[256] Author's note: The illustrations contain some text: *spetie de bonbarde* (types of

The Fortress of Salvador

In 1609, a uniform standard emerged in Spain, which also prevailed on the coast of Brazil. In *The First Book of the Government of Brazil* is an entry dated 1607 that deals with "the quality and type of artillery in the latest production [...]."[257] It shows clearly the classification presented below, organized according to the two main groups (Table 18).

A comparison of culverins and cannons allows us to understand the differences between the pieces. The double culverin, nicknamed dragon, was long (5.87 meters), heavy (5,508 kg), and had a long range: it shot cannon balls weighing 18.36 kg to a distance of 5,508 meters. The double cannon, affectionately called a "rouser," was shorter (4.13 meters), slightly heavier (5,894 kg), and launched extremely heavy cannon balls (44.06 kg) a distance of 4,502.3 meters. For great distances, especially at sea, the lighter, more direct cannon ball of the culverin was recommended. For shorter distances and fixed targets, the cannon was the most suited.

Cristóbal Lechuga, when faced with the choice between culverins and cannons, stated that he preferred the latter, unless he had to fire against ships from the beach. In this case, he recommended the culverin, since it had a straight shot; for other situations, however, he criticized this type of weapon because it consumed a great deal of powder and recoiled little, due to its heavier weight in relation to the ball, exposing the artillery to enemy fire. In Lechuga's experience, demi- and quarter-cannons were lighter in weight, easy to move from one side to another, and were accurate in hitting fixed targets.[258]

Around 1612, the city of Salvador had four culverins (three true culverins and one demi-culverin), all installed in the upper city: three in the São Diogo station, situated slightly below Misericórdia, and one in the station in the back of the Jesuits' Church, now the Sé Cathedral.[259]

---

bombards): *mortaio; passavolante; mezana; cortana; basalischo; cerbottana; spingarda.*
257 In: LIVRO PRIMEIRO do Governo do Brasil [First Book of the Government of Brazil], p. 28.
258 LECHUGA, Cristóbal. *Tratado de la Artillería [...]* [Treatise on Artillery], p. 423.
259 MORENO, Diogo de Campos. *Livro que dá Razão do Estado do Brasil* [Book Presenting the Reason for the State of Brazil], pp. 144-145.

Table 18 - Classification of Artillery According to Spanish Standards, 1607

Type	Name	Greatest Distance	Weight (kg)	Caliber (cm)	Length (meters)	Cannon Ball Weight (kg)
Culverins	Dragon or double culverin	5,951	5,508	18.92	5.87	18.36
	True culverin	5,236	—	14.66	4.69	9.18
	Demi-culverin	3,940	1,909	11.55	3.81	4.59
	Ordinary saker or quarter-culverin	3,065	1,131	9.92	3.37	2.30
	Falconet (1/8)	2,433	593	6.91	2.42	1.15
	Ribauldequin	1,800	344	6.51	2.37	0.57
	Esmeril	1,373	—	5.95	2.20	0.286
	Post musket	1,056	107	4.43	1.71	0.143
	Arquebus	619	37	2.56	1.05	0.028
Cannons	Double cannon, rouser, or wall-smasher	4,502	5,895	24.14	4.13	44.06

Cannons	Common cannon, wall-beater, or battering cannon	4,376	3,305	19.56	3.52	18.36
	Demi-cannon or denter	3,718	1,968	15.4	2.93	11.02
	One-third cannon	3,556	1,330	13.20	2.64	6.89
	Quarter-cannon, persecutor, or mojane	3,285	1,239	11.00	2.64	5.51
	One-eighth cannon	2,640	962	8.96	2.42	2.75

Source: *LIVRO PRIMEIRO do Governo do Brasil [First Book of the Government of Brazil]*, pp. 28-33.

The placement and the large size of these pieces of artillery indicate that they were intended to serve as long-range weapons against enemy ships. Another document, dated 1644, noted that the culverins had been brought down the hillside and were stationed around Preguiça, where they were in an excellent position for firing against ships that approached the port.[260]

The classification of artillery pieces into cannons and culverins does not exhaust the issue. Other denominations or types of artillery pieces existed that were not included in the Spanish typology: stone cannons and cannons with detachable chambers.

The term "stone cannon" refers to a class of weapons, indicating artillery pieces that shot stone spheres. The manuscript *Reason for*

---

260 Source: ROJAS, Cristóbal de. "Sumario de la Milicia Antigua y Moderna" [Overview of Ancient and Modern Militias]. In: *Tres Tratados sobre Fortificacion* [Three Treatises on Fortification], p. 337.

the State of Brazil, written in 1616 by Sergeant-Major Diogo de Campos Moreno, detailed the typology of stone cannons, clearly indicating that it was a class term used to designate various types of cannons that shot balls made of stone instead of iron. In 1609, there were three stone cannons in the city of Salvador: the savage stone cannon, the camel stone cannon, and the falcon stone cannon. They weighed 1760 kg, 822 kg, and 411 kg, respectively. The first two shot stone balls that weighed 8.26 kg and 6.43 kilograms.[261]

The falcon, verso, and demi-verso, pieces used on the coast of Brazil during the administration of the Governorate General, belonged to a little-known category: cannons with detachable chambers, a movable breech that allowed the piece to be reloaded with greater speed and safety. The process did not involve the mouth of the cannon. Each piece had an average of three chambers that were placed in a sort of basin at the rear of the cannon and which were removed after firing to be filled. The verso, a term borrowed from the Spanish for a swiveling cannon, was given a homonym in Portuguese, *berço*, apparently alluding to the resemblance of the piece to a cradle.

The sizes of the pieces with a chamber were small in comparison to other types; they were often used on board ships, as well as being employed in the defense of plantations and fortresses. Because they could be fired quickly and repeatedly, and because of their light weight and low cost, the falcon, verso, and demi-verso became the most representative types of artillery on the coast of Brazil, at least during the period from 1549 to 1553. Available studies do not suggest that chambered pieces were distinct from other kinds. They were considered lightweight pieces, but, due to their prominence on the coast of Brazil during the early years of the Governorate General, they should be treated as a separate category.

The falcon was three times heavier than the verso. Together, the falcon and verso, which nowadays are practically unknown, were hailed by some authors as the source of many Portuguese military victories in the first half of the sixteenth century. The term "falcon," when designating artillery pieces, followed a tradition of naming fire-

---

[261] MORENO, Diogo de Campos. *Livro que dá Razão do Estado do Brasil* [Book Presenting the Reason for the State of Brazil], pp. 144-145.

arms after birds of prey, representing speed and danger. Other pieces were named in a similar fashion: merlin, gyrfalcon, saker, and diver.

The smaller firearms employed in the sixteenth century were muskets, arquebuses, and rifles. The best description available that differentiates these pieces can be found in an old manuscript that sought to rethink the use of light firearms in Portuguese fortresses along the coast of India.[262] The musket was the most important one, as well as the most often recommended, due to the long range of its firepower. The author of the manuscript considered the musket to be the best protection against enemy rifles, as well as being a new and unknown firearm in that region. Its barrel should be 1.32 meters long, he said, using balls weighing two Portuguese ounces (57.2 grams). The arquebus, which he also recommended, should be 1.1 meters long and use balls weighing one ounce, that is, half the weight of the musket's ammunition.[263]

According to his manuscript, the rifle served only for "birding" and not for going to war. The arquebus could be loaded three times faster than the rifle.[264] During the Governorate General, the arquebus and rifle were the most commonly used, while any reference to the musket was unknown.

Turning to Martini, his classification is composed of ten different types of "bombards," which can be grouped into two kinds: a) pieces that shot stones (bombard, mortar, quarter-cannon, demi-culverin, and rifle); b) pieces that used iron balls, shot, or a combination of both (basilisk, passe-volante, cerbotana, arquebus, and musket). Over a century and a half, we can observe great technological evolution in each group, revealing intriguing aspects.

Stone is lighter in weight than iron or shot and, as such, was of smaller caliber, which required artillery pieces that were proportionately shorter; the shorter the piece, the shorter the range. The mortar was short and used for curving shots. As for rifles, it is interesting to note that, in the Italian case, these used stones as balls and had the smallest caliber among all the firearms that used this type of projec-

---

262 MEMÓRIAS de Um Soldado da Índia [Memories of a Soldier in India].
263 Idem, p. 222.
264 Ibidem, p. 223.

tile. In comparison with the cerbotana, which used shot, the rifle had a greater caliber and was shorter in length.

Pieces in the second group were longer and had a greater range. The greater density of shot and iron balls facilitated smaller calibers in comparison with the proportional shape of arms with mouths that shot stones, a detail that favored the use of iron balls and shot, replacing those of stone.

Like Martini, writers in Portugal often used the word "bombard" as a class term. Its meaning was never precise, but it usually corresponded to a piece with large dimensions that shot stone balls. On the Iberian Peninsula, this type of piece was also called a "stone cannon" and, for this reason, Cristóbal de Rojas, in the late sixteenth century, classified artillery into three types: large, medium, and small. In addition to culverins and cannons, he included stone cannons, which had a shorter range and were used less at a horizontal level[265]—this being the reason why the use of stone for projectiles was gradually abandoned.

The technological evolution of cannons went from stone to iron, and from iron to copper. Stone cannons were utilized during the sixteenth century, but they gradually lost their function. Economic factors suggest that, in response to growing demand, there was an increase in the production of iron and copper; little by little, the greater effectiveness of iron balls and copper artillery led to changes, with iron substituting stone as a projectile and copper supplanting iron as the raw material in the artillery piece.

The change is even more evident when we analyze the issue from the perspective of terminology: names of pieces that shot stone balls dropped out of use. In weapons classifications at the end of the sixteenth century, we no longer find the words "bombard" or "quarter-cannon." "Mortar" survived as a concept, a short piece with a curved shot. It adapted to the changes, as did the rifle. Pieces using iron balls survived: the basilisk, passe-volante, cerbotana, arquebus, and shotgun, names that can be found in the classification of artillery before King Felipe III's reforms (Table 19).

---

265 Source: ROJAS, Cristóbal de. "Sumario de la Milicia Antigua y Moderna" [Overview of Ancient and Modern Militias]. In: *Tres Tratados sobre Fortificacion* [Three Treatises on Fortification], p. 337.

Table 19 - Classification of Martini's "Types of Bombards"[266]

Name of Piece in Italian	Length (in Meters)		"Pondo Di Libre"		Type of Projectile
	Minimum	Maximum	Minimum	Maximum	
Bombarda	4.44	5.92	—	300.00	stone ball
Mortaro	1.48	1.78	200.00	300.00	stone ball
Cortana	—	3.56	60.00	100.00	stone ball
Mezzana	—	2.96	—	50.00	stone ball
Basilisco	6.5	7.40	—	20.00	balls made of any metal
Passavolante	—	5.33	—	16.00	lead shot
Spingarda	—	2.37	10.00	15.00	stone ball
Cerbottana	2.37	2.96	2.00	3.00	lead shot
Arco buso	0.89	1.18	—	0.50	lead shot
Scoppietto	0.59	0.89	0.25	0.38	lead shot

Source: MARTINI, Francesco di Giorgio, *Trattati Di Architettura Ingegneria e Arte Militare [Treatise on Architecture, Engineering, and Military Arts]*. II, pp. 418-420.

These general considerations give us a better understanding of the various types of firearms utilized when the Fortress of Salvador was constructed. Cannons and gunpowder were the tools of territorial conquest; they were brandished and wielded against indigenous peoples, easily subjugating them. While the Governorate General was being established, the procedures for storing and distributing weapons were well organized, illustrating how the system worked on the coast of Brazil. This will be explored in the next chapter.

---

266 Author's note: 1) The measurements were given in feet, which have been converted to meters (1 foot = 0.286 meter); 2) The expression *"Pondo di libre"* apparently indicates the caliber of the piece.

23. Artillery in the Fortress

> *And I say that this Storehouse has artillery munitions of every kind, which supplies all sites in India, Guinea, Mina, and in parts of Africa, and all the armadas that sail from this city to any place where they are sent, and everything else related to the armory.*
>
> João Brandão (1552)[267]

Statistics for Lisbon in 1552 described with great pride the royal Artillery Foundry, the Powder Factory, and the Weapons Storehouse.[268] Each year, the artillery foundries produced an average of 1,500 to 2,000 pieces, both large and small. The production of powder destined for cannons (bombards) amounted to 30 to 35 tons, which did not include gunpowder for rifles, which added 8.8 tons. The Storehouse had three rooms full of piercing weapons, which could arm 46,000 troops and 600 horses. In addition, there were 1,000 steel breastplates made for servants and officials who would serve the King in other places, and a stock of rifles and arquebuses that totaled 10,000 pieces. This array of military

---

267 BRANDÃO (DE BUARCOS) João. *Grandeza e Abastança de Lisboa em 1552* [Grandeur and Affluence in Lisbon in 1552], p. 173.
268 Idem, pp. 165-173.

weaponry controlled by the Crown provided powder, cannons, arquebuses, rifles, and piercing weapons that served to affirm the Portuguese hegemony on the coast of Brazil.

Governor Tomé de Souza brought a relatively uniform set of armaments, composed of weapons destined not only for the defense of the Fortress of Salvador, but as a standardized system of arms that was mandatory for all captaincies and plantations. Each was required to have a minimum arsenal of armaments, as follows: artillery, supplementary equipment for artillery, ammunition, powder, as well as a collection of piercing weapons and light firearms totaling 448 and 148 items, respectively.

The cost was not insignificant. We can do a simple calculation: the lowest wage paid during this era was 333.33 réis; converting this rate into today's minimum wage, the investments in armaments in the captaincies and plantations were equivalent to R$113,237.48 and R$35,955.07, respectively (Table 20). The sum of the total amounts spent on the coast of Brazil can be calculated by multiplying the number of captaincies and plantations. In practice, Governor Tomé de Souza ordered a certain quota to be delivered to meet urgent needs, then collected payments from treasurers in each captaincy.

The Supplies and Provisions Storehouse in the Fortress of Salvador functioned as a distribution center for the Lisbon headquarters. It followed a set price list, fixed according to some cost calculation that was not explicit. For example, the assessed valuation of gunpowder in Lisbon was 6,000 réis for one quintal. In the Fortress of Salvador, this price was differentiated: while it cost 4,840 réis to purchase gunpowder for use in cannons, the same amount of powder for a rifle cost 8,460 réis. Artillery pieces were assessed on the basis of prices by weight,[269] while other arms were sold by the unit. Sometimes people received part of their salary in swords, artillery pieces, or other items (Table 21).

---

269 The usual unit of weight was the quintal (58.75 kg), which equaled four arrobas.

Table 20 - Items for Defense Required in Captaincies and Plantations

Weapon	Captaincies		Plantations	
	Quantity	Value	Quantity	Value
I: Artillery	14	119,578.29	4	32,026.51
Stone cannon (795 kg)	—	—	—	—
Falcon (250 kg)	2	47,376.49	—	—
Verso (84.5 kg)	6	48,039.76	4	32,026.51
Metal demi-verso (42.5 kg)	6	24,162.01	—	—
II: Supplementary Equipment	70	34,569.00	20	9,068.00
Carriage, ladle, and rammer for stone cannon	—	—	—	—
Cascabel and knob of falcon	2	2,436.00	—	—
Vent pick for falcon	2	476.00	—	—
Chamber for falcon	6	11,034.00	—	—
Carriage for falcon	—	—	—	—
Cascabel and knob of verso	6	2,736.00	4	1,824.00
Vent pick for verso	6	444.00	4	296.00
Chamber for verso	18	10,422.00	12	6,948.00
Cascabel and knob	6	1,824.00	—	—
Vent pick for demi-verso	6	222.00	—	—
Chamber for demi-verso	18	4,975.00	—	—
III: Ammunition	280	2,040.00	80	640.00
Cannon ball for stone cannon	—	—	—	—
Cannon ball for falcon (7.5 kg)	40	600.00	—	—
Cannon ball for verso (1.5 kg)	120	960.00	80	640.00
Cannon ball for demi-verso (.75 kg)	120	480.00	—	—

IV: Gunpowder and Shot	4	4,890.00	4	4,890.00
Shot (in arrobas)	—	—	—	—
Gunpowder for rifles (in arrobas)	—	—	—	—
Gunpowder (in arrobas)	4	4,890.00	4	—
Iron bullets (in arrobas)	—	—	—	4,890.00
V: Piercing Weapons	60	13,800.00	30	6,900.00
Lance	20	1,800.00	10	900.00
Pike	—	—	—	—
Swords with scabbard	40	12,000.00	20	6,000.00
VI: Firearms	20	13,850.00	10	6,400.00
Arquebus	10	7,450.00	—	—
Rifle	10	6,400.00	10	6,400.00
Total	448	188,727.26	148	59,924.51

Note: 1 Portuguese arroba = 14.688 kg.
Source: The author.

  In the realm of arms, artillery was the most expensive and important item. The standard set consisted of a camel stone cannon, also known for short as a stone cannon; a falcon; a verso; and a demi-verso—basic pieces that were distributed among villages and plantations. Each piece had its own distinct size and purpose.

  The nomenclature for artillery pieces was extremely varied. In 1525, someone in Goa collected 45 names for artillery weapons. Despite this apparent profusion of names, we can see that, on the coast of Brazil during the administration of Tomé de Souza, there was a certain logical system to the names, materials (iron or copper), weights, and standard uses for the various pieces.

Table 21 - Prices for Weapons and Supplements

Weapon	Price (in Réis)	Minimum Price (in Salt)
Price of falcon per quintal (100 lbs.)	5,570.00	16.71
Price of stone cannon, verso, demi-verso per quintal	5,562.00	16.69
Price per quintal for falcon chamber, cascabel, and knob	1,635.00	4.91
Cannon ball for falcon	15.00	0.05
Cannon ball for stone cannon	11.33	0.03
Cannon ball for verso	8.00	0.02
Cannon ball for demi-verso	4.00	0.01
Quintal of gunpowder for bombard	4,840.00	14.52
Quintal of gunpowder for rifle	8,460.00	25.38
Arquebus, fully equipped	745.00	2.24
Rifle	645.00	1.94
Sword with scabbard	300.00	0.90
Pike	100.00	0.30
Lance	90.00	0.27
Value of contemporary minimum salary	333.33	1.00

Source: DOCUMENTOS HISTÓRICOS [Historical Documents], v. XII-XIII, Bibliotheca Nacional.

In 1546, during the second siege of Diu, Dom João de Castro recommended to Captain João de Mascarenhas that he defend the fortress using "heavy" artillery, citing the lion, serpent, and espera. With the help of such pieces, the captain could impede the enemy from drawing near to the fortress batteries.[270] During another episode in the siege of Diu, the São Tomé bulwark was demolished by the combined firepower of two basilisks, two camels, and three esperas.

In these examples, it is clear that esperas were utilized as of-

---

270 SANCEAU, Elaine. *Cartas de D. João de Castro* [Letters of Dom João de Castro], pp. 133-135.

fensive and defensive weapons in fortresses. In subsequent technical classifications dating from the beginning of the seventeenth century, this role was reserved for cannons. The espera—due to the combined features of weight, length, and caliber, according to later classifications—must have corresponded to the quarter-cannon or, perhaps more likely, the demi-culverin. The purpose of the espera in the fortress bulwarks was to fire at ships.

The second type of bombard listed in documents related to the administration of Tomé de Souza was the stone cannon, also known as a camel, a type of weapon with a specific caliber and length. Comparing the weight of stone cannons recorded in documents from Tomé de Souza's administration with the data presented by Diogo de Campos Moreno,[271] we may conclude that the weight of the camel stone cannon was more or less 800 kilos and fired stone balls weighing 14 pounds. In comparison to the espera, the camel stone cannon was lighter in weight and fired stone balls, which meant that the length of the piece was shorter, it used less material for the barrel, and it had a higher caliber.

The falcon, verso, and demi-verso on the coast of Brazil became legal standards (Fig. 41). All captaincies had to have two falcons, six versos, and six demi-versos, as well as three detachable chambers for each one. Plantations were exempted from having a falcon, but they had to have four versos available. These pieces, made of bronze and forged in Portuguese workshops, were loaded through the breech, which protected the gunners. Their use became indispensable on warships and caravels. Such pieces could be placed anywhere on a ship, which ensured that they could be fired independently of the ship's maneuvers. On a trip in 1550, the Jesuit Leonardo Nunes witnessed a skirmish near São Vicente with some Tupiniquin Indians, who confused the Portuguese with the French, during which one of the artillery chambers fell into the ocean.

The use of this type of artillery reveals certain aspects of military defense on the coast of Brazil during this period. During a period when the greatest threat to the Portuguese came from indigenous peoples, the use of lightweight pieces that could be reloaded quickly

---

271 MORENO, Diogo de Campos. *Livro que dá Razão do Estado do Brasil* [Book Presenting the Reason for the State of Brazil], pp. 144-145.

and docked anywhere, without exposing the gunner to arrows, was sufficient to meet their needs. Added to these factors was the range the artillery shots could reach. Battles at sea occurred between a large number of canoes and a caravel of two or three masts, or else from the edge of a town or fortress. In such battles, the Portuguese continued the tradition of using the same type of weapon employed since the beginning of the great voyages of discovery.

Figure 41 - Portuguese verso. Artillery piece widely used on the coast of Brazil in the mid-sixteenth century.
Source: Museu Militar de Lisboa.

In the bulwarks of Góes and Santa Cruz, heavy artillery was complemented by the rapid fire of the falcons and versos, such that the areas in front or on the flanks never lacked protection from firepower. This logic was illustrated by Dom João de Castro in his recommendations to the captain of the Fortress of Diu during the 1546 siege. In his opinion, bulwarks should be provided with "stone cannons and camels" to protect the lateral sides (*través*).[272] If there were

---

[272] SANCEAU, Elaine. *Cartas de D. João de Castro* [Letters of Dom João de Castro], pp. 134-135.

no more space on the side of the bulwark for another of these pieces, it would be necessary to "always have a falcon" so that, while one piece was being reloaded, another could be fired against invaders, keeping the walls protected at all times.

A few decades later, the system of artillery underwent a radical change as a result of the disappearance of the indigenous threat, the rise of pirate attacks, successive conflicts with the French and Dutch, and the technological development of artillery. In this new phase, the solution became long-range pieces with greater firepower that were permanently installed in fortresses or ships. Thus, when Diogo de Campos Moreno referred to "four bronze-covered falcons" he found in the fortress of the town of Ilhéus, he described them as "something antiquated" that should be sent back to the foundry in Pernambuco.[273] The falcons and versos of the Manueline era were considered a "lightweight invention" that provided less security for fortresses.

---

273 MORENO, Diogo de Campos. *Livro que dá Razão do Estado do Brasil* [Book Presenting the Reason for the State of Brazil], p. 135.

24. The Four Corners of the Fortress

Bless us, divine number, thou who generated gods and men! O holy, holy Tetractys, thou that containest the root and source of the eternally flowing creation! For the divine number begins with the profound, pure unity until it comes to the holy four; then it begets the mother of all, the all-comprising, all-bounding, the first-born, the never-swerving, the never-tiring holy ten, the key holder of all.

Pythagorean prayer

The Fortress of Salvador constituted a unified entity. On the upper level, it was divided into two opposite areas: north and south, on two plateaus—the former dedicated to religious and social services, the latter, to civic ones. Both were integrated with the third area of the fortress, the harbor, where the Customs House, Storehouse, Blacksmith Shops, and place for beaching boats were located. The three areas were connected in a circular, interactive relationship through the twin sloping access roads. Besides these areas, there was a fourth one around the bottom of the Ladeira da Praça, which had a well, gardens, garbage dump, and pastures. The urban network was divided into ten parallel blocks and six perpendicular to the coast; each area was assigned specific uses.

The fortress was originally conceived as a pentagon, but the terrain would not allow this. It was necessary to adapt the idea to the topography. Let us proceed to demonstrate this theory. The pentagonal model of Martini (Fig. 50) reinforces the idea of a vertex projecting forward into the surrounding area. The Fortress of Poggio Imperiale (1488-1511) in the Italian city of Poggibonsi formed a five-sided polygon with a typical anthropomorphic appearance (Figs. 42 and 43). It was designed by the architect Giulano da Sangallo, commissioned by Lorenzo de' Medici. Martini's model and the Fortress of Poggio may have inspired the design of the Fortress of Salvador. The result was a polygon with at least six unequal sides; it did not have right angles, but its lines were straight. It is tempting to try to imagine the design from the geometric perspective that inspired the planner. The vertices are found, in general, at the extreme points of the terrain that the fortress needed to dominate; in this respect, geometry and topography were combined through techniques of military engineering. Points, lines, and planes are tools of the trade in an architect's imagination.

Figure 42 - Fortress of Poggio Imperiale in Italy, showing anthropomorphic conception of the fortress (1488-1511).

If the Fortress of Salvador was a unified entity, it was also a whole that reconciles contraries, forming a synthesis out of many parts. In conceptualizing the fortress, the architect took the approach of dividing it up: he extended an imaginary line through the middle of the terrain and, intentionally or not, located the midpoint in the narrowest spot between the two plateaus, dividing the urban site in two and establishing the idea of opposition. Once two things are set up, they form opposites. The architect therefore had to identify the contrast in terms that would complement each other—the enduring notions of male and female, creator and created, sacred and profane. Given the basic rationality underlying the duality of the whole, the architect created a separation between two areas.

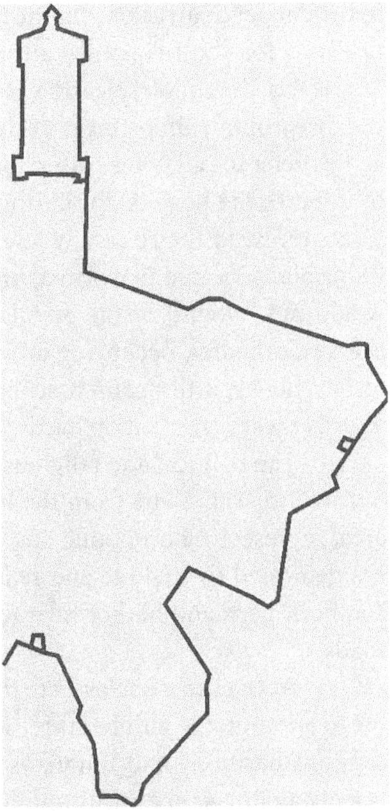

According to Vitruvius, the treasury, prison, and senate "ought to adjoin the forum, but in such a way that their dimensions may be proportionate to those of the forum."[274] The forum was the Romans' plaza, being the place where important authorities gathered.

Figure 43 - Design of the Fortress of Poggio Imperiale and the ramparts.

The plaza in the Fortress of Salvador brought together civil and military authorities. In precisely the spot where the two plateaus are connected, the plaza was established, with public buildings arranged according to the classical pattern: the governor's house, the citadel, the pillory, and the Municipal Council Building. The latter, situated on the eastern side, suggested the notion of internal jurisdiction: the council existed to take care of the body and, as such, was assigned to the center.

On the southern side, the smaller plateau was more exposed

---

274 POLLIO, Marcus Vitruvius. *Los Diez Libros de Architectura* [The Ten Books on Architecture], p. 112.

to the danger of invasion. On the northern side, the larger plateau was reserved for the religious, educational, and charitable institutions. There, too, the simple, pleasing notion of opposites was confirmed. In the foreground, almost next to the plaza, was the city hospital or, as some prefer to call it, the Misericórdia. In the Spanish model, inspired by Alberti, the hospital for curing noncontagious diseases should be located next to the church, while contagious ones should be treated in hospitals located in isolated, high places so that "harmful breezes" would not "wound"[275] the population. Beyond the city hospital was the Sé Cathedral, occupying a block and a half, and, next to it, the Jesuits' house, with a church, school, and residence. The northern side was also where the bishop lived.

The political and religious authorities could not survive without wealth. This came from the harbor, which gave rise to the third area, representing economic life, which complemented the other areas dedicated to civil life and religious life. The city's northern part, southern part, and harbor interacted by means of the sloping access roads.

At the three angles were the paths that led from one aspect of life to another; the number three is represented by the triangle, which suggests harmony and union, as in the trinity. The architect, when tracing an imaginary line through the middle of the fortress, reserved the beach for the Customs House and the Tax Collection House, with the Customs House located next to the port, at the vertex. In the middle of the area next to the ocean was the Royal Treasury, balanced by the Sé Cathedral in a second vertex, and the governor's house in the third, forming a triangle that was almost equilateral.

The division into three major areas was accompanied by a certain symmetry apparent in the headquarters of each of the three authorities—civil, religious, and economic—a feature that suggests the structure of thinking used in planning the fortress. The Customs House, being located near the middle and parallel to the edge of the

---

275 *RECOPILACION DE LEIS DOS REYNOS DE LAS ÍNDIAS* [Compilation of the Laws of the Kingdoms of the Indies]. Livro I, Título IV, Lei II. Law II dealt specifically with the ideal site for building hospitals, corresponding to Ordinance 122 issued by King Felipe II in 1573.

ocean, suggested protection and control in relation to each end of the port. Next to it was the Storehouse, where merchandise was securely stored. Their connection explains the reason why, in the future, a crane would be built there.

The number four stands for extension and totality, best represented by the idea of planes formed by the crossing of two lines: the cross and the square are excellent symbols for suggesting fullness and universality. There are four corners of the world, four cardinal points, four elements; so, too, there were four areas in the Fortress of Salvador. On the eastern side, the plateaus to the north and south slope down to the swamp, forming a large valley, where the architect built a large well for water. This constituted the fourth area, where nature, in the form of gardens, pastures, and a garbage dump, remained untouched for a long time.

The sum of 1, 2, 3, and 4 is 10—allowing the play of proportions—which, for many ancients, represented the perfect number. The Pythagorean *tetraktys*, or tetrad, symbolized totality and the return to unity after the completion of a cycle. Vitruvius, invoking ancestral thought, emphasized that, for some, ten was the perfect number, while, for others, six was given this honor. Accordingly, as mentioned earlier, the fortress was divided internally into ten blocks on the ocean side and six on the inland one.

The *tetraktys* was symbolized geometrically by a triangular figure made up of ten points. At the top, one point, the beginning; below it, two points, the first stage of development; then three points, the levels of human existence—physical, spiritual, and emotional; at the base, the earth and its four corners, elements, seasons, and cardinal points. The fortress of Salvador is unusual, therefore, in its ability to explain the distribution of its areas on the basis of Pythagorean geometry, making it an excellent exercise in metaphysical mathematics.

25. Symmetry and the Human Body

> *Symmetry is the appropriate correspondence among the units of a building and the harmony of each of its parts to the whole. Just as symmetry and proportion are found among the forearm, foot, palm, finger, and the other parts of the human body, the same applies to the construction of buildings.*
>
> Vitruvius

The construction of the city of the Fortress of Salvador combined symmetry and topography. The relief of the land determined the proportion of the various sections of the city, but the mathematical logic used in the project is visible. The city plan is related to standards based on the principle of symmetry developed by the Greeks and revived during the Renaissance. This is not surprising in light of the ancients' perception of proportion and its relationship to numbers—whether mystical or simply aesthetic, it was replete with logic and significance. The Fortress of Salvador was also inspired by the proportions of the human body. Through this perspective, it represents an excellent Renaissance model.

The ancients associated the number seven with various phenomena and formulated intriguing combinations. The entities of creation, for example, were divided into seven groups: those that have no body but only spirit, such as souls and angels; those that have simple bodies, which cannot be destroyed, such as the sky and stars; others with simple bodies that decay and are consumed, such as the elements—fire, air, earth, and water; the fourth, with bodies composed of "a soul that grows and has senses and reason, such as humans";[276] others composed of a soul that grows and has senses but no reason, which are animals; the sixth, trees and plants, endowed with "a soul that grows"[277] but without sensation or reason; and the seventh type, stones, without soul, sensation, or reason. In Aristotle's vision, the world's creations can be divided into seven: the soul, the firmament, elements, humans, animals, plants, and minerals.

Movement, inherent in all things, was also classified this way: up, down, forward, reverse, left, right, and around. The ancients were familiar with seven planets or stars: Saturn, Jupiter, Mars, the sun, Venus, Mercury, and the moon. Based on the seven heavens, they set up the seven days of the week. They also divided the world's climate and metals into seven groups, and made the same division among the arts and the ages of a human being.

In the Jewish and Christian religions, other intriguing indicators can be found: God directed Noah to put seven creatures of each kind in the Ark; Jacob served Laban for seven years and then another seven years, when he was given Rachel, the second daughter, as a wife; Joseph dreamed that, in the future, Egypt would have seven years of plenty and seven of scarcity; the candelabra of the Holy Temple had seven lamps; Jesus Christ had the seven gifts of the Holy Spirit; the Catholic Church has seven sacraments, all necessary for a person's salvation; and the Apocalypse of St. John counts things in sevens.

The number seven has an ancestral mystical nature, and other numbers with practical application in architecture reveal the metaphysical relationship of humans to mathematics. The notion of God as Reason arose from the abstraction of numbers; through them, the ancient Greeks created the logic of proportion and its effect on the symmetry of buildings. Imitation and observation of the human body led to the emergence of various units of measure: the digit, palm, foot,

---

276 *LEI DAS SETE PARTIDAS* [*Seven-Part Code*], Prólogo, Septenário.
277 Idem.

and cubit. The palm came from the hand, while the foot was derived from the lower limb.[278] The number ten was considered perfect, since hands have ten fingers and feet have ten toes; the number comprised the "unity of things" that the Greeks called *monads*.[279] The human body as a source of linear measurement was just the beginning: it was the origin of proportions guiding a great many classical buildings. For the Greeks, the body was the Creator's perfection, from which the ideal proportion was drawn. Vitruvius wrote, "No edifice can be well designed without symmetry and proportion, as in a well-shaped human body."[280]

Why was the human body considered the prime example of perfection with regards to symmetry? According to the classical conception, the various parts of the human body maintain a correlation with the whole, establishing perfect proportional measures and geometric shapes. Vitruvius wrote that the face is one tenth of the height of the body, as is the measurement of the palm of the hand (from the wrist to the tip of the finger). The head is one eighth of the body, while the distance from the chin to the beginning of the nose is one tenth of the face, and the foot is one sixth of the body's height. Similarly, many other parts maintain proportional relations. "On the geometric plane," wrote Vitruvius, "the navel is the center of the human body when someone with arms and legs extended, revolving in a compass, constructs a circle that touches the hands and feet. A square can be drawn from the opposition between the height and the extended arms."[281] This is the logic of the perfect proportions of the human body. The result is expressed in the famous "Vitruvian Man" of Leonardo da Vinci. If nature composed the human body in such a way that its parts reveal proportion and correspondence with

---

278 A palm (Portuguese *palma*) should not be confused with a span (Portuguese *palmo*): a palm is a linear measurement corresponding to four digits (7.33 cm), while a span represents the distance between the thumb and the small finger of an outstretched hand (22 cm). See Table 38 in the Table Appendix for correlations among the various measurements used in Renaissance Europe.
279 VITRUVIUS POLLIO, Marcus. *Los Diez Libros de Architectura* [The Ten Books of Architecture], p. 59.
280 Idem, p. 58.
281 Ibidem, p. 59.

the whole, Vitruvius asserted, then ancient architects attempted to imitate them, doing so "in all their works," mainly in temples of the gods and in columns. Such considerations demonstrate how the logic of these constructions functioned.

Although he expounded on and defended the notion of applying the proportions of the human body to temples, Vitruvius did not comment on applying the same rules to the planning of cities and fortresses. In the fifteenth century, especially after the work of Alberti, the relationship between city and body acquired a new, deeper dimension: "A building is a body and, like all bodies, consists of form and material."[282] For Alberti, just as the parts of an animal organism were adjusted in relation to each other, the parts of buildings were harmonized, such that larger buildings should have larger parts.

Alberti's vision was wide-reaching and abstract, with the body being that of any animal. Anthropomorphism as an architectural reference gained strength in the later works of Filarete and of Francesco de Giorgio Martini. Filarete praised the perfection of the human form and the proportions of its parts, repeating and exhaustively reviewing various standards, but Martini was the one who best theorized the relationship of the human body to cities and fortresses, creating a dogmatic model and graphically reproducing the ground plan of a fortress in the form of the body (Fig. 44). The theoretical models elaborated by Martini inevitably prompt comparisons with the layout of the Fortress of Salvador.

In the *Treatise on Architecture*, Martini offered a striking image of a man within a quadrilateral: the feet and elbows occupy the extremities of the geometric figure, where circular towers, which he called "turrets," are found; at the navel is a circle identified as the plaza; within the chest, precisely along the central axis, lies the temple and, on the head, the citadel, called a *bastion*; the door is located in the middle of the wall opposite the head.[283] The picture is a perfect fusion of the geometry associated with the maxim, "the city is a human body."

---

282 ALBERTI, Leon Battista. *L'Architettura* [Architecture]. Prólogo, p. 9.
283 MARTINI, Francesco di Giorgio, *Trattati Di Architettura, Ingegneria e Arte Militare* [Treatise on Architecture, Engineering, and Military Arts], I, folha 3, tábua I.

Two important ideas developed by Martini reveal parallels in the Fortress of Salvador. The first, briefly mentioned above, determined the location of buildings within the city according to certain parallels to the position of certain organs in the human body (for instance, if the temple lies at the heart, its position will be slightly above the middle of the body of the city). The second consisted of the proportional relationship among the parts of the human body. Martini opened the chapter on the city by stating, "Since the city has reason, I shall precisely describe the measure and form of the human body in its circumference and divisions."[284]

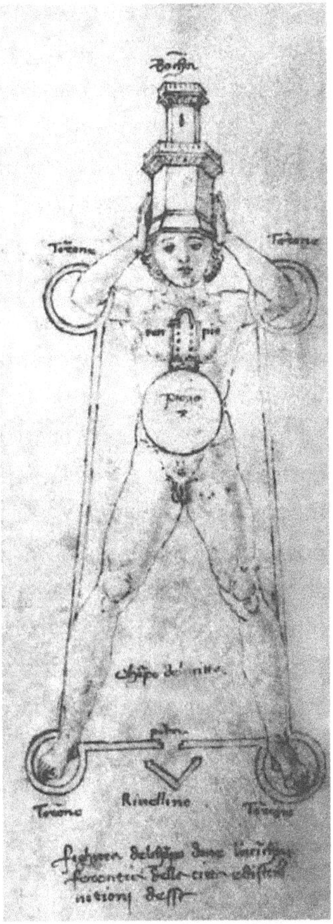

To plan a city, the architect should imagine a large human body lying down on the site and, from a central point on the navel, draw a circle using a string. For Martini, if the body had perfect measurements and proportion, the same should characterize the city. "Every time that some main part of the city or other buildings can be related to the measurement of some part of man, this part should have the same proportion to the city as in the relationship of the part to which it was compared,"[285] he asserted. He also offered some practical examples that integrated the two principles, which can be compared to the planning carried out in the Fortress of Salvador.

Figure 44 - The relationship of body and city, in the view of Francesco di Giorgio Martini. Source: MARTINI, Francesco di Giorgio, Trattati Di Architettura, Ingegneria e Arte Militare [Treatise on Architecture, Engineering, and Military Arts], I, folha 3, tábua I.

---

284 Idem. I, p. 20.
285 Ibidem. II, p. 362.

Martini associated, for example, the plaza to the "navel of the human body,"[286] recalling its origin in birth. However, the reason he gave for this comparison was the equal distance that should be preserved between the center and the periphery of the circumference, in which the main plaza should be placed in the middle of the city, following its format, whether round, square, or polygonal. If the site did not allow this, the architect should make adjustments. Martini made no reference to proportion in this text, but the pictures indicate a ratio of around 1:5; in other words, the plaza would occupy approximately 20% of the entire size of the city.

He said the city council chambers and the prison should be located in the plaza or as near to it as possible. He made a similar recommendation about the Lord's House, which, in the fortress would correspond to the governor's residence. The cathedral should be next to the plaza and opposite the Lord's House: Martini's picture shows it in the chest area, slightly above the navel. The streets should be straight and counterposed on the other side of the plaza, which cuts them in half, so that the parts appear as well-proportioned parts, "just as we see in the human body, where there is an equal correspondence between one part and another."[287] Parish churches could be located in the extremities, recalling feet and hands. A similar idea could be applied to the ramparts.

Martini valued the creative liberty of the architect, which indeed could not be otherwise. For him, each city had its own site and was planned according to specific objectives. Given the circumstances, the imagination of the architect should guide the vision of the human body at repose on the site, he suggested. The Bay of All Saints took full advantage of this liberty in creativity.

The main measurement in the Fortress of Salvador was its length along the coast: the distance from the northern edge of Praça da Sé to the top of the Praça Castro Alves was, at the time, approximately 528 meters (originally 240 *braças*, similar to fathoms). The northern edge could be extended toward Pelourinho, but for some reason the space was limited to that point. This entire measurement defined many other important proportions.

---

286 Ibidem. II, p. 363.
287 Ibidem. I, p. 21.

The Fortress of Salvador

To understand the logic of these proportions, it is necessary to follow the process of determining the urban layout step by step, a ritual that, to a certain extent, is familiar. The perimeter precedes the internal layout, although the point of departure is identifying the center, since the plaza should lie in the middle of the city. If we measure the Fortress of Salvador from the southern side of the Basilica to the end of Rua Chile, we will notice that the midpoint lies exactly along the line of the northern edge of Praça Tomé de Souza.

In the original vision of the site, the architect realized that, if he were to make the center of the plaza coincide with the center of the fortress, he would have problems with extra space along the edge of Misericórdia: on the northern side, the block located before the Ladeira da Misericórdia would be only 13 meters long, so that the plot would not be symmetrical. The abrupt slope of the Ladeira da Misericórdia impeded the formation of a new block. Two other problems arose: maintaining the symmetry of the access streets, and adjusting the urban layout to the slope located at the Ladeira da Praça.

What did the master builder do? He divided the length of the fortress into ten units and determined where the center would be. Along the northern edge, he made divisions between the blocks by following a standard unit of 24 fathoms. Slight variations can be observed, resulting from adjustments to the topography. Along the southern edge, the architect used an even more ingenious solution, due to the relief of the land. He divided the southern plot into five unequal parts, realizing that the steep valley at the Ladeira da Praça would impede any division using a ratio of 1:10, and elongated the ratio of the plaza to 1:6, creating two more blocks, measuring 1:15 and 1:10, behind the plaza, where the Municipal Council Chambers is located. The plaza was larger but, behind it, across from the slope of the Ladeira da Praça and taking advantage of the slanting surface of the plateau, was a block that preserved the general ratio of 1:10 (Table 22).

The result of putting together this urban layout is a mosaic in which the principles of symmetry and the proportion of its parts, imitating the model of the human body, can be perceived in certain aspects of the city. The Municipal Council Chambers sits at an oblique angle to the plaza, which can only be explained by the attempt to reproduce equivalences, which is another intriguing and typical aspect of models of Renaissance plazas. The fortress's plaza is situated where the direct lines converge from the legs of the sloping access streets, which are symmetrical and opposite each other, repeating the sinuous models presented by Martini. The combination of slopes and planes confers harmony on the design.

Table 22 - Blocks in the Fortress of Salvador: Proportions and the Human Body [288]

Blocks	1N	2N	3N	4N	5N	6S	7S	8S	9S	10S
Inland Line	1:10	1:10	1:10	1:10	1:10	1:15	1:10	1:8	1:10	1:9.2
Coastline	1:10	1:10	1:10	1:10	1:10	1:6		1:8	1:10	1:9.2
Cathedral and Plaza			Cathedral			Plaza				
Measurement (Braças)	24	24	24	24	24	40		30	24	26
Human Body	Hd	Nk	Ct	Ua	La	Thigh		Kn	Bkn	Ft

Source: The author.

The blocks were distributed in a balanced way. Triangles and quadrilaterals were combined in varied ways, and there was a general tendency toward squares and diamonds. The geometric shapes were adjusted with a certain degree of complexity, revealing the intellectual richness of the layout, which combined mathematics and topography. By looking carefully at the city plan, we can perceive a certain visual order in the distribution of the blocks, the position and shape of the plaza, the sinuosity of the slopes, the layout of the streets, the posi-

---

288 Abbreviations: N, north; S, south; CATH, Cathedral; HD, head; NK, neck; CT, chest; UA, upper abdomen; LA, lower abdomen; KN, knee; BKN, below knee; FT, foot.

tioning of the ramparts and customs offices, and the polygons of the walls.

The design is replete with rationality. This exploration of its geometry, however, is not the only aspect that stands out. A certain anthropomorphic quality can be perceived in the Fortress of Salvador, that is, revealing some inspiration from human proportions, an idea that the Renaissance exploited to the maximum, reaching poetic heights—reinforcing the architect's imagination, who tried to imitate the perfection of the human body in a creative endeavor.

In the human body, the navel is not found in the center of the body's height, but simply within the circle of the well-known image of Vitruvian Man (Fig. 45), as interpreted and eternalized by Leonardo da Vinci. Inserted within a square, the correct middle passes through the area of the groin. Leonardo studied the human figure, devising various anthropomorphic measurements. He contemplated the Vitruvian theory of the navel as the natural center of the body, then composed a human figure within a circle and a square: the center of *homo ad quadratum* is located in the lower abdomen, no longer in the navel, the center of *homo ad circulum*.[289]

Leonardo's Man departed from the evidence taken at first glance from Vitruvius, whom Martini echoed, and corrected the notion of the center of the body. This correction is apparent in the Fortress of Salvador: the center coincides with the northern side of the plaza, reinforcing the idea of representing and imitating the human body, an irresistible invitation to creativity.

This effort represents a concession to poetry and contemplation. So much beauty enchants the imagination. If Martini advocated and defended the location of a cathedral in the position corresponding to the chest, the location of the cathedral in the Fortress of Salvador followed this correspondence. The position of the plaza in the navel was adjusted in the design of the Fortress, where the plaza's northern side coincides with the median line. The ramparts were situated at the ends of the feet and hands.

---

289 ZOLLNER, Frank. *Leonardo da Vinci 1452-1519*, pp. 37-38.

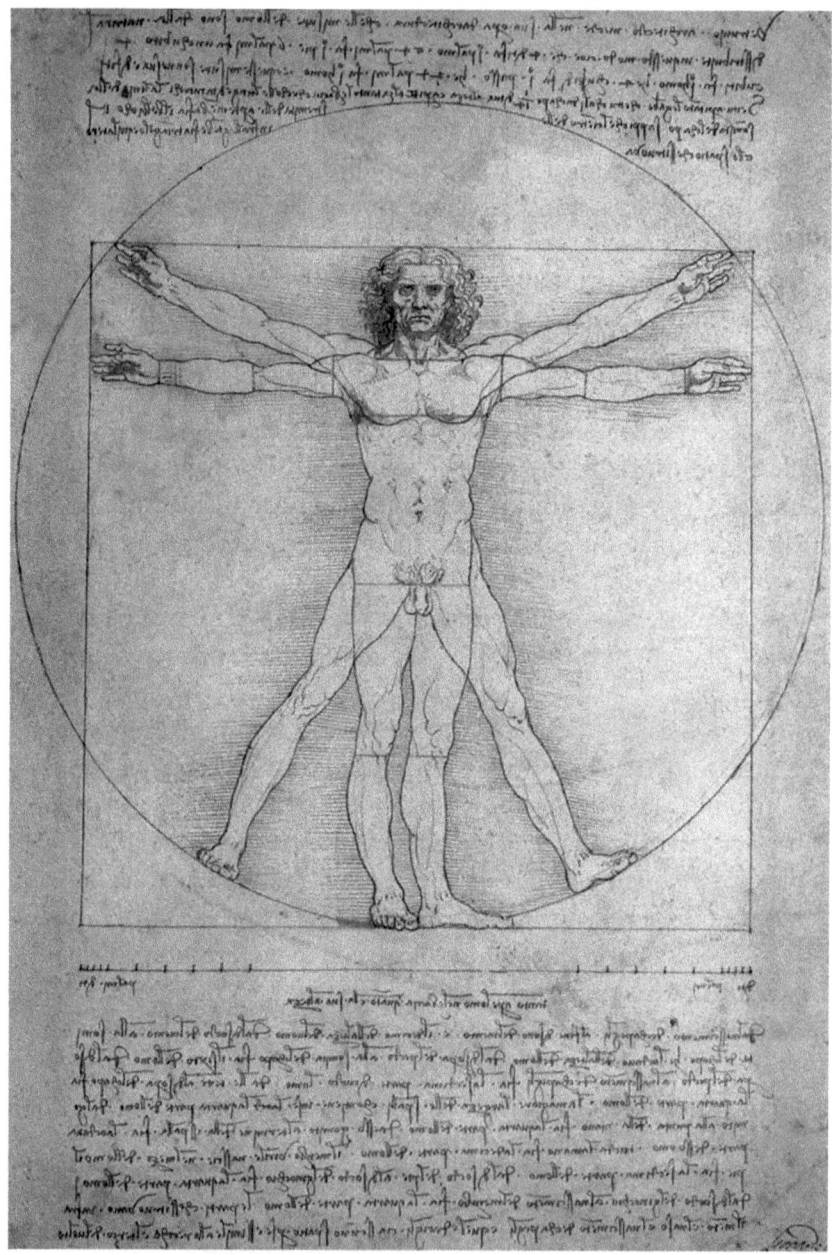

Figure 45 - Vitruvian Man as reconceptualized by Leonardo da Vinci.

26. The Urban Design

> *The town being fortified, the next step is the apportionment of house lots within the wall and the laying out of streets and alleys with regard to climatic conditions.*[290]
>
> Vitruvius

Cities were constructed by people and by mules. "A curved street is a donkey track, a straight street, a road for men," wrote Le Corbusier.[291] According to him, a mule wanders, avoiding boulders, dodging barriers, seeking shade, while a person has a goal and walks in a straight line. This radical vision, written in the twentieth century, illustrates the secular dilemma of urbanism: geometric planning versus natural expansion.

The Fortress of Salvador was constructed to be a path for people, although its subsequent growth occurred largely along the paths of donkeys. Tomé de Souza, in a report on his activities that he submitted to the King in 1553, stated that he had ordered "the straightening of some streets"[292] in various towns along the coast of Brazil. The

---

290 POLLIO, Marcus Vitruvius. *Los Diez Libros de Architectura* [The Ten Books on Architecture], p. 20.
291 LE CORBUSIER. *Urbanismo* [Urbanism], p. 10.
292 Carta de Tomé de Souza ao Rei Dom João III, datada de 1° de junho de 1553 [Letter from Tomé de Souza to King Dom João III, dated June 1, 1553]. In: MALHEIROS

expression "straight streets" reveals the concern with a new order in the urban design.

This model was fully realized in the fortress by submitting its entire design to the strict rules of geometry. The techniques used reveal sophistication and mastery of various concepts that are still used today in topographic planning: Euclidean geometry, serving as a theoretical foundation, was combined with a certain standard for dealing with proportions, a typically Renaissance practice. In its elegant translation of the special relationship between the human form and the line, angle, triangle, quadrilateral, and parallels, the urban design of the Fortress of Salvador is its richest feature.

The division of physical space (a plane) into regular geometric units (triangles and quadrilaterals) separated by straight lines (streets) was derived from mathematical knowledge. This made it possible to perceive the potential of the square, rhombus, or rectangle as a unit of a certain piece of land. To divide it into these shapes, it was necessary to develop techniques of measurement and transpose the abstract reasoning of postulates and geometric theorems to the field.

Classical literature attributes the invention of what is known as geometric urban planning to Hippodamos of Miletus. More than anyone else, the Greeks mastered the secrets of mathematics, being endowed with the necessary intellectual capacity for transposing geometric concepts to physical locations.

The city of Priene, located on the southern slopes of Mount Mycale, was an excellent example of what could be called the "Greek model" (Fig. 46). Its plan was conceived during the reign of Alexander the Great, on terrain that was relatively steep. By observing the city plan, we can see sixteen rectangular blocks from east to west, and seven from north to south.[293] The technique used to define the design was, apparently, to split the longer length into sixteen parts, each one forming a block of approximately 120 feet (35 meters). In the other direction, the width was divided into eight parts, comprised of seven

---

DIAS, Carlos. *História da Colonização Portuguesa no Brasil* [History of Portuguese Colonization in Brazil], III, p. 365.

293 ROBERTSON, D. S. *Arquitetura grega e romana* [Greek and Roman Architecture], p. 217.

blocks and a space, equivalent to a unit, for the gymnasium. We can perceive that the design is subjected to the proportion 16:8, although the overall measurements of the length and width do not maintain a ratio of 2:1.

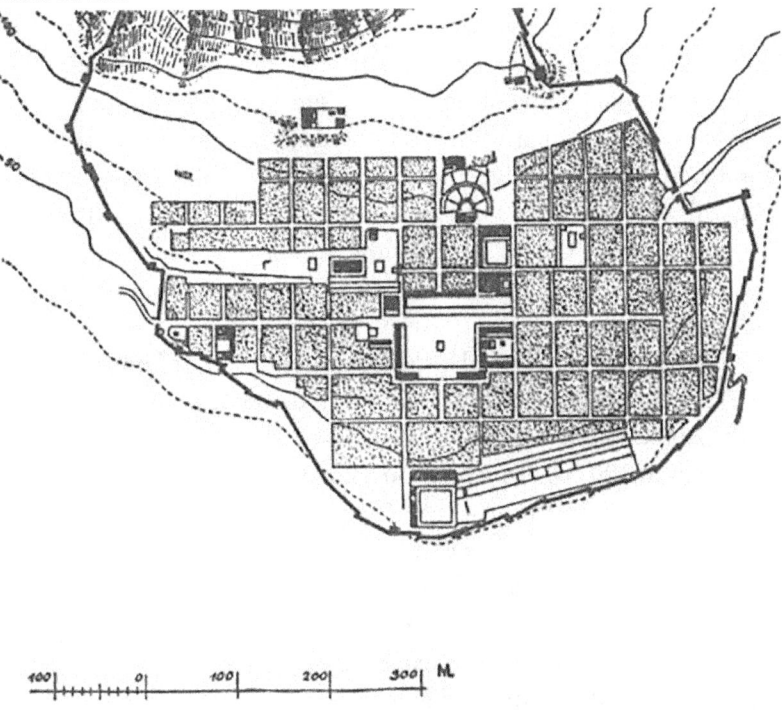

Figure 46 - Simplified city plan of Priene, Greece.
Source: ROBERTSON, D. S. Arquitetura grega e romana [Greek and Roman Architecture], p. 217.

The notable detail of the technique is the independence of each measurement, the length and width. The main reference points are not the actual size of the block or its square shape, but, rather, the number of parts into which the line would be split. This principle was also systematically employed in the Fortress of Salvador, but with greater sophistication in adjusting the blocks to the topography of the land. This standard differed, to an extent, from the strictly square model widely used by the Romans in their famous military camps.

The Roman technique consisted in determining the principle line, called the *decumanus maximus*, oriented in an east/west direction, which was intersected at its midpoint with a perpendicular line, called the *cardo*, oriented in a north/south direction. The design in the form of a cross, with two intersecting lines, represented the most ancient image of a meeting place. Its orientation could be adjusted to the cardinal points, the position of the site (with the *decumanus* parallel to the main dimension) or, if located along a river or the seacoast, parallel to the water's edge. In Brazil, the Fortress of Salvador was laid out with the *decumanus maximus* being the line that runs from the far side of Praça Castro Alves to the Terreiro de Jesus, but, strictly speaking, it did not have a *cardo*, due to its distinctive technique, as explained later.

The line was divided into blocks that were based on the square, although they did not always conform to this shape. A good example of the Roman model is the city of Tingad, Algeria, a colony founded by Trajan in 100 AD, which is considered one of the finest examples of Roman urbanism (Fig. 47).[294] The blocks were square, measuring twenty meters on each side, and comprised a whole that was nearly a square, made up of twelve blocks by eleven.

In describing the principles that guided the construction of Brasilia, Lúcio Costa articulated a simple and poetic statement: "It was born from the primordial gesture used by someone who is marking a place or taking possession of it: two axes crossing each other at right angles, that is, the sign of the cross itself."[295] This notion of an axis—which lay behind the construction of Greek and Roman cities and served as a basis for the design of Brasilia—was not present in the grid of the Fortress of Salvador. It had a design that was absolutely geometrical, but free of the notion of an axis, with its major streets crossing in the center, which may have obscured the perception of perfect order and regularity: its complexity bequeathed a veritable geometric puzzle to future generations.

---

294 Idem, p. 223.
295 BUCHMANN, Armando José. *Arquiteto Lúcio Costa, o inventor da cidade de Brasília* [Architect Lúcio Costa, inventor of the city of Brasilia], p. 61.

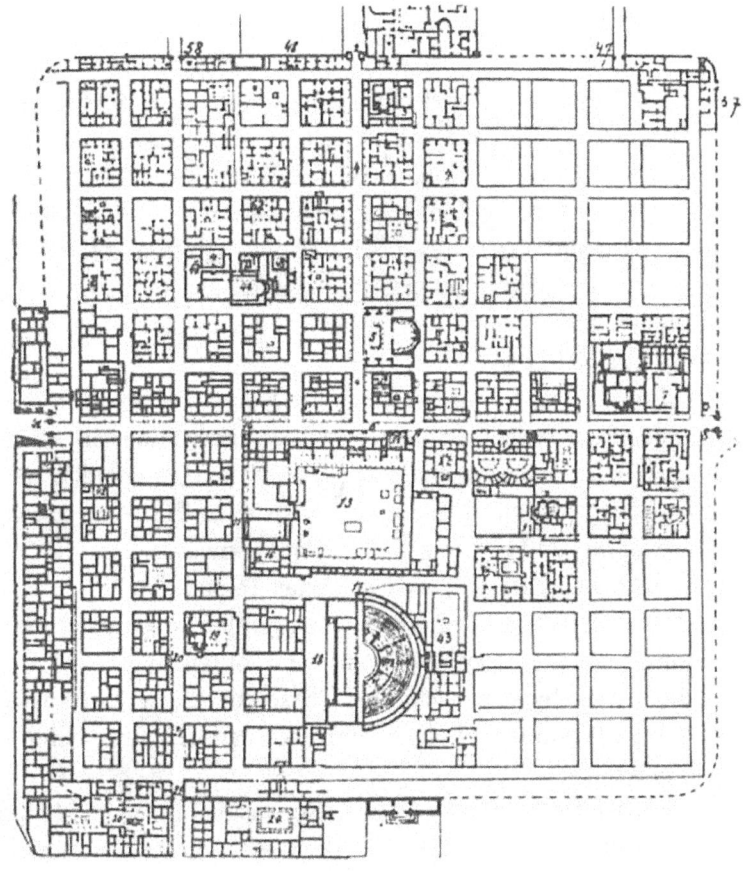

Figure 47 - Plan of the Roman city of Timgad, Algeria.
Source: ROBERTSON, D. S. *Arquitetura grega e romana [Greek and Roman Architecture]*, p. 223.

As a simple typological suggestion, the classic Roman chessboard contrasts with the Greek rectangular pattern, obtained through the division of the length and width into a certain number of units, according to the architect's vision. Although superficial, this difference correlates with a contrast between Priene and Tingad, as well as suggesting a certain opposition between Salvador and Hispanic-American cities. The well-known Spanish *damero* (square blocks), utilized in cities such as Lime and Santiago, retain a certain similarity with Rome, while the Portuguese version is guided by the Greek.

The geometric model of the Fortress of Salvador is not simple in appearance, but studying its measurements exposes the curious process of its conception, such as the notion of a polygon as a flat figure formed by segments of straight lines that cross each other, forming a closed internal area. Logically, the definition of the perimeter constitutes an operation prior to the internal arrangement, since it outlines the area of the site within which the division of streets and blocks will be planned.

The main unit of measure, the *decumanus maximus*, from the upper side of the Praça Castro Alves to the Terreiro de Jesus, formed the longest internal measurement of the polygon. It was parallel to the coast and enabled unimpeded travel and views. The defined length was more or less 240 fathoms (528 meters), a measurement that was almost exact, suggesting it was intentional. The number 240 is easily divided by 2, 3, 4, 5, 6, 8, and 10, a concern that is compatible with the notion that symmetry, as an expression of beauty, was obtained through division by perfect numbers, based on the proportions between the parts and the whole, with the constant reference being the human body.[296]

The width of the fortress was also reasonably exact (144 fathoms). The technique utilized indicates that the ordinates were derived from the *decumanus*, applied to the opposite vertices on the eastern and western sides of the polygon. The larger dimension was obtained in the direction of the northeast vertex (120 fathoms—5 blocks long), and the smaller one in the opposite direction, at the point of the present-day Praça do Palácio (24 fathoms).

It is curious to see that the design was subordinated to the

---

[296] According to Luca Pacioli, cited by Leonardo da Vinci, "The ancients, having taken into consideration the rigorous construction of the human body, elaborated all their works, as especially their holy temples, according to these proportions; for they found here the two principal figures without which no project is possible: the perfection of the circle, the principle of all regular bodies, and the equilateral square." In: BRAMLY, Serge. *Leonardo da Vinci 1452-1519*, p. 226.

topography and the combination of multiple variables. As a result, the Fortress of Salvador was rectangular in the relation between its length and width (240:144). The longest line was drawn in such a way as to take maximum advantage of the land overlooking the coast. To a certain extent, the breadth of the present-day Praça do Palácio oriented or delimited the other measurements: the breadth of the larger blocks along the coast is approximately 1/6 of the total figure. The *decumanus* line kept a certain distance from the coast, such that it was possible to obtain the desired proportions.

The rectangle of 240 by 144 fathoms was divided along each dimension, into 10 and 6 parts, respectively. The result would be the creation of as many quadrants as would fit into the polygon—although this general rule was attenuated due to the topography of the terrain, leading to a few adjustments in the proportion of the longer measurement (the *decumanus*). We can see that one block compensates for the other. The variants, in relation to the rationality of the project, are irrelevant.

The midpoint of the larger diagonal was determined. The median line passed more or less 48 meters beyond the Ladeira da Misericórdia, toward the Praça do Palácio. On the north side, five blocks were demarcated, representing 5/10 of the general measurement. On the north side of the fortress, starting with the midpoint, the division was more complex and interesting. The plaza was ideally situated in the most central point, following Vitruvian guidelines, amply repeated in Renaissance treatises. The architect Luís Dias endowed it with the measurement of 1/6.

Carrying out the division led to demarcating the block where the present-day Government Palace is located. In this case, the measurement was 1/8; however, for the last block in this alignment, the measurement reverted to approximately 1/10. The reason for adopting the division by 8 was simple: the alignment of the blocks in front, which started at the Municipal Council Building and ended at the Casa dos Sete Candeeiros, was oblique in relation to the coast and ran up against the row of the Palace blocks. The solution was to enlarge the measurement, so that the inland blocks would not be too narrow.

In the next alignment, the blocks went back to being 1/10

of the general measurement. The final set is the mathematical result of the proportions, representing a measurement of approximately 1/9.23. In the opposite direction, that is, farther up, the division by 6 was maintained. The result suggests the predominance of square blocks over those that are rectangular, trapezoid, or triangular.

The plaza—with a format that, respecting the best Renaissance tradition, reproduces the north side of the fortress—is a special space: this is why the Municipal Council building is oblique in relation to it. Its length is 1/6 of the fortress, while its width is 1/3. Another interesting fact is the proportion of 1/3 between the two lines (perpendicular and oblique), ensuring a neat symmetry between the whole and the part, a harmony that jumps out of the design. The original plaza was much larger than the present one. The necessity of occupying this privileged space probably led to its reduction, especially after the creation and integration of the Terreiro de Jesus into the urban space.

Two blocks on the north side were allocated to the cathedral; the segregation of the religious space was compatible with the Vitruvian principle of separating the religious and the civil. Erected in an isolated, but visible, locale—close to the chest, if we visualize the Fortress as a human body—invites comparison with Martini's design.

Vitruvius identified order as the first principle of architecture. He cited five other principles: arrangement, eurythmy, symmetry, propriety, and economy. He followed the Greek doctrine, according to which the "order" (*taxis*) of a building should be based on modules or "quantity" (*posótes*). Quantity was the "selection of modules from the members of the work itself and [...] constructing the whole work to correspond."[297] Order was the set of proportions of a building based on the consistent use of a certain unit; the best expression of this principle is consecrated in Greek temples. The module of temples corresponded, as a rule, to the diameter of the column in its thickest lower point; this determined the height of the column, the spacing among columns (called the "intercolumn"), the general measurements of the

---

[297] POLLIO, Marcus Vitruvius. *Los Diez Libros de Architectura* [The Ten Books on Architecture], p. 9.

temple, and various other proportions in relation to other parts of the building.

In the design of the Fortress of Salvador, there are grounds for suggesting that a module was utilized. The unit would be the width of the street, 1/100 of the greater measurement, which would correspond to 2.4 fathoms, from which the rest of the measurements would be derived, as deduced below:

> **I – greater length and width:** this would correspond, respectively, to 100 (240 fathoms) and 60 (144 fathoms) times the measurement of the module;
>
> **II – blocks:** for square blocks, 9 units of the module would form blocks of 21.6 fathoms, excluding the measurement of the width of the street; for the block where the Governor's Palace was located, the length would be 11.5 modules and 9 in the width;
>
> **III – plaza:** the unit would be 16.66 modules, equaling 40 fathoms;
>
> **IV – lots:** each block was divided into 6 or 8 lots, but it is not possible to determine whether this applied to each side or to the total; nine units divided by six results in 1.5 modules, equivalent to 3.6 fathoms; nine units divided by eight results in 1.125 modules, or 2.7 fathoms;
>
> **V – streets:** these would be based on the unit of the module (2.4 fathoms), while the main street may have been wider fathoms).

In Greek architecture, the relationship between the diameter of a column and its height gave rise to the well-known Doric, Ionic, and Corinthian orders. Vitruvius wrote that the origin of the Doric column was inspired by the measurements of the foot and the height of a person. The first measurement would correspond to the diameter; the second, to the height (six times the length of a foot). The ancient units of measure based on the human body constituted a series of numbers divisible by four (Table 23).

Table 23 - Linear Measurements with Anthropomorphic Roots

Measurement	Digit	Palm	Foot	Cubit
Digit	1	4	16	24
Palm		1	4	6
Foot			1	1.5
Cubit				1

Source: POLLIO, Marcus Vitruvius. *Los Diez Libros de Architectura* [*The Ten Books on Architecture*], p. 60.

The urban design of the Fortress of Salvador gracefully manipulated the subdivision of the number 240 into modules: 10, 8, 6, 5, 4, 3, and 2. Geometry, combined with topography, resulted in a mosaic of triangles, squares, lozenges, rectangles, and trapezoids. As an aesthetic element, symmetry exploited the repetition of certain patterns and the imitation of human proportions, in a project that was innovative, creative, and well-integrated with Renaissance ideas, a novelty that Portuguese urbanism bequeathed to the world.

27. Blocks and Lots

My footprint serves as the measure of Heaven and Earth.[298]

Inscription in the Holy Sepulcher

The Fortress of Salvador revealed something that, apparently, had not existed before: a Portuguese model for the geometric design of blocks and lots. With regard to urban design, Portugal and Spain displayed different tendencies in the sixteenth century. The Spanish followed their own path, probably influenced by the Aztecs, often utilizing the shape of a square for their city blocks and 1/4 of a square for their lots. The Portuguese, reflecting ideas from Vitruvius and the dominant orientation in Italy, applied models of proportion based on the fortress's overall measurements of length and width to derive the desired harmony.

Classical authors dealt little with the topic of blocks or their subdivisions, lots. The relationship of units to the general dimensions of the city was clearly supposed to be proportional. Vitruvius wrote that an architect should carefully consider "the exact proportions of

---

[298] In the twelfth century, a visitor claimed to have read this phrase on the outside wall of the building that consecrated the reputed place where Christ was crucified. The inscription was engraved in association with an image of Jesus. In: CUNHA, Rui Maneira. *As Medidas na Arquitetura* [Measurements in Architecture], p. 18.

his building," following "the standard of symmetry," and next consider the appearance of the building in relation to "the nature of the site."[299] Cataneo recommended that the spaces intended for dwellings be designed with "their compass proportionate" to other areas.[300]

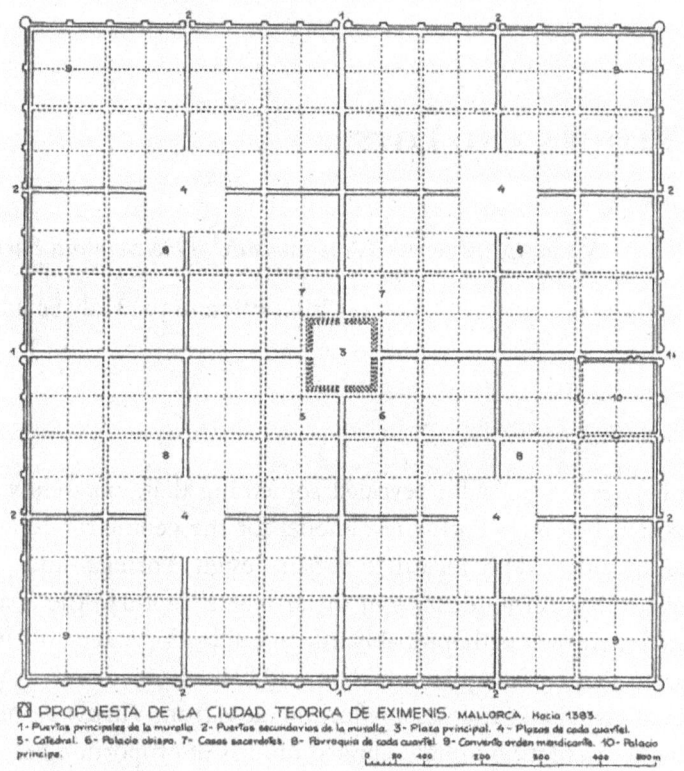

Figure 48 - Plan of Eximenes's theoretical city.
Source: FERNÁNDEZ, José Luis García. "Análisis dimensional de modelos teóricos ortogonales de las ciudades españolas e hispanoamericanas desde el siglo XII al XIX" [Dimensional analysis of orthogonal theoretical models of Spanish and Hispano-American cities from the twelfth to the nineteenth centuries], p. 162.

---

299 Idem, p. 58.
300 CATANEO, Pietro Dell'Architettura [On Architecture], p. 221.

In contrast to the Italian classics, the Spanish model adopted in Hispano-American cities made extensive use of blocks and lots. Speculation about urbanism had a precocious start in Spain in 1300, when the Mallorcan king, James II, published ordinances in which he established that lots (*cuartons*) were to form squares that measured 42.13 meters on each side. Around 1381, Eximenes wrote *Dotze del Crestiá*, in which he proposed square blocks divided into four lots, each measuring 40.75 meters on the sides (Fig. 48).[301] When Hispano-American cities were later built, the use of square blocks became entrenched, each of them being divided into four units, consolidating the "chessboard" model typical of Spanish America.

The units of Spanish urbanism are *manzanas* and *solares*—each *manzana* having four *solares* and the city having twenty *manzanas*. In Lima in 1535, one *solar* measured 62.7 meters on each side; this measurement was repeated in the Argentine cities of Mendonza (1561-1562) and San Juan de la Fronteira (1562). Spanish urbanism was considered innovative in its time: it established a new relationship to space, enlarging streets, blocks, and lots. Although this may seem to have been inevitable in historical terms, it was apparently also influenced by the monumental appearance of Mexico-Tenochtitlán, the Aztec city conquered by Cortes.

While the Spanish developed cities based on the square, the Portuguese worked with models guided by flexible rules of proportion, determining the dimensions of blocks and lots on broader geometric concepts. The design of the Fortress of Salvador encompassed ten blocks in length and six in width. The rules of proportion utilized for blocks were the following:

(1) **along the length** at the greatest distance, corresponding to the Basílica-Castro Alves axis, the midpoint was identified, forming two sides (south and north): on the southern

---

301 FERNÁNDEZ, José Luis García. "Análisis dimensional de modelos teóricos ortogonales de las ciudades españolas e hispanoamericanas desde el siglo XII al XIX" [Dimensional analysis of orthogonal theoretical models of Spanish and Hispano-American cities from the twelfth to the nineteenth centuries]. In: *La Ciudad Iberoamericana* [The Iberoamerican City], pp. 157-164.

side were five blocks of different sizes; on the northern side, five blocks of equal size, following the topography, since the gorge at the Ladeira da Praça required some geometric accommodation in the design;

(2) **in the width**, the greatest distance was on the northern side, corresponding to the perpendicular Basílica-São Francisco line, which was divided into five sections; added to these was the main plaza, closer to the hillside, for a total of six blocks.

Although a certain inspiration from Martini's designs is apparent, it is difficult to confirm definitively the source of influence for the Portuguese model. The evidence comes from the historical context, entailing various points of view, commentaries, designs, and ideas that were circulating at the time and contributed to the development of urban projects. The notion that each city or fortress should be adapted to the terrain constituted one of the pillars of Martini's work, a key concept that may have become a commonplace by the time the Fortress of Salvador was built. The play of proportions, worked out by Martini and echoed by Cataneo, had a strong geometric component and a common origin in Vitruvius. These made their imprint on the style of the era.

Just as limbs are proportional to the height of the body, city blocks were proportional to the length and width of the city. Similarly, lots were equal fractions of a block. In this respect, the Fortress of Salvador was not the only model in the Portuguese urban universe. The city-fortress of Daman (Fig. 49) in India apparently utilized a proportion based on two overall measurements and the size of each block: 1/8 of the city length and 1/6 of the width. An effort was made to have the blocks conform to squares, but they did not, precisely because the rule of proportion determined each side of the blocks.

The Sicilian city of Carlentini is another interesting example. Like a twin sister of the Fortress of Salvador, it constituted an exception to the usual urban design in Renaissance Spain. In 1550, Sicily was under the control of Spain, and the Viceroy Dom Juan de Vega ordered the construction of a fortress, with the status of a city, on a plateau near the city of Lentini. Given the name Carlentini, it was built in the context of a military strategy for protecting the island against incursions from the Turks and pirates. The plateau on which it was nestled lay somewhat inland, away from the coast, strategically located between the cities of Augusta and Catania.[302]

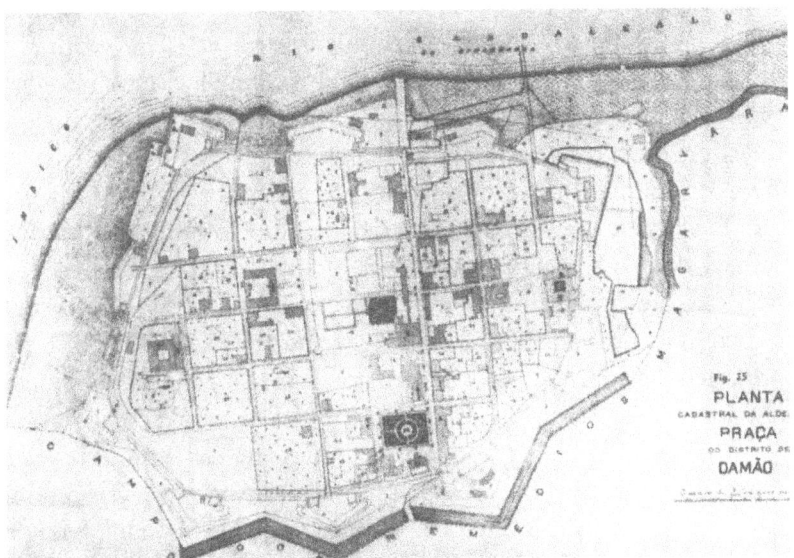

Figure 49 - Plan of the Portuguese city-fortress of Daman, India. Source: BRITO, Raquel Soeiro de. Goa e as praças do norte revisitadas [Goa and the northern cities revisited], p. 127.

In founding the city, Juan de Vega cited reasons of healthfulness, besides its advantages for defense. To attract residents from the area, especially from Lentini, he offered privileges, exemptions, and land to those who would take up residence in it. The project was elaborated by the engineer Pedro di Pietro, the successor to Antonio Ferramolino, the renowned military engineer who worked on the Spanish fortifications in Sicily.

Before Ferramolino died in 1550, he was consulted about the

---

302 BLOND, José Ramón Soraluce. *Las Fortificaciones Españolas de Sicilia en el Renacimiento* [The Spanish Fortifications of Sicily in the Renaissance], pp. 66-68.

fortification of Mount Seinal on the coast of Morocco. Miguel de Arruda was the person in charge of the works at Seinal and directed Luís Dias, who became the architect of the Fortress of Salvador. This illustrates the exchange of ideas in the Mediterranean region, where Italians, Portuguese, and Spanish were energetically engaged in constructing fortifications.

The surviving plan of Carlentini, dating from 1578, was drawn up by Tibúrcio Spanochi.[303] If we look at it carefully, we can see that the line of ramparts followed the curves of the hill. In only one stretch, it descended into a valley and returned to the plateau in the opposite direction. In the Fortress of Salvador, the perimeter was similarly determined by the profile of the mountain, crossing two valleys on the eastern side. In Carlentini, the five main bulwarks were concentrated near the gates, protecting the most vulnerable places; this likewise occurred in its sister fortress in Salvador, where the four bulwarks above protected the northern and southern access roads, a system that would also explain the alignment of the blocks in the Terreiro de Jesus.

Further examination of the design of Carlentini suggests more comparisons with Salvador. The plaza in Carlentini was central because the city was located in the interior, while Salvador, being a coastal city, needed its plaza to be close to the harbor. Carlentini's plaza boasted neither the size nor the majesty of the public spaces that became the norm in Hispano-American cities. The dimensions of its plaza were around 1/10 of the length of the fortress and 1/4 of its width. Although the plaza was not square, the architect worked with dimensions that approximated this proportion.

The construction of Carlentini revealed yet other intriguing aspects. The horizontal outline was longer and composed of blocks of three different sizes: the blocks of the first kind, from left to right to a point just beyond the plaza, were relatively equal; the second block after the plaza was shortened because of the depression in the land; beyond that, the blocks represented smaller, equal units. In Carlentini, the topography guided the play of proportions, a geometric feature that was also adopted in the Fortress of Salvador.

---

303 Idem, p. 69.

The Fortress of Salvador

Looking at the outline in the perpendicular direction, the blocks were equal, with the exception of the central one, which was double their size. In total, there were twelve blocks along the perpendicular line and thirteen along the horizontal one, each having some variations due to the topography and the aim of making the main avenue majestic. The size of blocks was another aspect that differentiated Hispanic cities: they were conceptualized as a "nonsquare complex orthogonal design," containing blocks that were between 30 and 50 meters on each side. The large dimensions that were "typical of the American continent were not applied in Carlentini."[304]

The blocks in the Fortress of Salvador were structured on the basis of the standard measurement of 24 fathoms (1/10 of a *decumanus*), combining larger and smaller dimensions that were determined by the topography. The measurements revealed in the Brazilian and Sicilian fortresses were similar. In both locations, the needs for defense were prioritized; the two were constructed to accommodate the topography of hilltops and make the best use of limited space. Carlentini and Salvador display similarities that constituted a particular style, confirming that ideas and standards were circulating during this period, leading to the construction of works that resembled each other.

This style used blocks that represented divisions of city dimensions by 10, 9, 8, 6, or 4, a geometric standard that, to a certain extent, was also applied to lots—the smallest unit of property which, as a rule, could not be further subdivided. The word *lote* (lot) was only recently introduced into the Portuguese language as a term associated with the division of properties. In the sixteenth century, the word usually appearing in deeds was *chão*, meaning "ground." Originating from the Latin *planu*, it also designated an agrarian unit (*chaô*), measuring 60 spans in length and 30 in width.[305]

---

[304] NICOLINI, Alberto. "La ciudad regular en la praxis hispanoamericana" [The geometric city in Hispano-American praxis]. In: *Universo Urbanístico Português 1415-1822* [The Portuguese Urban Universe, 1415-1822]. Colóquio Internacional, actas, p. 605.

[305] VITERBO, Frei Joaquim de Santa Rosa de. *Elucidário das palavras, termos e frases que em Portugal antigamente se usaram [...]* [Elucidation of words, terms, and phrases formerly used in Portugal], II, p. 94.

In the Fortress of Salvador, each block was apparently divided into 16 and 12, or 8 and 6 lots. Luís Dias reported that "in each *chão* that is occupied, there are 8 houses, and the smaller ones have 6 houses."[306] Two interpretations are possible: the first hypothesis is that here the word *chão* signified a quadrant in which six or eight houses fit; the second is that each *chão* corresponded to half a quadrant, so that there were twelve or sixteen lots in a block.

According to the first hypothesis, the lots in larger blocks would have been rectangular, being 7.2 fathoms in front and 10.8 fathoms deep. An interesting example is the block that faces the Terreiro de Jesus and the Praça da Sé: its current layout has seventeen houses, but an observer will notice that the boundaries can be grouped into six lots. In fact, the original *chão* may have been even larger, but the pressures exerted by new residences led to further subdivision, with the creation of houses having two windows and a door in front, a possibility that is worth considering (Table 24).

Table 24 - Measurements of Lots in Fortress of Salvador

Lots by Quadrant	Large Quadrants 27.6 x 21.6 fathoms		Small Quadrants 21.6 x 21.6 fathoms	
	length	width	length	width
16	3.45	10.8	2.7	10.8
12	4.6	10.8	3.6	10.8
8	6.9	10.8	5.4	10.8
6	9.2	10.8	7.2	10.8

Source: *The author*.

In Lisbon in the sixteenth century, the *Register of Deeds* of properties paying taxes to the Lisbon Municipal Council showed that houses measured four to seven meters on the side facing the street,[307]

---

306 MOREIRA, Rafael. "O arquiteto Miguel de Arruda e o primeiro projeto para Salvador" [The architect Miguel de Arruda and his first project for Salvador]. In: *Anais do 4° Congresso de História da Bahia*, V. I, p. 141. The letter from Luís Dias, the master architect, is dated July 13, 1551.
307 *LIVRO PRIMEIRO de Tombo das propriedades foreiras à Câmara desta insigne*

small by today's standards. Two windows and a door comprised the façade of the house, a well-known and widely-used model in Brazilian cities. However, the *Register of Deeds of the Jesuit School of Rio de Janeiro* reveals other facts about the first concessions of lots: for example, in October, 1567, Antonio de São Payo, a magistrate, received a land grant to a *chão* measuring twelve fathoms on each side, for the purpose of building houses.[308]

In the Bairro Alto neighborhood of Lisbon, the blocks were practically rectangular; their width was intended for two lots, adjacent along the middle and facing opposite streets. The length of each division was more variable, depending on whether there were six or eight lots.[309] The standards of the Bairro Alto were similar to those applied in the Fortress of Salvador; both followed geometric practices in which the proportional rectangle of blocks corresponded to the modern notion of lots. Notably, the Bairro Alto originated in the sixteenth century.

Vitruvius wrote that the principles of symmetry arise from proportion, "a correspondence among the measures of the members of an entire work, and of the whole to a certain part selected as a standard." In his view, just as symmetry and proportion exist between the cubit, foot, hand, finger, and other parts of the human body, the same should occur in architecture,[310] a classical technique applied in constructing the Fortress of Salvador. The process of identifying proportions can be an intriguing mathematical game, in which blocks and lots represent a rich colonial heritage.

---

cidade de Lisboa [Book One of the Register of Deeds of properties paying taxes to the Municipal Council of this eminent city of Lisbon].
308 *LIVRO de Tombo do Colégio de Jesus do Rio de Janeiro* [Register of Deeds of the Jesuit School of Rio de Janeiro], p. 270.
309 CUNHA, Rui Maneira. *As Medidas na Arquitetura* [Measurements in Architecture], p. 94.
310 VITRUVIUS POLLIO, Marcus. *Los Diez Libros de Archîtectura* [The Ten Books on Architecture], p. 11.

28. Streets

The arrangement of private houses is considered to be more agreeable and generally more convenient, if the streets are regularly laid out after the modern fashion which Hippodamus introduced, but for security in war the antiquated mode of building, which made it difficult for strangers to get out of a town and for assailants to find their way in, is preferable.[311]

Aristotle

The historical evolution of streets presents two major dilemmas:

— the first deals with whether they should be straight or curved, eloquently discussed by Aristotle, who, when commenting on the ideal form, praised both the straight and the curved; to him, the straight street was pleasing, but the sinuous lines of the curved street were better for internal defense due to the difficulty it posed to invaders; with respect to the Fortress of Salvador, the design combined straight streets in the upper city with winding, curved access roads ascending from the harbor;

---

311 Aristotle *Política* [Politics], 133, a.

— the second concerns whether they should be wide or narrow; in Salvador, the narrower streets indicate older neighborhoods, since the standard used in the original site of the fortress was distinct from that followed in the area beyond the Terreiro do Jesus; in other words, Pelourinho is more modern than the historic center of the city.

Hippodamus of Miletus has always been associated with geometric urban planning; his native city of Miletus was an example of streets crossing at right angles, forming rectangular blocks, with the city separated into two parts—north and south—and having the agora and other civic buildings in the center. Another Greek city with a regular pattern was Priene, which had three intriguing characteristics that warrant highlighting: the city was constructed at a height, the wall was an irregular polygon that followed the curves of the terrain, and its streets were straight, running in either a north-south or an east/west direction. In both Miletus and Priene, we can see a certain uniformity in the measurements of the streets and blocks, as well as the way in which the design is subordinated to the terrain (Table 25).

As for the Fortress of Salvador, the layout of the blocks was rectangular, its streets were straight, altered only when required by the topography, and the overall measurements closely followed those used in Miletus and Priene, which reinforces the identification of the fortress with Greek patterns. The sloping access roads in the Fortress of Salvador were designed to be winding, in accord with the tradition of making the approach of invaders as difficult as possible.

Vitruvius worked with the assumption that main streets should be distinguished from secondary streets, according to the layout of the design, which was a common practice. In 1596, in the city of São Sebastião in Rio de Janeiro, the official who served as a street planner, responsible for marking out where streets would run, reserved a certain strip of land that was 3.5 fathoms (7.7 meters) in width, which he said would be considered the main street of the city.[312] In the original design of the Fortress of Salvador, the streets were not differentiated in terms of measurements, that is, all the surviving original streets are around 2.5 arm's lengths in width. This conclusion, however, is not certain, since some streets were later widened.

Table 25 - Measurements of Streets in Greek, Spanish, and Portuguese Cities

City	Street (in Meters)				Block (in Meters)
Miletus (476 A.D.)	main	7.50	secondary	3.60	30 to 50
Priene (334 B.C.)	main	7.00	secondary	3.50	35 to 45
Lima (1535)	main	11.10	secondary	11.10	130
Santiago (1542)	main	11,20	secondary	11.20	130
Salvador (1549)	main	5.69?	secondary	5.69	40 to 48
Salvador (Pelourinho, 1565?)	main	6.40	secondary	6.20	52 to 65
Mazagan (1769)	main	8.80	secondary	8.80	123

Source: LAWRENCE, A. W. Arquitetura Grega [Greek Architecture], p. 191; ROBERTSON, D. S. Arquitetura grega e romana [Greek and Roman Architecture], p. 210; FERNÁNDEZ, José Luis García. In: La Ciudad Iberoamericana [The Iberoamerican City], pp. 168-171; TEIXEIRA, Manuel C. O Urbanismo Português [Portuguese Urbanism], p. 263.

Streets are like veins, enabling the movement of people and things. Alberti prioritized the aesthetic function of streets in large cities, stating that a thoroughfare, as it approached a famous and powerful city, should be straight and broad, in keeping with the decorum and dignity of its destination. For colonies or simple forts, security should take precedence in designing the means of access. The most

---

312 LIVRO de Tombo do Colégio de Jesus do Rio de Janeiro [Register of Deeds of Jesuit School of Rio de Janeiro], p. 250. The official notice concerning measurements stated, "[...] and in this plot, thirty-five spans are reserved for the street that the street planner assigned for the main street [...]."

secure road should not lead directly to the city gate, but, rather, should wind to the right and the left along the walls, preferably passing under their battlements. This advice is suggestive, since, in the Fortress of Salvador, the sloping access roads from the harbor to the summit were winding, heeding the need for security. It is also possible to picture some curves in the access road leading to the main gate by Praça Castro Alves. For the city's internal plan, Alberti defended the use of curved streets. According to him, they were longer, more attractive, and confused the enemy due to their obstructed sightlines. However, he recognized that straight streets were better adapted to the angles of city walls and buildings.

Alberti's speculative and theoretical concepts were superseded by Martini's pragmatic vision, which recommended straight streets on flat terrain and curved ones on hills. Martini proposed that cities situated in mountainous locations should have roads and streets that were circular or spiral, or were laid out in stages or as ramps composed of cross-cutting streets that would ease the climb for residents. For cities on flat terrain, he advised straight lines linked to the central plaza, where eight, six, or four streets should cross (Fig. 50), dividing them in half as they ran between the main gates. In both cases, the streets that opened up on the main plaza should be straight at this meeting point. If a city or castle were built on a hill, mountain, or valley that had flat areas, the part that was flat should follow the rules for cities that were entirely flat, while the sloping parts should follow those for mountainous cities.

Martini's theoretical vision is very pertinent to the realities of the design of the Fortress of Salvador, with its main plaza in the center and eight streets converging upon it. All these streets were straight, three of which linked the northern and southern gates, another three leading to the rear of the fortress on the eastern side, and two more being the sloping access roads. An interesting aspect is that the sloping access roads arrived at the plaza in a straight line, their curves having ended a block away from it. After a certain point, the switchbacks appeared in the access roads as they descended toward the harbor, tracing the northern and southern boundaries of the fortress.

Inside the city on the plateau, where the Rua José Gonçalves is now located, there used to be a sloping access road that wound back and forth up the hillside until reaching the Praça da Sé; the angle of the incline did not allow a straight street to be built. In this case, we can also see the principle applied to sloping roads, which added curves that make access less strenuous on steep inclines.

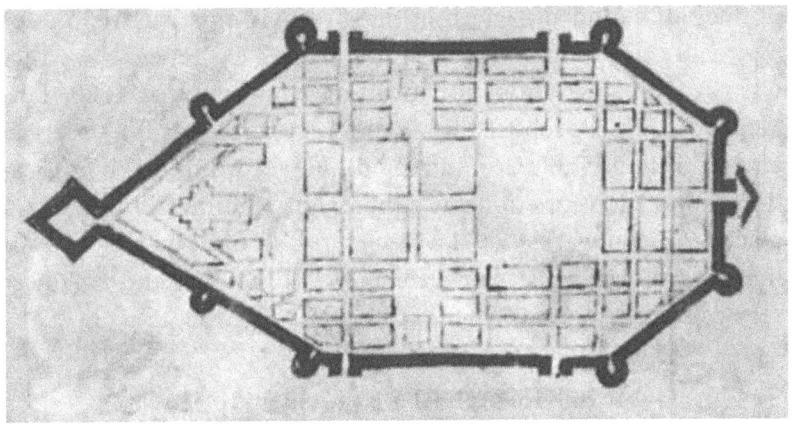

Figure 50 - Model of city with straight streets that cross in the main plaza, according to Martini.
Source: MARTINI, Francesco di Giorgio, *Trattati Di Architettura Ingegneria e Arte Militare [Treatise on Architecture, Engineering, and Military Arts]*, I, *folha 7v, tábua 10.*

Adaptations to the terrain are probably the most characteristic feature of the fortress's design. Here are a few examples:

— the main street cut across the Municipal Plaza and ended at the Praça da Sé, a contingency imposed by the curvature of the hillside;
— the Rua do Tesouro and Rua do Tira-Chapéu were built taking advantage of the plateau and, for this reason, were oblique in relation to the quadrangle of the city's design; the right angle was used only where the terrain allowed;
— when following a certain topographical line was justified, the design overrode right angles: this is perhaps the best

approach to understanding the logic of city planning in the fortress.

The blocks located behind the Praça da Sé have been preserved, being, in a certain respect, the oldest in the city. The size of the blocks and the width of the streets in this part reproduce the reality of the first years of the fortress's existence. Nevertheless, in a treatise about fortifications, published in 1680, Luís Serrão Pimentel proposed three different standards for streets in city-fortresses (Table 26), distinguished according to their location rather than function: straight streets leading from the main plaza to the bulwarks (9.9-11.55 meters); secondary streets heading toward the curtains or wall (8.25-9.9 meters); and narrower service streets (6.6-8.25 meters).

Table 26 - Theoretical Measurements of Streets

Model	Type of Route	Width (Meters)
Law of the Twelve Tables, 451 B.C.	Straight route	2.64
	Route along curves	5.28
Lusitanian Method, Luís Serrão Pimentel, 1680	Straight streets heading to the bulwarks	9.90 to 11.55
	Streets heading to the curtains	8.25 to 9.90
	Streets inside the city	8.25 to 6.60

Source: LEI DAS XII TÁBUAS [LAW OF THE TWELVE TABLES], tábua oitava; TEIXEIRA, Manuel C. O Urbanismo Português [Portuguese Urbanism], p. 130.

The data indicate that a clear distinction existed between the oldest measurements (2.4-2.5 fathoms) and the later standard used in the Pelourinho area (3 fathoms). There is a certain correspondence between the north/south length of the fortress and the width of the streets: the measurement of 2.4 fathoms corresponds to 1/100 of the fortress's length, which suggests a certain proportion and symmetry compatible with the standards of the era—yet another factor enriching our understanding of the geometric and mathematical conception of the Fortress of Salvador.

Recall that the ratio of 1/100 also existed in the wage structure of the Governorate General: the highest salary was one hundred times greater than the lowest wage, possibly an intentional ratio.

In Lisbon, the streets in the neighborhoods of Bairro Alto and Vila Nova da Oliveira (present-day Rua da Oliveira and Rua da Condessa) are around 2.4 fathoms in width.[313] Since these divide blocks that arose in the early sixteenth century, they may indicate some technical standard.

---

313 CARITA, Helder. *Lisboa Manuelina e a Formação de Modelos Urbanísticos da Época Moderna (1495-1521)* [Manueline Lisbon and the Formation of Urban Models in the Modern Era], p. 191.

29. The Plaza

If the city is on the sea, we should choose ground close to the harbour as the place where the forum is to be built; but if inland, in the middle of the town.

Vitruvius

Planned cities always had a main plaza, which the Greeks called the "agora" and the Romans called the "forum"; the Spanish called it the "great plaza" or "place of arms." The uses and traditions of each era determined its size and position in the layout of the city, obeying certain rules. It could have a military function, serving as an area for troops to assemble and perform maneuvers, or as a place for a market to be held, for gladiators to fight, or for horses or bulls to race.

The ideal city proposed by Aristotle contained two agoras: the first, called a "free agora," common in Thessaly, was for leisure; the second, a "commercial agora" separate from the former, was established in a site capable of receiving merchandise carried from the maritime ports and from inland sources,[314] and served as well as a place for public assemblies. In the areas adjacent to the commercial agora were buildings devoted to business and public services, such as the courts, police headquarters, and market administration.

---

314 Aristotle *Política* [Politics], 133, b.

If the "commercial agora" was supposed to be close to the port, where was the "free agora" assigned? The answer to this question allows us to suggest a clear Aristotelian pattern in the structure of the two public spaces in the Fortress of Salvador: the public plaza and the place where the Sé Cathedral was built. This conceptualization, an intentional one, came a few years before the Vitruvian model was adopted in the urban ordinances issued by King Felipe II.

The location of the public plaza in the Fortress of Salvador, being closer to the southern border, was dependent upon military and topographic factors. In Vitruvius's theoretical model, the plaza would be located in a central position at the port. In Salvador, as a maritime city, the plaza was built above and overlooking the ocean, near the southern border of the fortress and the harbor—located in the upper city, a variation on the concept presented by Vitruvius.

What was the reason for this? The top of the plateau offers the obvious answer: the fortress was on the upper level, while the beach served merely as the point of access to the harbor. The proximity of the plaza to the hillside also reveals the necessity of having the main area of the city be well articulated with strategic vistas, with visual access to the harbor area.

Aristotle stated that the buildings dedicated to religious worship and common meals should occupy the same area, adding, "The site should be a spot seen far and wide, which gives due elevation to virtue and towers over the neighborhood".[315] The free agora, he said, should be located somewhat below this spot. This separation between spaces dedicated to business and to faith, ensuring ample visibility for temples, was a pattern followed in the Fortress of Salvador. It preserved the original mystical sentiment that guided the construction of temples in urban spaces. This stood in marked contrast to the model of the first Spanish cities in the Americas.

In Santo Domingo, Lima, and Santiago, for example, the cathedral occupies one side of the main plaza, a feature due to the influence of certain theological doctrines applied to urban designs in the Middle Ages. These doctrines, a Medieval alteration of the traditional

---

315 Idem.

separation between spaces, sought to ensure that the Lord's temple would occupy a central position in the urbe.

If we examine the plan of the Fortress of Salvador, we will notice that the plaza was not located centrally, as one might expect. Mathematical data show that the master architect, Luís Dias, divided the city plan at the midpoint. However, on the northern side, there was a fifty-meter strip where the land descended toward the Ladeira da Misericórdia; to resolve the problem this posed, he transferred the plaza to the first block on the southern side, reserving space for it equal to 1/6 of the length, which was about 1/3 of the northern side. The boundaries of the fortress were fixed.

Locating the plaza in this spot presented clear military advantages: it was close to the southern boundary, which was the most dangerous, and it was centralized in relation to the two bulwarks on the beach. The western side "opened up with a large vista overlooking the ocean where a few pieces of heavy artillery are situated [...]."[316] Thus, the location of the plaza emphasized the division between the sets of artillery in the two levels of the fortress: the upper set, situated in the plaza and bulwarks, protected and watched over the lower set.

Another aspect to contend with was the lay of the land. The plaza was the only connection possible between the southern and northern sides of the fortress; on one edge of the plaza was the hillside, on the other, the dip where the Ladeira da Praça ran. The terrain was very narrow and favorable for defense, serving as a bottleneck in case of an invasion coming from any direction. Any enemy who invaded the fortress would have to pass through this narrow, well-defended passage. The plaza, being well situated, ensured an open field, which would assist in defense. Open spaces are conducive to accurate shots. The plaza, in combination with the marsh, with only the Municipal Council Building in between, created a sort of fortress within a fortress, a military fact that might explain why this building stood alone on the eastern face of the plaza.

The geometric shape of the plaza is another intriguing characteristic. Vitruvius wrote that "the Greeks lay out their forums in

---

316 SOUZA, Gabriel Soares. *Notícia do Brasil* [Report from Brazil], I, capítulo VII, p. 257.

the form of a square," which distinguished them from the Romans, where the custom of holding "gladiatorial shows"[317] in the forum determined its shape. In 1586, Gabriel Soares de Souza wrote that the city of Salvador had "an honest plaza, in which bulls are made to run when it is suitable," and that its shape was "in a square with the pillory in the middle of it."[318] Vilhena also stated that the Municipal Plaza was "a small square."[319]

In fact, the plaza was conceived as a six-sided polygon: the two sides running in a north-south direction were 88 meters long; on the southern side, the two sides running east-west were 24 and 6 fathoms, respectively; and on the northern side, the last two sides running east-west measured 24 and 12 arm's lengths, respectively. The internal angles were 90°, with the exception of the two corners that nowadays are crossed by Rua Chile, these two being 80° angles.

To explain the form of the plaza, there are two hypotheses possible: was it something random or an intentional design? The second option seems more likely, since the central space was always orderly. With a closer look, we can see that the Municipal Council Building was constructed on a spot that was somewhat recessed, allowing more space for the plaza and ensuring that its east-west dimension would be longer than the standard block of 24 fathoms.

While the dictates of the city plan caused the plaza to push back the Municipal Council Building, why did the building's façade lie at an oblique angle in relation to the alignment of the street? The historic engravings all show the Council Building larger at one of its ends. A possible explanation is that the city planner wanted to design the plaza with the same silhouette as the fortress at large, which was an irregular quadrilateral, the southern side being smaller than the northern. The plaza reproduced this silhouette. Harmony arose from the perception that the spaces representing the fortress and the

---

317 POLLIO, Marcus Vitruvius. *Los Diez Libros de Architectura* [The Ten Books on Architecture], p. 108.

318 SOUZA, Gabriel Soares. *Notícia do Brasil* [Report from Brazil], capítulo VII, p. 257.

319 VILHENA, Luiz dos Santos. *Recopilação de Notícias Soteropolitanas e Brasílicas* [Compilation of Reports from Salvador and Brazil], I, p. 107.

plaza were proportional repetitions that produced symmetry. Martini wrote, "And in the middle of the city is the main plaza, round, faceted, square, or any other shape that is so desired."[320] In his designs, we can observe a correlation between the shape of the plaza and the perimeter of the city.

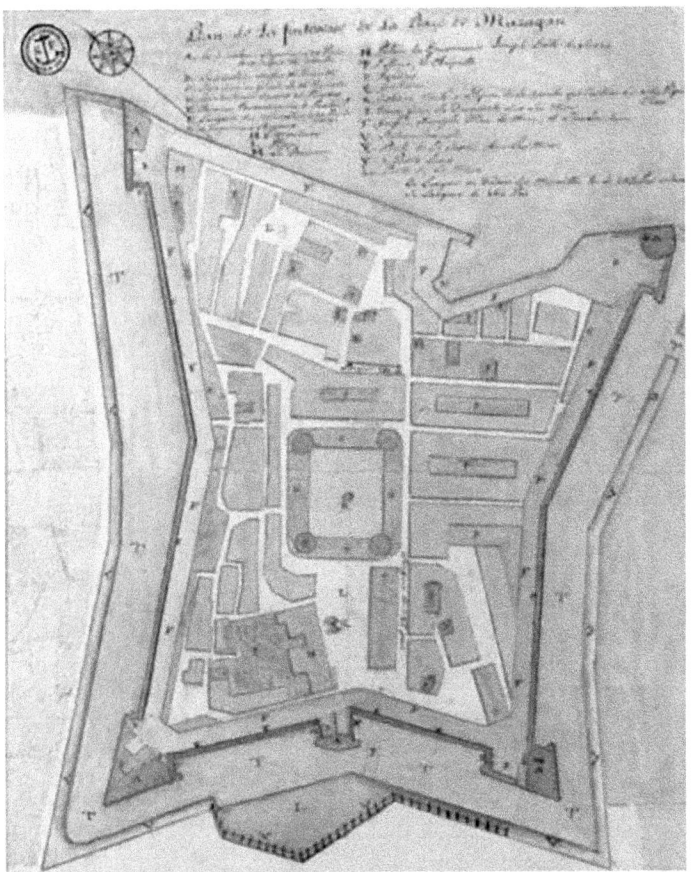

Figure 51 - Fortress of Mazagan, showing plaza in a trapezoid shape, 1757. Source: MOREIRA, Rafael. A Construção de Mazagão: Cartas Inéditas 1541-1542. [The Construction of Mazagan: Unpublished Letters, 1541-1542], p. 184.

---

320 MARTINI, Francesco Di Giorgio. *Trattati Di Architettura Ingegneria e Arte Militare* [Treatise on Architecture, Engineering, and Military Arts], I, p. 21.

Without a doubt, it is a suggestive image. The search for an aesthetic effect in the central plaza through the use of a trapezoidal shape was a Renaissance practice. In the Fortress of Mazagan, the main plaza was a trapezoid, which accentuated the visibility of the surrounding buildings. There was a certain harmony between the quadrilateral shapes of the fortress and of the plaza (Fig. 51), the format of the latter reproducing that of the former on a smaller scale. In this regard, there are parallels with the Piazza Pio II in Pienza, Italy, a trapezoidal space that was designed with the participation of Leon Batista Alberti and the Florentine architect Bernardo Rosselino. The measurements of the plaza observed geometric standards that accentuated the effect of perspective. The Capitol Square in Rome used a similar approach, utilizing a trapezoid to accentuate the size of the main building. Transposing these ideas to the Fortress of Salvador, the aim of the architect Miguel de Arruda may have been to amplify the apparent size of the Governor's Palace (Fig. 53).

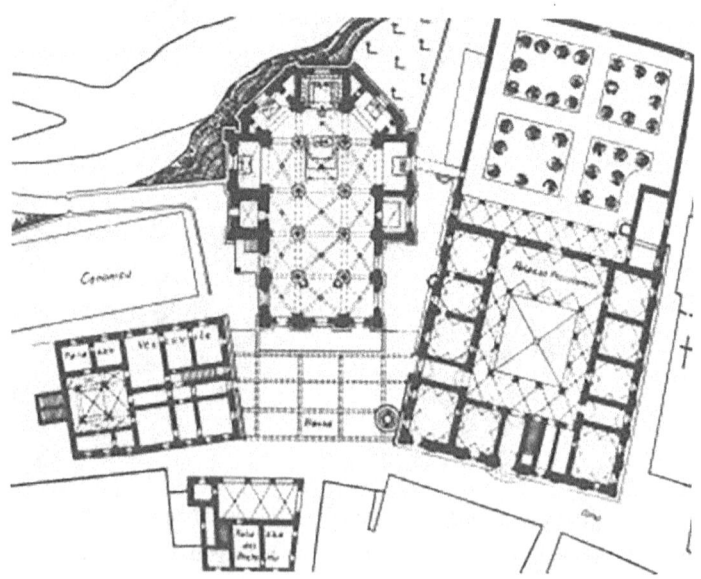

Figure 52 - Piazza Pio II, in Pienza, Italy, in the shape of a trapezoid, 1459-1462. Source: Benevolo, Leonardo. História da Cidade [History of the City], p. 428.

The Fortress of Salvador

Figure 53 - Current view of the Municipal Plaza of the city of Salvador.

The size and format of the plaza in the Fortress of Salvador were different than the standards observed in the Hispano-American cities (Table 27), in which the plazas were square and larger in size. These characteristics may have been linked to the Spaniards' astonishment when they first encountered the Aztec city of Mexico and its monumental central plaza. It is worth recounting the impressions the Spaniards had when they arrived, since these influenced the formation of urban spaces in many other Hispanic cities. The best description came from the military officer Bernal Díaz del Castillo, who accompanied Cortes during the conquest of Mexico.

After they had been in the city for four days, Cortes said that it would be good to go see the *plaza mayor*.[321] Accompanied by many of Montezuma's chiefs, they arrived at the great plaza, which was called *El Tlatelulco*. Since they had never seen such a wonder, they were

---

321 CASTILLO, B. Díaz del. *Historia Verdadeira de la Conquista de la Nueva España* [The True History of the Conquest of New Spain], p. 216.

amazed at the multitude of people and wares found there, with each type of item having its own spot marked out for display.

Table 27 - Dimensions of Plazas in Selected Cities in the Americas

City	Year Founded	Plaza (in Meters) Minimum	Maximum	Ratio
Santo Domingo	1502	78	106	1.36
Tenochtitlan (Mexico City)	1325	310	420	1.35
Mexico City (Cortes)	1524	240	350	1.46
Lima, Peru	1531	148	148	1.00
Puebla, Mexico	1531	117	208	1.77
Salvador, Brazil	1549	66	88	1.33
Caracas, Venezuela	1561	135	135	1.00

Source: NICOLINI, Alberto. *Universo Urbanístico Português* [The Portuguese Urban Universe], p. 605; FERNÁNDEZ, José Luis García. In: *La Ciudad Iberoamericana* [The Iberoamerican City], pp. 168-171.

    Díaz del Castillo described at length the great variety of goods sold in the plaza. They were so numerous and so diversified, and "the market was so crowded with people, and the thronging so excessive in the porticoes, that it was quite impossible to see all in one day."[322] Among Cortes's men were many soldiers who had been in different parts of the world, some in Constantinople, Rome, and other cities in Italy, who said that "they never had seen a market-place of such large dimensions, or which was so well regulated, or so crowded with people as this one at Mexico."[323]

    Then Cortes's entourage headed for the sacred courtyards where the temple was located; they climbed 114 steps of the monument built of stone, overlooking a wide vista of the city. Montezuma invited Cortes to contemplate "his vast metropolis, with the towns

---

322 Idem, p. 218.
323 Ibidem, p. 219.

which were built in the lake," as well as other towns on land surrounding the lake; he also said that, "from this place we should have a better view of the great market."[324] From the summit of the temple, they could observe the throngs of people in the plaza, some buying, others selling. According to Castillo, "The bustle and noise occasioned by this multitude of human beings was so great that it could be heard at a distance of more than four miles." The account reveals that the Spanish conquistadors experienced a new way of thinking.

Montezuma's plaza was 4.8 times larger than that constructed in the Fortress of Salvador. It represented an entirely new dimension and ended up influencing the construction of plazas and cities such as Puebla, Santiago, and Lima. Cortes, when he occupied Mexico, rebuilt it with smaller dimensions. Dazzled by what they saw, the Spanish absorbed a new urban standard and broke with certain aspects of the classical and Medieval tradition of reduced spaces—a new vision that did not get translated into the Portuguese world.

The size of plazas in relation to the length of the city or fortress provides another source of data that can be examined to shed light on the standards of the era. The theoretical models of Martini and Cataneo employ proportions of the plaza to the city that are between 1/6 and 1/4. The Spanish followed a standard of 1/5, meaning that the plaza corresponded to 20% of the longest dimension of the city. The relative size of the plaza in the Fortress of Salvador was small, revealing a unique style (Table 28). Its proportion of 1/6, the smallest of those included in the theoretical models, corresponded to the foot, a basic standard of the human body described by Vitruvius, representing 1/6 of a person's height.[325] The plaza in the Portuguese Fortress of Daman in India, constructed a few decades later, measured 1/4 of the total length.

---

324 Idem.
325 POLLIO, Marcus Vitruvius. *Los Diez Libros de Architectura* [The Ten Books on Architecture], p. 58. Vitruvius wrote, "The length of the foot is one sixth of the height of the body; of the forearm, one fourth; and the breadth of the breast is also one fourth. The other members, too, have their own symmetrical proportions [...]"..

Table 28 - Standard Proportions in Length of Plazas and Cities

City or Model	Ratio	Percentage (%)
Francesco Martini	1/6 to 1/4	16 to 25
Pietro Cataneo	1/5.5 to 1/3.57	18 to 28
Lima, Peru	1/5	20
Salvador, Brazil	1/6	16.66
Daman, India	1/4	25

Source: MARTINI, Francesco di Giorgio, Trattati Di Architettura Ingegneria e Arte Militare [Treatise on Architecture, Engineering, and Military Arts], I, f. 7v, táboa 10; CATANEO, Pietro. L'Architettura [Architecture], pp. 222, 224; FERNÁNDEZ, José Luis García. La Ciudad Iberoamericana [The Iberoamerican City], p. 168; BRITO, Raquel Soeiro de. Goa e as praças do norte revisitadas [Goa and the northern cities revisited], p. 127.

In conclusion, the facts suggest that the central plaza of the Fortress of Salvador drew its theoretical inspiration from the models of proportion and symmetry defended by Vitruvius. Adaptations were made with the aim of taking advantage of the topography of the terrain for defensive purposes, echoing the Greek tradition of adjusting the city to the site and planning it with proportions that would attain symmetry. To complete the typology, the only thing lacking on the perimeter of the plaza in Salvador was a colonnade, a sequence of porticos called *stoas*; however, if we consider the colonial arcades of the Municipal Council Building, we can perceive a certain resemblance. In sum, the Portuguese and the ancient Greeks had something in common.

30. The Pelourinho District

The royal houses, where the governors reside, are in front of the plaza, in the middle of which was the pillory [...].

Priest Vicente do Salvador

The pillory was the symbol of local power. A pillar of stone on top of a pedestal, with irons on the upper part, erected in front of the Municipal Council Building, it was the physical manifestation of the public right to punish. Every town had a jail and a pillory, structures designed to carry out criminal justice. Some authors argue that the act of erecting a stone column symbolized taking possession of land, a point of view they support with classical references. This is plausible: stone pillars on pedestals are associated with various other religious or cultural manifestations, a notable example being the maypole festival, when people danced around a tree trunk or pole erected in the middle of a town commons. This is still celebrated in many places in the interior of Brazil; another variant was practiced in the Nile River Delta, during which the population danced around a pole, believing that a prophet or saint lived inside or on top of the trunk. For certain authors, the maypole festival represented the community's authority over its space.[326]

---

326 Idem, p. 205.

The act of erecting a pillar, trunk, or column in the center of a particular piece of land carries multiple and complex meanings: Osiris, for example, was represented in Egypt in the form of a pillar; among the Celts, a column signified the world axis. The base and chapter of the pillar convey the notion of a tree of life, in which the base represents the roots, the shaft stands for the trunk, and the chapiter symbolizes the leaves.

To set a pillar on a piece of land can also be perceived as an act of self-affirmation. Strabo's historical reference is relevant: "It was an old custom to raise posts or poles for the duration of a trip, an example of which is the column in the shape of a tower erected in the Strait of Messina, in front of Messina, called the Tower of Peloro."[327] This last word comes from the Greek term meaning something of "enormous girth." In the age of the great voyages, the Portuguese used stone pillars to assert their claims to conquered lands. In this way, they hoped to achieve certainty and primacy with a form of proof that only stone could afford, due to its weight and durability.

Such symbolic meanings pale, however, in light of the function of the pillory in the Iberian justice system. Dictionaries are in agreement in defining *pelourinho*: "A column of stone or wood, in a plaza or public place, associated with exposing and punishing criminals."[328] Historical documents often used another term for the pillory, *picota*, a designation from the Iberian Peninsula that referred to a post to which rings were attached, serving the same purpose. In the Viterbo dictionary, *picota* is defined as a "sign of jurisdiction," that is, the power to administer justice, through which "criminals were exposed to humiliation."[329] In Portugal and Brazil, the *pelourinho* continued to bear a direct relationship to the power to administer punishment through whippings or public exposure, as determined by the Council. Public humiliation held the wrongdoer up as an example to be avoided.

---

327 SANTO, Moisés Espírito. *Origens Orientais da Religião Popular Portuguesa* [Oriental Origins of Portuguese Popular Religion], p. 203.
328 Online Aurélio Dictionary.
329 VITERBO, Frei Joaquim de Santa Rosa de. *Elucidário das palavras, termos e frases que em Portugal antigamente se usaram [...]* [Elucidation of words, terms, and phrases formerly used in Portugal], II, p. 478.

The Fortress of Salvador

The Viterbo dictionary states that the noun *picota* is derived from the verb *empicotar*, "to expose a criminal or wrongdoer to humiliation by cuffing him to the rings of a pillory [*picota*] when he is not a defendant in cases warranting greater punishment than whippings or humiliation."[330] There is no doubt that the *picota*, later called the *pelourinho*, was the place where these punishments were carried out, but it could only be set up in locations that were authorized for meting out justice and exercising administration over a particular territory. In this sense, building a pillory was preceded by a formal act of constituting or authorizing power.

In the captaincy of Ilheus in 1547, Jorge de Figueiredo Correia granted powers to Lucas Giraldo to build, as he saw fit, towns and fortresses in authorized land grants, and giving him "jurisdiction and control" over "terminals, councils, fora, pillories, and other insignia, liberties, and honors."[331] Similarly, in 1496, King Dom João II decided that the town of Vale de Prados in Portugal should have a "noose, pillory, and post"[332]—such was the royal power to delegate judicial and administrative power.

An appropriate comprehension of the role of the pillory in the historical penal system requires knowledge of the mechanism of punishments, and the best description of it can be found in the *Seven-Part Code*. There were seven forms of punishment for crimes, four of which were considered grave and three of less significance. The gravest punishment was the death penalty or amputation of limbs. Next came the penalty of enslavement in mines or other kinds of forced labor, with the criminal being bound in chains or fetters. The third mode of grave punishment was exile or banishment and confiscation of property. The fourth was confinement to jail and fetters, that is, being chained in a cell, a punishment applied only to slaves. Free men did not suffer the same confinement, but were given intermittent sentences while they awaited judgment.

---

330 Idem, p. 214.
331 COELHO FILHO, Luiz Walter. *A Capitania de São Jorge e a Década do Açúcar* [The Captaincy of São Jorge and the Decade of Sugar], p. 157.
332 VITERBO, Frei Joaquim de Santa Rosa de. *Elucidário das palavras, termos e frases que em Portugal antigamente se usaram [...]* [Elucidation of words, terms, and phrases formerly used in Portugal], II, p. 478.

Among the three lesser forms of punishment, the first was exile without confiscation of property; the second was dishonor and dismissal from office, permanently or temporarily; the third and final one, considered less grave according to the values of that era, consisted of a set of three different punishments: whippings, confinement to "the dishonor of the pillory," and exposure to the sun, unclothed, for a certain number of hours, with honey applied to the body for flies to feed upon.[333]

This hierarchy of punishments was also observed in Portugal. Naturally, some adjustments were made, since the ordinances set forth the punishment applicable to each case with precision. For instance, exposure to the sun, the last punishment described, was not included in the ordinances. Classic crimes had their usual sentences, almost always exile or death, but carrying them out depended on the pragmatic considerations of populating colonies in the kingdom. In this respect, exile was the most prominent and common form of punishment.

In Portugal, corporal punishment and exposure to public humiliation were called *penas vis*, punishments of degradation. One type was whipping the criminal while in a pillory or walking through the town. Another form of *pena vil* included exposing the criminal to the town while bound with a tether tied around the neck, and publicly proclaiming the criminal's sentence. Public exposure could also take place at the pillory. In practice, the pillory was sometimes, but not always, used in applying the *pena vil*, since being forced to walk through the streets emphasized the public and degrading nature of the punishment.

Noblemen, clergy, judges, councilmen, prosecutors and their children, shipmasters and pilots, wealthy merchants, and people who owned horses and stables might be excluded from such punishments, substituted by exile for two years. Exclusion from the *penas vis* could not be granted if the crimes were lese majeste, sodomy, false witness, counterfeiting currency or other counterfeits, theft, sorcery, or pandering (being a go-between in amorous adventures). In practice, the

---

[333]*LAS SIETE PARTIDAS* [*Seven-Part Code*]. Sétima Partida, Título XXXI, lei IV.

victims of *penas vis* were laborers, slaves, simple people, or common criminals.

In the Fortress of Salvador, the pillory was built in the main plaza; Gabriel Soares de Souza reported its presence in 1586. In 1603, Governor Diogo Botelho landed in the city of Salvador and assumed residence in the Governor's Palace. In front, in the middle of the plaza, was the pillory. The Governor ordered that it be transferred to another site where he would not have to see it: simply looking at it made him sad, remembering how he was almost beheaded at the foot of a pillory when the throne passed to the control of Spain, allied with Dom Antônio do Crato and his group opposing King Felipe. Diogo Botelho was saved through a providential marriage with the sister of the Court Secretary.

The Franciscan friar Vicente reported that Salvador was left without a pillory, since Diogo Botelho was not the only one who despised it. Despite the protests by Frei Vicente, who believed that crimes should not go without punishment, it was not rebuilt by the Governor's successors,[334] a fact that can be confirmed by examining the records of the Municipal Council, in which there are few references to the site. Punishments by whipping, however, were still practiced.

In 1542, a person who sold wine without a license from the Municipal Council would be sentenced to fifty lashes, if he were a laborer.[335] In 1650, a new law setting the price of wine was passed: anyone who charged above this amount would be imprisoned in the dungeon and whipped "publicly through the public streets of this city with a tether and public proclamation [...]."[336] In the same year, it was determined that whoever refused to respect the price of oil would be sentenced to "whippings through the public streets."[337] In

---

334 SALVADOR, Frei Vicente do. *História do Brasil 1500-1627* [History of Brazil, 1500-1627], p. 346.
335 DOCUMENTOS históricos do Arquivo Municipal [Historical Documents of the Municipal Archive], V. 2º, p. 104.
336 DOCUMENTOS históricos do Arquivo Municipal [Historical Documents of the Municipal Archive], V. 2º, p. 63.
337 Idem, p. 108.

1652, the penalty of whippings "through the public streets" was renewed for crimes against price controls.[338]

Reports about the pillory in Salvador are scarce. At some point, it was rebuilt in the Terreiro de Jesus, but the cries of those being punished disturbed the religious activities of the Jesuits, so, in 1727, it was transferred to the public square by the São Bento gate.[339] In 1742, it was rebuilt elsewhere, although it is not possible to identify the location. However, it is possible to describe it: the column was reinforced inside with brass spikes for greater security; on top was a decorative piece in the form of a sphere upon which a dove stood. Portuguese pillories traditionally had simple or armillary spheres placed on top.[340] The dove represented the city of Salvador, a symbol bestowed to it by King Dom João III.[341]

In 1807, the pillory was transferred to the Carmo gate, nowadays the Largo do Pelourinho, where it remained until 1835. In a resolution passed on September 7, 1835, at the request of the Second of July Society, the Municipal Council decided to remove it, leaving its trace only in the place name.[342] The relationship between the general public and the pillory had never been peaceful: it represented the memory of a form of justice that no one wanted to preserve.

The end of the pillory did not, however, mean the extinction of *penas vis*, which were not outlawed until the abolition of slavery. The Imperial Constitution of 1824 banned the use of whips, torture, and other cruel penalties, but the Criminal Code of 1830 allowed the use of whips as a moderate form of punishment for slaves.

In Portugal, pillories survived as cultural heritage; they can

---

338 Ibidem, p. 199.
339 MATTOS, Waldemar. *Evolução Histórica e Cultural do Pelourinho* [Historical and Cultural Evolution of Pelourinho], p. 117.
340 A historic astronomical instrument composed of numerous metal rings representing the main circles of a celestial sphere.
341 DOCUMENTOS históricos do Arquivo Municipal [Historical Documents of the Municipal Archive], V. 9 º, p. 197.
342 MATTOS, Waldemar. *Evolução Histórica e Cultural do Pelourinho* [Historical and Cultural Evolution of Pelourinho], p. 118.

be seen to this day in small towns as a decorated pillar in the center of the plaza. But in Brazil, social history did not allow this memory to survive in the sublimated form of cultural heritage—an intriguing difference between the two countries.

31. The Citadel and the Governor's House

First of all, the ruler's palace should be in the supreme part of the main plaza, in an eminent place [...]

Francesco di Giorgio Martini

In cities, castles, and fortresses, it was common to construct houses fortified with towers and ramparts with the purpose of providing a stronghold, command post, and point of resistance in case of invasion. Another purpose was to protect the most powerful person from threats emanating from his own community. In the Middle Ages, such structures were called *castelejos*, a designation that was later replaced with "*cidadelas*" after the emergence of military engineering. In simple terms, it was a fort inside a fortress. In the Portuguese military tradition, the citadel coincided with the captain's house; it was always strategically located in relation to the overall defense of the plaza or city. At the Fortress of Salvador, the governor's house was planned to fulfill this role as a command post and stronghold of resistance.

The citadel originated in the notion that the king, tyrant, captain, or governor constituted the head of defense of a particular place and therefore needed a strong, well-situated structure from which to do combat with invaders or to defend against adversaries. This double notion—internal and external defense—depended on the specific situation of each city or plaza. Aristotle, for example, emphasized that the citadel was best suited to monarchical or oligarchic governments, which needed internal defense.[343]

The logic of double defense, both internal and external, was followed in the sixteenth century. Leonardo Torriani, an Italian engineer who assisted in the fortification of the city of Salvador, wrote at the end of the century that the issues involved in fortifying any island, kingdom, or province should be considered on two planes, "those inside and those outside": as protection against the population within—enemy vassals, staff, or relatives—there should be castles and fortresses within the city; as protection against neighboring populations, "the same cities, at enormous expense, encircle themselves with thick ramparts and towering bulwarks and watchtowers."[344]

According to the *Seven-Part Code*, when an army had to encamp, the leader's tent was assigned to the center, with those of his officials lying in a wider circle, constituting a sort of protective wall. Between the leader and his officials was a space devoted to the movement of people on horseback in the service of the king or who came to defend the leader if a threat arose.[345]

The notion that a citadel should be constructed in the center of a fortress was widespread, although not compulsory. Eximenes, a Medieval theoretician, argued that the citadel or prince's palace should be situated next to the ramparts; this allowed the prince to mobilize troops freely, without disturbing the daily life of the city. In the city-fortresses constructed by the Portuguese from the sixteenth century onward, citadels were common, although their location did not follow any regular pattern.

To illustrate, let us examine the locations of citadels in Chaul, Bassein, and Daman. In Chaul, the citadel was next to the beach and close to the commercial establishment, having been the nucleus spur-

---

[343] Aristotle. *Política* [Politics], 1330, b.
[344] TORRIANI, Leonardo. *Descrição e História do Reino das Ilhas Canárias* [Description and History of the Kingdom of the Canary Islands], p. 64.
[345] *LAS SIETE PARTIDAS* [*Seven-Part Code*], Segunda Partida, Título XXIII, lei XX.

ring growth in the city. The citadel of Bassein was on the beach, but it was more centralized in relation to the urban network than in Chaul. The case of Daman is the most intriguing: the fortress construction was well planned, with a centrally located citadel, which, in a certain way, oriented the geometric design of the city. Taking advantage of the earlier Moorish fort, the citadel formed a square with a plaza in the center, surrounded by walls with four bulwarks in the corners, one of which was the captain's residence. A peculiarity of this fortress was that the captain's residence and the plaza both occupied the citadel, a fact that explains its size and proportions: the ratio of the dimensions of the citadel to the fortress as a whole was 1:4 (Table 29). The measurements of the Fortress of Daman were extrapolated from a map and should be viewed as approximations.

Table 29 - Measurements of the Fortress of Daman

Fortress of Daman	Measurement (in Meters)	Proportion
Largest diameter of the fortress	638.88	1
Smallest diameter of the fortress	455.55	1.4
Measurement of the side of the citadel	155.55	4.1
Average measurement of blocks	80.55	7.93

Source: BRITO, Raquel Soeiro de. *Goa e as praças do norte revisitadas* [Goa and the northern cities revisited], p. 127.

For an adequate comparison among Portuguese fortresses, it is necessary to understand the evolution of each one. However, the lack of correct information about the evolution of most constructions *in situ* hampers the comparison; the Fortress of Daman, on the other hand, seems to offer a solid point of reference. Housing the captain or governor in the citadel was a pattern followed in both the Daman and Salvador fortresses, coinciding with the theories about military urbanism. In Martini's opinion, the ruler's palace should be located in the main plaza in a place that was "prominent and elevated on its own,"³⁴⁶ communicating with the citadel through covered, secure means of access.

The area chosen for the citadel of the Fortress of Salvador was the block currently called the Governor's Palace, on a piece of land that, in relation to the total area of the fortress, occupied the most strategic position, being on high ground closer to the vulnerable southern boundary. Equidistant from the two bulwarks on the beach, the citadel overlooked the entire harbor of Salvador. On the corners, it controlled the access roads coming from the southern side; on the west and south, the Ladeira da Conceição; and, on the east, the streets now known as Rua Chile and Rua Ajuda. It was difficult to reach the northern side without being exposed to the control of the citadel. Notably, the terrain is flat and narrow on the northeastern corner, creating a natural defense.

The position of the citadel, closer to the southern boundary, indicates the weight given to defending this side of the fortress, underscoring the military characteristics of its design. There are few records about the original building, but its function as a citadel was clear in the works carried out by Mem de Sá. Through certain declarations, he ordered the construction on the site of a "tower of stone and lime in the style of a bulwark with its portholes and embrasures, and which is next to the houses where the governors live."³⁴⁷ With "battlements and domes" as well as portholes, the tower was treated as a fortress.³⁴⁸ This military construction illustrates well the role of the citadel reserved for the governor's residence.

In the oldest maps of the city, the governor's residence, although occupying the entire front of the plaza, took up 1/3 or perhaps 2/3 of the north/ south side of the block that nowadays is completely

---

346 MARTINI, Francesco Di Giorgio. *Trattati Di Architettura Ingegneria e Arte Militare* [Treatise on Architecture, Engineering, and Military Arts], I, p. 22.
347 INSTRUMENTOS de serviços de Mem de Sá [Service Declarations of Mem de Sá]. In: *Anais da Biblioteca Nacional*, V. XXVII, p. 162.
348 In the military jargon of the era, a porthole was a circular, square, or rectangular opening in a wall or at the top (on the parapet), through which cannons fired. Embrasures were vertical openings in walls with the same purpose. Battlements were notched projections on the top of walls, which, according to the standards of the era, could assume various forms.

occupied by the Government Palace. There used to be a plot in the middle that took up a third of the block and another building occupying the rest of it. In 1772, measurements were taken that showed that the side of the block facing what is now Rua Chile was 19.3 fathoms long, that is, 2/3 of the entire block.

The perception that the site had an excellent citadel lasted throughout the following centuries. The city grew and its boundaries drifted in two opposite directions: toward Santo Antônio Além do Carmo and toward São Pedro. Furthermore, the system of fortification of the city underwent an evolution, and documents demonstrate that this expansion also modified the physical notion of the citadel. The system grew in successive rings; the citadel, first located on the block with the governor's house, expanded toward the entire southern crown of the fortress and, later, toward the boundaries from the Praça Castro Alves as far as the Largo do Pelourinho.

The model of strong citadels was faithful to the vision of Leonardo Torriani, who, around 1605, designed a new system of defense for the growing city. The new plan included the "citadel which Your Majesty ordered built," the objective being the creation of a secure stronghold. This plan, later merged with the original fortress, corresponded to the crown of the southern plateau.

The defense systems of the city of Salvador that were built until at least 1720 included citadels as reinforced sites where those defending the city could take shelter in extreme situations. The block containing the Rio Branco Palace, or at least part of it, was the first citadel in the Fortress of Salvador; its original military function should not be forgotten. It has a special history as the only space that, from the very beginning, was chosen for a citadel; its location is due to the fact that the master architect Luís Dias identified that particular block as best suited for the military functions of a citadel.

32. Municipal Council Building, Jail, and Butcher's Market

> *The treasury, prison, and assembly ought to adjoin the forum, but in such a way that their dimensions may be proportionate to those of the forum.*
>
> Vitruvius

In the Roman world, "forum" referred to the plaza, while "assembly" was the room where senators and municipal councilors held meetings on public affairs. Vitruvius defined the forum as the place where magistrates performed their duties, making decisions on public and private issues. The assembly was usually a large rectangular room, with adjoining rooms devoted to the administration of civil affairs. There was another type of building, also located "next to the forum," called a "basilica," so named because it was a royal building; *basileu* in Greek means "king," which explains the origin of the term. Erected in the most protected part, the basilica housed the activities of merchants during the winter. The forum and its porticos, along with the assembly, jail, and basilica, constituted the set of buildings where politics, justice, and business were handled and resolved. This represented the center of the civic life of the city.

The arrangement of political powers around the main plaza had not altered by the sixteenth century, a pattern repeated in the Fortress of Salvador with only small variations. In the fifteenth century, Alberti commented with great clarity on the specialization of urban spaces. In his view, public life was composed of a sacred part, where the divinity was honored, and a profane one, dedicated to the administration of social affairs. In times of peace, senators and judges were the representatives of the community; in times of war, this role fell to the generals.[349] Senators worked in the assembly; judges, in the court; and generals, in the military camp.

Alberti recalled that, in antiquity, senators held meetings in the temple. There was a period when they would meet outside urban areas, but, subsequently, they preferred to assemble in the city in a place built specifically for this purpose. The assembly, Alberti believed, should be situated in the center of the city, near the judicial curia, which should be larger in order to accommodate all parties. The assembly building should be secure and reinforced to withstand any threats from the population. The architect distinguished between the space dedicated to meetings—*curia senatoria*—and the place for the administration of justice—the *curia judiciaria*.[350]

The center of the city was also appropriate as a site for the provisions storehouse and the public treasury, Alberti maintained, since it was more secure and accessible to everyone. The jail should be in a part of the city that was sufficiently secure and well-traveled, suggesting the possibility of situating it near the main plaza as well. Echoing the ancients, he argued that there should be three types of jail: the first, used for minor offenses, suited for promoting good discipline and public calm; the second, a civil prison for holding debtors; and the third, a place where dangerous criminals were held. With a humanist vision, Alberti repudiated the type of jail that was a "dark underground similar to a frightening sepulcher," and suggested instead a prison with walls dividing the main section, with guards posted around it.[351]

---

349 ALBERTI, Leon Battista. *L'Architettura* [Architecture]. Livro V, capítulo VI, p. 188.
350 Idem. Livro V, capítulo IX, pp. 195-196.
351 Ibidem. Livro V, capítulo XIII, p. 209.

The Fortress of Salvador

Martini's view did not diverge from Alberti's. The former proposed that "the officials' building, the prison, the customs house, and the salt storehouse" should be near the public plaza,[352] a guideline that also applied to the ruler's palace for the "convenience of holding audiences and civil congregations"; next to it, instead of a basilica, should be a spacious shop or portico where merchants and citizens could meet. He also suggested a plaza for the market, which should be surrounded by a portico and shops, forming a space dedicated to buying and selling.

Pietro Cataneo was more emphatic on the subject, stressing the need to avoid "the same error of Rome and other cities," which, for some reason, did not surround the main plaza with the appropriate public buildings. He determined that, first and foremost, the ruler's palace should be in the most privileged spot on the plaza. In the Fortress of Salvador, this guideline was observed; the governor's house, on the southern side of the plaza, overlooked the ocean, while its front windows faced the northeast, taking advantage of shade and good ventilation. Cataneo situated the council, treasury, and public armory in the facilities of the ruler's palace, but located the court in a nearby building, while the prison was in an even more discrete spot. He said the salt storehouse should also be situated on the main plaza, near which should be currency exchanges and merchants' stalls.[353]

If Vitruvius, Alberti, Martini, and Cataneo presented similar ideas about the arrangement of spaces surrounding the main plaza, their theoretical concepts seem to have been fully applied in the Fortress of Salvador. On the elite side was the Governor's Palace, while on the other side, to the east, was the block where local powers were stationed. The hierarchy of power can be reconstructed through the areas chosen for each building.

The block where the Jail and Municipal Council Building was located, as well as the butcher's market, showed some interesting features: it was on the inland side, as if in the rear part; and its design was different from the others, being originally in the shape of a lozenge (a

---

352 MARTINI, Francesco Di Giorgio. *Trattati Di Architettura Ingegneria e Arte Militare* [Treatise on Architecture, Engineering, and Military Arts]. I, p. 22.
353 CATANEO, Pietro *Dell'Architettura* [On Architecture], pp. 203-204.

parallelogram with four equal sides and different angles). To ensure the symmetry or harmony of the shape of the plaza with the northern line of the fortress, the architect integrated half of the area of the lozenge into the public space. By observing the design of the fortress, we can see that approximately half of the block was subtracted in order to form the shape of the plaza, a six-sided polygon. A straight line was drawn through the lozenge, cutting it into two parallel sides. The result was the formation of two trapezoids (quadrilaterals with one pair of parallel sides) that were the same size but in inverted positions.

The block covered approximately half the area that the standard-sized blocks did, a geometrical peculiarity noted by Paulo Thedim Barreto. In commenting on the shape of the Municipal Council Building in Salvador, he defined it as a regular trapezoid and called attention to some of its geometric characteristics, describing the design as an "exceptional example of the application of the trapezoidal shape."[354]

Originally, the Municipal Council Building did not take up the entire block; the trapezoid was divided into lots. A study by Paulo Ormindo de Azevedo showed that a later renovation took advantage of the "retaining walls of existing houses," resulting in the size of the building as it now stands.[355] In the words of Azevedo, "given the differences in the thickness of the walls of the current City Hall, the variation in its spaces, and other details of its construction, we can clearly identify the four houses that originally occupied the block."

We know with relative certainty that, in the first lot on the north side, a well-ventilated spot forming a corner with the present-day

---

354 BARRETO, Paulo Thedim. "Casas de Câmara e Cadeia" [Municipal Council Building and Jail]. In: *Revista do Patrimônio Histórico e Artístico Nacional* [Journal of National Historic and Artistic Heritage]. V. 11, p. 162. Barreto states, "[...] the existing plan of the Municipal Council Building in Salvador has the form of a rectangular trapezoid. The upper side of the trapezoid is twice as long as the base and, with only a slight difference, is almost equal to the diagonal of the square formed by the larger base. It is beyond our present study to investigate this particular divergence in shapes or the exceptional example of this application of the trapezoidal shape."
355 AZEVEDO, Paulo Ormindo de. "O Traço Hispânico do Paço Municipal de Salvador" [The Hispanic Design of City Hall in Salvador]. In: *Anais do 4º Congresso de História da Bahia.* V. I, p. 408.

Ladeira da Praça, the building that housed the Municipal Council and jail was built. Azevedo states that it was "relatively narrow on the rear side" and "must have been longer on the front, up to seventeen meters, to contain not only the council chambers, but also the vertical access and scribe's office."[356] This measurement, derived from an examination of the site, suggests a lot that occupied one-third of the front of the block. According to Luís Dias, the work was composed of "a very good, well-finished jail, with a hearing room and council chambers above, all made of stone and clay plastered with lime and roofed with tiles."[357]

In commenting on the construction of the Jail and Municipal Council Building, Azevedo praised the precision of its geometric design, noting that even the "rear façade of the wall has a trapezoidal section to absorb the angle of the Rua da Ajuda and prevent it from reverberating into the council chambers," a characteristic that still exists. He concluded that the precision was the work of the architect and revealed fifteenth-century characteristics.[358]

The building housing the jail and Municipal Council was not the only structure on the block. Luís Dias also built a butcher's market and probably a house for the mayor and jailkeeper. The butcher's market was built by the stonemason Belchior Gonçalves, who received a payment of 6,880 réis for 21.5 fathoms of construction, according to a receipt dated February 26, 1552.[359] Another payment, recorded April 7, 1551, was made for the construction of 12 fathoms of wattle and daub for the mayor's and jailkeeper's house.[360] The Jail and Municipal Council Building, the butcher's market, and the mayor's and

---

356 AZEVEDO, Paulo Ormindo de. "O Traço Hispânico do Paço Municipal de Salvador" [The Hispanic Design of City Hall in Salvador]. In: *Anais do 4º Congresso de História da Bahia*. V. I, pp. 408-409.
357 Letter from Luís Dias to King Dom João III, dated August 15, 1551. In: MALHEIROS DIAS, Carlos. *História da Colonização Portuguesa no Brasil* [History of Portuguese Colonization in Brazil]. III, p. 363.
358 Idem, p. 409.
359 DOCUMENTOS HISTÓRICOS [Historical Documents], V. XIII, Bibliotheca Nacional, order of payment nº 974.
360 DOCUMENTOS HISTÓRICOS [Historical Documents], V. XII, Bibliotheca Nacional, order of payment nº 560.

jailkeeper's houses belonged to the set of buildings associated with the administration of the collective good.

The butcher's market, for example, reveals intriguing particularities that completely escape modern understanding. The Portuguese term for butcher, *açougue*, is derived from the Arab word *assoq*, which signified market, fair. In Medieval Portuguese, the term was used for places where merchandise was bought and sold in markets composed of small shops, which usually belonged to the municipal council or the king. Besides meat, these markets could include the sale of fruits, vegetables, bread, and other items. In that era, there was a tribute imposed on consumption, known as *açougagem*, or butcher's tax. In standards closer to the sixteenth century, the butcher's market was the place authorized by the municipality for selling meats, fruits, and vegetables.

A good example was the regulation on new butcher's markets in the Praça de Évora in 1470, when the King, at the request of the Municipal Council, established a tax to be collected from merchants conducting business there. Bakers, sellers of fruits and vegetables, fishermen, and butchers paid daily fees, receiving a spot to exercise their trade. Nobody was permitted to sell in the plaza. The only place of business allowed was the butcher's market. Actually, the tax seems to have corresponded to a daily rent for the physical space. The council assured the butcher's market a monopoly on provisions for the city and, in return, received a valuable source of income.[361]

This system, with historically dependent variations, was present in the city of Salvador. In the first place, the butcher's market belonged to the Municipal Council and was sometimes rented out, yielding substantial economic profit. In 1630, Simão Alves leased two stalls[362] in the market for one year, for which he paid 100,000 réis,[363] slightly more than half the amount spent on carpentry work on the new Municipal Council Building in 1636. Rents financed city construction projects,

---

[361] PEREIRA, Gabriel. *Documentos Históricos da Cidade de Évora* [Historical Documents of the City of Évora], pp. 108-109.

[362] Stalls could be tents or square enclosures.

[363] DOCUMENTOS históricos do Arquivo Municipal [Historical Documents of the Municipal Archive]. V. 1º, p. 152.

and profits from the butcher's market also served to ease shortages in provisions and to prevent conflicts associated with speculation.

The minutes of Salvador's Municipal Council reveal that the butcher's market, located on the same block, was considered a significant part of the infrastructure for provisioning the city. In 1634, a contract was drawn up for constructing a new space for the Municipal Council Building, "above the butcher's market,"[364] a project that lasted until 1639, when a passageway was built connecting the old and the new council buildings.[365] The length of the wooden walk indicated that the buildings were near each other, although perhaps not contiguous (Table 30).

Table 30 - Progress of Work on Jail and Municipal Council Building, 1626-1639

Date	Value (in réis)	Type of Service
April 29, 1626	35,000	Work on jail and council building.
May 8, 1630	1,500	Work on roofs of jail and council building and tiled corridor floor. Repair of roof tiles coated with lime, replacing them where needed, and tiling corridor floor in jail.
November 22, 1634	14,000	Repair and replacement of roof tiles on council building and jail and new council building beyond the butchers' markets, covering all costs of lime as well as of tiles.
November 23, 1635	171,000	The work of the stonemason on the new council building, specifically, eaves, sills, roof tiles, and plaster trim inside and outside and on the front parts of the building.

---

364 Idem, p. 260.
365 Ibidem, p. 404.

December 23, 1635	82,740	Work on the new council building, specifically: install beams, floor planks, build staircase and door and front part of the house above and below, install rafters and new cornices, with attic.
September 20, 1636	170,000	Work on the new council building, specifically: cedar lining, windows with openings and doors and closets, over the stairs, and finish lining the two corridors.
October 13, 1638	32,000	Roof tiles on jail and tiled corridor floors.
May 28, 1639	45,000	Two tea doors of good wood with hardware and hinges and a wooden passageway to lead from the old council building to the new, cover with limestone, then cover with roof tiles, and open walls for both doorways and put up wooden grilles along the passageway.

Source: DOCUMENTOS históricos do Arquivo Municipal [Historical Documents of the Municipal Archive]. V. 1º, pp. 34, 260, 293, 294, 384, 404.

Paulo Ormindo has identified four units in the block: the first, as mentioned above, was the Jail and Municipal Council Building; the second, in the far south, faced the plaza; the third, in the rear, opened up onto Rua do Tira-Chapéu; and the final, a single-story building in front, lay between the buildings to the north and south. The single-story building may have been the butcher's market, with the new council building located just to the north.

In 1660, another expansion was undertaken. The jail was too small for the number of people who were brought in from various places, and the butcher's market could no longer meet the needs of the population. Plots and a house on the far side of the block were purchased, completing the Municipal Council's ownership of the entire block.

Notably, the alignment of the façade of the Municipal Council Building was preserved; all the renovations took advantage of the pre-existing masonry and built over it. The foundations of the imposing building we see today were mostly constructed in the sixteenth century, and, due to this simple fact, the oblique façade was conserved. This strange alignment, which, surprisingly, has drawn little attention or few commentaries, reflects the elements of symmetry at play during the founding of the city. As Azevedo notes, "The different thicknesses of the internal wall of the entryway prove that the façades of the original houses were preserved."[366] The only addition was the entryway that projected toward the plaza; indeed, the records, as well as the geometric design of the fortress, excluded it from the original area of the block assigned to the council building.

---

366 AZEVEDO, Paulo Ormindo de. "O Traço Hispânico do Paço Municipal de Salvador" [The Hispanic Design of City Hall in Salvador]. In: *Anais do 4º Congresso de História da Bahia*, V. I, pp. 410-411.

33. Infrastructure at the Harbor

Around the pier and harbor are a storehouse, station, and reservoir, adequate for the characteristics of the site.

Francesco di Giorgio Martini

On the Góes stream, along the section currently situated between the churches of Conceição and Corpo Santo, a space was reserved for the following services: construction and repair of ships, on the site for beaching boats; storage and safekeeping of goods belonging to the Crown, to be distributed from the Storehouse and Powder Vault; collection of duties imposed on merchandise, in the Customs House; administration of accounting, personnel, and assets, functions assigned to the Treasury and Accounting House; and the Blacksmith Shop, where metal items were forged. This early distribution of functions obeyed a certain logical order, although, over time, certain modifications were made. The structures and buildings, according to the original design of the Fortress of Salvador, were located on the ocean front.

Bulwarks were placed on each end of the Góes stream:

— on the side next to the Conceição da Praia was the Santa Cruz station, the smaller bulwark; the section beyond the

present-day Conceição da Praia, toward the Largo da Preguiça, was known as the Pescadores ("Fishermen's") stream;
— on the end across from the stream or cove was the Góes bulwark, the larger of the two, built by the team of the Captain Major Pero de Góes.

Between the two defensive bulwarks were the public buildings and, in a separate section, places for naval activities, an arrangement compatible with the rational system adopted in the fortress plans.

In 1586, Gabriel Soares reported that the "general wharf for merchandise" was located at this site.[367] Some deeds entered in the Old Register of Charters and Deeds of the São Bento Monastery refer to the boat beaching site. For instance, one deed deals with a plot of land measuring 20 by 6 fathoms (44 x 13.2 meters) on the "beach of Nossa Senhora da Conceição to the boat beaching site where goods are unloaded from ships," where there was a house of wattle and daub, in which a carpenter lived, which was transferred in accordance with the legal title conveyed to Baltazar Ferraz in 1596, as discussed earlier.[368] On this beaching site, carpenters from the river built and repaired ships, caravels, and galleys.

Beyond the beaching site, in a location that was more central and almost aligned with the main plaza, a set of buildings was constructed along the beach on a north/south axis, according to the sequence described by Luís Dias, which appears to have been the following: Blacksmith Shop, Storehouse, Powder Vault, Customs House, and Treasury and Accounting House (Table 31). "And thus we are constructing [...] on the Góes stream the treasury and customs house and storehouses and blacksmith shops, all of stone and clay plastered with lime and roofed with tiles [...],"[369] Dias wrote. However, we cannot categorically affirm that this was the original sequence of buildings, only that it is a hypothesis.

---

367 SOUZA, Gabriel Soares, *Notícia do Brasil* [Report from Brazil], capítulo VII, p. 256.
368 LIVRO *Velho do Tombo* [Old Register of Charters and Deeds], p. 318.
369 Letter from Luís Dias to King Dom João III, dated August 15, 1551. In: MALHEIROS DIAS, Carlos. *História da Colonização Portuguesa no Brasil* [History of Portuguese Colonization in Brazil]. III, p. 363.

Table 31 - Buildings Constructed on Góes stream, 1549-1552

Building	Function
Treasury and Accounting House	**Accounting, personnel, and assets**: agreements on rights and duties. Records of income, orders, and provisions for officials in captaincies. Contracts and leases. Register of personnel.
Customs House	**Tax collection:** orders and collection of taxes on merchandise.
Supplies and Provisions Storehouse	**Storage and safekeeping** of ship gear, provisions, weapons and ammunition, construction materials, and other items.
Powder Vault	**Storage and safekeeping** of gunpowder.
Blacksmith Shop	**Workshop** for blacksmiths.

Source: The author.

The Blacksmith Shop was not discussed by Luís Dias, but, on August 8, 1550, a carpenter named Antonio Gonçalves was paid for the "contract work of covering the Blacksmith Shop and Customs House with wood."[370] The activities at the Blacksmith Shop were connected to the Storehouse, since the raw material, iron, and the finished products had their origin and destination in the repository.

The Supplies and Provisions Storehouse was controlled by an overseer, who was responsible for guarding, preserving, and controlling almost all the goods belonging to the Crown. Four different types of goods can be identified in the array of merchandise:

> **1. Provisions:** all wheat, manioc, wine, vinegar, salt, oil, meat, and other foodstuffs necessary for supplying officials and residents of the fortress; food stocks had to be stored in the appropriate building; and distribution was based on a particular order, in which each person who performed services

---

[370] DOCUMENTOS HISTÓRICOS [Historical Documents], V. XIII, Bibliotheca Nacional, order of payment nº 646, p. 30.

for the Crown was allotted certain provisions and other necessities determined by the Governor's mandates;

2. Equipment for ships: cloth for sails, rope, tar, pitch, tallow, nails, and other accessories; if a ship sank or was wrecked, the official was responsible for retrieving and taking in materials that could be saved;

3. Arms and ammunition: artillery pieces, falcons, versos, rifles, cannon balls, gunpowder, and other accessories;

4. Construction materials, metals, tools, and related items: iron and copper were safeguarded by an overseer, who supplied the blacksmiths and also controlled distribution of lime, tiles, scales, and various tools.

A 1529 regulation for the Overseer of Provisions and Supplies in the Fortress of São Jorge da Mina on the coast of Africa ordered the construction of two separate buildings, one for provisions and the other for artillery and ammunition.[371] In Lisbon in 1552, there were even more specialized buildings: a storehouse or building for provisions, controlled by an overseer; a river storehouse, which held materials for building and repairing ships; and an armory, in which arms and ammunition were manufactured, stored, and maintained by blacksmiths and gunsmiths.[372]

The size of the storehouse could not be small. In 1517, in the town of Safi, on the Coast of Morocco, the regulations for the construction of the fortress ordered that two structures be built within the castle, one as a granary and another as a storehouse. The measurements were relatively large (Table 32). By examining the historic plans of Salvador, we can see two blocks on the beach with similar measurements. Probably, the Storehouse, Treasury and Accounting House, and Customs House occupied the entire site on the beachfront. They represented functions analogous to those in the city center where the plaza and Governor's Palace were located.

---

371 "Regulation pertaining to the Overseer of Provisions and Supplies," dated February 8, 1529. In: BALLONG-WEN-MEWUDA, J. Bato'ora. *São Jorge da Mina 1482-1637*. V. II, pp. 592-595.
372 BRANDÃO, João. *Grandeza e Abastança de Lisboa em 1552* [Grandeur and Affluence in Lisbon in 1552], pp. 174-178.

Table 32 - Measurements of Storehouses in the Fortresses of Safi and Salvador[373]

City	Length (in Fathoms)	Width (in Fathoms)	Height (in Spans)
Safi (granary)	20 (44 m)	3.5 (7.5 m)	16 (3.52 m)
Safi (storehouse)	12 (26.4)	3.5 (7.5 m)	16 (3.52 m)
Salvador (first block on beachfront)	25.7 (56.5 m)	5.7 (12.5 m)	—
Salvador (second block on beachfront)	22.1 (48.7 m)	5.7 (12.5 m)	—

Source: Carita Helder. Lisboa Manuelina [Manueline Lisbon], p. 234; RAZÃO do Estado do Brasil [Reason for the State of Brazil] (c. 1616). Códice 126 da Bibliotheca Pública Municipal do Porto.

In June of 1549, wood, palm leaves, and other items were acquired for the house on the "river from which salt is collected and other things for the storehouse."[374] On January 21, 1550, André Rodrigues Romeiro did work clearing "a small area of brush next to the storehouses by the stream." [375] On October 22, 1551, Pero de Carvalhaes received compensation in payment "for the storehouse buildings, which were built on the stream of this city."[376]

The Powder Vault represented a special situation. In his letters, Luís Dias said nothing about it, but the practice current at the time was to build a distinct place for storing gunpowder. The risk of fire meant there should be little movement at the site and, if one broke out, other goods in storage would not be destroyed. Gunpowder was therefore segregated from other supplies, a rule compatible with the technical standards of the era. The Powder Vault may also have served

---
373 For Salvador, the author estimated the measurements based on those used in the map in Codex 126.
374 DOCUMENTOS HISTÓRICOS [Historical Documents]. V. XII, Bibliotheca Nacional, order of payment nº 35, p. 286.
375 Idem, order of payment n º 298, p. 372.
376 DOCUMENTOS HISTÓRICOS [Historical Documents]. V. XIII, Bibliotheca Nacional, order of payment nº 840, p. 119.

as a repository for weapons, a hypothesis drawn from the number of payment records related to the building (Table 33). Many stonemasons worked on the building, which was rather unusual.

Table 33 - Cost of Contract Labor on Powder Vault, 1550-1552

Date	Value (in réis)	Beneficiary	Description
October 2, 1550	1,350	Belchior Gonçalves, stonemason	Owed "for work on the powder vault, built on the stream of this city."
October 2, 1550	566	Francisco Pires Verdelho, stonemason	Owed "for the rest of the contract labor for the work done on the powder vault, built on the stream of this city."
October 19, 1551	11,120	Belchior Gonçalves, stonemason	Owed for 25 fathoms of wattle and daub and roofing for the powder vault.
October 1, 1551	3,340	Francisco Gomes, lime burner	Owed for 8 fathoms of wattle and daub for the powder vault.
October 20, 1552	2,600	Francisco Pires Verdelho, stonemason	Owed for 7.66 fathoms of "a wall of stone and clay" for the powder vault.
Total	18,976	—	—

Source: DOCUMENTOS HISTÓRICOS [Historical Documents]. V. XII, Bibliotheca Nacional, orders of payment nº 811, 830, 857, 858, and 1201.

The last pair of buildings were assigned to the Treasury and the Customs House, built at the order of the Chief Purveyor, Antônio Cardoso de Barros in 1553. These were two distinct buildings, housing specific government agencies: the Customs Office, charged with collecting tariffs, and the Treasury and Accounting Office, responsible for the administration of public property, accounting, and personnel. Each building had two stories, the ground floors leading to the pier. They measured 8.8 meters on the side facing the ocean, and 6.6 meters in width;[377] between them was a covered wooden platform forming a veranda. In the outlying captaincies, one building housed both Customs and Accounting; in the Fortress of Salvador, there was not a strict separation between the two, although it is likely that the pair of buildings, joined by the veranda, housed each agency in its respective side, similar to the arrangement in the town of Santos.

In Portugal in the sixteenth century, the customs house was "the house where merchandise is brought in, whether unloaded or in the process of being loaded, national or not, destined for or originating from ships, for the purpose of charging duties, when applicable." The concept used to be applied more widely than nowadays, since the obligation to pass through customs as the first and last act of shipping also applied to coastal routes within the same country. In Lisbon in 1551, for example, duties of 10% were charged in the customs house on all merchandise entering through the mouth of the Tagus River. A tribute of 5% was imposed on cloth and silk that came overland from Castile.

A regulation authorized by King Dom João III to the Provisioner Major Antônio Cardoso de Barros ordered that he construct a "customs house, near the ocean, in an advantageous place, for the proper dispatch of parties and collection of my duties [...]" and another house "[...] in which the business related to my Treasury and Accounting is conducted." [378] These were two distinct divisions, each with its own responsibilities, desks, books, and officials.

Many orders of payment did not specify the object, but only referred to the works undertaken. The volume of entries indicates that most of the works involving walls and public buildings were

---

377 DOCUMENTOS HISTÓRICOS [Historical Documents]. V. XII, Bibliotheca Nacional, order of payment n° 67, p. 423.
378 MENDONÇA, Marcos Carneiro de. *Raízes da Formação Administrativa do Brasil* [Roots of the Administrative Structure of Brazil], p. 92.

constructed along the stream. The ramparts and bulwarks consumed most of the resources; after they were built, most of the disbursements were for expenses relating to the public buildings on the beach and occasionally for some work on the piers.

The early plans of the port of Salvador show that this set of buildings was aligned with the main plaza and the block where the Governor's Palace was located. Apparently there was a small cove with flagstones where stairs and large houses were built along the beach or stone piers. The alignment between the main blocks in the upper city—the plaza and citadel—and the public service buildings in the harbor was a technical detail of the morphology of the Fortress of Salvador, constituting yet another element in the game of symmetry. In a certain respect, it still serves nowadays to compose the main picture-postcard vista of the city, the view from the ocean of the upper and lower city, with the plaza in the center and the Public Storehouse, Customs House, and Treasury being nearby. Another likely reason for this location was public access, which allowed responsibilities to be spread out.

When Tomé de Souza's fleet landed, the lower section was merely a sliver of land squeezed between the hillside and the beach. The position chosen for the Storehouse, Customs House, and Treasury was not directly in the site that served as the port, the Conceição beach. Instead, a more central place was preferred, below the plaza and the citadel. The exact location of the buildings must have offered some topographical feature that made it desirable. The oldest plan of the city of Salvador reveals something curious: to the right of the construction there was apparently a water fountain or reservoir.

The proximity of the Customs House, Storehouse, and plaza represented one more element of the urban planning proposed by Vitruvius, Alberti, and Martini, who recommended locating public buildings along the central axis of the city to facilitate access by residents and outsiders. The location of the plateau between the space for the plaza and that for the public buildings was a detail that did not compromise the logic behind their distribution: there was a technical, geometric rationality that guided the organization of the urban grid and the placement of each building within it.

The stratification of the services of the Treasury, Customs

House, and Storehouse in the harbor zone apparently did not survive for much time. In 1586, according to information from Gabriel Soares de Souza,[379] the buildings had been relocated to land on the north side of the main plaza. It was a new era: private storehouses along the Preguiça beach served as merchandise storehouses, while duties were collected at the new site. The primitive buildings on the beachfront still served as armories.

At the end of the sixteenth century, a large-scale renovation was planned and carried out on the port structures of the city of Salvador, following a design drawn up by the engineer Leonardo Torriani. The Storehouse was relocated to the place where the old Customs House had stood, improvements were made to the structures for mooring ships and storing goods, and a pier and fort were built. The first port of the city was on the Praia da Conceição, but the simple structures originally built there were substantially altered as the city constructed a modest port infrastructure with additional fortifications. At the beginning of the seventeenth century, a new history unfolded, in which the growth of the city imposed major changes on the size and location of each building.

---

379 SOUZA, Gabriel Soares, *Notícia do Brasil* [Report from Brazil], I, capítulo VII, p. 256.

34. The Sé Cathedral

For the temples, the sites for those of the gods under whose particular protection the state is thought to rest and for Jupiter, Juno, and Minerva, should be on the very highest point commanding a view of the greater part of the city.

Vitruvius

The tops of mountains have long served as places for worship. The heights promote spirituality, stimulate contemplation, and approach the sky. Mountains have a divine dimension, being "the encounter between the sky and the earth, the home of the gods and the aim of human ascension."[380] This significance was shared by peoples who constructed their temples in high places and with ample visibility.

Some ancestral forms of worship were described in the Old Testament: "Mountains tremble at the presence of the Lord—even Sinai!—at the presence of the Lord God of Israel."[381] Moses was called by the Lord on Mount Sinai. On the third day, "there was thunder and lightning, with a heavy cloud over the mountain, and the very loud

---

380 CHEVALIER, Jean. *Dicionário de Símbolos* [...] [Dictionary of Symbols], p. 616.
381 Bible, *Judges*, 5:5.

sound of a ram's horn [...]" and "Mount Sinai was completely enveloped in smoke because the Lord had come down in fire on it."[382]

This notion of the sacredness of mountains was shared by the Hebrews and Greeks. "Olympus," in the language of the early inhabitants of Greece, probably signified "mountain." In Hellas, many mountains carried this name.[383] Mount Olympus became firmly identified with the official residence of the immortals, especially Zeus. Over time, the physical notion of the mountain became more abstract, such that Olympus came to be seen as the celestial residence of the divinities. This illustrates the movement from the concrete to the abstract followed by Greek religious culture ever since Aristotle. In Greek cities, temples were built in places that were prominent, visible, and segregated from spaces dedicated to business affairs.

The best example of this concept is the Acropolis of Athens—the city on high, sanctuary of the gods—and especially the Parthenon. In Rome, the situation was no different; on top of the Capitol was the Temple of Jupiter, as Vitruvius recommended, following the "precepts and rites of Etruscan soothsayers"[384] who guided the religious conduct of the Romans.

Other peoples and cultures have also used this symbolism. Fujiyama in Japan, Meru in India, Kuen-Luen in China, Macchu Pichu in Peru, Alborj in Persia, and Qaf in Islamic lore are a few examples of mountains replete with mystical significance. It has been said that the high places "among the Canaanites, Hebrews, Arabs, and Mesopotamians are, par excellence, sanctuary sites."[385] The relationship between height and the cult of a god constituted an ancestral sentiment and, for this reason, was passed on to Christianity.

---

382 Idem, *Exodus*, 19:16.
383 BRANDÃO, Junito de Souza. *Dicionário Mítico-etimológico da mitologia grega* [Mythical-Etymological Dictionary of Greek Mythology]. II, p. 183.
384 POLLIO, Marcus Vitruvius. *Los Diez Libros de Architectura* [The Ten Books on Architecture], p. 25.
385 Santo, Moisés Espírito. *Origens Orientais da Religião Popular Portuguesa* [Oriental Origins of Portuguese Popular Religion], p. 3.

In choosing the site where a church was to be constructed, locations that were high, isolated, and segregated became part of sacred ritual. The mystical principle of heights and the associated idea of the isolation and segregation shaped the thinking of philosophers and architects. They believed that the location and the temple should be visible as something distinct, specific, grandiose—a gateway to the heavens. The relationship with the gods was enhanced by heights, but it also implied isolation. Temples were supposed to suggest calmness and silence, stimulating contemplation; they could not share the same space with mundane activities. In Salvador, such notions were evidenced, presenting some interesting peculiarities.

The Portuguese followed the ancestral pattern that, on a rational plane, hearkened back to Aristotle. The site chosen for the Sé Cathedral in the city of Salvador, constructed around 1551, was a place overlooking the Bay of All Saints, separated from the main plaza by a church plaza and two blocks. Gabriel Soares de Souza gave the best description of it: "The Sé Cathedral of the city of Salvador is situated with its face toward the ocean of the Bay, across from the ships' anchorage, with a walkway in front of the main door, with a sheer drop down to the landing, offering a wide vista."[386] The report conveys how impressive the location was, with its excellent view and visibility. Another passage reflects on the cathedral's isolation, the open areas around it, and the church plaza that separated it from other buildings: "[...] this Sé Cathedral is encircled with land."[387]

The transition from the mystical to the rules of urban design required adaptations. The relationship with God could be considered a type of intimacy with nature, and isolation was incompatible with the city. While mountains exposed human beings to the power of the elements, the city made them seek refuge in the maternal protection of the family. Correlating the urban space with the spiritual necessities that promoted faith was not easy. How could spirituality be developed in the midst of buildings and people? This challenge

---

386 SOUZA, Gabriel Soares, *Notícia do Brasil* [Report from Brazil]. Idem, capítulo VII, p. 258.
387 Idem, p. 258.

resulted in the rules formulated by Aristotle and Vitruvius, which were accepted in the Iberian Peninsula with a few important alterations.

The cities planned and constructed in the Middle Ages generally segregated churches in plazas or provided special church squares for them. This can be confirmed in the urban designs of the French and English *bastides*, a study that would require meticulous and exhaustive analysis. In the Iberian Peninsula, it appears that, until the mid-sixteenth century, Spain and Portugal followed different principles for determining the appropriate site for the city's main church.

In Spain, the church was located in the main plaza, usually to one side. The place of worship was the most important building in the city and, as such, had to be placed in the center; thus spiritual power came to share the same space in the *plaza mayor* as the civil powers. In Portugal, the separation of the spiritual and civil spaces did not alter the Greek and Roman heritage it received. The two countries, being leaders of European expansion, conveyed their respective patterns to the cities they constructed in the Americas and elsewhere.

The Spanish model was apparently rooted in popular culture: the *Seven-Part Code* determined that a church should be built in an "honest and fitting" location, but did not specify a particular site in the city other than to say that it should not be near the house of "women of ill repute" and butcher shops. It also excluded high places, from where damage could be inflicted on the city, given the military advantage of such locations.

The greatest theoretical influence can be credited to Frei Francisco Eximenes (*circa* 1330-1409), whose work explained his ideas about urban planning. He recommended that the city be square, with the cathedral in the center on the main plaza, a notion that was the fruit of theocentrism. He relocated the prince's palace to the periphery, next to the city wall, while the church took over the main plaza, which it shared with other powers (Table 34).

Table 34 - Location of the Main Temple: Theoretical Patterns

Name	Theoretical Pattern
Vitruvius (Rome, 1 A.D.)	Outside the central plaza. The temples for the gods of the cities, Jupiter, Juno, and Minerva, should be erected in the highest site, where they can be seen from any point in the city.
Frei Francisco Eximénez (Spain, 1383)	In the middle of the city should be the church, and next to it should be a large, attractive plaza surrounded by high columns on all sides. Thus, if an enemy tries to besiege it, it will be well defended: in honor of the church and the sacraments that are kept there, no dishonest house should be built there, nor should there be allowed any small animals, nor fighting, nor punishing, nor sentencing.
Leon B. Alberti (Italy, 1450)	The place where the temple is built should be busy, well known, and, as they say, prominent; moreover, in all ways it must be kept immune from contact with the profane.
Francesco Martini (Italy, 1490)	The cathedral should not be far from the plaza, in a place where people from the entire city could easily visit.
Pietro Cataneo (Italy, 1554)	The cathedral should be located in a prominent place, on the highest ground where it can be seen, and not far from the main plaza.
Ordinances (Spain, 1573)	In Mediterranean locations, in a plaza separated from any building. On raised ground where it can be seen and worshiped. In coastal cities, in a place where it can be seen from the sea, with no structures impeding the view.

Source: POLLIO, Marcus Vitruvius. *Los Diez Libros de Architectura* [*The Ten Books of Architecture*], p. 25; FERNÁNDEZ, José Luis García. "Análisis dimensional de modelos teóricos ortogonales de las ciudades españolas e hispanoamericanas desde el siglo XII al XIX" [Dimensional analysis of orthogonal *theoretical models of Spanish and Spanish-American cities from the twelfth to the nineteenth centuries]. In: La Ciudad Iberoamericana [The Ibero-American City];* ALBERTI, Leon Battista. *L'Architettura [Architecture];* MARTINI, Francesco Di Giorgio. *Trattati Di Architettura Ingegneria e Arte Militare [Treatise on Architecture, Engineering, and Military Arts].* I, p. 22; CATANEO, Pietro. *L'Architettura [Architecture].*

This standard prevailed in the cities constructed in Spanish America until at least the mid-sixteenth century. The Ordinances of 1573—a consolidation of the Spanish laws applied to the Americas and issued by King Felipe II—altered this concept, adopting the model of the separation of plazas, as influenced by Vitruvius. Santo Domingos, for example, was founded in 1503 on the right bank of the Ozama River. The cathedral stood on the central axis of the city, to the side of the largest plaza. In cities such as Lima and Santiago, the situation was no different: the church was always located in the main plaza (Table 35).

Table 35 - Location of Main Cathedral in Selected Spanish Cities

Spanish Cities	Location of the Cathedral
Santo Domingo (1503)	In the central plaza and on the southern side.
Lima (1535)	In the central plaza and on the western side.
Santiago (1541)	In the central plaza and on the western side.
Carlentini (1551)	In the central plaza and on the southern side.

Source: FERNÁNDEZ, José Luis García. *La Ciudad Iberoamericana [The Iberoamerican City],* p. 168; MORRIS, A. E. J. *Historia de la Forma Urbana [History of the Urban Form],* pp. 348, 364; BLOND, José Ramón Soraluce. *Las Fortificaciones Españolas de Sicilia en el Renacimiento [The Spanish Fortifications of Sicily in the Renaissance],* p. 69.

In general, Portuguese cities maintained the Greco-Roman tradition of segregating the main place of worship in a separate area (Table 36). In the Fortress of Salvador, the space reserved for the construction of the Sé Cathedral took up one and a half blocks on the northern side, where the Misericórdia and the Jesuit School were also located—bringing together religious power, health care, and education, suggesting the idea of a certain specialization in the areas.

Table 36 - Cathedral Location in Selected Portuguese Cities

Portuguese Cities	Location of the Sé Cathedral
Angra do Heroísmo, Terceira Island, Azores (town, 1478, and city, 1534).	The cathedral was located in a specific block on the western side of the city. It was separate from the central plaza, where the Municipal Council Building and the pillory were located.
Goa, India (1510)	The cathedral was located in a specific block in the center of the city, bordered by the Terreiro do Sabaio. It shared this space with the Municipal Council Building.
Funchal, Madeira Island (fifteenth century)	The cathedral, built from 1493 to 1514, was located in the center of the city on its own block with its own plaza in front.
Ponta Delgada, São Miguel Island, Azores (city, 1546)	The cathedral was located in its own area with its own plaza. It was built from 1531 to 1545.
Salvador, Brazil (1549)	Outside the central plaza. The cathedral was located in a specific site located on the northern side and facing the ocean.

Source: VAN LINSCHOTEN, Jan Huygen. Itinerário, Viagem ou Navegação para as Índias Ocidentais ou Portuguesas [Itinerary, Voyage, or Navigation to the West or Portuguese Indies]. Engravings 36 (Angra) and 6 (Goa); TEIXEIRA, Manuel C. O Urbanismo Português [Portuguese Urbanism], pp. 63, 75.

The northern side of the fortress was, in theory, the safest and most tranquil. The central plaza, where the routes to the harbor began, was the center of the circulation of civil powers. The streets did not pass by the door of the Sé Cathedral, which was in an isolated spot; it could only be observed by people below, gazing up at its façade, sovereign and serene, far from everything but visible from everywhere.

The original plans selected the western quadrant to orient the façade, a choice that was clearly inspired by Vitruvius. The altar had to face the west to create the impression that God emerged from the east. Although this orientation was not a universal pattern of the Catholic Church, it did represent a tendency during the Renaissance; likewise, the churches of Ajuda and Conceição were built with their front facing the direction where the sun set.

The space chosen for the Sé Cathedral in the Fortress of Salvador and its subsequent construction, looking out over the hillside and visible from any point around the Bay of All Saints, revealed a classical inspiration (Fig. 54). We can see the application of Vitruvius's guidelines, enriched by Alberti, Martini, and Cataneo: proximity to the main plaza, isolation, prominence, visibility, and distance from civic buildings. It was the desired image for spiritual power, a Renaissance version of the original relationship between human beings and God, represented in the mountain.

Figure 54 - Location of the original Sé Cathedral in the city of Salvador.

35. Construction of the Cathedral

The quarter toward which temples of the immortal gods ought to face is to be determined on the principle that, if there is no reason to hinder and the choice is free, the temple and the statue placed in the cella should face the western quarter of the sky.

Vitruvius

The cycle of construction projects undertaken during the administration of Tomé de Souza drew to a close with the building of the Sé Cathedral. The bishop and his chapter landed at the Fortress of Salvador in June, 1552. Three months later, in September, the first payments were made for constructing the cathedral's foundations. Soon thereafter, Pero de Carvalhaes, a stonemason, was contracted to work for the princely sum of 200,000 réis. The cathedral was built of stone at a site specifically reserved for it, located next to the infirmary. It was demolished in the early twentieth century. Today, its exposed foundations can be seen exactly where Pero de Carvalhaes placed them in the long-ago year of 1552.

The arrival of the bishop and the construction of the Sé Cathedral constituted the final pair of acts for consolidating the Portuguese state on the coast of Brazil. Work on the cathedral began in 1552. After the stonemason received the funds to build the foundations, he set to work. Thirty years later, when Mem de Sá listed services rendered to the Crown, he included the completion of the cathedral.

A certain amount of the funding was derived from bonds paid by people accused of crimes to obtain their release from jail. This situation, which historical studies have not yet fully documented, deserves further discussion.

In 1551, Pero Borges, the Chief Ombudsman, returned to the Fortress of Salvador after traveling for a year throughout the captaincies lying to the south, administering justice and issuing sentences. He identified serious problems associated with the effectiveness of sentencing in a region that was so sparsely populated and had so few European colonists. A critical factor aggravated the situation: the possibility that a Portuguese colonist, accused of a crime, could flee to an indigenous group or join the ranks of the Spaniards. This risk had precedents on the coast of Brazil, when Gonçalo de Acosta, like many other Portuguese, performed invaluable services for the Spaniards in settling the lands in what is now the State of São Paulo.

The efforts of the Governorate General to penalize crimes faced major hurdles. When political authorities came into contact with the vast lands and forests devoid of colonists, occupied by native peoples who were often hostile, dotted here and there with French traders and threatened in the south by the Spanish, they realized they would have to revise traditional concepts linking each crime to a penalty. A strange social phenomenon occurred: since Portuguese colonists were so scarce in relation to the necessity of populating the land, it was better to make punishments flexible than to run the risk of losing people to Spain or other countries, or even to the Indians, given the possibility of their fleeing into the dense, impenetrable forests. The dilemma of the Court lay between the need to punish crimes and the possibility of losing contingents of colonists. What could be done?

The drama was communicated to the Portuguese Court by various sources, being the topic of divers letters, many of which have been lost. King Dom João III did not vacillate. The solution came through two royal edicts issued in August, 1551, which established momentous changes into the rules for applying justice on the coast of Brazil. The first edict issued a general amnesty by granting pardon to all criminals whose offenses occurred before the arrival of Governor Tomé de Souza. The second delegated powers to the Ombudsman General to issue bond papers to people accused of crimes if they wanted to remain free during criminal proceedings. Some exceptions could be made in both cases, although they were of minor importance relative to the total range of crimes committed. These royal edicts, which are published here for the first time, are indispensable to comprehending the grave difficulties that hampered efforts to effectively administer criminal justice on the coast of Brazil in light of the population factor.[388]

The most important edict was that adopted through a provision dated August 6, 1551, concerning the issuance of pardons. In his explanation, the King emphasized that he had been informed that, before Tomé de Souza's arrival, many Christians who roamed the coast of Brazil "committed crimes and made errors in their duties and positions and were guilty because they were held responsible [...]" in the eyes of the law. The monarch added that, when the Ombudsman General traveled through the captaincies to hear cases, many of the guilty "[...] took flight and some joined the pagans of the land and are living among them, setting a bad example and following their customs." Others returned to the kingdom and set sail for the Antilles or other destinations, fearful of being "[...] imprisoned and punished as their crimes warrant." The King issued a general amnesty, collectively applied to all people who had committed crimes before the date of the edict.

He recognized that, because so many crimes had been committed and because of the population dispersal and possibility of flight, it would be difficult to punish them. His primary concern was that the lands be populated and cultivated, which, in his opinion, meant removing any impediments to such aims. Nevertheless, he made two exceptions to the general pardon and stipulated an obligation:

— crimes could only be pardoned when there was no party who brought forward an accusation; if there were, then

---

[388] These texts can be found in the Documentary Appendix of this book.

the right of the victim to seek punishment for the offender prevailed; however, the Indians, victims of numerous crimes, were not allowed to make accusations;

— there would be no pardons for five specific crimes: heresy, sodomy, treason, counterfeiting, and murder of a Christian, but all crimes against native peoples were pardoned;

— as a condition for a pardon, he stipulated that the beneficiaries were required to reside for a certain length of time in a Portuguese settlement of their choosing, the duration being determined by the Governor. Pardons would be granted through a standard procedure: the Governor was to send a letter containing a transcript of the provision and defining the period of time and place of residence; each pardon would be promptly recorded in a log; after the completion of the time specified in the letter, the person granted a pardon would be required to present a certificate of compliance, to be recorded below the entry for the corresponding pardon.

The King's second act allowed bond papers to be issued, the same means used today to avoid or reduce prison time, through a payment of a certain sum or a monetary guarantee, with an agreement to meet certain conditions to ensure that the legal case duly moved forward. During the period of the Manueline Ordinances, bonds were an exceptional measure, applied only to crimes in which the accused pleaded not guilty or alleged legitimate self-defense, in which case the accused could present a letter of guarantee. The extreme measure of granting liberty to the accused before a verdict was reached in a criminal case was a privilege reserved to the King.

In cases involving deportation for less than six years, convicted criminals could fulfill the sentence in liberty, through a ruling by a judge, county magistrate, or ombudsman. This required that a guarantor post a bond of money or goods that would ensure the fulfillment of additional obligations imposed on those convicted. For Brazil, the King decided to institute special arrangements for bail applicable to all crimes except heresy, sodomy, counterfeit, treason, and murder of a Christian.

The Fortress of Salvador

The decision taken by King Dom João III took the form of an authorization, dated August 5, 1551, which he justified in light of the possibility that colonists accused of crimes might flee or seek refuge, pointing out their "fear of being unable to avoid being imprisoned." The guarantee that those accused of crimes could remain free was yet another concession made to the particular conditions of colonization on the coast of Brazil.

In an earlier letter to the King written from Porto Seguro in January, 1550,[389] Pero Borges had called attention to how little value there was in holding a man in prison, given that the land was in a state of war and thinly populated, that a prisoner would have to be fed, and that someone would have to look after him. After the decree, the Ombudsman was authorized to issue bond papers so that accused people could remain free while their case was pending. The papers had to limit the period of validity, which could be renewed according to the nature of the crime and the conduct of the accused, and all facts had to be recorded in a specific book. If the accused failed to meet the requirements stipulated in the bond papers, the bail was forfeited, with the sum being applied to works of a religious nature. In the city of Salvador, these resources were used for the construction of the Sé Cathedral.

King Dom João III was a figure who leaned toward liberality and viewed pardons favorably. The measures he adopted reflected the practical sensibility of the era, revealing a certain tolerance and accommodation of various interests inherent in any process of brusque change, whether social or political. Any other approach would most likely have seriously hampered the project of settling Brazil, especially in light of the fact that so many customs were considered crimes and the penalties were disproportionate. Previously, the absence of a justice system had been the cause of public uproar, but its arrival began to sow panic and problems. To bolster the system, crimes in the past were granted amnesty, and the money raised from bail money helped to construct the Sé Cathedral of the Fortress of Salvador.

---

389 Letter from Pero Borges to King Dom João III, dated February 7, 1551. In: MALHEIROS DIAS, Carlos. *História da Colonização Portuguesa no Brasil* [History of Portuguese Colonization in Brazil]. III, p. 267.

36. The Churches of Our Lady

The ecclesiastic history of Portugal is the most abundant in prodigious successes, which affirms the special care given by Blessed Mary to these kingdoms, which, furthermore, are perhaps the more eminent in Europe in the number of sanctuaries dedicated to the Mother of God.

Royal letter, November 18, 1844.[390]

The Holy Child and the Mother of God inspired the founding of the Fortress of Salvador as a substantial stronghold. The fortress was intended to nurture and support the Portuguese domination over the coast of Brazil, affirming the youthful vigor of the Lusitanian empire, a center from which its Catholic culture would spread.

In this sense, the fortress was masculine. The Portuguese were sons committed to the mission of salvation, for which they needed the discreet protection of their mother—Mother Mary, Our Lady. They sailed over to Brazil in three ships named Salvador, Conceição, and Ajuda ("Savior, Conception, and Help"); when they arrived, they christened the fortress in honor of Jesus the Savior and constructed the first

---

390 ALMEIDA, Fortunato de. *História da Igreja em Portugal* [History of the Church in Portugal]. III, p. 446. Royal letter to Councilor João Pedro Miguéis de Carvalho, Envoy Extraordinary and Minister Plenipotentiary at the Court of Rome.

two churches inspired by Mother Mary—the churches of Nossa Senhora da Conceição and Nossa Senhora da Ajuda ("Our Lady of the Immaculate Conception" and "Our Lady of Good Help")—as if they were asking for permanent vigilance, something that only a mother could provide.

The relationship between the Portuguese and Our Lady is a special one, going beyond typical Catholic practices: "The great majority of the Portuguese are convinced that the Heavenly Mother is charged with the task of coming to visit her Lusitanian children from time to time."[391] They believe they are the chosen ones, who are protected from external threats as they arise.

The feeling of being a special child reveals a certain messianic relationship with the Mother of God, which gets expressed in another specific belief: the notion that Our Lady appears on earth, performs miracles, and provides protection in a thousand different places. She is one, but has a thousand names. Although one, each village has its own Marian apparition, stronger and more powerful than that of the neighboring village, a curious phenomenon of the multiplication of the singular, which is manifested physically and confers individuality to each place. It might be a tree, a hill, a grotto, or a bush—all sites of a manifestation or apparition that conveys its prestige through a new name: Our Lady of Lapa, of Fatima, of Tocha, of Culcorinho, of Montserrat, of the Waves, of the Star. In her names, "Our Lady" designates her general nature, but the nominal qualifier restricts it, as if to proclaim that *this one* is distinctive and special.

If a specific place is able to ensure a certain individuality to its manifestation of Our Lady, other names may be added as a means of calling attention to the characteristic that is most essential to her, such as Our Lady of the Needy, of Mercy, of Good Help, conveying the action inherent in the verb "to help." In other cases, the theological principle of conception without sin, or divine conception, may also serve as inspiration for the title often used, Our Lady of the Immaculate Conception or, more simply, of Conception.

Our Lady does not have only one form, as the saints do; she

---

391 SANTO, Moisés Espírito. *Origens Orientais da Religião Popular Portuguesa* [Oriental Origins of Portuguese Popular Religion], p. 21.

is approached with requests that differentiate her aspects through a qualifier added to the head noun—an ever-repeated particularization, suggesting the incessant search for an individual relationship. Each place, each individual needs its own Our Lady; she protects each one or each group according to local beliefs.

This individualization of Mary occurs not only in her names: it also appears in artistic representations of the image of the Virgin as well as in the mystical origins of each cult. Our Lady of Mercy, for example, is represented with an open cloak, sheltering the faithful within, a well-known iconography that has been adopted by many brotherhoods to transmit the idea of a specialized form of protection.

The origin of the cult of the Virgin of Mercy with an outspread cloak goes back to a dream recounted in a thirteenth-century book. A Cistercian monk who was devoted to Our Lady had a dream in which he was carried aloft to heaven, where he saw angels, patriarchs, prophets, saints, and members of all the religious associations, but he could not find anyone from his own order. Anguished over his abandonment, he asked Our Lady, "What is happening, Holy Virgin, why do I see no Cistercians here?" The Queen of Heaven responded, "To the contrary, the Cistercians are so dear and beloved that I nurture them under my arms." And, opening her extraordinarily ample cloak, she showed him a multitude of monks.[392]

Image, cult ritual, and name demonstrate the idiosyncrasies of each manifestation, the particular quality that arouses the sense of the mystical and provides support to some sentiment or supplication. She is one, but she is many: she is Our Lady of Good Help—to whom Father Manuel da Nóbrega continually appealed for assistance; she is Our Lady of Refuge—the mother who rescues and protects her chosen children, especially worshiped by Afro-Brazilians; she is Our Lady of Sorrows—recalling her enormous suffering and anguish over the crucifixion of her Son; she is Our Lady of Bethlehem—kneeling before the Holy Child and gazing upon him with wide-open eyes; she is Our Lady of the Assumption—with her hands raised and held close

---

392 CAETANO, Joaquim Oliveira. "Sob o Manto Protetor. Para uma Iconografia da Virgem da Misericórdia" ["Under the Protective Cloak: Toward an Iconography of the Virgin of Mercy."] In: *Mater Misericordiae* [Mother of Mercy], p. 26.

to her chest, wearing a crown and robe and seated on a throne of seraphims; she is Our Lady of Good Voyage—whom sailors beseech for prosperous travels or safety in storms; she is Our Lady of Good Counsel—petitioned for grace and solutions to problems; she is Our Lady of Springs, originating in the Alentejo region of Portugal, where the Mother of God appeared to a shepherd; and she is Our Lady of Conception—having conceived Jesus without conjunction but through divine conception. The faithful call on Our Lady of the Good Hour for special attention and grace in their last moments, and on Our Lady of the Good Death, shown lying in her sumptuous, celebrated tomb on the day when her body and soul ascended to heaven. Our Lady of Exile recalls her flight to Egypt with the baby Jesus in her arms, while Our Lady of Guadalupe memorializes her miraculous appearance in mountains of that name in Spain, like that of Our Lady of Montserrat in Catalonia. And so it was with many other names and meanings in Marian worship, each one specific and replete with traditions, rituals, and representations.

The mother's joy at seeing the newborn child, the serenity of the mother with the child in her lap, and the grief of the mother at the feet of the deceased son represent common life passages. Appeals for help, support, pity, and health are sentiments and supplications from those who are in need. In building the Conceição chapel in the Fortress of Salvador, the founders affirmed the primacy of the Portuguese cult to the dogma of immaculate conception; in building the Ajuda chapel, they appealed for support in undertaking their colonization project—both erected, interestingly enough, near the two main means of access to the fortress. In this respect, cult and faith were intermingled with urban planning patterns, forging intriguing symbolic associations. This will be demonstrated in the following chapter.

37. The Peripheral Churches

At the hands and feet, other temples and plazas will be built.

Francesco di Giorgio Martini

The first two churches built in the Fortress of Salvador, those of Conceição da Praia and Ajuda, reveal intriguing similarities: they were both given alternative names of the Virgin, which replicated the names of two ships in Tomé de Souza's armada. Built on the southern side of the fortress, they were situated in symmetrical positions, one on the eastern side and the other on the western, both guarding the access points. What was the reason for this?

The answer seems to lie in the mystical, symbolic sense of protection. The southern side was the point where people landed on shore and arrived in Salvador. The road that connected the port and the upper city provided access to the first points of contact with the settlement. Similarly, the protection received during the voyage, invoked through the names of the ships (Ajuda, named for "Our Lady of Good Help," and Conceição, for "Our Lady of the Immaculate Conception") most likely served as further religious inspiration to the city founders.

Examining the question from the perspective of sixteenth-century urbanism, it is notable that the location of the churches obeyed a customary model: the Sé Cathedral was in a central, visible spot, while the smaller churches were in peripheral locations. As such, the main cathedral and the parish churches were distinguished, one being central and the others satellites, following a general orientation followed in the urban network of the Fortress of Salvador. The model provided a small plaza for each parish church, a pattern that was also followed in Salvador.

Greco-Roman traditions oriented the construction of temples in honor of the gods, according to the stature and role of each one. For instance, the temple of Venus was usually located close to the city ports, while that of Mars was farther away in order to avoid warfare and civil discord. This logic of separating levels of spiritual power was reproduced in the transition from ancient mythology to Catholicism by Giorgio Martini, the Renaissance engineer and architect whose designs and texts considered various references for positioning the parish church in the design of cities. Martini reviewed many hypotheses, always relating them to associations with the human body.

In the first place, he advised that the architect imagine the human body lying down on the ground, with the navel being the point anchoring the main plaza; from this point, an imaginary line would be extended to the extremities, such that a circle or a square could be drawn around the body. Next, the proportional measurements of the parts of the body were calculated.[393] As a general rule, Martini proposed that, in cities where a citadel was not necessary, the cathedral church (*cattedral chiesa*) should occupy the spot usually assigned to the citadel. Notably, the citadel in Martini's model corresponded to the head of the human body. Regarding parish churches, he stated that their location should correspond to the hands and feet: "At the hands and the feet will be constructed other temples and plazas."[394] The relationship of center and periphery was perfectly represented in the Fortress of Salvador: the Conceição da Praia and Ajuda churches were the religious feet of the architectonic body—providing support for the spiritual protection desired by the community—with the cathedral on the opposite end, symbolizing its role as the head of the

---

393 MARTINI, Francesco Di Giorgio. *Trattati Di Architettura Ingegneria e Arte Militare* [Treatise on Architecture, Engineering, and Military Arts]. I, p. 20.
394 Idem, p. 20.

diocese. The devotional churches, dedicated to the exercise of pure Marian faith, were built in critical sites associated with the central one, having the most intimate contact with the earth.

Martini's designs portrayed parish churches in different settings: on gently sloping hills, they were located next to the city walls; on steeper hills accessed by switchback roads, they were situated somewhat farther from the walls. In designs for cities on flat land, the arrangement of parish churches did not undergo any significant alteration. The model was always symmetrical with extensions, having "arms" and "legs" that revealed a certain stylization of design. This was because each temple, cathedral, or parish church reproduced the proportions of the human body, laid out graphically in the form of a cross. Each church was served by its own plaza.

In Martini's model, parish churches were supposed to be next to well-traveled streets, maintaining a close relationship with the population. In the architect's words, such churches should be easily accessible to the city inhabitants. He also said they should have certain features in common: the entrance to the church should be in front, not on the side, with the door in the middle, conveniently reached from the plaza. The temple should be separated from neighboring dwellings as well as apart from the parsonage.

The Ordinances of King Felipe II, applicable to the construction of Spanish cities in the Americas, stated that smaller plazas should be reserved for "parish churches and monasteries."[395] This rule may seem straightforward, but it reveals special significance when considered in light of its imitation of the human body. In the city plan of the Fortress of Salvador, it is possible to identify the shape of the human body lying down, with the navel coinciding with the main plaza. Harmony existed because the distances between the center of the plaza and the extremities allowed the formation of a circle, with the measurements being almost exact, suggesting something more than mere coincidence. In fact, this pattern is yet one more among many that reveal near-total subordination of the designs to Greco-Roman

---

395 *RECOPILACION DE LEIS DOS REYNOS DE LAS ÍNDIAS* [Compilation of the Laws of the Kingdoms of the Indies]. Livro IV, Título VI, Lei VIII. Law VIII dealt specifically with the type of site that was appropriate for houses of worship.

models, with Renaissance adaptations and contributions. The theoretical design brought from Portugal that guided the master architect Luís Dias undoubtedly inspired the general lines of the patterns observed in the Fortress of Salvador.

Tomé de Souza's armada reportedly did not bring priests belonging to the regular clergy, but only Jesuits. However, this fact should be considered with some latitude, since King Dom João III appointed a seminary graduate, Manoel Lourenço, on February 18, 1549, "to be the perpetual vicar of the church that I have ordered to be built in honor of Our Lord Jesus Christ in the Fortress of Salvador [...]."[396] The armada departed Lisbon on February 2, 1549. The vicar was not able to board, but the position was already included in the array of posts planned for the Fortress of Salvador.

The vicar, Manoel Lourenço, landed in Salvador in the latter half of 1549 and, by October 8, he was serving as the prior of the church of the city of Salvador.[397] Early the next year, he received two altar screens, one for the Church of Conceição da Praia, at the time a mere chapel, and another for the "main church in this city of Salvador,"[398] that is, the Ajuda Church. Before the arrival of this church official, the two churches, as rustic and poor as could be, were the responsibility of the Jesuits; after he arrived, they were turned over to the administration of the regular clergy. With Manoel Lourenço appointed as the new spiritual power in the Fortress of Salvador, religious spaces and orders were separated. The Company of Jesus migrated to the locale next to the old Sé Cathedral, while the vicar assumed control of the Ajuda Church.

Some people may find it hard to imagine that Luís Dias, the master architect, would plan the fortress in the shape of a human body lying on the turf of the plateau, or that he would delineate and build two small chapels at the feet of this giant. Nevertheless, members of modern society may not be capable of fully understanding the domination of Renaissance theories in Italy, Portugal, Spain, and oth-

---

396 RUBERT, Arlindo. *A Igreja no Brasil. Origem e Desenvolvimento (Século XVI)* [The Church in Brazil: Origin and Development (Sixteenth Century)], p. 74.
397 Idem, p. 75.
398 Ibidem.

er countries in the fields of geometry, engineering, and architecture. The mystique about the perfection of the human body, although not always conscious in the minds of those designing or viewing architectural projects, was one of the strongest ingredients in sixteenth-century thinking. It was altogether natural that the models drawn up by architects and lovers of knowledge would reflect such concepts.

38. The Hospital and the Infirmary

When founding or settling some city, town, or place, the hospitals for the poor and the ill who do not have contagious illnesses should be put next to the churches where they can be cloistered; hospitals for the ill who have contagious illnesses should be in high places where no harmful wind can pass through and endanger the settlement.[399]

Ordinance 122 of Felipe II (1572)

The hospitals in the Portuguese cities of Goa in India, Angra do Heroísmo in the Azores archipelago, and Salvador and Rio de Janeiro on the coast of Brazil reveal a curious pattern: in Goa, the King's Hospital was located next to the Santa Catarina piers; in Angra, the hospital, near the infirmary, stood on the first parcel of land after the gate to the piers; and the oldest drawings of Rio de Janeiro show the infirmary next to the port. In all these Portuguese cities, the site assigned to the hospital was always near the port. This was a practical decision arising from the strong association between illness and sailing: ships would land with men who had become ill, injured, or weakened, so hospital beds for their recuperation were provided in a nearby building.

---

399 *RECOPILACION DE LEIS DOS REYNOS DE LAS ÍNDIAS* [Compilation of the Laws of the Kingdoms of the Indies]. Tomo I, Livro I, Título 3, Lei II.

In his memoirs, a solder in the late sixteenth century wrote about his arrival in Goa, where "the sick lead us to the hospital."[400] The rest survived "gum decay, pestilent fevers, diarrhea, and a great many other similar illnesses."[401] Health policy distinguished between contagious and noncontagious diseases, segregating only critical cases. In the Fortress of Salvador, the site chosen for the hospital was on the corner at the top of the Ladeira da Misericórdia, the sloping access road that led to the "people's wharf."

The ancients appealed to Aesculapius, Apollo, and the goddess Health, to whom they attributed the art of curing diseases and the power to keep them healthy. Temples dedicated to them were built in locales that were not only healthy, but also provided with pure air and clean water. This would allow the ill to recuperate not only with divine help, but also with the effects of the local climate, which would accelerate recuperation.[402] Alberti praised the splendid "houses of healing" in Tuscany, "the land of ancient religious piety,"[403] and commented on the necessary segregation of curable and incurable illnesses. Lepers and those stricken with a plague might "infect and pass on contagious diseases to healthy people."[404] He recommended that sites reserved for curing contagious diseases should be constructed and maintained distant "not only from the city, but also from public roads";[405] noncontagious diseases could be treated within the city in hospitals that should be divided into two parts: one for treating patients with curable diseases, the other for cases of mental disabilities that were incapable of total recuperation. Alberti further recommended some sort of segregation between rooms and wards. We can perceive similar approaches in the Spanish Ordinances consolidated in 1573 by King Felipe II, intended to ensure good governance in the colonies.

---

400 *MEMÓRIAS de Um Soldado da Índia* [Memoirs of a Soldier in India], p. 16.
401 Idem, p. 16.
402 ALBERTI, Leon Battista. *L'Architettura* [Architecture]. Livro V, capítulo VIII, p. 194.
403 Idem.
404 Ibidem.
405 Ibidem.

The Fortress of Salvador

The appropriate locale for the sick to recuperate was closely associated with healthful conditions. According to Alberti, such a place should be dry, rocky, and exposed to constant breezes. The heat could not be scorching; on the contrary, the climate should be mild, since "Nature in every Thing loves a Medium."[406] The enjoyment of good health required a combination of all factors in moderation.

Alberti's theoretical references and the Spanish regulations provide evidence of the prevailing standards. In Portugal, the Royal Hospital of All Saints, which was founded by King Dom João II and constructed beginning in 1492, was an example both majestic and practical of a building devoted to curing noncontagious diseases. It had three wards forming a cross that centered on the main altar; one ward treated "men with fevers," having twenty beds, each in front of a door to a room where patients went to relieve themselves and where waste products were removed "through a corridor without bothering other patients with bad odors";[407] another ward had sixteen beds for men who "suffered injuries"; and a separate third ward had sixteen beds for sick and injured women. In another wing of the hospital, two more wards were used for syphilis patients, one for men, with twenty-four beds, and the other for women, with nineteen beds. There were also wards specifically for mendicant friars and traveling pilgrims, having a total of fifty-two beds. The Royal Hospital therefore had around 147 beds, each one with its own "curtains and mattresses, with well-prepared pillows."[408]

The tradition of establishing royal hospitals was carried over to the Portuguese colonies. In Goa and Salvador, they were incorporated into the administration and property of the infirmaries (known as *Misericórdia*). A few documentary records contemporaneous with the founding of the fortress referred to the "hospital of the city of Salvador"; we know little about it other than that its first financial administrator was the nobleman Diogo Moniz and that the Crown paid for some expenses for construction and maintenance (Table 37).

---

406 Ibidem.
407 BRANDÃO, João. *Grandeza e Abastança de Lisboa em 1552* [Grandeur and Affluence in Lisbon in 1552], p. 125.
408 Idem.

Table 37 - Hospital: Orders of Payment, 1549-1552

Date	Order of Payment or Transfer of Goods
October 5, 1549	Payment to the financial administrator of the hospital of the city of Salvador in the amount of 900 réis, derived from a fine imposed on the court official João Lopes for the benefit of the "work on said hospital."
November 6, 1549	Payment in the name of Diogo Moniz, financial administrator of the hospital of the city of Salvador, derived from a fine imposed by the governor on three people "for said hospital."
December 14, 1549	Payment to Diogo Moniz, financial administrator of the hospital of this city of Salvador and executor for the sailor Estêvão Fernandes, deceased, derived from his salary for June and July of 1549.
February 25, 1550	Order for delivery to the "administrators of the hospital of the city of Salvador" of a donation of 35 rods and hemp cloth for "some curtains for said hospital."
July 15, 1552	Payment to the "administrators of the hospital of this said city" of 4,000 réis for construction work, in accord with a letter from the King providing a total of one hundred cruzados (40,000 réis) for the work.
November 5, 1552	Payment to the "administrators of the hospital of this said city" of 8,900 réis for construction work, in accord with a letter from the King providing a total of one hundred cruzados (40,000 réis) for the work.

Source: DOCUMENTOS HISTÓRICOS [Historical Documents]. Bibliotheca Nacional, V. 12, 13.

During his administration, Governor Duarte da Costa named the hospital Nossa Senhora das Candeias ("Our Lady of the Lamps") and proposed to the King that he authorize that fines derived from commuting sentences be applied to its maintenance. For some time (the exact period is unknown), the hospital of the Fortress of Salvador existed separately from the infirmary. Mem de Sá may have been the one responsible for incorporating the hospital into the infirmary, although no surviving documentation clarifies this point.

In the city of Goa, the hospital was incorporated into the administration of the infirmary in 1542 by an order from Governor Martim Afonso de Souza, which ensured some income to cover expenses and certain facilities and privileges. The administrators were motivated to make this decision due to the "disorder and poor organization prevailing in the care of the sick in the hospital which Your Highness ordered be built in this city."[409] The Governor's letter reveals that the Crown was obligated to provide care and medicine for Portuguese patients who arrived on ships or fell ill while in the city. In later years, the Goa Hospital reverted to the administration of the Crown.

The budget for the State of India in 1571 showed separate budgetary allocations for the hospitals in large Portuguese fortresses; at least seven[410] were granted sums to cover food for the patients and salaries for the employees. The infirmaries in each fortress were supported by "alms for the poor and crippled";[411] the sums earmarked for the hospitals were much higher, demonstrating that the two institutions, hospital and infirmary, were generally independent.

In Salvador, the tracts assigned to the hospital and the infirmary were adjoining but separate, located in the block at the top of the northern access road (Fig. 55), which, according to Gabriel Soares de Souza, went down to the "people's wharf." People who were ill when they landed at the port would ascend to the upper city, where, on the first corner, they would find shelter in the hospital—the probable rationale for choosing the site assigned to the fortress hospital.

---

409 DOCUMENTAÇÃO para a História das Missões do Padroado Português do Oriente [Documentation on the History of Missions under Portuguese Patronage in the Orient], volume II, p. 313.
410 Ormuz, Diu, Daman, Bassein, Chaul, Goa, and Kochi.
411 O ORÇAMENTO do Estado da Índia 1571 [Budget of the State of India, 1572], p. 33.

Figure 55 - Corner where the first hospital in the city of Salvador was built.

39. The Jesuits' Buildings

> *I labored to choose a good place for our school within the fence and found only one, which, as Your Highness can see in the model, has many inconveniences, because it is very close to the cathedral and two churches next to each other is not good.*
>
> Padre Manuel da Nóbrega

In 1581, the Jesuits sold Helena Borges a group of houses made of wattle and daub on pylons, with tile roofs, located on the "Paulo Serrão road coming from the cathedral." There was a large house in the front and a garden. In the rear was a slope descending to the ocean, bordering the path by the Pereira Fountain, nowadays known as the Ladeira da Misericórdia. The front side of the set of buildings lay along a public street. To one side lived Gaspar Luiz and his wife Maria Rabela, and, on the other, Antônio Rodrigues Vaqueiro. The Jesuits lived there until they moved to the Terreiro de Jesus.

During the first few months after the fortress was founded, the Jesuits, having arrived with Tomé de Souza, exercised parish functions. They constructed the Ajuda Church and lived there for a while. In Father Manuel da Nóbrega's second letter, dated April 15, 1549—a mere seventeen days after their landing—he wrote that the Governor had chosen "a good valley" for the Jesuits, apparently the only one that had water.[412] Given the short period of time, the uncertain information, and the ill-defined plans, it seems that the site allocated for the Jesuits may have been on the side of the hill that slopes down to the Ladeira da Praça. Another possible site may have been outside the fortress fence (there was as yet no wall).

The construction of the fortress moved ahead, adapting to the locale. On August 9, 1549, Father Manuel da Nóbrega described the new situation: the lot would be located inside the city fence, adjacent to the Sé Cathedral, and smaller than Nóbrega expected. This suggests, not surprisingly, that the location of the cathedral was determined during the planning stages, the site being reserved for its future construction. The lot allocated for the Jesuits measured 10 fathoms (22 meters) along the street, and 40 fathoms (88 meters) along the hillside. These dimensions were inadequate, especially since it was all on "a very steep incline" and with no place for gardens (Fig. 56).[413]

In protesting the site next to the cathedral, Nóbrega expressed interest in another location "right outside the fence," also overlooking the ocean, with a source of water near the school and room for gardens and orchards. He was unsuccessful, however, in obtaining permission from the Governor, since this alternative site would be outside the fortress. He reconciled himself to their assigned place only as a temporary measure, going so far as to state that the Jesuits would leave the Ajuda site and move to the new one as soon as the vicar arrived.[414] By January, 1550, a church was completed on the site, where mass was conducted, and next to it was a building where the priests taught classes for boys. Nevertheless, Father Manuel da Nóbrega had not forgotten the site outside the fence and continued to reiterate this preference in his letters.[415]

---

412 LETTER from Father Manuel da Nóbrega to Father Simão Rodrigues, dated April 15, 1549. LEITE S. I., Serafim. *Cartas dos Primeiros Jesuítas do Brasil* [Letters of the First Jesuits of Brazil]. I, p. 117.
413 LETTER from Father Manuel da Nóbrega to Father Simão Rodrigues, dated August 9, 1549. *Op. cit.*, p. 125.
414 Idem, p. 126.
415 LETTER from Father Manuel da Nóbrega to Father Simão Rodrigues, dated January 6, 1550. *Op. cit.*, p. 158.

Figure 56 - Probable location of the Jesuits' buildings in the present-day Praça da Sé.

In July, 1552, the Jesuits' church, made of wattle and daub and a thatched roof, was in ruins; a new one was built of stone and lime, with help from the population. In December 1554, the church served as the burial site for Father Salvador Rodrigues. At this point, it still had a simple thatched roof; the Jesuits believed that a permanent church could be constructed only after the issue of their school and monastery would be settled. Nóbrega never forgot the plot outside the city walls, which, in a certain sense, had been promised to the Jesuits; it was the only site capable of meeting the needs of the school and monastery.

By 1557, the situation had apparently become critical, echoed in the frustration of Nóbrega's letters. His major complaint was how the small plot cramped their living quarters, allowing no separation between the priests and the boys. For strategic reasons, he did not want to completely separate the school's facilities from those devoted to the monastery, insisting that moving outside the wall to the spot chosen for it would resolve the precarious situation once and for all.

A promise to allow the move had already been made, and the design for the new school and monastery was ready. Nóbrega was irritated because, although the Governor showed the new design in Salvador, it never made its way to Lisbon. He understood, however, that the volume of investments made in the Sé Cathedral and fortifications made it impossible for any funds to be left over that could be spent on building the school.[416]

In the best religious tradition, the Jesuits constructed a set of one-story houses forming a quad, a square around a courtyard. One quarter of the square served as a church, possibly facing the street. In the rear was another section with the sacristy, study, and priests' dormitory, which were connected by a corridor. On the third side were the boys' dormitory, kitchen, dining hall, and pantry. On the fourth side, probably facing the street, was a schoolhouse with two classrooms, one for teaching grammar and the other for teaching reading.

Each section of the square measured 17.38 by 6.38 meters. The width of the houses measured 2.9 fathoms, compatible with the usual standard for houses with two windows and a door. The sum of the two measurements indicates that the front of the tract was 23.76 meters. It originally measured about 10 fathoms (22 meters), according to Nóbrega. He recorded these measurements on two occasions—the first in 1549, the second in 1557—showing they were relatively consistent. The difference between them can be attributed to various factors that are not relevant here.

The site where the Sé Cathedral was situated, on the side overlooking the slope, had significant topographic features. The first half of the plot was wider than the other and contained buildings that were slightly more than twenty meters in depth. In the second half, up to the Plano Inclinado Gonçalves, the plot was narrow. In light of the measurements indicated by Father Manuel da Nóbrega, as well as other sources, the location of the first quad of the Jesuits was probably at the site where nowadays the Excelsior Cinema stands.

The priests needed to break through the wall to expand, but they were unsure if that had permission to do so. They adamantly

---

416 LETTER from Father Manuel da Nóbrega to Father Miguel Torres, dated September 2, 1557. LEITE S. I., Serafim. *Op. cit.* II, pp. 407-411.

wanted to move outside the city walls from the spot allocated to the school, complaining about how close it was to the cathedral. The churches were so close to each other that "no matter how softly people speak, what is said in one can be heard in the other." The solution was to transfer their church to the other side of the wall, where they would be farther from the Sé Cathedral.[417] They awaited the arrival of Mem de Sá, the third governor, at the Fortress of Salvador, and through him they finally managed to get the necessary support for their move.

The year 1561 was decisive: in September, records indicate that Mem de Sá had taken upon himself the project of constructing a new church for the Jesuits. It was to be a spacious one built of stone and lime,[418] suggesting that the Jesuits had achieved their goal of acquiring the tract they had proposed since the beginning. The new church was officially inaugurated on May 23, 1572.[419] In subsequent years, deed records show that the Jesuits came into possession of more adjoining plots. In 1573, for example, they acquired some lots belonging to the family of Paulo Dias, son-in-law of Diogo Álvares Caramuru, including a piece of land bordering that of André Pereira,[420] probably located at the curve in the Ladeira da Misericórdia near the present-day Plano Inclinado Gonçalves. The Jesuits prayed for Caramuru.

Relatives of Portuguese shipwreck victims were concentrated near the northern side of the fortress, indicating that they had received the original land grants in strips of land that were later subdivided. Although the Graça Church was merely a chapel without the status necessary for conducting burials, an exception was made for Diogo Álvares Correia, known as Caramuru. He enjoyed prestige among the Jesuits and, in his will, left some inheritance to them as a donation, so he was buried at the Jesuit monastery on October 3, 1557, according to the burial certificate. His bones were later transferred to the new

---

417 Idem, p. 410.
418 LETTER from Father Luis da Grã to Father Miguel de Torres, dated September 22, 1561. LEITE S. I., Serafim. *Op. cit.* III, p. 431.
419 LEITE, Serafim. *História da Companhia de Jesus no Brasil* [History of the Society of Jesus in Brazil]. I, p. 26.
420 DOCUMENTOS HISTÓRICOS [Historical Documents]. V. LXIV, Bibliotheca Nacional, Códice I (19,18,2), p. 24.

church inaugurated in 1572, but the site where the Excelsior Cinema now stands was probably both a church and a cemetery.

In the late sixteenth century, the Jesuits acquired properties located along Pelourinho to ensure that the monastery could be expanded. In 1575, the old set of buildings next to the Sé Cathedral, after having served from more than a decade as the Jesuits' residence and school, was rented for the reasonable sum of 38,000 réis a year. The property inventory described the set of buildings as being situated "between our school and the Sé Cathedral," with a "garden above the sea."[421] The sale of the property to Helena Borges for 90,000 réis brought the chapter of the Jesuits' first expansion to a close.

---

421 LEITE, Serafim. *História da Companhia de Jesus no Brasil* [History of the Society of Jesus in Brazil]. I, p. 152.

40. Cemeteries

All the earth is a grave, and nought escapes it; nothing is so perfect that it does not fall and disappear. The rivers, brooks, fountains and waters flow on, and never return to their joyous beginnings; they hasten on to the vast realms of Tlaloc, and the wider they spread between their marges the more rapidly do they mould their own sepulchral urns.

Nezahualcóyotl, Aztec king

A great many languages of Europe and Asia had a common origin in Indo-European; at least that is what some linguists argue. They cannot specify precisely when or where it was spoken, nor do they know of any text using it. They surmise its existence only through the curious technique of comparing shared or similar words. They have drawn the conclusion that the people who spoke it had a patriarchal society and worshiped the memory of the great father, a reference to the god that inhabited the home, lending the family a surprising divine dimension. Each family had its own tomb erected on its property, thus symbolizing the relationship among human beings, religion, and burial.

Fustel de Coulanges wrote on the origin of the supernatural and its connection to the family and death: "It was perhaps while looking upon the dead that man first conceived the idea of the supernatural, and began to have a hope beyond what he saw."[422] The grave was the house of the dead, whose soul resided there, and it was there that the family worshiped and nourished it. During the funeral rites, the soul was invoked three times; the family wished it a happy life, adding, "May the earth rest lightly on you,"[423] which was also inscribed as an epitaph on the tomb. In 1533, André de Resende related the words of one of the inscriptions he saw on a certain tower in the city of Sines in Portugal:

> "Consecrated to the Manes gods. Here lies Júlia Marcelina, daughter of Gaio, 30 years old. May the earth rest lightly on you."[424]

The word "lares," a synonym for the Manes, signified the deities who looked out for the family—which the Romans viewed as the soul of the parents—and who lived in the tomb always located next to the house. It was necessary to care for them and nourish them. If they were abandoned, they would leave their graves to wander as ghosts and their moaning would be heard in the dead of night. They would punish the living by sending them diseases or threatening them with sterile earth. With the reinstatement of sacrifices, food offerings, and libations of wine or milk spilled on the tomb, they returned to their graves and resumed their role as protectors of the household.

The religion of the household worshiped the ancestral father. Each house had a hearth and an altar, and from this cult arose the strength and the power of the family, not as a mere natural grouping, but as a religious association. For this reason, the ancient Greek term for the family was *epistion*, "that which is near an altar." The father was the interpreter and the pontiff of the religion, and each family had its own rites and secrets. This was echoed in India, where the

---

422 COULANGES, Fustel de. *A Cidade Antiga* [The Ancient City], p. 18.
423 Idem, p. 9. The epitaph was placed on the urn with the inscription, S. T. T. L. SILVA, Justino Adriano Farias de. *Tratado de Direito Funerário* [Treatise on Funerary Law]. I, p. 438.
424 RESENDE, André de. *As Antiguidades da Lusitânia* [Antiquities of Lusitania], p. 202.

Brahmins would say, "I am strong against my enemies from the songs which I receive from my family, and which my father has transmitted to me."[425]

From father to son, the cult was handed down from one generation to the next. Reproductive power was thought to reside in the male, therefore leading to the establishment of the masculine line of succession. Curiously, the man was not the owner but the guardian of the land and the house. He could not divide it or dispose of it. The eldest son could not refuse the inheritance; in fact, he had to remain in the house and perpetuate the cult, in which his role was merely transitory. The ancient Aryans used to say, "The oldest was begotten for the accomplishment of the duty due the ancestors; the others are the fruit of love."[426]

Through succession, the heritage was transmitted and with it, the *paterfamilias*, which should not be confused with the simple notion of the father. The latter was called the *gânitar*, *ghennetér*, and *genitor* by the Greeks, Romans, and Hindus, respectively. The *paterfamilias* was the patriarch, the one responsible for the cult and for pursuing justice in his territory, as well as being a father, a husband, and the head of the family with authority over his siblings. With respect to property, he exercised his power and watched over the sacred markers placed along its boundaries. Religion constructed private property and made it immutable for the enjoyment and shelter of the household gods.

Historical references indicate that, long ago, graves were situated in the center of the house, not far from the door, so that "the sons, in entering and leaving their dwelling, might always meet their fathers, and might always address them an invocation."[427] Cicero observed the relationship between the tomb and the family, emphasizing, "[...] for it is worth a great deal to have common ancestral monuments, to employ the same religious rites, and to possess common burial places."

As cities grew, this tradition changed. People realized that

---
425 COULANGES, Fustel de. *A Cidade Antiga* [The Ancient City], p. 33.
426 Idem, p. 82.
427 Ibidem, p. 31.

it would be necessary to segregate the space of the dead in a place outside the city walls. The Law of the Twelve Tables ordered that no person could be buried or cremated in the city. An ancient Roman *senatus consultum* also prohibited burials within city walls, with the exception of vestal virgins and the emperor. Plato, when contemplating the rules of social life, recommended burials in locations outside the walls in lands that were not used for agriculture.

A multitude of customs and funeral rites were formulated to maintain hygienic conditions by segregating the space of the dead from that of the living. The Roman custom of raising tombs and mausoleums along military roads, notably the Via Appia, became famous. A traveler, upon leaving or arriving in a city, could pause and contemplate the deeds of each family and its heroes. In other regions, tombs were built on top of small hills with the intention of gaining visibility and isolation. Suetonius, when recounting the history of the Vespasii family, said that there was "on the top of a mountain, near the sixth milestone on the road from Nurcia to Spoletium, a place called Vespasiae, where many monuments of the Vespasii are to be seen."[428]

The variety of customs in the ancient world did not entirely abolish burials inside city limits. Lycurgus, a Spartan legislator, ordered that the dead be interred around the temples. The objective was to combat superstition and fear among the young. By making such sights familiar, they would lose their fear of seeing the tomb of a deceased person and have "[...] no horror of death as polluting those who touched a corpse or walked among graves."[429]

The advent of Christianity and the consolidation of spiritual power by the Catholic Church enabled the temple and its surroundings to be viewed as an appropriate place for burial grounds. Authority over the dead and the rituals of death came under Canon Law, and ample regulations arose to discipline each and every act: the wake, the funeral procession, the grave, and the corresponding alms. The Catholic Church appropriate death and transformed the concept of the temple, which was no longer simply a house of prayer; its floor also

---

428 SUETONIUS. *A Vida dos Doze Césares* [The Lives of the Caesars], p. 456.
429 PLUTARCH. *As Vidas de Homens Ilustres* [Lives of the Noble Greeks and Romans]. I, p. 248.

served as a sepulcher and its surroundings were required to include space for a cemetery. These were two socially distinct spaces: within the church were those who could afford to give alms; in the cemetery was everyone else. Wealth was what made the difference.

The canonical control over death and the identification of church space as the locale appropriate for burials led to a type of financial transaction: people began buying graves with alms and donations, which could be quarters, thirds, or halves, according to the custom. This economic tendency helps explain, to a certain degree, the proliferation and wealth of the churches over time. It was forbidden to charge for services to the dead or for a spot in the cemetery, but donations were accepted.

Eyewitness accounts within the Catholic Church on the relationship between burials and donations are revealing. In the Goa hospital, according to the account of the traveler Van Linschoten, the dead were carried to the cemetery by two slaves, without any bell-ringing or chanting, unless "the deceased had left some goods and the priests had arranged a means to accompany him to the grave and to say mass for his soul. In such cases, a throng appears, while the deceased is buried honorably, some in the church or chapel, depending on the request in the last will and testament [...]."[430]

In Rome, the last will was intended primarily to secure the continuity of the *paterfamilias*: this was the principle of preserving the family clan and the reason why they avoided dying *ab intestato*. The Catholic Church transformed this notion and linked the belief in atonement for sins with the provisions of the last will intended for the salvation of the soul. The will became the proper instrument for determining the place of burial, the masses for the salvation of the soul, and, consequently, the appropriate donations for such services. The will came to be a canonical institution under mixed responsibility of both civil and religious authorities.

Having rehabilitated the urban space as the place for burials, Catholicism gave rise to the curious idea that the living were walk-

---

430 Source: VAN LINSCHOTEN, Jan Huygen. *Itinerário, Viagem ou Navegação para as Índias Ocidentais ou Portuguesas* [Itinerary, Voyage, or Navigation to the West or Portuguese Indies], p. 169.

ing over the dead. Church dignitaries were aware that the ancients had expelled the dead from the city so that "their stench would not corrupt the air or kill the living,"[431] but they elaborated a powerful religious argument to justify the placement of sepulchers in the church. Four reasons were presented: the religion of Christians "is closer to God than that of other peoples," and therefore, their tombs should be close to the churches;[432] the living, upon seeing the graves of their relatives and friends, would remember to "pray to God for them"; the prayers would call upon the protection of the saint in whose honor and name each church was founded, who would intercede on behalf of those who were buried in the cemetery; the final reason was to provide a refuge for the dead, who, being within church grounds, were protected from the devil, who could not come near the bodies.

The bishop had the task of assigning and consecrating a space for a cemetery for each church. For the main cathedral and the monastery church, the space measured 200 feet on each side; in the parishes, it was 150 feet.[433] The general rule was that the deceased should be buried at the church where he or she was a parishioner and had received the sacraments. Nonetheless, there was some freedom of choice. Other options were burial by the main cathedral, a monastery, or another place where the graves of the deceased's lineage were located. These rules were set forth in the *Seven-Part Code*, the Spanish statutory code written between 1256 and 1263, acquiring legal force in 1348 through the Ordinance of Alcalá issued by Alfonso XI. Four centuries later, the Constitutions of the Archbishop of Bahia reproduced similar norms: "It is a pious, ancient, and praiseworthy custom of the Catholic Church to bury the bodies of deceased faithful Christians in the churches and their cemeteries [...]."[434]

Church land, being sacred, could not be sold; alms could be accepted inside the temple for sepulchers or the construction and

---

431 LAS SIETE PARTIDAS [*Seven-Part Code*], Primeira Partida, Título XIII, lei II.
432 Idem.
433 Ibidem, lei IV. The text expressed the measurement in paces, explaining that each pace covered five feet.
434 CONSTITUIÇÕES DO ARCEBISPADO DA BAHIA [Constitutions of the Archbishop of Bahia], 1707, Livro Quarto, título LIII.

maintenance of the building, but no sums could be received in the church plaza or cemetery. With the passage of time, urban churches grew and took over space in the cemeteries. We can deduce that there were enough alms to finance the sumptuousness of the church edifice, which undoubtedly led to the disappearance of side properties.

A few small churches and their associated cemeteries survived over time. A good example is the Church of Vera Cruz on the Island of Itaparica. On the floor of the little church, a gravestone was laid out, which, according to some, is the oldest in Bahia. Its inscription read,

> "Sepulcher of Francisco Nunes
> who is with God and of his wife
> Joana Barreta and their descendants
> Deceased in grace 1579."

Recall that Caramuru was buried at the church of the Jesuits' School in 1557, at some spot in the section of the Praça da Sé that overlooked the ocean. Mem de Sá was buried at the Jesuits' new church, which is now the Sé Cathedral; Garcia D'Ávila, at the Church of São Francisco; and Gabriel Soares de Souza, at the Monastery of São Bento. Usually the deceased's last will determined the burial place and the alms to be given in gratitude and acknowledgment for the site.

During the Dutch occupation, senior officers killed in battle were buried in the Sé Cathedral, while soldiers were buried in the Terreiro de Jesus. The properties of the churches of Ajuda, Conceição da Praia, Misericórdia, São Francisco, the Sé Cathedral, the old Sé, and the many other sites where chapels were built, such as that of Santa Luzia or the original Jesuit church, served as sepulchers and cemeteries. They perpetuated the image of the living walking about over the dead.

The growth of the city and the evolution of medical knowledge led to a radical change in the religious and economic model of burying the dead, reviving, in a certain sense, what the Greeks and

Romans had known. Starting in France, the theory of miasmas was disseminated, according to which emanations from decomposing bodies caused harm to the population, so cadavers should be buried in places that were far from the city, at a height, and exposed to winds. This theory held that the pits should be deep and arranged in an orderly fashion, and that the cemeteries should be surrounded by walls that could prevent animals from digging up the bodies.

In the city of Salvador, the debate over the issue arose in the nineteenth century. In 1835, Provincial Law nº 17 granted a monopoly over burial grounds to private parties, giving rise to the cemetery known as Campo Santo. The concession was controversial, with strong opposition from the brotherhoods, religious orders, and clergy. Many of them foresaw a financial crisis and organized a popular revolt called the Cemetery Rebellion. When the church bells rang, a mob of 1,400 people destroyed the new graveyard.[435]

Some of the reports on conditions in the burial grounds are disturbing. The parish priest of the Vitória church, in a letter to the Legislative Assembly, reported that the situation at its church grounds was critical, being "saturated with cadavers," so a small plot behind the sacristy was being utilized, but it was already "heaped up with bodies [...], exuding miasmas that threaten great ills [...]."[436] To avoid leaving them unburied, the priest began putting his deceased parishioners in graves dug in nearby plots located between residential houses. Eyewitness accounts in other parishes referred to cases of morbid odors, "greasy substances" oozing through the walls of nearby houses, and skulls and bones rolling down the bluff in front of the old Sé Cathedral.

The popular revolt may have slowed the impetus for change, but it did not solve the problem. Campo Santo was sold to the infirmary in 1840. After renovations were compete, burials at the new cemetery were initiated for people of simple means who became sick and died at the Santa Casa. Once the situation was accommodated, churches were able to maintain adequate conditions for performing burials. In 1851, a German cemetery was inaugurated in front of Campo Santo.

---

435 REIS, João José. *A Morte é uma Festa* [Death is a Festival], pp. 292-306.
436 Idem, p. 292.

Then, in 1855, a terrible epidemic of cholera-morbus broke out, giving a preeminent role to the new cemetery. In nine months, 30,000 people died, of whom 8,000 were residents of the capital city. This generated panic in the population. In August, 1855, at the recommendation of the School of Medicine, burials in churchyards were once again prohibited. This time, there were no protests. Everybody was afraid of the epidemic and fled from the dead.[437]

Thus, the second union of the living and the dead, motivated by the desire to be close to saints and martyrs, came to a close, as had the first one long before, based on the cult of the ancestors. To deal with the situation, the government gave the brotherhoods a piece of land on a hill in the Quinta dos Lázaros so they could set up their cemeteries.

Regarding the city of Salvador, it is reasonable to argue that each church, conceived as a house of God and a house of the dead, grew and took over the land originally used for shallow graves. The center of Salvador is replete with cemeteries: few people are aware of them, as society has forgotten them. The question becomes, what is the importance of remembering them? The answer may be found in the words of Nezahualcóyotl, poet-king of Texcoco, a city-state near Tenochtitlan: "All the earth is a grave, and nought escapes it."

---

437 Ibidem, p. 338.

41. The Anguish of the Master Architect

[...] the building of a city shall establish a name [...]

Ecclesiasticus 40:19

His name was Luís Dias. Here was a man who rejected what he created, but was never forgotten by his creation. In July, 1551, he wrote to his patron in Lisbon, saying that his service was almost concluded and asking him to intercede with the King to summon him back to the kingdom when his three years' mandate was over. The letter is full of complaints, many of them expressing a surprisingly uncharacteristic aggressiveness: "In all the lands of creation with all things of this world, there is nowhere that compares with this, but the pagans who live here are demons."[438] He was referring to Bahia de Todos os Santos, the Bay of All Saints

Nor did Dias spare his countrymen whom he met there: "There never was a man we found in this land who spoke the truth, but who caused sorrow to all of us upon our arrival with the evil of their

---

438 Letter from Luís Dias to Miguel de Arruda, dated July 13, 1551. In: *Anais do 4º Congresso de História da Bahia*. I, pp. 140-144.

ways."[439] He was probably referring to the custom of polygamy practiced by the Diogo Álvares Caramuru's men, which the Jesuits soon tried to prohibit and eradicate. The nostalgia that the master architect felt for Portugal, along with his pain after his nephew disappeared in a shipwreck on his return to Lisbon, brought him to the brink of despair, which pervaded his entreaties: "In one way or another, if it pleases Your Majesty, order me to go, for the love of the Madonna, because I swear that, if I die here, I will go straight to hell [...]." [440]

Besides his nostalgia for Portugal and hostility to the customs of the native peoples, he was exasperated with the meager food he received and the medium in which his salary was issued. Although he had been promised a basic food supply, he was given "a little bit of woody flour with a little bit of vinegar and oil, without any meat, not even fish [...],"[441] he wrote, referring to the ration of provisions given to all men who earned fixed wages or salaries. Concerning the salaries, he asserted that the men had been deceived, since what "comes from the Kingdom is old metal like that sold in the market in Lisbon and this is used to pay the poor fellows who work here."[442]

In the words of the master architect, it was sad to consider the handling of "proceeds in Brazil," which were itemized in the royal appointments: "Everything is circumvented because there is no way to pay even half the salary of one of these men."[443] On this point, his complaints were true. The orders of payment confirm the low standards of the provisions, the delays in salaries, the issuance of iron, the payment of only a few privileged men in Pernambuco, and the inability of the Treasury to pay the salaries of the superior officers.

Even though he was the first architect, urban planner, and engineer assigned to the coast of Brazil, responsible for executing the construction of the Fortress of Salvador, his words expressed pessimism and a lack of identification for what he was creating. "Many houses could be built on these sloping access roads, if that is nec-

---

439 Idem, p. 142.
440 Ibidem, p. 143,
441 Ibidem, p. 142.
442 Ibidem, p. 140.
443 Idem.

essary later [...],"[444] he said, referring to the Ladeira da Misericórdia and Ladeira da Conceição da Praia, the original means of entering the city. However, he had his doubts about population growth: "And I tell you this, Sir, the only thing that can be told about this place is the hunger and work we endure. As long as this Bay has no more than one hundred residents, if fifty arrive on horseback, none of them will fare well or eat a decent meal."[445] It did not take long for this figure to be reached, but Dias's assignment and his primary concern, besides returning to Lisbon, were to complete the defensive walls of the city. In his opinion, it was sufficient to build them of wattle and daub, then whitewash and reinforce them with wood, in order for them to last twenty years with only annual maintenance.

The architect's dilemma was not confined to paper: Father Manuel da Nóbrega communicated it to the King, omitting any personal identifying information. Undoubtedly, because of his private conversations and the confessions he heard, he was familiar with the moods and motivations of each official. In 1552, Nóbrega wrote some disconcerting words in his report: "This land is so poor, even now, that it will cause much grief to Your Highness's officials [...]."[446] He acknowledged that there were many expenses in Portugal and little revenue to send from Brazil. He then asked that so many officials with high salaries be recalled, since there was nothing else they wanted than "to end their time here and earn their salaries [...],"[447] using some excuse to importune the monarch. He faulted the officials' desire for wealth: "As this is their main goal, they do not love this land, since their affection is for Portugal [...]."[448] They were not working to benefit Brazil, but instead seeking to take advantage of it in any way they could.

---

444 Ibidem, p. 141.
445 Ibidem, p. 143.
446 Carta do Padre Manuel da Nóbrega ao Rei Dom João III, datada de julho de 1552 [Letter from Father Manuel da Nóbrega to King Dom João III, dated July 1552]. LEITE S. I., Serafim. *Cartas dos Primeiros Jesuítas do Brasil* [Letters of the First Jesuits of Brazil]. I, p. 344.
447 Ibidem, p. 344.
448 Ibidem, p. 345.

The coast of Brazil presented a curious contrast: it brought suffering and vexation to both common people and the well-born in the Kingdom, among them, Luís Dias, the weary and afflicted master architect; yet it also served as a refuge for outcasts from Portuguese society and aroused Christian ideals in the virtuous. It attracted some types of people due to the liberty of action it offered, and other types whose sights were set on enrichment.

Nóbrega concluded his correspondence by pronouncing this to be the general rule in Brazil, although there were some exceptions. In the final analysis, the difference lay between ordinary people and those who obstinately sought meaning in their life and in their work.

Documentary Appendix

The criterion for selecting the documents transcribed and translated in this appendix was that of being previously unpublished; research conducted for this book was unable to discover any prior source where they may have been published. Evidently, the texts are either unknown or absent from the standard bibliographies on the history of Brazil.

The first two documents are authorizations granted by King Dom João III in 1551 concerning policies for dealing with crimes on the coast of Brazil. They were transcribed from Codex 112, a book found in the Arquivo Histórico Ultramarino Português (the Portuguese Overseas Historical Archives). The Instituto Histórico e Geográfico Brasileiro (Brazilian Institute of History and Geography) has manuscript copies of documents drawn up by order of King Dom Pedro II, but, apparently, these two decrees were not published.

The third is a letter from the governing bishop in Lisbon, which contains information about exiles sent to Brazil in Tomé de Souza's armada. The source for this letter is the *Corpo Cronológico do Instituto dos Arquivos Nacionais, Torre do Tombo* (Chronological Corpus of the Institute of National Archives, Deeds Annex).

The last two documents describe the city of Salvador in the seventeenth century. The texts were originally translated from French and represent a useful contribution to knowledge about the city's history.

Document 1
Authorization from King Dom João III permitting Governor Tomé de Souza to issue bond papers to people who committed crimes and wished to remain free, issued August 5, 1551.

Transcript of the authorization that Our Lord the King granted to Thomé de Sousa, Governor of the lands of Brazil, allowing him to grant authorizations for bond papers to guilty parties to secure their release by appearing before the ombudsman general in the city of Salvador.

I, the King, apprise you, Thome de Sousa, in my council, captain of the Bay of All Saints and governor of the other captaincies and lands of Brazil, that I have been informed that some of the Christians resident in those parts who have been found guilty and sentenced in my courts have fled from the settlements and taken refuge among the pagans, setting a bad example to them and following their customs, and that others have left for other parts out of fear of being unable to avoid being imprisoned. I wish to provide measures to prevent such flights and allow the accused to gain their release, it being very important in service to God and to myself that the land be settled by Christians, so it is for the better that those who were thus accused in any court actions of crimes they committed up to now or will commit from now on, with the exception of the crimes of heresy, sodomy, treason, counterfeiting, or deliberate murder of a Christian, can obtain their release in the city of Salvador by appearing before my ombudsman general, whom you may authorize to grant bond papers so that they may obtain their release and be free for the period specified in the bond papers, except for those as you see fit according to the nature of the crime and the person. This will be recorded using the transcript of the form for granting authorization for bond papers to them in my court and entered into the book that I have sent for recording pardons, in which bond papers will be recorded under a separate heading. For those who cannot obtain their release within the time that you specified and who have good cause for this, you may allow more time that you consider necessary for them and the periods of their release shall be recorded in the aforementioned book so that they will not be in violation. If some of them forfeit their bonds, you shall execute the papers and collect the money from their guarantors and that which you have collected shall be delivered to the person who is in charge of the construction of the cathedral in that city and who shall be responsible for spending what he receives on such work, since it is right that such penalties be applied to this project. Notice shall be sent to all my justices, officials, and people in charge of such matters that they shall thoroughly obey what I have ordered and that they must have forms authorizing bond papers, which they shall grant without any doubt whatsoever and, to ensure that this notice reaches everybody, this authorization shall be registered and published in my chancellery in that captaincy, and, in each of the other ones in that land, you shall have it published and registered, which shall carry the same force as if it were a letter in my name, despite the ordinance in the second book, title XX, stating the contrary. Executed by Bento Perez in Almeirim on August 5, 1551. Fernão d'Alvarez put it in writing, and, in the cases in which more time is calculated, the parties will recalculate their bond papers or issue new ones.

Source: Codex 112. Book in which regulations, provisions, official letters, and favors that Our Lord the King issues to people who go to Brazil are recorded, beginning on the 1st of January, 1549, in Almeirim, page 174v-175. Portuguese Overseas Council. Paleographic transcription by Luiz Walter Coelho Filho.

DOCUMENT 2
AUTHORIZATION FROM KING DOM JOÃO III PERMITTING GOVERNOR TOMÉ DE SOUZA TO PARDON PEOPLE WHO COMMITTED CRIMES ON THE COAST OF BRAZIL ON DATES PRIOR TO HIS ARRIVAL, ISSUED AUGUST 6, 1551.

Transcript of a provision that Your Highness granted to Thomé de Sousa allowing him to grant pardons to the residents of the lands of Brazil for crimes for which they were sentenced in court before he arrived.

I, the King, apprise you, Thome de Sousa, member of my council, captain of the Bay of All Saints and governor of the other captaincies and lands of Brazil, that I have been informed that, before your arrival in those parts, many of the Christians who lived there committed crimes and errors in their duties and positions and were guilty because they were held responsible by the court and that, when my ombudsman general went there last year in fifteen hundred and fifty to administer justice in towns and places in those captaincies, many of those who were guilty took flight and some joined the pagans of the land and are living among them, setting a bad example and following their customs, and others came back to these Kingdoms and went to the Antilles out of fear of being imprisoned and punished as their crimes warrant. Because my intention is to have those lands be settled and ennobled and to avoid the inconveniences that might impede this, it is the will of God and myself to pardon through my court any persons who were sentenced through any court actions of crimes that they committed in those parts before your arrival, as long as there are no parties that have accusations against them, and if they have been residing in those settlements for some time, as long as they are not guilty of any of these five cases: heresy, sodomy, treason, counterfeiting, or deliberate murder of a Christian, because it is not my desire to pardon such crimes. They may be released through the court ordinarily according to the law and my ordinances, and to each one of them who is thus pardoned, you shall issue a pardon in my name using a transcript of this authorization and, instead of punishment, you shall define the length of time, as you see fit, that he must be restricted to residing in Christian settlements in those captaincies, each one in the place he prefers, because, with such conditions, it is right to pardon them. These pardons shall be summarily registered in a book that you shall use for this purpose and, after such parties have fulfilled the period of time that you restricted them, they will be responsible for bringing a certificate of how they fulfilled it and have it recorded underneath their pardon. I hereby order all my justices, officials, and people in charge of such matters to issue pardons and releases, and they must thoroughly fulfill such pardons without any doubt whatsoever and, to ensure that this notice reaches everybody, this authorization shall be registered and published in my chancellery and you shall have it published and registered in each of the captaincies of that coast, and it shall carry the same force as if it were a letter in my name, despite the ordinance in the second book, title XX, stating the contrary. Executed in Almeirim by Bento Perez on August 6, 1551, and I, Fernão d'Alvarez, put it in writing.

Source: Codex 112. Book in which regulations, provisions, official letters, and favors that Our Lord the King issues to people who go to Brazil are recorded, beginning on the 1st of January, 1549, in Almeirim, page 174v-175. Portuguese Overseas Council. Paleographic transcription by Luiz Walter Coelho Filho.

Document 3
Letter from the Governing Bishop to King Dom João III, reporting that the city of Lisbon was peaceful and that exiled persons had departed in Tomé de Souza's fleet headed for Brazil, on February 15, 1549.

Gaspar Lopez, university graduate and criminal judge in this city, showed me a letter from Your Highness in which Your Highness ordered that he bring the wife of Entremoz to Santarém. He will go with a mayor, as the judge is a man diligent in his office, serving and overseeing this city a great deal; Your Highness should remember his service and show him favor. The Brazilian armada took all the exiles who were in the jails in this city to Brazil, so no more than seven or eight are still here who will later follow the exiles to such places in the coming days when many caravels will be leaving, as I ordered all the exiles to leave and none are to remain.

The city, praise be to the Lord, is very safe and sound. May the royal state of Your Highness Our Lord keep well and add many more long and prosperous days of life to your sainted service. From Lisbon, February 15, 1549.

The Governing Bishop

Source: Corpo Cronológico [Chronological Corpus], parte 1, maço 82, doc. 52, ANTT. Paleographic transcription by Luiz Walter Coelho Filho.

Document 4
Copy of a letter written by Jacques Raynard from Brazil and the Bay of All Saints to his wife, on October 30, 1634.

Dear wife,

I think you heard about my departure from Ilha de Madeira, headed for Brazil, which took place on July 29, my intention being to go to the Cabo de Santo Agostinho, near Pernambuco, in hopes of finding better business dealings than in any other location. We arrived in Brazil, in a place called Lagos, on September 2, which is a small sandbar that we could not enter, since there we heard that the Cabo de Santo Agostinho was held by the Dutch, just like all the ports on the coast of Pernambuco, such that no trade could be conducted on that coast, given that there were many Dutch warships all along it, which made us decide to go to the Bay of All Saints. Arriving in the Bay, about two leagues from its entrance, at daybreak on September 7, the eve of the Nativity of the Mother of God, we encountered four Dutch warships, one with 32 cannons, one with 28, another with 22, and the last with 8 cannons, most of them made of cast iron. We engaged in a battle so furious that they approached and fired more than 300 cannon shots toward us, at the body of the ship as well as at the masts and sails. For our part, we fired more than two hundred shots, most of them hitting their ships. They managed to come up against the side of our ship and dominate it, with more than 30 men coming aboard the first time. We engaged in hand-

to-hand combat and overcame all of them, throwing them into the sea and killing many people, to the point where the enemies were obliged to raise their sails, cut loose, and leave us. We did them a lot of harm and killed the captain of the main ship and the two other captains as well, and by the end, we had killed a large number of them and injured more than sixty people, which we heard about from the sailors of a Portuguese ship that they seized and whom they left on land. They fled from us and did not kill anyone, thank God, although they had injured many of our crew, most of whom have recuperated by now. This happened in full sight of many people in the Bay who came to the edge of the sea, more than two thousand armed men, to see the battle, which lasted more than eight hours in calm seas, with so little wind that, if it were not visible to so many people, it would not be believable. Thus, it is possible that anyone who did not see it would not believe it. In the end, we were well received in this country, by the Governor, the Court, as well as everyone else, rich and poor, because of the battle we fought in front of them. We were welcomed by the fortresses with cannon shots, just like when the Governor comes from Portugal. We did achieve victory, but it must be attributed to God and the Blessed Mother who gave us enough courage to do battle against those large ships, since no men could have done so without the assistance of God. If only you could have seen how we entered the port with all the sails, rigging, and yards damaged. So we have to replace all the masts and sails. Without mentioning the numerous cannon shots in the body of the ship, our victory is a great miracle, given that the enemies fled after being so badly mistreated. As for business dealings, they are not going so well because of the 80 ships we see in this city, which have brought a great quantity of all types of merchandise. For two years, no ship has been allowed to leave for any place, even those that go to Angola, the main business destination of this city. We will give out our merchandise little by little and get our ship repaired during this time until Lent arrives. This will surely take some three months, by which time we will have finished selling our merchandise and will immediately ask permission for detained ships to leave. We are waiting for a governor from Portugal who is coming with a squadron of warships. The old governor will board and take 80 ships with him in a fleet to navigate *with safety. As soon as we are ready, the Governor promised us that he would give us permission to leave because of the battle we fought. If we are released, we will not fail to take a long trip and make good profits, if it please God. If we could have gone to the Cabo de Santo Agostinho or some port on the coast near Pernambuco, we would have taken a longer trip and our merchandise would have been sold for twice as much as in this city, but we must consider everything in the best light. I will close here, hoping I remain in your good graces and those of your mother, sisters, brothers-in-law, relatives, and friends. Your husband, Jacques Raynard, his signature. From Brazil and the Bay of All Saints, on October 30, 1634.*

Source: SERRÃO, Joaquim Veríssimo. O Tempo dos Filipes em Portugal e no Brasil (1580-1669) [The Philippine Dynasty in Portugal and Brazil, 1580-1669], pp. 303-305. The original text is in French, consisting of a copy extracted from Codex 1777 of the Inguimbertini collection, f. 358, 358v, in the library of the French city of Carpentras. The text was first translated from French to Portuguese by Catherine J. Tresgots.

Document 5
Report from Brazil, probably written by Jacques Raynard, dated 1635.

Report from Brazil, 1635

We arrived in the Bay of All Saints with a wind coming from the east. The entrance to the gulf of this Bay (where one goes by Gree and Tramontana) is at least eight miles wide. It is necessary to enter in the middle, due to the banks and reefs that are found on the left side. Upon entering, one passes on the right side in front of three towers that defend the mouth, all situated within reach of musket shots of each other, well armed and guarded. One can anchor safely in any part of the gulf, with the tide coming every six hours, generally eight to twelve spans high.

As for the city, it is not much smaller than Toulon, furnished with bastions and moats. Those on the eastern side going two-thirds of the way to the other side of the city are filled. There is a Portuguese Governor representing the King of Spain in command of a thousand men in garrison. With regards to the inhabitants, the people are a mixture, that is, there are white people, who are called Portuguese, bronze-black people who have been taken from the country of Angola and who are used for every kind of servile labor, and savages, who are called "Gentiles." The majority of the inhabitants follow the laws and customs of Portuguese way of life. One can see an attractive palace for the Governor's residence, an Episcopal Church that used to be pretty, as one can see from the ruins caused at the hands of the Dutch. Besides this, there are the houses for the Jesuits, Observants,

Carmelites, and Benedictines. The city and its houses are all built of stone and are quite good. There are two fountains providing water for the entire city. Although they are a little bit salty, people like to draw their water from them, since they are excellent.

One can see many orange trees and lemon trees inside the ramparts and even more in the fields outside the city. Through the ebb and flow, the largest ships can go very far, up to a hundred and fifty miles inland, using, however, boats appropriate for this and bearing a weight of five hundred quintals.

Besides this, one may count thirty-six plantations that operate to supply this city.

The terrain is elevated in some places with small hills.

In the Gulf I mentioned (which contains an area of at least a hundred and some miles), there are a number of islands that are very pretty, fertile in wood, and which serve as pastures for cattle, pigs, and horses. One can see no donkeys, mules, or wolves, except in some of the plantations, which carry a large quantity of sugarcane, watermelons, and very good white melons, which lack for nothing in comparison with ours. The islands are usually inhabited and we could circulate among them with the greatest liberty.

The land along the ocean is almost entirely used for sugarcane and you would think they were vineyards, I might say, or else in some places, the cane may be separated by small woodlots. When it is the rainy season, the sugar harvest is much better.

Other pieces of land are used for cultivating manioc, which is a certain plant that I would compare to the largest turnips in our country. In that country, cuttings of the plant are inserted in the soil to reproduce, as we do in our vineyards, since their foliage is similar, not completely the same in thickness as that of agnus castus, *but similar in their flowers and leaves. The roots of this manioc are removed from the soil (which can be done at any time and in any season, as is the case with planting it) after having remained in the soil usually for a period of two years. It is grated with a knife, in the same way that we do with horseradish roots, and then placed in a type of device made for this purpose, which could be compared to a large lathe for reeling wool, covered with prongs that are the exact length to grate close to a board (of a propor-*

tionate size). At an opening in the board, a man holds the root securely, out of fear of being injured, and pushes it in until it is completely grated. The shreds of manioc fall into a wooden box, where they are stored and then pressed to squeeze out all the liquid, which has a terrible smell and a worse taste, which one dare not sample. After that, it is put into immense copper kettles with a round shape of more or less ten spans in circumference and half a foot thick. Underneath these kettles is a good fire for drying and preparing the manioc, during which time a man must constantly stir it from one side to the other with an instrument made for this purpose, similar to those in our country with which we clean out our tanks, which we call "redables." The manioc is then removed and put on mats made of reeds and saigne *to cool it. After this, all the common folk of this country as well as the most powerful partake of it in the same way that we do with bread. When it is well prepared, you would think it made of pounded almonds, being very close in its taste and aroma, or even better. Some mix it with sugar, and it is also added to various kinds of soups, whether of meat, fish, or other kinds, as we do with cheese, only in larger amounts. It grows abundantly and its flesh does not spoil. It is not perfect when it is hot or about to boil, but only in medium and moderate heat. The usual price for it is up to two* liards *a pound, although it is true that one can see it for up to six* liards. *Among other noteworthy things are the trees that are seen on the banks of the rivers that the ocean creates from its ebb and flow. They are the same height as our common pines and their leaves look like those of the laurel. Usually the ebb and flow cover them halfway and often damage their limbs. After they are uncovered, their smallest roots can be seen, which are many times cut because of the amount of oysters that are found attached to them, of a taste and size of those found in our country One can observe in these trees and in a few others that the limbs grow from the roots and keep on piling up, with the soil getting lodged in them. They start growing again and sending out new shoots, like other limbs, although they do not bear fruit. In the midst of the trees that grow in this country, one may find the rosewood, which, besides being lovely in appearance, has the advantage of not being subject to worms.*

There is also another species of tree that, by its nature, is square in shape, like one would describe the remaining core of a felled tree, and its thickness is no more than such a core. It is naturally white but, if gouged, becomes red.

Along the seacoast normally covered up by the ebb and flow of water grow certain trees called "piedsane," which are quite thick and which one might say are the common oaks of this country, from which the bark (used on the yards that come from Spain) is made into ropes and cables for the largest ships, for all kinds of purposes. The cables prove themselves to be especially good and strong, very durable and not easily degraded by water. Without them, it would be very difficult to sail in that country, given that the heat is excessive and the sea water is so strong and corrosive that it would cause all other rigging on the ships to deteriorate in short order.

The vineyards bear fruits three times a year, as I have witnessed for myself and eaten these grapes, and they are also cut three times a year; however, wine is extremely expensive, given that a large barrel with a volume of six meilleroles costs up to a hundred coins of eight [francs]. What impedes the cultivation of vineyards in this country is the large quantity of ants, since, if they have a few stocks like those we saw, it is thanks to a special practice. The stock is put in a container with holes, which is filled with soil to serve as food, and it is necessary to have it inside another, well sealed and able to hold water, serving as a barrier full of water to impede attacks by ants. If this were not done, it would not be possible to prevent its destruction. It is necessary to practice the same technique for conserving lemon trees, sweet orange trees, as well as pomegranate trees and all delicate trees that bear sweet fruits. The fig tree, for its part, is safe from attack by these creatures, due to the bitterness of either its bark or its leaves, or some other quality or peculiarity. There are not a lot of them, but they become so laden with fruits that they can hardly bear more.

We can see a large quantity of those we call Adam's fig trees. As for other fruit-bearing trees, there is one that could be compared to our jujube trees and which bears a fruit called a "mangano," similar to our rowans in all ways, whether in color or in taste. There is another tree that has a fruit they call pineapple, like a medium-sized cone; the husk is removed from the fruits, and, after being cut into slices, they are submerged in wine to make it even better, like we do here with our peaches.

The Fortress of Salvador

When it is nearing ripeness, if we stick a knife inside it, it is capable of damaging the metal of the knife. Moreover, if anyone has some wounds or ulcers and continues to eat this fruit, he will prolong the curse of his ailment. A large quantity of tobacco can be collected, which is generally worth about six soldos *per pound.*

Also, a certain herb can be seen that is composed of many tiny leaves that are scattered about the ground; it displays a property of recoiling and contracting if it is touched.

Ginger is also collected from a plant that is similar to what we call "gramo," the roots of which we use to make ginger. However, it is necessary to plant this ginger in a foot of cultivated soil that is good and fertile, placing the plant half a foot under the soil, with one square span between each one. It is necessary to divide the ginger into small pieces, as long as the pieces have one or two eyes. They must be left this way for eight months and will only grow after forty days. They grow in the same way as a small shoot of a cattail, but there is no risk in leaving it in the soil without transplanting it for two seasons, which will not stop it from growing and will even increase its growth.

The soil is also very appropriate for growing cotton, and the trees that grow in it are incomparably taller and higher than those in the east. There is also a large amount of rice and beans. Especially noteworthy is the whale hunting that begins at São João. With this objective, five or six boats leave the Bay, each holding seven to eight men, each man engaged in rowing except for the one who will stab the whale with his trident or pitchfork. This is done in the following manner, going out in search of this fish and then taking care to see if it is a male, which is recognized by the sound of its breathing in the water, the way it lifts its head, and how it beats its tail. Seeing as it is too dangerous to try to capture one of these, they attack only the females. After they have discovered one, the man whose role it is throws his weapon and secures his target. This being done, the pitchfork is tied to a strong cable, three inches thick, which is allowed a certain amount of play while waiting for the animal's fury to pass. As its strength diminishes, the men try to pull in the rope, and, with the help of a few other companion boats, it is hauled between two rows until reaching land. If by chance the whale is cut underwater, then it is a lost cause, since even before the order to pull it out is given, sharks, which are found in prodigious quantity, will have devoured it. Depending on circumstances, in general up to twenty-five or thirty whales will be killed, from which their oil is extracted. From some it is possible to extract twenty-five to thirty bottles of oil and from others, less, while from some not even eight will be extracted. The fat of this fish is used for its oil. From the remains, the blacks and other peoples in the country make merchandise, some cook it and eat it, others salt it and produce a good amount for the home. The ribcage looks as big as the hull of a boat holding a thousand quintals in this country. They say that it has a throat that is so small that it measures no more than a foot in diameter, but its tongue looks like a shroud and its eye is similar to that of an ox. Its worst enemy is a fish called a swordfish, which has a spike on the top of its head like a sword, with which it pierces the whale from under its belly and thus attacks it.

Snakes with two heads have been seen here.

Also seen are those fish that have a tiny head and are nevertheless fat and round like a ball.

In a hermitage dedicated to Our Lady of Exile, a serpent was seen that was twenty-seven spans long, with a proportionate thickness. Many of these are seen in this country, which are not much smaller. I already mentioned how ants cause a lot of trouble, but certainly the small animals that we call "lingastes" [lizards] cause no less trouble.

Moreover, there is a certain type of small worm that is almost impossible to see, called beasties, which grow in the toes of one's foot, or below the soles of the heel or in the ankles. These must be removed as soon as possible, given that in a short time they will grow to a large size and even cause gangrene.

There is a constellation in the sky that can be seen at night in the form of a cloud, the size of a shield that remains fixed and stationary, and lies to the south, just as in this country the east is where Tramontana lies.

Source: SERRÃO, Joaquim Veríssimo. *O Tempo dos Filipes em Portugal e no Brasil (1580-1669)* [*The Philippine Dynasty in Portugal and Brazil, 1580-1669*], pp. 305-310. The original text is in French and consists of a copy extracted from Codex 715 in the library of the French city of Carpentras. The translation from French to Portuguese was commissioned by the author from Catherine J. Tresgots.

TABLE APPENDIX

Renaissance Measurements

Although Renaissance measurements of length were usually based on the human body, the actual dimensions varied greatly from region to region. To get an idea of this variability, the following table indicates the approximate dimensions of common units of measurement in Renaissance Portugal, Spain, Italy, and ancient Rome.

Table 38 - Correlation of Units of Measurement[449]

Unit in English (Portuguese, Spanish, Italian, Latin)	Portugal (Meters)	Spain (Meters)	Italy (Meters)	Rome (Meters)
Span (palmo, palmo, palmo, palmus)	0.220	0.210	0.230	—
Foot (pé, pie, piede, pes)	0.330	0.280	0.296	0.290
Cubit (cúbito/côvado, codo, cubito, cubitus)	0.660	0.418	0.440	0.435
Yard (vara, vara, n/a, vara)	1.100	0.836	—	—
Pace (passo, paso, passo, passus)	1.650	0.650	1.480	1.450
Rod* (cana/aguilhada, caña, canna, canna)	3.960	1.670	2.320	—

---

[449] The Moliner dictionary states that the Spanish cana is equal to two *varas*; see *Diccionario de uso del español*.

Fathom (braça, braza, bráccio, brachia)	2.200	1.670	0.580	—
Furlong (estádio, estadio, stádio, stadium)	206.250	201.200	185.000	181.250
Mile (milha, milla, miglio, miliarium)	2200.000	1375.000	—	1450.000

Sources: *I) Portuguese measurements:* CUNHA, Rui Maneira. *As Medidas na Arquitetura [Measurements in Architecture];* FERREIRA, Aurélio Buarque de Holanda. *Novo Dicionário Aurélio [New Aurélio Dictionary]. II) Spanish measurements:* LECHUGA, Cristóbal. *Tratado de la Artilleria y de Fortificación [Treatise on Artillery and Fortification]*, p. 451; MOLINER, María. *Diccionario de uso del español [Dictionary of Spanish Usage]; III) Italian and Latin measurements:* ALMEIDA, Napoleão Mendes de, *Gramática Latina [Latin Grammar],* p. 459; ALBERTI, Leon Battista. *L'Architettura [Architecture],* pp. 41, 93.[450]

---

[450] *Translator's note:* Although the concepts behind the English term "rod" and the Romance terms show parallels, they are not strictly equivalent. The unit called *cana* or *aguilhada* in Portugal (and *caña* or *canna* in Spain and Italy, respectively) was probably derived from the length of a cattle prod, while the English rod may have been derived from a pole used to goad teams of oxen and was much longer, 5.029 meters. See http://www.unc.edu/~rowlett/units/index.html.

Bibliography

ACTAS DEL SEMINARIO "LA CIUDAD IBEROAMERICANA" [Acts from the Seminar "The Iberoamerican City"]. Buenos Aires: Ministerio Español de Obras Públicas y Urbanismo de Madrid, 1985.

ACTAS DO COLÓQUIO INTERNACIONAL "UNIVERSO URBANÍSTICO PORTUGUÊS, 1415-1822" [Acts of the International Colloquium, "The Portuguese Urban Universe, 1415-1822"]. Coordenação de Renata Araújo, Hélder Carita e Walter Rossa. Lisboa: Comissão Nacional para as Comemorações dos Descobrimentos Portugueses, 2001.

ALBERTI, Leon Battista. *L'Architettura* [Architecture]. Milano: Edizioni Il Polifilo, 1989.

ALMEIDA, Fortunato de. *História da Igreja em Portugal* [History of the Church in Portugal]. Nova edição preparada e dirigida por Damião Peres. Porto: Portucalense Editora, 1967.

ALMEIDA, Napoleão Mendes de. *Gramática Latina* [Latin Grammar], 26ª edição. São Paulo: Saraiva, 1995.

AQUINO, São Tomás. *Escritos Políticos* [Political Writings]. Petrópolis, RJ: Vozes, 1995.

ANAIS do 4° Congresso de História da Bahia: Salvador 450 anos [Annals of the Fourth Congress on the History of Bahia: Salvador 450 Years], 27 de setembro a 1° de outubro de 1999. Salvador:

Instituto Geográfico e Histórico da Bahia; Fundação Gregório de Matos, 2001.

ANCHIETA, José de. *Monumenta Anchietana—Obras Completas* [Anchieta Collection: Complete Works]. São Paulo: Edições Loyola, 1988.

ANDRADA, Francisco de. *Crônica de D. João III* [Chronicle of Dom João III]. Introdução e revisão de M. Lopes de Almeida. Porto: Lello & Irmão Editores, 1976.

ARISTÓTELES. *Política*. Brasília: Editora Universidade de Brasília, 3ª edição, 1997. English translation: ARISTOTLE. *Politics*. Translated by Benjamin Jowett. Oxford: Oxford University Press, 1902 [1885]. http://classics.mit.edu/Aristotle/politics.html

AS GAVETAS da Torre do Tombo [Royal Files of the Torre do Tombo]. Lisboa: Centro de Estudos Históricos Ultramarinos, 1962.

BALLONG-WEN-MEWUDA, J. Bato'ora. *São Jorge da Mina 1482-1637*. Lisbonne/ Paris: Fundação Calouste Gulbenkian, 1993.

BARATA, Felipe Themudo. *Navegação, Comércio e Relações Políticas: os Portugueses no Mediterrâneo Ocidental (1385-1466)* [Navigation, Commerce, and Political Relations: The Portuguese in the Western Mediterranean, 1385-1466]. Lisboa: Fundação Calouste Gulbenkian e Junta Nacional de Investigação Científica e Tecnológica, 1998.

BARROS, Henrique da Gama. *História da Administração Pública em Portugal nos Séculos XII a XV* [History of Public Administration in Portugal in the Twelfth to Fifteenth Centuries]. Lisboa: Livraria Sá da Costa Editora, 1945.

BARROS, João de. *Ásia* [Asia]. Lisboa: Imprensa Nacional --Casa da Moeda, 1988.

BARROS, José Teixeira de. "Muros da cidade do Salvador" ["Walls in the City of Salvador"] In: *Revista do Instituto Geográfico e Histórico da Bahia*, V. 36. Salvador: 1909.

BENEVOLO, Leonardo. *História da Cidade* [History of the City]. São Paulo: Editora Perspectiva, 1999.

BLOND, José Ramón Soraluce. *Las Fortificaciones Españolas de Sicilia en el Renacimiento* [Spanish Fortifications in Sicily during the Renaissance]. Coruña: Universidade da Coruña/Servicio de Publicaciones. 1998.

BRAMLY, Serge. *Leonardo da Vinci 1452-1519*. Tradução de Henrique de Araújo Mesquita. Rio de Janeiro: Imago Ed., 1989.

BLANCO, Ricardo Roman. *Las Bandeiras— Instituciones Bélicas Americanas* [The Flag Companies: American War Institutions]. Brasília: Universidade de Brasília, 1966.

BOCARRO, Antôno. *O Livro das Plantas de Todas as Fortalezas, Cidades e Povoações do Estado da Índia Oriental* [Book of Plans of All Fortresses, Cities, and Settlements in the East Indies]. Lisboa: Imprensa Nacional --Casa da Moeda, 1992.

BRANDÃO (BUARCOS), João. *Grandeza e Abastança de Lisboa em 1552* [Grandeur and Affluence in Lisbon in 1552]. Lisboa: Livros Horizonte, 1990.

BRANDÃO, Junito de Souza. *Dicionário Mítico-etimológico da Mitologia Grega* [Mythical-Etymological Dictionary of Greek Mythology], 4ª edição. Petrópolis, RJ: Vozes, 1991.

BRINTON, Daniel G. *Ancient Nahuatl Poetry*. Briton's Library of Aboriginal American Literature, number VII, 1890. http://www.gutenberg.org/files/12219/12219-h/12219-h.htm

BRITO, Raquel Soeiro de. *Goa e as praças do norte revisitadas* [Goa and the Northern Cities Revisited]. Lisboa: Comissão Nacional para as Comemorações dos Descobrimentos Portugueses, 1998.

BUCHMANN, Armando José. *Arquiteto Lúcio Costa, o inventor da cidade de Brasília: centenário do nascimento* [Architect Lúcio Costa, Inventor of the City of Brasilia: Centennial of His Birth]. Brasília: Thesaurus, 2002.

CALMON, Pedro. *História da Fundação da Bahia* [History of the Founding of Bahia]. Salvador: Publicações do Museu do Estado, nº 9, 1949.

_____. *História do Brasil* [History of Brazil], 4ª edição. Rio de Janeiro: Livraria José Olympio Editora, 1981.

CARITA, Helder. *Lisboa Manuelina e a Formação de Modelos Urbanísticos da Época Moderna (1495-1521)* [Manueline Lisbon and the Formation of Urban Models in the Modern Era (1495-1521)]. Lisboa: Livros Horizonte, 1999.

CARNEIRO, Edison. *A Cidade do Salvador 1549: Uma reconstituição Histórica: A Conquista da Amazônia* [The City of Salvador, 1548: A Historical Reconstruction: The Conquest of Amazonia], 2ª edição. Rio de Janeiro: Civilização Brasileira, 1980.

CASAS, Fray Bartolomé de las. *Historia de las Indias* [History of the Indies], 2ª edición. México: Fondo de Cultura Económica, 1995.

CASTILLO, B. Díaz del. *Historia Verdadera de la Conquista de la Nueva España*, 2ª edición. México: Editores Mexicanos Unidos, 1992. English translation: CASTILLO, Bernal Diaz del. *The Memoirs of the Conquistador Bernal Diaz del Castillo, Written by Himself Containing a True and Full Account of the Discovery and Conquest of Mexico and New Spain*, Vol. 1. Translated by John Ingram Lockhart. London: J. Hatchard and Son, 1844. http://www.gutenberg.org/files/32474/32474-h/32474-h.htm

CATANEO, Pietro. "L'Architettura" [Architecture]. In: *Trattati, de Pietro Cataneo e Giacomo Barozzi da Vignola, com l'agiunta degli scritti di Architettura di Alvise Cornaro, Francesco Giorgi, Claudio Tolomei, Giangiorgio Trissino e Giorgio Vasari*. Milano: Edizioni Il Polifilo, 1985.

CENTRO Histórico de Salvador, Bahia: patrimônio mundial [Historic Center of Salvador, Bahia: World Heritage Site]. São Paulo: Horizonte Geográfico. 2000.

CHEVALIER, Jean. *Dicionário de Símbolos (mitos, sonhos, costumes, gestos, formas, figuras, cores, números)* [Dictionary of Symbols: Myths, Dreams, Customs, Gestures, Shapes, Forms, Colors, Numbers], 16ª edição. Rio de Janeiro: José Olímpio, 2001.

CICERO, Marcos Tullius. *De Officiis: On Duties*. Translated by Harry D. Edinger. Indianapolis: Bobbs-Merrill, 1974.

COELHO FILHO, Luiz Walter. *A Capitania de São Jorge e a Década do Açúcar* [The São Jorge Captaincy and the Decade of Sugar]. Salvador: Editora Vila Velha. 2000.

COLECCIÓN de Documentos Inéditos Relativos al Descubrimiento, Conquista y Organización de las Antiguas Posesiones Españolas de Ultramar [Collection of Unpublished Documents on the Discovery, Conquest, and Organization of the Former Spanish Overseas Possessions]. Madrid: La Real Academia de La Historia, 1897.

CORTESÃO, Jaime. *História da Expansão Portuguesa* [History of Portuguese Expansion]. Lisboa: Imprensa Nacional --Casa da Moeda, 1993.

COSTA, Francisco Augusto Pereira da. *Anais Pernambucanos* [Pernambuco Annals], 2ª edição. Recife: FUNDARPE, 1983.

COSTA, Leonor Freire. *Naus e Galeões na Ribeira de Lisboa. A Construção naval no século XVI para a Rota do Cabo* [Ships and Galleons on the Lisbon River: Shipbuilding in the Sixteenth Century for the Cape Route]. Cascais: Patrimonia Histórica, 1997.

COULANGES, Fustel de. *A Cidade Antiga*, 4ª edição. São Paulo: Martins Fontes, 1998. English translation: COULANGES, Fustel de. *The Ancient City*. Translated by Willard Small. Boston: Lee & Shepard, 1874 [1864].

COUTO, Jorge. *A Construção do Brasil* [The Construction of Brazil]. Lisboa: Edições Cosmos, 1995.

CUERPO DEL DERECHO CIVIL ROMANO [Corpus of Roman Civil Law], a doble texto, traducido al castellano del latino por D. Ildefonso l. Garcia del Corral. Edición facsímil. Valladolid: Editora Lex Nova S/A, 1988.

CUNHA, Rui Manuel Manera. *As Medidas na Arquitetura, séculos XIII-XVIII. O Estudo de Monsaraz* [Measurements in Architecture in the Thirteenth to Eighteenth Centuries]. Lisboa: Caleidoscópio. 2003.

DE VARAZZE, Jacopo, Arcebispo de Gênova. *Legenda Aúrea: vida de santos* [The Golden Legend: Lives of the Saints]. Tradução do latim, apresentação, notas e seleção iconográfica de Hilário Franco Júnior. São Paulo: Companhia das Letras, 2003.

DIAS, Carlos Malheiro. *História da Colonização Portuguesa no Brasil* [History of Portuguese Colonization in Brazil]. Porto: Litografia Nacional, 1924.

DOCUMENTAÇÃO para a História das Missões do Padroado Português do Oriente [Documentation on the History of Portuguese Church Missions in the East], 2ª edição. Coligida e anotada por António da Silva Rego. Lisboa: Fundação Oriente e Comissão Nacional para as Comemorações dos Descobrimentos Portugueses, 1991.

DOCUMENTOS HISTÓRICOS [Historical Documents]. V. 12 e 13. Bibliotheca Nacional do Rio de Janeiro. Rio de Janeiro: Officinas Gráphicas da Bibliotheca, 1929.

DOCUMENTOS HISTÓRICOS [Historical Documents]. V. 35, 36, 63, 64 e 74. Bibliotheca Nacional do Rio de Janeiro. Rio de Janeiro: Officinas Gráphicas da Bibliotheca, 1937.

DOCUMENTOS HISTÓRICOS do Arquivo Municipal [Historical Documents of the Municipal Archive]. Atas da Câmara. V. 1 a 5. Salvador: Prefeitura Municipal do Salvador.

DOCUMENTOS para a História do Açúcar [Documents on the History of Sugar]. Rio de Janeiro: Instituto do Açúcar e do Álcool, 1963.

DOMINGUES, Francisco Contente; Barreto, Luís Filipe (org.). A abertura do mundo—estudos de história dos descobrimentos europeus [Opening the World: Studies in the History of European Discoveries]. V. II. Lisboa: Editorial Presença, 1987.

ENEAS, o Tácito. *Poliorcética*. Biblioteca Clásica Gredos, 157. Madrid: Editorial Gredos, 1991. English translation: TACTICUS, Aeneas. *Aineiou Poliorketika: Aeneas on Siegecraft*. Translated by Hunter, L.W. and Handford, S.A. Oxford: Clarendon Press, 1927.

EVOLUÇÃO FÍSICA DE SALVADOR. 1549 a 1800 [Physical Evolution of Salvador, 1549-1800]. Salvador: Fundação Gregório de Mattos e Universidade Federal da Bahia, 1998.

FERREZ, Gilberto. Apresentação Kátia Queirós Mattoso. *BAHIA—Velhas Fotografias 1858/1900* [Bahia: Old Photographs, 1858-1900]. Rio de Janeiro: Kosmos Ed; Salvador: Banco da Bahia Investimentos S/A, 1998.

HERRERA, Antonio. *Historia General de los Hechos de los Castellanos en las Islas y Tierrafirme del Mar Oceano que llaman Indias Occidentales* [General History of the Deeds of the Spaniards in the Islands and Mainland of the Ocean Sea Known as the West Indies]. Madrid: Academia de la Historia, 1950.

HIPÓCRATES. "Sobre los Aires, Aguas y Lugares" [On Airs, Waters, and Places]. In: *Tratados Hipocráticos, II*. Biblioteca Clásica Gredos, 90. Madrid: Editorial Gredos, 1997.

HISTÓRIA DA ARTE PORTUGUESA [History of Portuguese Art], 3ª edição. Direção Paulo Pereira. Lisboa: Temas e Debates, 1999.

HISTORIA DE LA ARQUITECTURA Y EL URBANISMO MEXICANOS [History of Mexican Architecture and Urbanism], coordinador Carlos Chanfón Olmos. Ciudad de México: Fondo de Cultura Económica, 1997.

HISTÓRIA NAVAL BRASILEIRA [Brazilian Naval History]. Rio de Janeiro: Ministério da Marinha. Serviço de Documentação Geral da Marinha, 1997.

HISTÓRIA DAS FORTIFICAÇÕES PORTUGUESAS NO MUNDO [History of Portuguese Fortifications Around the World]. Direção de Rafael Moreira. Lisboa: Publicações Alfa, 1989.

HOLANDA, Francisco de. Álbum dos Desenhos das Antiguidades [Album of Designs of Antiquities]. Lisboa: Livros Horizonte, 1989.

JALDÚN, Ibn. *Introducción a la Historia Universal* [Introduction to Universal History]. Al Muqaddimah. México: Fondo de Cultura Económica, 1997.

JOSEFO, Flávio. *História dos Hebreus* [History of the Hebrews]. Tradução de Vicente Pedroso. Rio de Janeiro: CPAD, 1990.

JUSTINIAN. *Justinian's Institutes.* Translated by Peter Birks and Grant McLeod. Ithaca: Cornell University Press, 1987. http://books.google.com/books?isbn=0801494001

KAUFMANN, J. E.; KAUFMANN, H. W. *The Medieval Fortress: Castles, Forts and Walled Cities of the Middle Ages.* London: Greenhill Books, 2001.

LAS SIETE PARTIDAS de Sabio Rey Don Afonso el nono *[Seven-Part Code of King Alfonso IX the Wise]*, nuevamente Glosadas por el Licenciado Gregório Lopez del Consejo Real de Indias de su Majestad. Reprodução fac-símile da edição feita em 1555. Madrid: Boletin Oficial del Estado, 1974.

LAWRENCE, A. W. *Arquitetura Grega* [Greek Architecture]. Tradução de Maria Luíza Moreira de Alba. São Paulo: Cosac & Naify Edições, 1998.

LECHUGA, Cristóbal. *Tratado de la Artilleria y de Fortificación* [Treatise on Artillery and Fortification]. Madrid: Ministerio de Defensa, Secretaria General Técnica, 1990.

LE CORBUSIER. *Urbanismo* [Urbanism], 2ª edição. São Paulo: Martins Fontes, 2000.

LEIS EXTRAVAGANTES e Repertório das Ordenações de Duarte Nunes do Lião [Supplementary Laws and Repertoire of the Ordinances of Duarte Nunes do Lião]. Notas de Apresentação Mario Júlio de Almeida Costa. Reprodução fac-símile da edição feita em 1569. Lisboa: Fundação Calouste Gulbenkian, 1987.

LEITE, José. *Santos de Cada Dia* [Saints for Every Day], 3ª edição. Braga: Editorial A. O., 1993.

LEITE, Osmário Rezende. "Evolução Fisiográfica e da Ocupação do Território da Baía de Todos os Santos" [Physiographic Evolution and the Settlement of the Territory of the Bay of All Saints]. In: *Baía de Todos os Santos; diagnóstico sócio-ambiental e subsídios para a gestão*. Salvador: Germen/UFBA-NIMA, 1997.

LEITE S. I., Serafim. *Cartas dos Primeiros Jesuítas do Brasil* [Letters of the First Jesuits in Brazil]. São Paulo: Comissão do IV Centenário da Cidade de São Paulo, 1954. (Cartas de 1553-1558).

_____. *História da Companhia de Jesus no Brasil* [History of the Society of Jesus in Brazil]. Lisboa: Livraria Portugália; Rio de Janeiro: Civilização Brasileira, 1938.

LIVIO, Tito. *História de Roma* [History of Rome]. São Paulo: Editora Paumape S/A, 1989.

LIVRO DO TOMBO do Colégio de Jesus do Rio de Janeiro [Register of Deeds of the Jesuit School of Rio de Janeiro]. Rio de Janeiro: Divisão de Publicações e Divulgação da Biblioteca Nacional, 1968.

LIVRO DO TOMBO da Prefeitura Municipal do Salvador [Register of Deeds and Charters of the Municipal Office of Salvador], 1º volume. Salvador: Publicação da Diretoria do Arquivo, Divulgação e Estatística da Prefeitura do Salvador, 1953.

LIVRO PRIMEIRO do Governo do Brasil 1607-1633 [Book One of the Government of Brazil, 1607-1633]. Rio de Janeiro: Ministério das Relações Exteriores, 1958.

LIVRO PRIMEIRO do Tombo das propriedades foreiras à Câmara desta muy insigne Cidade de Lisboa [Book One of the Register of Deeds of Properties Paying Taxes to the Municipal Council of this Eminent City of Lisbon]. Documentos para a história da Cidade de Lisboa. Lisboa: Câmara Municipal de Lisboa, 1952.

LIVRO VELHO do Tombo do Mosteiro de São Bento da Cidade do Salvador [Old Book of Deeds of the Monastery of São Bento of the City of Salvador]. Salvador: Tipografia Beneditina, 1945.

LOTZ, Wolfgang. *Arquitetura na Itália 1500-1600* [Architecture in Italy, 1500-1600]. Tradução de Cristina Fino. São Paulo: Cosac & Naify Edições, 1998.

LUZ, Francisco Mendes da Luz. *Regimento da Casa da Índia: manuscrito do Século XVII existente no Arquivo Geral de Simancas* [Procedures of the House of India: Manuscript from the Seventeenth Century in the General Archive of Simancas], 2ª edição. Lisboa: Ministério da Educação-Instituto da Cultura e Língua Portuguesa, 1992.

MAPA: Imagens da Formação Territorial Brasileira [Map: Images of the Territorial Formation of Brazil]. Pesquisa, textos e seleção cartográfica de Isa Adonias. Rio de Janeiro: Fundação Emílio Odebrecht, 1993.

MACHIAVELLI, Niccoló. *Comentários sobre a Primeira década de Tito Lívio* [Discourses on the First Ten Books of Titus Livy]. Tradução de Sergio Bath, 3ª edição. Brasília: Editora Universidade de Brasília, 1994.

_____. *Epistolario 1512-1527* [Correspondence 1512-1527]. Traducción, edición y notas de Stella Mastrangelo. Mexico: Fundo de Cultura Económica, 1990.

_____. *Del Arte de la Guerra*, 3ª edicion. Madrid: Editorial Tecnos, 2000. English translation: MACHIAVELLI, Niccoló. *The Seven Books on the Art of War*. Translated by Henry Neville. London: Harper and Amery, 1675 [1521]. http://en.wikisource.org/wiki/ The_Art_of_War_%28Machiavelli%29

MARIA, Frei Agostinho de Santa. "Santuário Mariano e História das Imagens Milagrosas de Nossa Senhora" [The Marian Shrine and the History of Miraculous Images of Our Lady]. In: *Revista do Instituto Geográfico e Histórico da Bahia*, tomo IX, n º 74. Salvador, 1947.

MARIÁTEGUI, Eduardo de. *El capitan Cristóbal de Rojas, Engenheiro Militar del Siglo XVI* [Captain Cristóbal de Rojas, Military Engineer of the Sixteenth Century]. Madrid: Comissión de Estudos Históricos de Obras Públicas, 1985.

MARTINI, Francesco Di Giorgio. *Trattati Di Architettura, In-*

gegnaria e Arte Militare [Treatise on Architecture, Engineering, and Military Arts]. Milano: Edizioni Il Polifilo, 1967.

MATER Misericordiae. *Simbolismo e Representação da Virgem da Misericórdia* [Symbolism and Representation of the Virgin of Mercy]. Santa Casa da Misericórdia de Lisboa. Lisboa: Museu de São Roque e Livros Horizonte, 1995.

MATOS, Gastão Melo de. *Memória sobre o alcance das armas usadas nos séculos XV e XVIII* [Memoir on the Range of Arms Used in the Fifteenth to Eighteenth Centuries]. Separata dos anais, volume IX. Lisboa: Academia Portuguesa da História, 1944.

MATOS, Luís de. *No IV Centenário da Fundação do Rio de Janeiro* [On the Fourth Centennary of the Founding of Rio de Janeiro]. Lisboa: Fundação Calouste Gulbenkian, 1965.

MATTOS, Waldemar. *Evolução Histórica e Cultural do Pelourinho* [Historical and Cultural Evolution of Pelourinho]. Rio de Janeiro: Serviço Nacional de Aprendizagem Comercial --SENAC, Departamento Regional da Bahia, 1978.

MEMÓRIAS de Um Soldado da Índia [Memoirs of a Soldier in India], compiladas de um manuscrito português do Museu Britânico por A. de S.S. Costa Lobo, 2ª edição. Lisboa: Imprensa Nacional, 1987.

MENDONÇA, Marcos Carneiro. *Raízes da Formação Administrativa do Brasil* [Roots of the Administrative Formation of Brazil]. Rio de Janeiro: Instituto Histórico Geográfico Brasileiro e Conselho Federal de Cultura, 1972.

MOREIRA, Rafael. *A Construção de Mazagão. Cartas Inéditas 1541-1542* [The Construction of Mazagan: Unpublished Letters 1541-1542]. Lisboa: Instituto Português do Património Arquitectónico, 2001.

_____. "A época manuelina" [The Manueline era]. In: *História das fortificações portuguesas no mundo* [History of Portuguese Fortifications Around the World]. Direção de Rafael Moreira. Lisboa: Publicações Alfa, 1989.

MORENO, Diogo de Campos. *Livro que dá razão ao Estado do Brasil–1612* [Book Presenting the Reason for the State of Brazil]. Edição crítica com introdução e notas de Helio Vianna. Recife: Arquivo Público Estadual, 1955.

MORRIS, A. E. J. *Historia de la Forma Urbana; desde sus orígenes hasta la Revolución Industrial* [History of the Urban Form: From its Origins to the Industrial Revolution]. Barcelona: Editorial Gustavo Gill, 1984.

NONATO, José Antonio; SANTOS, Nubia Melhem. *Era uma Vez o Morro do Castelo* [Once Upon a Time there was a Castle on a Hill]. Rio de Janeiro: IPHAN, 2000.

OLIVEIRA, Cristóvão Rodrigues de. *Lisboa em 1551—Sumário em que brevemente se contêm algumas coisas assim eclesiásticas como seculares que há na cidade de Lisboa (1551)* [Lisbon in 1551: Summary that Briefly Tells of Some Things Both Ecclesiastical and Secular Found in the City of Lisbon (1551)]. Lisboa: Livros Horizonte, 1987.

OLIVEIRA NETO, Luiz Camilo de. "Notícias Antigas do Brasil 1531-1551" [Historical Reports from Brazil, 1531-1551]. In: *Anaes da Biblioteca Nacional do Rio de Janeiro*. V. 57. Rio de Janeiro: Serviço Gráfico do Ministério da Educação, 1939.

OLIVEIRA, José Teixeira de. *História do Espírito Santo* [History of Espírito Santo]. Vitória: Fundação Cultural do Estado do Espírito Santo, 1975.

O ORÇAMENTO do Estado da Índia 1571 [Budget of the State of India, 1571]. Direção e prefácio Artur Teodoro de Matos. Lisboa: Centro de Estudos Damião Góes. Comissão Nacional para a Comemoração dos Descobrimentos Portugueses, 1999.

ORDENAÇÕES Afonsinas [Alfonsine Ordinances]. Lisboa: Fundação Calouste Gulbenkian, 1984

ORDENAÇÕES Manuelinas [Manueline Ordinances]. Reprodução fac-símile da edição feita na Real Imprensa da Universidade de Coimbra, no ano de 1797. Lisboa: Fundação Calouste Gulbenkian, 1984

ORDENAÇÕES Filipinas [Philippine Ordinances]. Reprodução fac-símile da edição feita por Candido Mendes de Almeida, Rio de Janeiro, 1870. Lisboa: Fundação Calouste Gulbenkian, 1985

OVIEDO, Gonzalo Fernandes de. *Historia General y natural de las Indias* [General and Natural History of the Indies]. Edición y estudio preliminar de Juan Perez de Tudela Bueso, 2ª edición. Madrid: Ediciones Atlas, 1992.

PAULINO, Francisco Faria, coord. *A Arquitetura Militar na Expansão Portuguesa* [Military Architecture in the Portuguese Expansion]. Porto: Comissão Nacional para as Comemorações dos Descobrimentos Portugueses, 1994.

PEREIRA, Gabriel. *Documentos Históricos da Cidade de Évora* [Historical Documents of the City of Évora]. Lisboa: Imprensa Nacional, Casa da Moeda, 1998.

PEREIRA, João Cordeiro Pereira. *Para a História das Alfândegas em Portugal* [Toward a History of Customs Houses in Portugal]. Lisboa: Universidade Nova de Lisboa, 1983.

PISO, Guilherme. *História Natural e Médica da Índia Ocidental* [Natural and Medical History of the West Indies]. Rio de Janeiro: Ministério da Educação e Cultura, Instituto Nacional do Livro, 1957.

PLATÃO. *As Leis* (incluindo Epinomis). Bauru, SP: Edipro, 1999. English translation: PLATO. *Laws*. Translated by Benjamin Jowett. Oxford University Press, 1892. http://classics.mit.edu/Plato/laws.html

PLUTARCO. *As Vidas de Homens Ilustres*. São Paulo: Editora das Américas. English translation: PLUTARCH. *Lives of the Noble Greeks and Romans*. Edited and translated by Bernadotte Perrin. Loeb Classical Library 46. Cambridge, Mass.: Harvard University Press, 1914.

POLÍBIO. *Histórias* [Histories]. Libros V-XV. Biblioteca Clásica Gredos, 43. Madrid: Editorial Gredos, 1996.

POLIENO. *Estratagemas*. Biblioteca Clásica Gredos, 157. Madrid: Editorial Gredos, 1991. English translation: POLYAENUS. *Stratagems*. Adapted from the translation by R. Shepherd [1793]. http://www.attalus.org/translate/polyaenus

POLIÓN, Marco Vitruvio. *Los Diez Libros de Archîtectura*. Edición de José Ortiz y Sanz, 1787. Toledo (Espanha): Antonio Pareja Editor, 1999. English translation: VITRUVIUS POLLIO, Marcus. *Ten Books on Architecture*. Translated by Morris Hicky Morgan. Cambridge, Mass.: Harvard University Press, 1914. http://www.gutenberg.org/files/20239/20239-h/29239-h.htm

PORTUGALIE MONUMENTA CARTOGRAPHICA [Portuguese Cartographic Collection]. Direção de Armando Cortesão, 2ª edição. Lisboa: Imprensa Nacional, Casa da Moeda, 1987.

RAZÃO DO ESTADO DO BRASIL (C. 1616) [Reason for the State of Brazil (c. 1616). Códice 126 da Biblioteca Pública Municipal do Porto, seguido de estudo cartográfico de Armando Cortesão e A Teixeira Mota. Lisboa: Edições João Sá da Costa, 1999.

RECOPILACION DE LEYES DE LOS REYNOS DE LAS INDIAS [Compilation of Laws of the Kingdoms of the Indies]. Mandadas imprimir y publicar por la majestad católica del Rey Don Carlos II. Edición facsímil. Madrid: Imprenta Nacional del Boletín Oficial de Estado, 1998.

REIS, João José. *A Morte é uma Festa: ritos fúnebres e revolta popular no Brasil do século XIX* [Death is a Festival: Funeral Rites and Popular Revolt in Brazil in the Nineteenth Century]. São Paulo: Companhia das Letras, 1991.

REIS, Nestor Goulart. *Imagens de vilas e cidades do Brasil colonial* [Images of Towns and Cities of Colonial Brazil]. São Paulo: Editora da Universidade de São Paulo --Imprensa Oficial do Estado, Fapesp, 2000.

RENATO, Flavio Vegécio. *Instituciones Militares* [Military Institutions] Madrid: Ministerio de Defensa, 1988. English translation: VEGETIUS RENATUS, Flavius. *The Military Institutions of the Romans (De Re Militari)*, Books I-III. Translated by Lieutenant John

Clarke. Harrisburg, PA: Telegraph Press, 1965 [1767]. http://www.digitalattic.org/home/war/vegetius/

RESENDE, André de. *As Antiguidades da Lusitânia* [The Antiquities of Lusitania]. Lisboa: Fundação Calouste Gulbenkian, 1996.

REVISTA STUDIA. *Biblioteca Virtual dos Descobrimentos Portugueses* [Virtual Library of Portuguese Discoveries]. Lisboa: Comissão Nacional para as Comemorações dos Descobrimentos Portugueses, volumes 1 a 53, CD-ROM.

REVISTA DO PATRIMÔNIO HISTÓRICO E ARTÍSTICO NACIONAL [Journal of National Historical and Artistic Heritage]. V. 11. Rio de Janeiro: Ministério da Educação e Saúde, 1947.

RICARD, Robert. "Documents de l'Archivo General de Índias, de Séville, relatifs au Brésil" [Documents of the General Archive of the Indies, in Seville, regarding Brazil]. In: *Arquivo de História e Bibliografia (1923-1926)*. Lisboa, Portugal: Imprensa Nacional, Casa da Moeda, 1976.

ROBERTSON, D. S. *Arquitetura grega e romana* [Greek and Roman Architecture]. Tradução Júlio Fischer. São Paulo: Martins Fontes, 1997.

ROJAS, Cristóbal. *Tres Tratados sobre Fortificación y Milicia* [Three Treatises on Fortification and Militias]. Madrid: CEHOPU—Comisión de Estudios Históricos de Obras Públicas y Urbanismo, 1985.

ROSSA, Walter. *Cidades Indo-Portuguesas—Indo-Portuguese Cities*. Lisboa: Comissão Nacional para as Comemorações dos Descobrimentos Portugueses, 1997.

ROSENAU, Helen. *A Cidade Ideal—Evolução Arquitetônica na Europa* [The Ideal City: Architectonic Evolution in Europe]. Lisboa: Editorial Presença. 1988.

RUBERT, Arlindo. *A Igreja no Brasil. Origem e Desenvolvimento (Século XVI)*[The Church in Brazil: Origin and Development (Sixteenth Century)]. Volume I. Santa Maria: Livraria Editora Pallotti, 1981.

SALDANHA, António Vasconcelos de Saldanha. *As capitanias. O Regime Senhorial na Expansão Ultramarina Portuguesa* [The Captaincies: The Authority Structure in the Portuguese Overseas Expansion]. Funchal: Centro de Estudos de História do Atlântico, 1992.

SALVADOR, Frei Vicente. *História do Brasil 1500-1627* [History of Brazil, 1500-1627], 5ª edição. São Paulo: Edições Melhoramentos, 1965.

SAMPAIO, Theodoro. *História da Fundação da cidade do Salvador* [History of the Founding of the City of Salvador]. Salvador: Tipografia Beneditina, 1949.

SANCEAU, Elaine. *Cartas de D. João de Castro* [Letters of Dom João de Castro]. Lisboa: Agência Geral do Ultramar, 1954.

SANTO, Moisés Espírito. *Origens Orientais da Religião Popular Portuguesa* [The Eastern Origins of Portuguese Popular Religion]. Lisboa: Assírio & Alvim, 1988.

SANTOS, Paulo F. "Formação de Cidade no Brasil Colonial" [Formation of the City in Colonial Brazil]. In: *Actas do V Colóquio Internacional de Estudos Luso-Brasileiros*. Volume V. Coimbra, 1968.

SERRÃO, Joaquim Veríssimo. *O Rio de Janeiro no Século XV* [Rio de Janeiro in the Fifteenth Century]. Lisboa: Documentos dos Arquivos Portugueses, 1965.

_____. *O Tempo dos Filipes em Portugal e no Brasil (1580-1668)* [The Time of Philippine Rule in Portugal and Brazil, 1580-1668]. Lisboa: Edições Colibri, 1994.

SILVA, Elvan. *A Forma e A Fórmula. Cultura, Ideologia e Projeto na arquitetura da Renascença* [Form and Formula: Culture, Ideology, and Project in Renaissance Architecture]. Porto Alegre: Sagra, 1991.

SILVA, De Plácido e. *Vocabulário Jurídico* [Legal Vocabulary]. Rio de Janeiro: Forense, 1980.

SILVA, Ignacio Accioli de Cerqueira e. *Memórias Históricas e Políticas da Província da Bahia* [Historical and Political Memories of the Province of Bahia]. Com notas de Braz do Amaral. Salvador: Imprensa Oficial do Estado, 1919.

SILVA, Justino Adriano Farias de. *Tratado de Direito Funerário* [Treatise on Funerary Law]. São Paulo: Método Editora, 2000.

SOUSA, Frei Luís de. *Anais de D. João III* [Annals of King Dom João III], 2ª edição. Lisboa: Livraria Sá da Costa Editora, 1951.

SOUTHEY, Robert. *História do Brasil* [History of Brazil], 4ª edição brasileira. São Paulo: Melhoramentos, 1977.

SOUZA, Gabriel Soares de. *Notícia do Brasil* [Report from Brazil]. São Paulo: Livraria Martins Editora, 19.

SUTEÔNIO. *A Vida dos Dozes Césares*, 2ª edição. São Paulo: Ediouro, 2002. English translation: SUETONIUS. *The Lives of the Caesars*, Vol. II. Edited and translated by J. C. Rolfe. Loeb Classical Library 38. Cambridge, Mass. Harvard University Press, 1914.

TEIXEIRA, Manuel C. e Margarida Valla. *O Urbanismo Português. Séculos XIII-XVIII Portugal-Brasil* [Portuguese Urbanism, Thirteenth to Eighteenth Centuries, Portugal and Brazil]. Lisboa: Livros Horizonte, 1999.

THOMAZ, Luís Filipe F. R. *A Lenda de S. Tomé Apóstolo e a Expansão Portuguesa* [The Legend of Saint Thomas the Apostle and Portuguese Expansion]. Série separatas 233. Lisboa: Instituto de Investigação Científica Tropical, 1992.

TORRIANI, Leonardo. *Descrição e História do Reino das Ilhas Canárias* [Description and History of the Kingdom of the Canary Islands]. Estudo e tradução de José Manuel Azevedo e Silva. Lisboa: Edições Cosmos, 1999.

TUECHLE, K. Bihlmyer H. *História da Igreja* [History of the Church]. São Paulo: Edições Paulinas, 1965.

VALDÉS, Francisco de. *Espejo y Disciplina Militar* [Reflections and Military Discipline]. Madrid: Ministerio de Defensa, Secretaria General Técnica, 1989.

VAN LINSCHOTEN, Jan Huygen. *Itinerário, Viagem ou Navegação para as Índias Ocidentais ou Portuguesas* [Itinerary, Voyage, or Navigation to the West or Portuguese Indies]. Lisboa: Comissão Nacional para as Comemorações do Descobrimento Portugueses, 1997.

VARNHAGEN, Francisco Adolfo de (Visconde de Porto Seguro). *História Geral do Brasil* [General History of Brazil], 9ª edição. São Paulo: Melhoramentos; Brasília: INL, 1975.

VIDE, D. Sebastião Monteiro da. *Constituições do Arcebispado da Bahia* [Constitutions of the Archbishop of Bahia]. São Paulo: Typografia 2 de dezembro de Antonio Louzada Antunes, 1853.

VILHENA, Luiz dos Santos. *Recopilação de Notícias Soteropolitanas e Brasílicas* [Compilation of Reports from Salvador and Brazil]. Salvador: Imprensa Official do Estado, 1921.

VITERBO, Sousa. *Dicionário Histórico e Documental dos Arquitetos, Engenheiros e Construtores Portugueses* [Historical and Documentary Dictionary of Portuguese Architects, Engineers, and Builders]. Reprodução em fac-símile do exemplar com data de 1904 da Biblioteca da INCM. Lisboa: Imprensa Nacional - Casa da Moeda, 1988.

_____. *Trabalho Náutico dos Portugueses. Séculos XVI e XVII* [Naval Work of the Portuguese, Sixteenth and Seventeenth Centuries]. Lisboa: Imprensa Nacional, Casa da Moeda, 1988.

ZOLLNER, Frank. *Leonardo da Vinci 1452-1519*. Colonia: Taschen, 2000.

/pod-product-compliance

B/1642